WAR IN THE
HELLENISTIC WORLD

Ancient World at War

The books in this series are authoritative surveys of the relationship between warfare and the economy and culture of ancient Near Eastern and Mediterranean societies. The series explores the impact of military organization on social life and the place of war in the cultural and imaginative life of communities. It also considers the "face of battle," examining the experiences of combatants and civilians.

Published

War in the Hellenistic World
Angelos Chaniotis

War in Ancient Egypt
Anthony J. Spalinger

In Preparation

War in the Ancient Greek World
John Buckler

War in Late Antiquity
Doug Lee

War in the Assyrian Empire
Mario Fales

War in the Roman Republic
John Serrati

War in the Ancient World
Philip de Souza

War in the Byzantine World
Frank Trombley

WAR IN THE HELLENISTIC WORLD

A Social and Cultural History

Angelos Chaniotis

Blackwell
Publishing

BLACKWELL PUBLISHING
350 Main Street, Malden, MA 02148-5020, USA
108 Cowley Road, Oxford OX4 1JF, UK
550 Swanston Street, Carlton, Victoria 3053, Australia

First published 2005 by Blackwell Publishing Ltd

Library of Congress Cataloging-in-Publication Data

Chaniotis, Angelos.
War in the Hellenistic world : a social and cultural history / Angelos Chaniotis.
p. cm. — (Ancient world at war)
Includes bibliographical references and index.
ISBN 0-631-22607-9 (hardback : alk. paper) —
ISBN 0-631-22608-7 (pbk. : alk. paper)
1. Military art and science—Middle East—History. 2. Wars of the
Hellenistic Monarchies, 301–146 B.C. I. Title. II. Series.

U31.C49 2005
938'.08—dc22

2004008897

A catalogue record for this title is available from the British Library.

Set in 10/12pt Galliard
by Graphicraft Limited, Hong Kong

The publisher's policy is to use permanent paper from mills that operate
a sustainable forestry policy, and which has been manufactured from pulp
processed using acid-free and elementary chlorine-free practices. Furthermore,
the publisher ensures that the text paper and cover board used have met
acceptable environmental accreditation standards.

For further information on
Blackwell Publishing, visit our website:
www.blackwellpublishing.com

To Professor Fritz Gschnitzer
on the occasion of his 75th birthday

CONTENTS

FIGURES

MAPS

ABBREVIATIONS

1. Ancient authors

Appian, *Syr.*: Appian, *Syrian Wars*
App., *Mithr.*: Appian, *Mithridatic Wars*
App., *b. civ.*: Appian, *Bella civilia* (*Civil Wars*)
App., *Illyr.*: Appian, *Illyrian Wars*
Arist., *Ath. Pol.*: Aristotle, *Athenaion Politeia* (*Constitution of the Athenians*)
Arist., *Polit.*: Aristotle, *Politics*
Athen.: Athenaios, *The Deipnosophists*
Cic., Flacc.: Cicero, *Pro Flacco*
Demosth.: Demosthenes
Diod.: Diodorus Siculus
FgrHist: F. Jacoby et al., *Die Fragmente der griechischen Historiker*, ++1923–
Jos., *Ant. Jud.*: Josephus, *Antiquitates Judaicae*
Just., epit.: Justinus, *Epitome historiarum Philippicarum*
Maccab.: *Maccabees* (Old Testament)
Paus.: Pausanias
Plut., *Demetr.*: Plutarch, *Demetrios*
Plut., *mor.*: Plutarch, *moralia*
Plut., *Philop.*: Plutarch, *Philpoemen*
Polyb.: Polybios
Theophr., Char.: Theophrastos, *Characteres*
Xen., *Cyr. paed.*: Xenophon, *Cyropaedia*

2. Works of reference

Amyzon: J. Robert and L. Robert, *Fouilles d'Amyzon en Carie. I. Exploration, histoire, monnaies et inscriptions*, Paris 1983.
BE: *Bulletin épigraphique* in *Revue des Études Grecques*.
BGU: *Ägyptische Urkunden aus den königlichen Museen zu Berlin. Griechische Urkunden*, Berlin 1895–1976.
CAH VII.1²: F. W. Walbank, A. E. Astin, M. W. Frederiksen, and R. M. Ogilvie (eds) *The Cambridge Ancient History. Volume VII. Part I. The Hellenistic World*, Cambridge 1984 (second edition).

CAH VII.2²: F. W. Walbank, A. E. Astin, M. W. Frederiksen, and R. M. Ogilvie (eds) *The Cambridge Ancient History. Volume VII. Part 2. The Rise of Rome to 220 B.C.*, Cambridge 1989 (second edition).

CAH VII.3²: A. E. Astin, F. W. Walbank, M. W. Frederiksen, and R. M. Ogilvie (eds) *The Cambridge Ancient History. Volume VII. Part 3. Rome and the Mediterranean to 133 B.C.*, Cambridge 1989 (second edition).

CIG: *Corpus Inscriptionum Graecarum*, Berlin 1828–77.

DGE: E. Schwyzer, *Dialectorum Graecorum exempla epigraphica potiora*, Leipzig 1923.

EBGR: A. Chaniotis et al., Epigraphic Bulletin for Greek Religion, *Kernos* 4, 1991– .

F.Delphes: *Fouilles de Delphes. III. Épigraphie*, Paris 1929– .

Gonnoi: B. Helly, *Gonnoi*, Amsterdam 1973.

I.Arykanda: S. Sahin, *Die Inschriften von Arykanda* (*IGSK* 48), Bonn 1994.

I.Beroia: L. Gounaropoulou – M. B. Hatzopoulos, Ἐπιγραφὲς Κάτω Μακεδονίας (μεταξὺ τοῦ Βερμίου Ὄρους καὶ τοῦ Ἀξιοῦ Ποταμοῦ). Τεῦχος Α'.Ἐπιγραφὲς Βεροίας, Athens 1998.

I.Byzantion: A. Lajtar, *Die Inschriften von Byzantion. Teil I. Die Inschriften* (*IGSK* 58), Bonn 2000.

I.Cret.: M. Guarducci, *Inscriptiones Creticae*, Rome 1935–50.

I.Ephesos: H. Wankel et alii, *Die Inschriften von Ephesos* (*IGSK* II), Bonn 1979–81.

I.Erythrai: H. Engelmann and R. Merkelbach, *Die Inschriften von Erythrai und Klazomenai* (*IGSK* 1–2), Bonn 1972–73.

IG: *Inscriptiones Graecae*, Berlin 1873– .

IGBulg: G. Mihailov, *Inscriptiones Graecae in Bulgaria repertae*, Sofia 1956–1997.

IGR: *Inscriptiones Graecae ad res Romanas pertinentes*, Paris 1911–1927.

IGSK: *Inschriften griechischer Städte aus Kleinasien*, Bonn 1972– .

I.Iasos: W. Blümel, *Die Inschriften von Iasos* (*IGSK* 28), Bonn 1985.

I.Ilion: P. Frisch, *Die Inschriften von Ilion* (*IGSK* 3), Bonn 1975.

I.Kalchedon: R. Merkelbach, *Die Inschriften von Kalchedon* (*IGSK* 20), Bonn 1980.

I.Kourion: T. B. Mitford, *Die Inschriften von Kourion*, Philadelphia 1971.

I.Lampsakos: P. Frisch, *Die Inschriften von Lampsakos* (*IGSK* 6) Bonn 1978.

I.Laodikeia: T. Corsten, *Die Inschriften von Laodikeia am Lykos I* (*IGSK* 49), Bonn 1997.

I.Lindos: C. Blinkenberg, *Lindos. Fouilles et recherches. II. Fouilles de l'acropole. Inscriptions*, Berlin 1941.

I.Magnesia: O. Kern, *Die Inschriften von Magnesia am Mäander*, Berlin 1908.

I.Mylasa: W. Blümel, *Die Inschriften von Mylasa. I. Inschriften der Stadt. II. Inschriften aus der Umgebung der Stadt* (*IGSK* 34–5), Bonn 1987–88.

I.Oropos: B. C. Petrakos, Οἱ Ἐπιγραφὲς τοῦ Ὠρωποῦ, Athens 1997.

IOSPE: B. Latysev, *Inscriptiones antiquae orae septentrionalis Ponti Euxini Graecae et Latinae*, St. Petersburg 1885–1901.

I.Pergamon: M. Fraenkel, *Die Inschriften von Pergamon*, Berlin 1890–95.

I.Perge: S. Sahin, *Die Inschriften von Perge. Teil I. Vorrömische Zeit, frühe und hohe Kaiserzeit* (*IGSK* 54.1), Bonn 1999.

I.Priene: F. Hiller von Gaertringen, *Inschriften von Priene*, Berlin 1906.

I.Prusa: Th. Corsten, *Die Inschriften von Prusa ad Olympum I–II* (*IGSK* 39–40), Bonn 1991–93.

IscrCos: M. Segre, *Iscrizioni di Cos*, Rome 1994.

ISE: L. Moretti, *Iscrizioni storiche ellenistiche I–II*, Florence 1967–75.

I.Selge: J. Nollé and F. Schindler, *Die Inschriften von Selge* (*IGSK* 37), Bonn 1991.

I.Sestos: J. Krauss, *Die Inschriften von Sestos und der thrakischen Chersones* (*IGSK* 19), Bonn 1980.

I.Side: J. Nollé, *Side im Altertum. Geschichte und Zeugnisse. Band II* (*IGSK* 44.2), Bonn 2001.

I.Stratonikeia: S. Sahin, *Die Inschriften von Stratonikeia* (*IGSK* 21–22), Bonn 1981–82.

I.Tralleis: F. B. Poljakov, *Die Inschriften von Tralleis und Nysa. I. Die Inschriften von Tralleis* (*IGSK* 36), Bonn 1989.

IvO: W. Dittenberger and K. Purgold, *Die Inschriften von Olympia*, Berlin 1896.

Labraunda: J. Cramba, *Labraunda. Swedisch Excavations and Researches. III 1/2. Greek Inscriptions*, Lund–Stockholm 1969–72.

LBW: P. Le Bas and W. H. Waddington, *Voyage archéologique en Grèce et en Asie Mineure fait pendant les années 1834 et 1844. Inscriptions grecques et latines*, Paris 1870.

LGPN: P. M. Fraser and E. Matthews (eds), *The Greek Lexikon of Personal Names, Vol. I–IIIb*, Oxford 1987–2000.

MAMA: *Monumenta Asiae Minoris Antiqua*, London 1928–93.

Milet I.2: C. Friedrich, Die Inschriften, in H. Knackfuß (ed.) *Milet. I 2. Das Rathaus in Milet*, Berlin 1908.

Milet I.3: A. Rehm, *Die Inschriften*, in G. Kawerau and A. Rehm, *Milet I. 3. Das Delphinion in Milet*, Berlin 1914: 162–406.

OGIS: W. Dittenberger, *Orientis Graeci Inscriptiones Selectae*, Leipzig 1903–5.

PH: W. R. Paton and E. L. Hicks, *The Inscriptions of Cos*, Oxford 1891.

RC: C. B. Welles, *Royal Corresopondence in the Hellenistic Period*, New Haven 1934.

SB: *Sammelbuch griechischer Urkunden aus Ägypten*, Strassburg-Wiesbaden 1915– .

Sardis VII: W. H. Buckler and D. M. Robinson, *Sardis VII. Greek and Latin Inscriptions*, Leiden 1932.

SEG: *Supplementum Epigraphicum Graecum*, Leiden 1923– .

Select Papyri II: A. S. Hunt and C. C. Edgar, *Select Papyri. Non-literary Papyri. Public Documents*, London–Cambridge, Mass. 1934.

SGO I: R. Merkelbach and J. Stauber, *Steinepigramme aus dem griechischen Osten. Band 1. Die Westküste Kleinasiens von Knidos bis Ilion*, Stuttgart-Leipzig 1998.

SGO II: R. Merkelbach and J. Stauber, *Steinepigramme aus dem griechischen Osten. Band 2: Die Nordküste Kleinasiens (Marmarameer und Pontos)*, Leipzig 2001.

SGO III: R. Merkelbach and J. Stauber, *Steinepigramme aus dem griechischen Osten. Band 3: Der "ferne Osten" und das Landesinnere bis zum Tauros*, Leipzig 2001.

SGO IV: R. Merkelbach and J. Stauber, *Steinepigramme aus dem griechischen Osten. Band 4: Die Südküste Kleinasiens, Syrien und Palaestina*, Leipzig 2002.

Staatsverträge: *Die Staatsverträge des Altertums.*

H. Bengtson, *Die Staatsverträge des Altertums. Zweiter Band. Die Verträge der griechisch römischen Welt von 700 bis 338 v. Chr.*, Munich 1975 (second edition).

H. H. Schmitt, *Die Staatsverträge des Altertums. Dritter Band. Die Verträge der griechisch-römischen Welt von 338 bis 200 v. Chr.*, Munich 1969.

Syll.³: W. Dittenberger, *Sylloge Inscriptionum Graecarum*, Leipzig 1915–24 (third edition).

TAM: *Tituli Asiae Minoris*, Vienna 1901– .

Tod, *GHI*: M. N. Tod, *Greek Historical Inscriptns*, Oxford 1933–1948.

TABLE OF IMPORTANT EVENTS

	murdered by his ally Ptolemaios Keraunos, who becomes king of Macedonia.
280–275	Wars of Pyrrhos in Italy.
280–278	Invasion of the Gauls (Galatians). Victory of the Aitolians and Antigonos Gonatas over the Gauls. Antigonos Gonatas becomes king of Macedonia.
278	The Gauls invade Asia Minor; continual raids against the Greek cities.
275/4–271	First Syrian War (Antiochos I against Ptolemy II).
274–272	War of Pyrrhos of Epeiros against Antigonos Gonatas.
272	Pyrrhos invades the Peloponnese and is killed in Argos.
268–261	Chremonidean War (Antigonos Gonatas against Ptolemy II, Athens, Sparta, and their allies).
ca. 263/2–229	Antigonos Gonatas occupies Athens.
260–253	Second Syrian War (Antiochos II, Rhodes, and Antigonos Gonatas against Ptolemy II).
255–254	War between Apollonia and Kallatis (west shore of the Black Sea).
255–254	Bithynian Succession War. Kappadokia breaks from the Seleukid kingdom.
ca. 250	Baktria breaks from the Seleukid kingdom, which also looses its eastern satrapies to the Parthians.
249–245	Revolt of Alexander (in Korinth) against Antigonos Gonatas.
245–243	Aratos becomes general of the Achaian League (245) and expels the Macedonia garrison from Korinth (243).
246–241	Third Syrian War or War of Laodike (Ptolemy III against Laodike).
239	Death of Antigonos Gonatas. Alliance of the Aitolian and Achaian Leagues.
239–229	War of Demetrios (Athens against Demetrios II of Macedonia).
238	Victories of Attalos I of Pergamon in wars against the Gauls in Asia Minor.
231–229	Invasion of Dardanians in Macedonia.
229	Liberation of Athens from Macedonian garrison.
227–222	Kleomenes' War (Sparta against the Achaian League).
ca. 229–220	Aitolian raids on the Peloponnese and in Central Greece.
227	Military operations of Antigonos Doson of Macedonia in Karia (Asia Minor).
224–222	Panhellenic alliance under the leadership of Antigonos Doson; war against Kleomenes of Sparta.
222	Defeat of Kleomenes in the Battle of Sellasia.

221–219	War of Lyttos on Crete (Knossos and Gortyn with their allies against Lyttos, civil war in Gortyn).
220–217	Social War (Philip V of Macedonia and his allies against the Aitolian League, Sparta, and Elis). Dardanian invasions in Macedonia (220–219, 217).
220	War of Rhodes against Byzantion for the abolishment of duties on vessels passing through the straits.
219–217	Fourth Syrian War (Antiochos III invades Koile Syria and Egypt).
217	Victory of Ptolemy IV over Antiochos III in the Battle of Rhaphia.
216–213	War between the Seleukid Antiochos III and the usurper Achaios in Asia Minor.
215–205	First Macedonian War (Philip V, ally of Hannibal, against Rome and the Aitolian League).
212–205	The "Anabasis" of Antiochos III. Temporary recovery of the eastern provinces.
207	War of Machanidas of Sparta against the Achaian League (under Philopoimen).
ca. 206–185	Revolt of the natives in the Thebaid (Ptolemaic Egypt).
205–201	First Cretan War (Cretan cities against Rhodes, Kos, and other islands).
202–200	Fifth Syrian War (Antiochos III against Ptolemy V). Military operations of Philip V in south Asia Minor. War of Philip V against Rhodes.
200–197	Second Macedonian War (Philip V against Rome and her allies Pergamon, Rhodes and Athens).
197	Victory of Titus Quintius Flamininus over Philip V at Kynos Kephalai.
197–185	Revolt of the native population in lower Egypt.
196	Antiochos III occupies Macedonian and Ptolemaic possessions in Asia Minor and Thrace.
195	War of the Romans against king Nabis of Sparta.
191–188	Antiochos' War (Antiochos III against Rome and her allies).
189	Defeat of Antiochos at Magnesia.
188	Peace of Apameia. Antiochos III looses his possesions in Asia Minor. Eumenes II of Pergamon and Rhodes gain territories.
189–ca. 183	Local wars in Asia Minor.
ca. 187–185	Eumenes II of Pergamon against Prousias I of Bithynia.
183–179	War of Eumenes II against Pontos.
171–168	Third Macedonian War (Rome and her allies against Perseus of Macedonia).

170–167	Wars on Crete (Kydonia against Apollonia, Gortyn and Knossos against Kydonia, Gortyn against Knossos, Gortyn and Knossos against Rhaukos).
169–168	Sixth Syrian War. Antiochos IV invades Egypt.
168	Victory of Aemilius Paullus over Perseus in the Battle of Pydna. The end of the Antigonid monarchy. The Romans force Antiochos IV to leave Egypt.
ca. 167–163	Revolt of the Maccabees in Judea.
156–154	War between Prousias of Bithynia and Attalos II of Pergamon.
155–153	Second Cretan War (Cretan cities against Rhodes).
149–148	Revolt of Macedonians against Rome.
146	Achaian War (the Achaian League against Rome).
146	Sack of Korinth. Macedonia becomes a Roman province. Greece under Roman rule.
133	Attalos III of Pergamon bequeathes his kingdom to the Romans.
132–129	Aristonikos' War: Aristonikos, illegitimate son of Attalos II of Pergamon, fights against the Romans supported by lower social strata.
132–124	Dynastic wars in Ptolemaic Egypt (Kleopatra II against Ptolemy VIII and Kleopatra III).
129	Antiochos VII is killed in a war against the Parthians. The Seleukids loose Mesopotamia to the Parthians. Judea regains its independence.
ca. 121–114	Territorial conflicts in Crete (Gortyn against Knossos, Hierapytna against Itanos, Lato against Olous).
88–83	First Mithridatic War (Mithridates VI, king of Pontos, and his Greek allies against Rome).
77–85	Sulla besieges and sacks Athens.
83–81	Second Mithridatic War (Mithridates VI against Rome).
73–63	Third Mithridatic War (Mithridates VI against Rome).
69–67	Conquest of Crete by the Romans.
63	Suicide of Mithridates VI. The Seleukid kingdom becomes Roman province.
49–48	Roman civil war (Caesar against Pompey) fought in Greece (Pharsalos) and Egypt (Alexandria).
42	Battle of Philippoi. Marc Antony and Octavian defeat the murderers of Caesar.
42–39	Raids of the Roman renegade general Labienus in Syria and Asia Minor.
31	Battle of Actium. Octavian defeats Marc Antony and Kleopatra VII of Egypt.
30	Suicide of Kleopatra. The end of the Ptolemaic kingdom.

PREFACE

One of the best experts on the Hellenistic period, Michel Austin, once criticized the widespread perception of war as an intrusive external force, purely destructive and negative, and never adequately explained (Austin 1986: 451–2). Few historical periods can better demonstrate the complexity of war as a social and cultural force than the 300 years between Alexander's victories and Kleopatra's defeat (323–330 BC). The continual and often confusing wars of the Hellenistic Age confront those who study this period, either in academic courses or in scholarly research, with unusual challenges. The geographical range is huge: from Italy to Afghanistan and from the north shore of the Black Sea to the coast of Africa. The sources, especially the hundreds of historical inscriptions (particularly from Asia Minor), and the thousands of papyri from Ptolemaic Egypt, provide an abundance of information, but very frequently uncertain clues (if any) about the historical context in which the information should be placed. The reconstruction of this period resembles a huge jigsaw puzzle, most of the pieces of which have been lost for ever. This explains why scholarship has concentrated on the wars of the kings and the conflicts between the great Hellenistic powers and Rome, for which the sources are somewhat better, rather neglecting the importance of local conflicts and the part played by war in the life of the populations of small urban centres and of the countryside. I hope that this book will demonstrate how rewarding it is, despite the aforementioned difficulties, to turn our attention to these areas of the Greek world.

This book has primarily been written for students of classics and history. It does not aim to cover every aspect of Hellenistic warfare (e.g., tactics and weapons), but rather surveys the various ways in which war shaped Hellenistic society, mentality, and culture, and also the ways in which wars corresponded to contemporary social conditions and reflected the cultural peculiarities of this era.

Let me warn the reader about the faults I am aware of – reviewers will probably discover more. None of the aspects selected for presentation could be discussed in an exhaustive manner. In addition, this study does not cover the entire geographical range of the Hellenistic world. The reader will immediately notice a focus on the world of the cities in mainland Greece, the Aegean islands, and Asia Minor – although I have included examples from Magna Graecia, the Black Sea, the Seleukid Empire, and Ptolemaic Egypt. Important subjects, such as the emergence of a Galatian state in Anatolia, the cultural background of the wars of the Maccabees, or warfare in the periphery of the Hellenistic world (e.g., in the Greek-Baktrian kingdoms) could not be discussed. The Hellenistic world is a well-defined historical period, but despite the impression of unity, a close study of the evidence always reveals local peculiarities and historical developments. Hellenistic Crete is very different from Hellenistic Ionia or Hellenistic Mesopotamia, and the warfare during the period of the Successors (322–281 BC) differs in aims, dimensions, and form from, for example, the wars of the Roman expansion (ca. 220–146 BC). Although I often draw the reader's attention to the necessity of such distinctions, I could not always avoid some of those more or less misleading generalizations which are inherent in general introductory surveys.

This is a book without footnotes, but the reader will find references to the sources and to modern scholarship, either in the main text or in the section on "Further Reading" which concludes every chapter. The Bibliography is long, but not exhaustive. I have preferred to include recent publications (where the reader can find further bibliographies), as well as the books and articles on which my discussion of specific subjects relies. Technical terms (e.g., sympolity, liturgy, etc.) are usually explained the first time they are used; the reader can find the explanation with the help of the index (under Greek terms).

Among the sources, the inscriptions take the lion's share in my discussions, including some very recent finds. This preference is easy to explain: it is through the discovery of new documentary sources (inscriptions and papyri) that our knowledge of essential aspects of the Hellenistic world is continually enlarged and modified. Many of the texts presented here in translation have already been included in two invaluable selections of sources, compiled by Austin (1981) and Bagnall and Derow (2004). If not otherwise indicated, all translations of Greek texts are mine; sometimes I have modified the translations of other scholars.

I hope that this book will increase the knowledge and interest of students in Hellenistic history, will enable scholars who study the wars of other periods and areas to take the Hellenistic examples into consideration, and will invite my fellow classicists and historians to provide better explanations of some of the questions which have intrigued and puzzled me.

I have never met some of the people I feel the need to thank. F. Walbank's seminal work on the Hellenistic Age and W. K. Pritchett's fundamental surveys on Greek warfare have helped me write this book more than I have been able to recognize in bibliographical references. J. W. Lendon allowed me to consult his forthcoming article on war and society in the Hellenistic and Roman worlds. Charalambos Kritzas (Epigraphical Museum,

Athens), Maria Akamati (Department of Antiquities, Pella), and A. Peschlow (German Archaeological Institute, Berlin) as well as the Numismatic Museum of Athens, the Rhodes Archaeological Museum, the École Française d'Athènes, and the British Museum provided photographs. My research assistant Volker Schmidt contributed substantially to the compilation of the bibliography and the preparation of the manuscript. My graduate research assistants Manolis Skountakis and Johannes Stahl offered valuable help in the collection of sources. The source index was compiled by Dr. Gian Franco Chiai. I am very grateful to Jon Ingoldby, who undertook the copy-editing and substantially improved the text, and to Sue Hadden for her patient and attentive work on the production of the manuscript. Without Al Bertrand's continual encouragement and help I would have never started writing this book, and without Angela Cohen's effective assistance in practical matters (and regular reminders), I would have never finished it.

From Fritz Gschnitzer I have learned to read inscriptions as sources for historical phenomena, and to pay attention to the tensions and complexities revealed by the choice of words. To him I gratefully dedicate this book on the occasion of his seventy-fifth birthday.

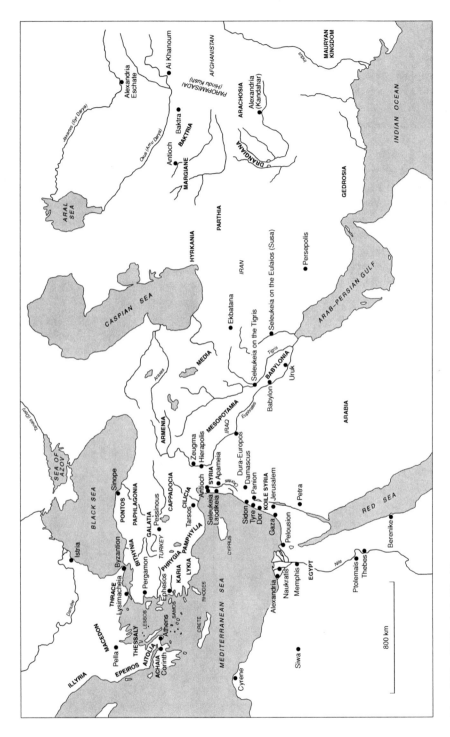

Map 1 The Hellenistic World

1

THE UBIQUITOUS WAR

1.1. The Visibility of War

If we are to believe the healing miracles of Epidauros, inscribed in the Asklepieion around the mid-fourth century BC, a visitor to that most famous Greek sanctuary would not only admire the newly-built temple and the sumptuous dedications, but also see, among the pilgrims seeking healing in that place, men whose bodies and faces had been marked by the wounds inflicted in war (LiDonnici 1995): "Euhippos bore a spear head in his jaw for six years" (A12); "Gorgias of Herakleia . . . was wounded in the lung by an arrow in some battle, and for a year and six months it was festering so badly, that he filled sixty-seven bowls with pus" (B10); "Antikrates of Knidos . . . had been struck with a spear through both his eyes in some battle, and he became blind and carried around the spearhead with him, inside his face" (B12).

Shortly after 197 BC, a traveller in North Thessaly would see, reaching the plain of Kynos Kephalai, the remains of 8,000 unburied Macedonians, killed at the decisive battle of the Second Macedonian War between Philip V of Macedonia and the Romans. It was not until 191 BC that King Antiochos III gave instructions to built a tomb for their bones (Livy 36.8; Appian, *Syr.* 16). Along the streets that led from the countryside to the city walls of a Hellenistic city, one would see the graves of men who had fallen in war. And a visitor to the Aitolian federal sanctuary of Thermon shortly before 218 BC would have been able to count more than 15,000 *hopla* – unidentifiable pieces of armor, dedicated by victorious parties in wars (Polyb. 5.8).

Travelling in Hellenistic Greece meant travelling in a landscape marked by war. The modern viewer of an aesthetically pleasing Hellenistic statue such as the Nike of Samothrace tends to forget that this statue decorated a victory monument (see chapter 11, section 6) and that ancient warfare could take unpleasant forms of visibility. Burned fields and farms next to trophies, cenotaphs in front of ruined or hastily built fortifications, plundered temples next to statues of war heroes – these are some of the impressions the Hellenistic landscape must have left on a contemporary traveler.

No detailed description of the Hellenistic world survives, but even if such a description had been written, it is doubtful whether the author would have bothered to inform his readers about the devastations caused by war – so familiar would these have been to his eyes, it would be more rewarding to describe impressive monuments. The only lengthy fragment of a Hellenistic periegesis, a work of the late third century attributed to a certain Herakleides, does not say a single word about warfare.

Despite this, among the factors that shaped the Hellenistic world, war seems without doubt to be the most important. The genesis of the Hellenistic world is itself the result of a war – the campaigns of Alexander the Great – and the end of this historical period is also marked by a battle – the Battle of Actium and the defeat of the last Ptolemaic monarch, Kleopatra. Between the violent beginnings, with the Wars of the Successors (322 BC), and the bloody end (31 BC), we have three centuries in which major and minor wars provided contemporary historians with the material for their books, and artists with assignments for grave monuments, war memorials, and dedications. These wars demanded thousands of mortal lives and the attention of those deities who were believed to be the patrons of war. There is hardly any moment in which a geographical region was not directly involved, or indirectly affected, by a military conflict; in fact, the most influential historian of this period, Polybios, regarded the entire Mediterranean as a single battlefield from the late third century onwards, and introduced the notion of the *symploke* ("interweaving") to characterize the "world history" of his times. The Hellenistic Age is not only the period of a global culture (*koine*), but also – indeed, more so – the period of the ubiquitous war.

The Hellenistic Greeks were surrounded by images of war (see chapter 10). The coins they used were decorated not only with the portraits of kings with military attributes, but also with weapons, war monuments, trophies, and divine patrons of war (especially Athena holding the Victory). Demetrios the Besieger, for example, minted silver coins after his victory in Salamis on Cyprus (307 BC) with the representation of Nike (Victory) standing on the prow of a warship and blowing a trumpet (see figure 1.1), and coins of the Syracusan tyrant Agathokles were decorated with the winged Nike erecting a trophy (see figure 11.1). The public areas of urban centers, such as the market-place, the buildings of the administration, and the sanctuaries, were decorated with the statues of war heroes and memorials of victorious battles, and war booty was dedicated to the gods. Inscriptions praising benefactors who had saved their own or foreign cities during wars were exhibited in the same public areas, and if the passers-by did not have the leisure to read the text of the honorary inscription, a representation would often provide a hint of the military context. For example, the honorary decree for Euphron of Sikyon in Athens (see figure 1.2) is decorated with the images of Athena and the grateful Demos (the personification of

Figure 1.1 Silver coin issued by Demetrios the Besieger after his victory in Salamis (Cyprus), 306 BC. Nike stands on the forecastle of a galley's prow holding a trumpet. Numismatic Museum of Athens (courtesy of the Museum).

the people) on one side, and Euphron, in military attire, standing in front of his horse, on the other.

Military parades were an integral part of public ceremonies, and one of these may be portrayed on the famous mosaic of Praeneste (Pollitt 1986: figure 222; cf. Coarelli 1990). In many regions, the graves of people who had spent a long period in military service were decorated with their images in military attire (see chapter 10, section 2). Even houseware was decorated with military themes – for example, with war elephants (see e.g., Ducrey 1985: 105, figure 76), and it is highly likely that paintings with representations of battle scenes would have adorned private houses.

There are a variety of reasons for the ubiquity of images of war, military equipment, and military personnel: an interest in dramatic changes of fortune, the feeling of compassion, the love of the exotic, and a fondness for the paradoxal (see chapter 10). But in addition to these reasons, which are closely connected with major trends in Hellenistic culture, there is a more pragmatic one: wars were extremely frequent in the Hellenistic period.

Figure 1.2 Athenian honorary decree for Euphron of Sikyon, an ally of the Athenians in their wars for freedom against the Macedonians (323–18 BC). The relief shows Demos (the personification of the people) on the one side and Euphron, in military attire, standing in front of his horse, on the other. Athens National Museum (courtesy of the Museum).

1.2. The Frequency of Wars

To narrate the history of Hellenistic wars would mean covering the history of the entire Hellenistic period, and this is well beyond the scope of this book. Even to compile a list of the wars which were fought between 322 and 31 BC, and of the regions which were affected by these wars, is beyond the possibilities of a modern historian. Almost all the works of Hellenistic historians have been lost (see chapter 11, section 2), and what survives directly (fragments of Polybios, Diodoros, and Poseidonios), and indirectly in later historiography – for example, in Livy (late first century BC), in Appian (early second century AD), and in Plutarch's *Lives* (late first/early second century AD) – only allows a partial reconstruction of the "great wars." The focus on these major wars, in which usually more than two states were involved, often results in our overlooking the far more numerous regional and local conflicts, territorial disputes, civil wars, revolts of indigenous populations or mercenary soldiers, and invasions of barbarian tribes. In a conference of the Hellenic Alliance in Korinth in the spring of 219 BC, under the presidency of Philip V, the allies brought forth accusations against the Aitolians (Polyb. 4.25.2–5; Austin 1981: no. 58). They had plundered in peace-time the sanctuary of Athena Itonia in Boiotia, attempted to sack Ambrysos and Daulion in Phokis, ravaged Epeiros, and attacked Thyrreion in Akarnania at night. In the Peloponnese, they had seized Klarion on the territory of Megalopolis, ravaged the territory of Patrai and Pharai in Achaia, sacked Kynetha, plundered the temple of Artemis at Lousoi, besieged Kleitor, and attacked Pylos by sea and Megalopolis by land. All these were recent wars that had occured shortly before the summer of 220 BC, and all had taken place in the narrow geographical region in which the interests of the Hellenic Alliance were concentrated.

Rather than summarizing the political history of the Hellenistic world (see pp. xvii–xx), I will attempt to give an impression of the frequency of wars by focusing on four selected areas, which seem more or less representative and are certainly well documented: a kingdom (Antigonid Macedonia); a major city state (Athens); a "middle power" in the Aegean (Rhodes); and an island on the periphery of the Greek world (Crete). (Readers who do not wish to be confronted with dates and names and are willing to accept my general statement concerning the frequency of wars may skip the following section.)

Counting wars in Antigonid Macedonia

Antigonos the One-Eyed, the founder of the dynasty of the Antigonids, who ruled over the kingdom of Macedonia and its external possessions, aquired the title of king after a military victory during one of the Wars of the Successors (307/6 BC). He lost his kingdom and his life at the Battle of

Ipsos (301 BC), but his son, King Demetrios the Besieger, continued until 287 BC to try to re-establish himself on the throne of the Macedonians, and for a short period of time (294–287 BC) he was successful. The Antigonids firmly established their rule when Demetrios' son, Antigonos Gonatas, exploited a vacuum of power during the invasion of Gaulish tribes (277/6 BC) and was recognized as king of the Macedonians. In the following years he gained control over Thessaly as well as over a series of Macedonian garrisons in southern Greece (Euboia, Attika, and the Peloponnese). In the 111 years between his victory over the Gauls and the defeat of the last Antigonid, Perseus, at the Battle of Pydna (167 BC), there is hardly any period in which the Antigonid kings or members of their families were not involved in a war: throwing back an invasion of barbarian tribes, subduing revolts, helping their allies against enemies, or attempting to increase their territory. These wars were not only fought in Antigonid lands, but affected areas as distant as the Adriatic coast and Karia in Asia Minor. The highlights of these wars were: the invasion of Macedonia by King Pyrrhos and the subsequent wars in the Peloponnese (274–273 BC); the Chremonideian War against Ptolemaic Egypt, Athens, Sparta, and their allies, which was primarily fought in Attika, on the Peloponnese, and in Macedonia, but also in the Aegean (268–261 BC); the revolt of Antigonos' nephew Alexandros, who controlled the garrisons in Korinth and Chalkis (252–245 BC); the expulsion of the Macedonian garrisons in the Peloponnese (243 BC); the War of Demetrios, with operations in central Greece (Akarnania), Attika, and in the Peloponnese (239–233 BC); the invasion of the Dardanians in Paionia (231–229 BC); the revolt of the largest part of Thessaly and the loss of the garrison in Athens (229 BC); the expedition of Antigonos Doson in Karia (Asia Minor, 227 BC); the War of Kleomenes on the Peloponnese (224–221 BC); the wars against Illyrian tribes (221 BC) and the Dardanians (220–219, 217, 209 BC); the Social War against the Aitolians with operations in the Peloponnese, in Akarnania, Aitolia, Epeiros, Illyria, Thessaly, and Macedonia (220–217 BC); the war in Illyria (217–215 BC), which directly led to the First Macedonian War against the Romans, with military activities in Illyria, Akarnania, Phokis, Lokris, Thessaly, and the Peloponnese (215–205 BC); the expansion wars of Philip V in Thrace, the northern Aegean, Marmaris, and northwest and west Asia Minor (202–200 BC); and the Second Macedonian War, provoked by these activities and mainly fought in Illyria, Thessaly, and Macedonia (200–197 BC). The defeat at Kynos Kephalai in 197 BC imposed a short interruption of this policy of aggresson, without bringing peace. Macedonian troops participated in the Roman wars against Nabis in Sparta (195 BC), and against the Aitolians in Thessaly (191 BC), in addition to sporadic operations in Thrace, which culminated in wars against Thracian tribes (183–179 BC). Philip's successor, Perseus, had fought a war against the Dolopians (174 BC) before the Third Macedonian War (171–167 BC) sealed the fate of the Antigonids.

Counting wars in Athens

Athens was once a hegemonial power, but during the Hellenic War (323–322 BC), an uprising against the Macedonians after Alexander's death, it lost its fleet, and along with this its influence. It did, however, remain strategically important and politically influential until the first century BC. During the Wars of the Successors, Athens and Attika – especially their harbors and fortresses – were time and again the scene of battle, but Athenian soldiers also participated in battles outside Athens, among them the siege of Piraeus (318 BC); skirmishes during the conflict between Polyperchon and Kassandros (317 BC); the sea-battles at the Bosporos (317); and Kassandros' attack against and occupation of Salamis and Panakton (317 BC). As an ally of Kassandros (317–307 BC), Athens sent ships which participated in naval expeditions in the Cyclades and in Lemnos (315–314 BC). In 307 the fortress of Mounychia fell to Demetrios the Besieger and Athens regained its independence, after which the Athenians fought with Demetrios in the Battle of Salamis in Cyprus (307/6 BC). Kassandros attempted to regain Athens at least twice (306 and 304 BC), and the second time the city was besieged, the territory ravaged, and the island of Salamis plus the fortresses of Panakton and Phyle were occupied. A year later (303 BC), Athenian soldiers fought against Kassandros in the Peloponnese, and possibly in the same year Piraeus and Mounychia were attacked by Macedonian troops. Demetrios' defeat in the Battle of Ipsos (301 BC) led to the tyranny of Lachares, and in connection with it to unrest in Athens, as the harbor of Piraeus was held by Athenians who opposed him. The first attempt of Demetrios to regain the city in 296 failed, but the second attack (295 BC), connected with a long siege and the plundering of the countryside, was successful. A rebellion of the Athenians in 287 removed Demetrios' troops – but not from Piraeus – and the following decades were by no means free of wars, of which the Galatian invasion (279–278 BC) and the Chremonidean War (268–262 BC) caused the greatest losses. Under the Macedonian subjugation (262–229 BC) Athens – and especially Piraeus, Salamis, and the countryside – repeatedly suffered during the wars of Antigonos Doson, especially during the revolt of the king's nephew, Alexandros (ca. 251–244 BC), and during the wars with the Achaians (242 and 240 BC).

Athens was also involved in military combat during the War of Demetrios (239–233 BC). After the removal of the Macedonian garrison in 229, and following a policy of neutrality, Athens was able to enjoy, for the first time, a rather long period of peace (229–200 BC), which came to an end with its active participation in the Second Macedonian War against Philip V (200–197 BC). As allies of the Romans, the Athenians were involved (on a very modest scale) in the Roman wars against Antiochos III and the Aitolians (192–188 BC). With the exception of Athenian raids on Oropos in the 150s, Roman rule in Greece established a further period of peace. However,

Athens broke with Rome in 88, supporting Mithridates VI in his war against the Romans, and this ultimate expression of independence ended in 86 with the sack of the city and terrible bloodshed.

Counting wars in Rhodes

Several things led to the rise of Rhodes: its strategic position in the southeast Aegean, its great harbor, a significant fleet, an intelligent internal policy, and skillful diplomacy. However, none of these attributes protected the island from attacks and wars. After Alexander's death, the Rhodians expelled the Macedonian garrison (323 BC), and Rhodes managed to avoid direct involvement for most of the Wars of the Successors – except for an attack by one of Perdikkas' generals in 321, the participation in naval operations of Antigonos the One-Eyed (314–312 BC), and the famous siege by Antigonos' son Demetrios the Besieger (305–304 BC). Rhodes did not fall, and it not only recovered from the destructions of the long siege, but was also active in the third century on the opposite coast of Asia Minor, in part subjecting territories and in part gaining influence, both by diplomatic means and with military action.

The limited sources do not allow us to fully reconstruct the history of Rhodian expansion in Karia, but at least one major battle is directly reported (a victory over a fleet of Ptolemy II near Ephesos), possibly during the Second Syrian War (ca. 260 BC). There are also reports of fights against "Tyrrhenian" pirates in the early third century. The trade interests of the Rhodians led to active military engagement from the late third century onwards: against Byzantion, which had imposed duties on vessels passing though the straits (220 BC); against Illyrian pirates (220 BC); and against the Cretan cities, which organized raids in the southeast Aegean (219 and ca. 205–201 BC). Philip V's adventures in southwest Asia Minor (202–201 BC) brought the Rhodians into conflict with the Macedonians, which ultimately contributed to the Second Macedonian War, in which Rhodes was one of the most important allies of Rome (200–198/97 BC). Its participation in the War of Antiochos on the side of Rome (191–188 BC) brought to Rhodes the domination of Lykia and Karia (with the exception of a few cities). However, these areas required an intensive military presence following their subjugation. These military efforts culminated in the supression of two revolts in Lykia (ca. 188–178 and ca. 174–171 BC). Rhodes' contribution to the Third Macedonian War (171–167 BC) was limited to the dispatching of a few ships, and this half-hearted support of Rome was punished with the loss of Lykia and Karia. The last years of Rhodian domination there (167–166 BC) were not free of military conflicts, but this period marked the end of Rhodes' power and its participation in intensive warfare. With the exception of a second "Cretan War" (ca. 155–153 BC), only sporadic military activities are attested – for example, a limited participation in the

Third Punic War on the side of Rome (147 BC), and occasional piratic raids and attacks during the civil wars of the late Roman Republic.

Counting wars in Hellenistic Crete

Finally, turning to Hellenistic Crete (see map 2), this island gave the contemporary observer the confusing picture of a region affected by endemic wars. Ancient historians were puzzled by this situation, as the following comment by Polybios shows (24.3.1): "This year [181 BC] witnessed the beginning of great troubles in Crete if indeed one can talk of a beginning of trouble in Crete. For their continual civil wars and their excessive cruelty to each other make beginning and end mean the same thing." Since in this case we are not dealing with one state, but with some 50 or 60 independent city-states concentrated in a limited space, a more detailed discussion is necessary. It should be remarked that in many cases we know of a war only from its results – i.e., the conquest and/or destruction of a city. The causes of the continual war in Hellenistic Crete were mainly territorial expansion and the involvement of foreign powers.

In the late fourth or early third century BC, Praisos (east Crete) conquered the harbors of Setaia and Stalai, and Dragmos suffered the same fate somewhat later. Cretan cities were involved in the Chremonidean War (ca. 268–261 BC) as allies of both parties, and this division of Crete may have also resulted in conflicts within the island. The greatest war in Cretan history is the "War of Lyttos" (ca. 222–218 BC). Here, the cities of Gortyn and Knossos joined forces to attack the third major city, Lyttos. Because its warriors were busy attacking the neighboring city of Dreros, Lyttos had been left defenseless. The Knossians attacked, sacked the city, destroyed it entirely, and captured all the women and children (Polyb. 4.54). When the Lyttians returned and saw what had happened, they lamented the fate of their fatherland, turned their backs on it and retired to Lappa.

However, the situation soon changed. Several allies of the Knossians left the alliance and joined with Lyttos, while the other major power, Gortyn, was divided due to a civil war. Contemporary inscriptions allude to further civil wars (*SEG* XLIX 1217; *I.Cret.* I, ix 1), and it seems probable that at the end the anti-Knossian alliance was victorious. A small episode of this war was the attack of Milatos against Dreros for the occupation of a border area (*I.Cret.* I, ix 1); the Drerians were able to defend it, but both cities were conquered and destroyed by Lyttos some time later. The fact that the protagonists of this war were also allied with major powers makes the "War of Lyttos" look like a local episode of the "Social War" of Philip V of Macedonia and the Achaians against the Aitolians (222–217 BC). Knossos was allied with the Aitolians, while Gortyn and its allies supported Philip and the Achaians. To make things more complex, we also hear of an attack of Eleutherna against Rhodes, an ally of the Knossians (219 BC), and many

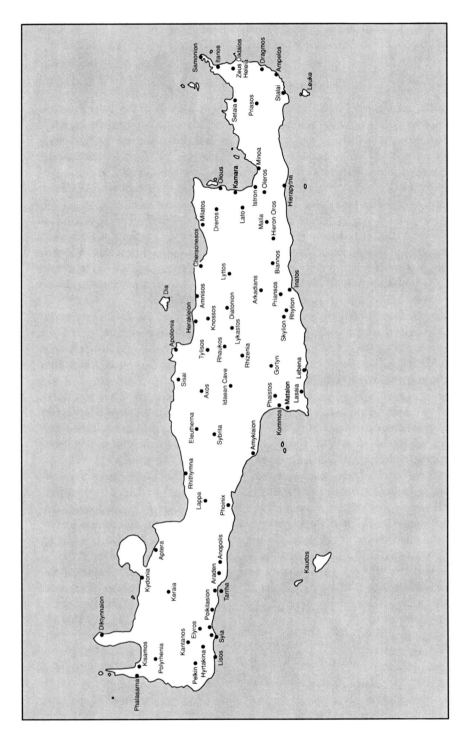

Map 2 Hellenistic Crete

Cretan mercenaries fought in the war between Ptolemy IV and Antiochos III (219–217 BC).

A very short period of peace was then followed by the "Cretan War," which was probably part of Philip V's strategy to use his Cretan allies to control the eastern Aegean. This war (ca. 206–201 BC) had the form of attacks of Cretan ships – probably of Gortyn and her allies – on the islands of the Dodecannese (especially Rhodes and Kalymna), and the coastal cities of Asia Minor. Crete was divided into two camps, under Gortyn and Knossos respectively, and there are direct references and allusions to local wars, especially in the eastern part of the island. The "Cretan War" ended around 201 BC, but the wars continued on Crete itself, this time between Gortyn and Knossos (ca. 200–195 BC). As in most cases, we do not know what the outcome of these wars was, but in 189 BC the two opponents joined forces to attack the most important city in western Crete: Kydonia. The causes of a civil war in Phalasarna (ca. 185 BC) are not known; its strong neighbor, Kydonia, took the opportunity and occupied the city for a short period. Soon after (184 BC), Gortyn conquered Knossian territories (Lykastion and Diatonion), but had to return them as soon as the peace was established.

Another war in 174 BC was obviously so important that the Romans had to send Q. Minucius to arbitrate between the anonymous opponents. The next major war can be dated to around 170–167 BC. This time, Kydonia attacked Apollonia (ca. 170 BC), destroyed the city, and occupied its land. This caused the intervention of Knossos and Gortyn, who fought against each other for this same land until 168 BC. When this conflict was resolved, the earlier enemies joined forces to attack Rhaukos, which was finally taken and destroyed. An inscription describes the line which divided the territory and the town between the conquerors (Chaniotis 1996a: no. 44). This line follows the course of a street that goes through the center of the lower town, passes in front of the town hall, and leads through one of the gates to the citadel, and from there to the countryside. Everything south of the line belonged to Gortyn, the rest to Knossos (166 BC). Phaistos, the only remaining city in the central plain of Crete (the plain of Mesara), was destroyed by Gortyn some time later (ca. 150 BC). After Knossos and Gortyn had achieved their primary aim – i.e. to conquer all the cities in their vicinity – and had fixed their borders, peace was finally established, but only on the island itself. Cretan troops still fought outside Crete, in the wars between Ptolemy VI and VIII (ca. 158–154 BC) and in the "Second Cretan War" against Rhodes (ca. 155–153 BC).

The period of internal peace on Crete ended with the death of Ptolemy VI and the retreat of his troops from east Crete (Itanos, 145 BC). Only a local episode of the next great war around 145 BC is known: the conquest and destruction of Praisos in east Crete by Hierapytna (see chapter 7, section 3). By occupying the territory of Praisos, Hierapytna inherited the dispute that had been raging between Praisos and Itanos for many decades concerning land near the sanctuary of Zeus Diktaios and the island of Leuke. A Roman arbitration brought peace in 140 BC, but did not solve the problem. When a new war between Knossos and Gortyn broke out around 121 BC, the traditional and unsettled territorial disputes in east Crete caused a new series of wars between Lato and Olous (121–118 BC), and between Itanos and Hierapytna (115–114 BC). It was only with repeated arbitrations under the auspices of Rome that peace was established around 110 BC.

We hear of no other wars among the Cretans, but their military operations did not stop; rather, they took the form of raids against ships and coastal cities in the south Aegean. Cretan piracy was the cause of (or the excuse for) two Roman wars against the Cretans in 74 and between 69 and 67 BC, which finally led to the island's subjugation.

In addition to the aforementioned wars, which are directly recorded, we may assume that conquest was the fate of many small cities, the autonomy of which is attested in the late Classical and early Hellenistic periods through coins and decrees, but which either disappear in the course of the Hellenistic period or are only known as subordinate communities. Istron must have been conquered by Lato, Matalon by Phaistos (ca. 260–220 BC), Tylisos by Knossos, and Eltynia by Knossos or by Lyttos. If to these wars one adds the service of Cretan mercenaries abroad (see chapter 5, section 2), it becomes clear that war was the most important feature of Cretan everyday life (and a frequent cause of death).

A study of the political history of other areas – for example, the major kingdoms (Ptolemies, Seleukids, Attalids, the kingdom of Bithynia, the Bosporan kingdom, and the Greek-Baktrian kingdoms in the East); of the Peloponnese, Aitolia, and Boiotia; of most cities of Asia Minor (e.g., Magnesia on the Maenander, Xanthos, Miletos, Teos); of the Greek colonies along the coast of the Black Sea; and of course of the Greek cities of south Italy and Sicily – would only confirm the impression of ubiquitous war. Even if some (perhaps most) military operations described by our sources as "wars" were no more than skirmishes, sudden attacks against forts, and raids in the more or less defenseless countryside, they still substantially affected the everyday life, economy, political institutions, and culture of the Hellenistic populations.

1.3. Reasons to Fight

Modern tourists who visit the picturesque Cretan city of Agios Nikolaos in east Crete probably pay hardly any attention to the islet of Nikolonisi and the rock, Mikronisi, next to it. If we happen to know the ancient name of this islet (Pyrrha), it is thanks to a long dossier of inscriptions which concerns a dispute between the cities of Lato (Agios Nikolaos, ancient Kamara, was its harbor) and Olous (modern Elounta). The object of the dispute, for which the two cities fought a war in the late second century (ca. 121–118 BC), is described in the final verdict of the arbitrators: "a dispute concerning [a piece of] land, the sanctuary at Dera and all the adjacent sacred precincts, the island of Pyrrha and the adjacent rock, the quadrireme and the silverware from this ship and the silver coins and the bronzeware and the other items, of all kind, and the persons who were sold, two free persons and a slave" (Chaniotis 1996a: 327). The Latians and the Olountians fought for all the usual reasons: material profit (in this case land and the booty from a captured ship), safety, symbolic capital (the control of an old sanctuary, which also owned land), and – often more important than the rest – pride, honor, and justice.

The frequency of wars in the Hellenistic period can be attributed to a variety of factors, and these have already been alluded to in the overview of the wars of Antigonid Macedonia, Athens, Rhodes, and Crete (see section 1.2): the expansionist endeavors of kings; the attempts of cities to regain their autonomy; disputes over territories and their resources; conflicts over a hegemonial position; defensive wars against invading barbarians or raiding pirates; and civil wars.

A major factor of instability was that the conquests of Alexander the Great had destroyed a great empire – the empire of the Achaemenids. Alexander's premature death left this huge geographical area without unified rule. The outcome of 40 years (322–281 BC) of continual war for the succession of Alexander's empire was the creation of new rival kingdoms (especially those of the Ptolemies, Seleukids, Antigonids, and Attalids), the conflicts of which affected not only the populations who lived in the kingdoms and the contested areas, but also had much wider consequences because of a complex network of alliances and dependencies. War was of vital importance for the monarchies, both for material reasons (control of terrirories and their resources, gain and redistribution of booty), and because of the ideology of kingship, which was primarily based on military victory (see chapter 4). In addition to this, the achievements of Alexander served as a model for ambitious adventurers (e.g., Pyrrhos, Demetrios the Besieger). Most of the "great wars" of this period – the wars of the longest duration, the greatest mobilization of troops, and the largest numbers of victims, but also the wars which are better represented in our sources – were either wars between two or more kingdoms and their allies (e.g., the Chremonidean War and six Syrian Wars) or wars provoked by the efforts of a king to re-establish control over a territory (e.g., the various wars of Antiochos III). To these we may add dynastic conflicts (e.g., the war between Antiochos III and Achaios, 216–213 BC, or the civil war between Ptolemy VI and Ptolemy VIII).

The revolt of the Maccabees (168–164 BC) had its origins in internal Jewish conflicts rather than in any fundamental opposition between Hellenism and Judaism (Gruen 2003: 267–8). It was more of an "ethnic" conflict within the realms of a kingdom, as were the repeated revolts of the native population in Ptolemaic Egypt in the second century (McGing 1997; Thompson 1999, 2003: 115).

Among the external enemies of the Hellenistic world, the Celtic tribes, which invaded Greece in 280 BC, and from there crossed to Asia Minor, certainly occupy the most prominent position (Strobel 1991; Mitchell 2003). Their raids in Greece and Asia Minor in the third century BC were among the most traumatic experiences of the Greeks, and the wars against these Galatians were assimilated with the Persian wars. In the periphery of the Hellenistic world, on the northern border of Macedonia, in the Greek cities of the Black Sea, and in Kyrenaika (Libya), barbarian attacks were very frequent, albeit not well represented in our sources. On the eastern border, the wars of the Greek-Baktrian kings against the local tribes of Iran and Afghanistan have left their traces in the representation of military themes on their coins (cf. Lévêque 1991).

However, the most important external factor influencing Hellenistic wars from the late third century onwards was the expansion of Rome and the increasing importance of imperialism for the Roman political, social, and economic elite. In addition to the wars of the Roman expansion (especially the three Macedonian wars, the war against Antiochos, the occupation of Achaia, and two Cretan wars), the intrusion of the Romans into the Hellenistic world provoked the resistance of some populations (e.g., the revolt in Macedonia between 148 and 146 BC, and revolts in Asia Minor and Greece during the Mithridatic wars). An additional external factor in the first century BC was the civil wars of the late Roman Republic, which in part were fought in the East.

Despite the focus of Hellenistic (and later) historians on the royal wars and the wars of Rome, for the majority of Hellenistic populations, wars were predominantely local affairs. To mention only a few examples, the Samians violently expelled Athenian settlers (*klerouchoi*) from their island in 322 BC (*IG* XII.6.1 43); a Macedonian garrison was expelled from Sikyon in the same year (*IG* II² 448 = Austin 1981: no. 26); and the incursions of the Galatians, joined by Thracian tribes and other warlike Anatolians, terrorized Tlos in Lykia, Laodikeia on the Lykos (Paus. 10.32.4), and Kelainai (Paus. 10.39.9) in the 270s. In addition, in the early second century, hostilities between cities of the Achaian League and the Boiotians were caused because of unsettled private suits between Boiotian and Achaian citizens and consequent reprisals (Ager 1996: 281; cf. Pritchett 1991: 94–100). Around 188 BC, a fort seceded from Alabanda in Karia and around the same time Termessos and Isinda (probably also Aspendos and other Pamphylian cities) were involved in a local war (Ma 2000c: 339), and Berenike (Kyrenaika) "was under siege by the bandidts" in 62/1 BC (*SEG* XXVIII 1540).

If the social causes of war are hard to grasp, economic factors are a clearer, and predominant, cause of military conflicts. Even on the eve of Alexander's campaign, Greece was in a state of economic distress (Fuks 1972). The concentration of land in a few hands has always been an endemic problem in Greek history. If we look beyond Athens and a few other cities, agriculture was the most important source of income for the citizens, and certainly the most respectable. Political theorists and reformers alike never tired of including the redistribution of land in their programs.

The reality was very different. A bad harvest, a wedding or a funeral, an enemy attack and the destruction of the olive trees and the vineyards, forced those who could not produce enough surplus into debt. When the debts were not paid (and this was usually the case), farmers lost their land. Time and again in their history, the Greeks had to deal with the problem of large numbers of citizens without land. The Peloponnesian War and the subsequent wars on mainland Greece made the situation worse. One of the phrases that was heard in Greek cities from the mid-fourth century onwards was *ges anadasmos* (redistribution of land). Greek cities had always had the same set of solutions to the problems created by the existence of citizens without landed property: they usually sent them abroad to found colonies or to serve as mercenaries (see chapter 5, section 2), or they conquered the territory of a neighbor, or – in rare cases – they enacted reforms.

With the campaigns of Alexander, thousands of Greeks had the opportunity first to serve as mercenaries and later to man the newly-founded cities and acquire land there (see chapter 5, section 3). One would expect that this would improve conditions in Greece, and this holds true for large parts of the mainland, but not necessarily for the islands and the cities of Asia Minor. The numerous inscriptions that concern themselves with territorial conflicts show that disputes over the ownership of land were the most frequent issue faced by Hellenistic interstate arbitration (see chapter 7, section 3). In some cases the relevant texts directly inform us that the disputed territory was important for agricultural activites. But very often – and this should not surprise us, given the mountainous nature both of the borders of Greek cities and of the largest part of their territories – the disputed land was beyond the cultivated area. This land (*eschatia*) still had economic importance for the exploitation of natural resources (such as timber and metals), but most of it functioned as pasture land during the summer months.

The control of strategically important areas (e.g., on trade routes) could also provoke wars. When, in the mid-third century, Kallatis (on the west shore of the Black Sea) attempted to establish a trade monopoly at the port of Tomis, Byzantion put an end to these plans after a war (Memnon *FgrHist* 434 F 13; Ager 1996: no. 34). Byzantion itself was attacked some time later by the Rhodians, when it attempted to impose duties on vessels passing through the straits.

In areas in which neither colonization could be practiced nor territorial expansion was possible, part of the population had war as its actual occupation: some men offered their services as mercenaries (see chapter 5, section 2), others participated in raids (see chapter 7, section 3), and many occupied themselves with both activities. Unpaid mercenaries, like the Macedonian soldiers who marched from Egypt to Triparadeisos (320 BC) without pay, were a constant element of instability.

In addition to economic factors, the ideology of the independent city-state provoked conflicts. The importance of military training for the young men of free citizen communities (see chapter 2, sections 1 and 2 and chapter 3) and the continual effort to defend their autonomy from the interventions of Hellenistic kings (e.g., through the expulsion of garrison troops), tyrants, and later the Romans, left only limited possibilities for a lasting peace.

Finally, rival political groups within a city would occasionally try to defeat their opponents with the help of a foreign ally, promising in exchange to offer support themselves after their victory. Many of the political upheavals in late third- and second-century Athens (see section 1.2) originated in such a nexus of internal political aspirations and external alliances. Siege and war could endanger the social equilibrium and bring to the surface latent conflicts (Garlan 1974: 42–3; Will 1975: 301). Many civil wars broke out in the context of larger conflicts, with the representatives of different political groups in the same city supporting different opponents. During the Lamian War (the revolt of Greek cities against Macedonian control, 323–322 BC), the propertied classes opposed the war and appeared to be in favor of a collaboration with Macedonia (cf. $Syll.^3$ 317, line 10). Thisbe (Boiotia) was divided during the Third Macedonian War (170 BC), and Roman supporters had to flee from the city and occupy a citadel (IG VII 2225; Sherk 1969: no. 2; Bagnall and Derow 2004: no. 45). The socio-political components of "Aristonikos' War" in Asia Minor (133–129 BC), between Aristonikos and his supporters (allegedly the poor and recruited slaves), and the Romans and their Greek allies, are a matter of controversy. Even if the interpretation of this war as a "social revolution" is improbable, it still shows – like the Mithridatic wars – the coexistence of many different causes and hopes, ranging from the aspiration of monarchical rule to the hope of freedom.

Our contemporary sources recognize the most important causes of war in human nature. Polybios makes the greed (*pleonexia*) of the Cretans responsible for the continual wars (van Effenterre 1948: 285–92), and a lesser-known historian, Philippos of Pergamon (IG IV.1² 687; FgrHist 95 T 1; Goukowski 1995), introduced his history of the last wars of the late Republic with these words:

> With my pious hand I delivered to the Greeks the historical narrative of the most recent deeds – all sorts of sufferings and a continual mutual slaughter having taken place in our days in Asia and Europe, in the tribes of Libya and in the cities of the islanders; I did this, so that they may learn also through us, how many evils are brought forth by courting the mob and by love of profit, by civil strifes and by the breaking of faith, and thus, by observing the sufferings of others, they may live their lives in the right way.

Looking for the origins of wars in the love of (material) profit and in courting the mob, Philippos certainly failed to comprehend the complexity of war. But his didactic endeavor was noble, and the *Pax Romana*, established in the largest part of the Roman world, could indeed create the (wrong) impression that people had learned from the sufferings of others.

Further Reading

1.1. The Visibility of War. *The periegesis of Herakleides*: Pfister 1951. *The notion of symploke in Polybios*: Walbank 1975; Vollmer 1990.

1.2. The Frequency of War. *General books on the political history of the Hellenistic world*: Will 1979 and 1982; *CAH* VII²; Green 1990; Shipley 2000; Erskine 2003: 19–174. *Antigonid Macedonia*: Walbank 1984: 221–56, 446–81; Buraselis 1982; Errington 1986: 133–95; Derow 2003; Scholten 2003. *Athens*: Habicht 1997. *Rhodes*: Berthold 1984: 59–232; Gabrielsen 1997; Bresson 1999; Reger 1999; Wiemer 2002. *Crete*: Chaniotis 1996a: 14–15, 27–56.

1.3. Reasons to Fight. *The dispute between Lato and Olous*: van Effenterre 1942; Baldwin Bowsky 1989; Chaniotis 1996a: 51–5, 318–32. *Examples of wars between neighbors*: Livy 38.15.1–6 (Termessos-Isinda); *I.Mylasa* 102 (Mylasa-Heraklein); *I.Side* 227 (Side-Aspendos); *SEG* XXIX 1130 bis (Temnos-Klazomenai); Baker 2001 and Herrmann 2001 (the wars of Miletos). *The revolt of the Maccabees*: Bringmann 1983; Bar-Kochva 1989; Hyldahl 1991. *The Roman expansion*: Gruen 1984. *Aristonikos' war*: Mileta 1998; Briant, Brun and Varinlioglu 2001; Ferrary 2001: 98–100; Daubner 2003; Dreyer and Engelmann 2003; Brun 2004.

2

BETWEEN CIVIC DUTIES AND OLIGARCHIC ASPIRATIONS: DEVOTED CITIZENS, BRAVE GENERALS, AND GENEROUS BENEFACTORS

2.1. Fighting Against a Neighbor: A Privilege of the Polis

In the Hellenistic period, no less than in the Classical period, war was more than the means by which a city protected its territory – it was an essential privilege of the free and autonomous city (Will 1975). Since we lack an ancient definition of what constitutes the autonomy of a city, we have to infer the importance of the right to make war from indirect sources. The right to fight wars is more clearly formulated in civic oaths. The oath of the Athenian *ephebes* (Tod, *GHI* no. 204; cf. Lycurgus, *contra Leocraten* 77) begins with a reference to their military duties and to their duty to increase the civic territory: "I will not dishonour the sacred weapons and I will not abandon the comrade on the flank, whomever I may be placed next to; and I will fight to defend the sacred and holy things; I will not deliver the fatherland diminished, but larger and stronger." The same invitation to expansion – certainly through war – is to be found in the oath of the inhabitants of the island of Kalymna when it joined the island of Kos in joined citizenship (*sympolity; Staatsverträge* 545, lines 26–7): "I will not allow Kos to become smaller, but on the contrary I will increase it to the best of my capacity."

The belief that the ability to successfully avert attackers and to attack others is a fundamental right of an autonomous civic community also explains why any limitation of this ability, such as the destruction of fortification walls, or the occupation of citadels and forts by foreign garrisons, was regarded as an "amputation" of freedom. In an epigram, the city wall is called "the crown of free children" (Ma 2000c: 365, n. 31), and the envoys of Kytenion in Doris, who requested financial support for the reconstruction of their city walls in the late third century BC, made it clear that their city would be extinguished if it lacked such walls (*SEG* XXXVIII 1476, lines 101–2). If the lack of a fortification wall makes a community vulnerable, the presence of a garrison limits its ability to express its own free will. From the early fourth century onwards the term *aphrouretos* – i.e., "ungarrisoned" – is almost a synonym for *autonomos* in the diplomatic language of the Greeks. The words *autonomos* and *aphrouretos* appear alongside one another in several treaties which aimed at guaranteeing the independence of a polis (Chaniotis 2002: 101–2). For Plutarch (i.e., for his Hellenistic source) the Achaians were "bridled like a horse" (*hosper chalinoumenous*) when they accepted a Macedonian garrison and delivered hostages to King Antigonos Doson (Plut., *Aratos* 38.10).

The Greeks were conscious of the incompatibility of autonomy and the presence of foreign troops in a polis. Foreign troops were then, as they are now, an instrument of subordination: they implemented a more or less direct control over the political institutions of a civic community (e.g., Apollodoros, *FgrHist* 244 F 44; cf. Dreyer 1999: 167, n. 224). To some extent they controlled or exploited the community's economic resources, and they occupied its military facilities (e.g., forts, citadels, and harbors). A foreign garrison prevented military activities by the garrisoned city. As Diodoros (18.18.3–5) reports, after the capitulation of Athens to Antipatros in 322 BC, the Athenians had to accept a garrison so that they would not attempt a violent revolt (*neoterizein*).

It should not come as a surprise that many local conflicts, suppressed by direct or indirect royal control, flared up again almost immediately after the eclipse of the said royal power. A document concerning an arbitration of Magnesia on the Maeander in a long territorial conflict on Crete illuminates the conditions under which this conflict started again. The Itanians:

> were at times pressed hard by the neighboring Praisians and invited Ptolemy, the former king of Egypt, for help and protection of their city and territory as well as of the islands . . . ; in this way they continued occupying the aforementioned areas. When King Ptolemy Philometor died [145 BC] and those who had been sent in order to jointly look after the territory and the islands for the Itanians left, the Itanians protected their land by themselves as they could, making use also of the benevolence of their friends. When a great war broke out in Crete, and the city of Praisos which lies between the Itanians and the Hierapytnians had been sacked, the Hierapytnians started a dispute with the Itanians concerning the island and the land.
>
> (*I.Cret.* III.iv 9, lines 39–58)

Similarly, when Antiochos III was defeated by the Romans in 189 BC and lost control and later ownership of his territories in Asia Minor, a series of local conflicts was reported in Alabanda, Termessos, Isinda, Aspendos, and other Pamphylian towns (Ma 2000c: 339) – the unexpected vacuum of power had presumably revived old disputes.

An essential expression of the autonomy of a city is its right to conclude treaties. The Hellenistic treaties cover a large variety of subjects, from the administration of sanctuaries to international arbitration and economic co-operation. The lion's share is made up of treaties of alliance, which are directly connected with war. One third of the treaties concluded between a Greek city and another partner (city, king, or league) from 323 to 200 BC (the treaties contained in the third volume of *Staatsverträge*) are treaties of alliance. Most of the remaining treaties also have a military background (peace treaties, capitulations, arbitrations, delimitations, etc.). In Crete, which admittedly is a particular case because of the predominantly military charac-ter of its civic communities, at least 30 of 63 Hellenistic treaties between Cretan cities are treaties of alliance. It should be noted that several of these treaties were explicitly concluded for offensive wars. If to the treaties of alliance one adds the peace treaties or agreements of delimitation after the end of a war, one immediately recognizes how seriously Greek states took their right to fight defensive and offensive wars.

Treaties of alliance between unequal parties are instructive in this context, since they show that a limitation of the weaker party's freedom in warfare means its subordination. From the Classical period onwards, such unequal treaties obliged the hegemonial power to help the dependent city only in her *defensive* wars, whereas the dependent city was required to follow the hegemonial power against whichever enemy the latter might choose (Chaniotis 1996a: 89–90). In the Hellenistic period, the relevant clause is found in Cretan treaties of alliance – for example, in a treaty between Gortyn and Lappa (Chaniotis 1996a: no. 31): "the Lappaian shall follow the Gortynians in both peace and war, against whomever the Gortynians ask him to." Of course, this does not mean that Lappa did not have the right to start its own wars, but it shows its inferior position.

Some time in the late second century BC, a poet described in a poem of 60 lines what constitutes the glory of Halikarnassos (*SGO* I 01/12/02; *SEG* XLVIII 1330). The poem begins with a narrative of the most important local god myths (lines 5–22), continues with the deeds of heroes (lines 23–42), lists the greatest native historians and poets (lines 43–56), and con-cludes: "[Halikarnassos] accomplished many splendid deeds on land; and many noble exploits at sea, carried out together with the generals of the Hellenes, are spoken of" (lines 57–8). Even though alluded to with only two lines, military achievements could not be absent from the praise of a city.

2.2. Warfare as a Citizen's Duty

One can hardly deny the fact that military service in most Hellenistic poleis was no longer the fundamental requirement for citizenship rights as it had been in Archaic and Classical Greece. The "military" revolution of the fourth century BC, which gave a greater significance in battle to the light-armed soldiers (*peltastai*), to mercenaries, and to trained military specialists (cavalry, archers, slingers, artillerists) than to the old-style citizen militias, had consequences for the defensive strategy of many cities. In this area one should, however, beware of any kind of generalization: there is little in common, for example, between the Cretan city of Lyttos, where the prerequisite of citizenship was military service almost to the exclusion of all other activities, and the city of Messena in Sicily, which relied for its defense on mercenaries and was eventually taken over by those it had hired to provide that defense (Polyb. 1.7.1–2). We should also take into consideration changes within the same city (e.g., the temporary revival of citizen militias as an expression of autonomy). Nevertheless, a study of the documentary evidence shows that in many, if not most, Hellenistic cities, citizen armies survived and were an important element of local pride (Vidal-Naquet 1981: 126–7; Ma 2000c). Military service was regarded as an honor, and only priests were temporarily exempted from it (Gauthier 1991). The importance of war and military service in the mentality of citizens is also alluded to by the many personal names which were composed with the words *polemos* ("war," e.g., Neoptolemos, Polemon, Polemarchos, Polemakles, Polemokrates, etc.), *stratos* ("army," e.g., Stratokles, Stratokydes, Straton), *nike* ("victory," e.g., Kallinikos, Sosinikos, Kleonikos, Laonikos, Stratonikos, etc.), and other words with a military connotation (e.g., *syle*, "spoils," *tharsos/tharros*, "courage"). Such names were extremely popular in the Hellenistic period, admittedly in part because they were traditionally transmitted within the family, but in part also because of the values they expressed.

The following, rather impressionistic examples of a citizen's duty and military service should be read with the explicit warning against generalization in mind.

Among the Greek regions in which the old tradition still lived on that citizenship depended on military duty, Crete takes a prominent place. More than 60 independent poleis existed there in the Classical period (Chaniotis 1996a: 12–13, n. 36; Perlman 1996: 282–3), and although their number decreased dramatically in the Hellenistic period due to conquest (and, in a few cases, peaceful arrangements), Crete remained until its conquest by the Romans in 67 BC the paradise of the small polis. All of them had their own citizen army, and military training was the basic occupation of the young men. As we can infer from the abundant evidence concerning the oath ceremony for new citizens, a successful participation in military education was one of the requirements for citizenship (Chaniotis 1996a: 124–6). To the best of our knowledge, the Cretan cities never employed mercenaries, although they often invited allied troops. On the contrary, Crete was one of the major sources for the *recruitment* of mercenaries for almost all the Hellenistic armies (see chapter 5). The main magistrates of the Cretan cities were military officials, the *kosmoi* ("those who set the army in array"), who were elected every year, each year from a different tribe. The tribes were also primarily military groups, and one of their designations was *startos* (= *stratos*), the "army." The continual Cretan wars were in part the result of an economic and social crisis (see chapter 1, section 2, chapter 5, section 2), but in part also the result of a civic ideology which made war the most important civic duty – and the most profitable occupation.

Besides Crete, Sparta is another famous example of a militarist society. Here, the archaic military institutions were declining and were artificially brought to life with the reforms of Kings Agis IV and Kleomenes III (Cartledge and Spawforth 1989: 38–58). By the mid-third century BC the Spartan army was undermanned because of the rapid decline of citizen manpower (from 1,000 men in 370 BC to ca. 700 in 244). The famous education focusing on military training (*agoge*) was not rigorously followed, and property concentration and debts had degraded many Spartans to the class of "inferiors." In 242 BC, Agis started introducing measures, such as the cancellation of debts and a redistribution of land, that would bolster the number of full Spartan citizens, and he also reimposed the traditional military education and lifestyle. His efforts failed and he was executed, but his work was continued in 227 BC with the very ambitious socio-political program of Kleomenes III. Debts were cancelled and civic land was redistributed to 4,000 new and old citizens, including foreign merceneries. The new citizen army adopted Macedonian weapons and tactics, but it was also based on the old tradition of an austere lifestyle and military education for the citizens' children. These social and military reforms made Sparta a major military power on the Peloponnese once again. It required the joint armies of Antigonos Doson of Macedonia and the Achaian League to defeat Kleomenes at the Battle of Selassia (222 BC), and to put an end to his reform work. One year before his defeat, Kleomenes had liberated 6,000 *helots* (serfs), 2,000 of which were armed, thus increasing the manpower of the Spartan army. This policy was also followed by King Nabis in the late third century (Cartledge and Spawforth 1989: 70). Four thousand men of the Spartan army (citizens, but also mercenaries and possibly light-armed *helots*) had lost their lives at the Battle of Mantineia in 207 BC, and only the liberation of *helots*, some of which were also given citizenship, could effectively restore the size of the army. With this army, Sparta remained a substantial military factor in the Peloponnese until the Roman conquest in 146 BC.

Turning to another conservative region, Boiotia, regular military training and the recruitment of citizen troops persisted to the end of Greek freedom. The citizens served in various divisions (Feyel 1942b: 200–4), as light-armed troops (*peltophoroi* and *thyreaphoroi*), elite infantry (*agema* and *epilektoi*), cavalry-men (*hippotai*), archers (*pharetritai*), and slingers (*sphendonitai*). The numerous military catalogs, in particular from Hyettos, Orchomenos, and Thespiai, which list the names of 20-year-old men who were registered as light-armed soldiers and in the cavalry (ca. 245–167 BC), show the care given to this institution by the authorities. Unlike Athens, where the military training of the *ephebes* had become voluntary by the end of the fourth century, in Boiotia all the young men of citizen status seem to have been enrolled (Étienne and Knoepfler 1976: 202). The importance of military service can be seen, for example, in the fact that in the federal Boiotian festival of the Panboiotia, military teams of the various cities competed in "good maintenance and use of arms" (*euhoplia*; *SEG* III 355) and in "discipline" (*eutaxia*; *SEG* XXVI 551).

In other areas, the existence of citizen militias depended on several factors – for example, the demographical evolution and the existence of manpower, institutional developments, the control by a king and the presence of a garrison, or the financial situation. Hellenistic kings did not generally discourage the existence of citizen armies in allied cities, since they could rely on their support in case of war. In addition to this, they could be relieved of the obligation to protect the cities with their own troops. Of course, too large a citizen army could become a problem, especially when royal power was on the wane. Literary sources and inscriptions alike mention citizen military units in passing. We know, for example, that in Thessaly the forts of Mopsion, Gonnoi, and Atrax were manned by citizens, and the same observation can be made in Asia Minor – for example, the citadel of Teloneia in Priene, the Teian fort of Kyrbissos, and the forts of Kolophon and Miletos. In larger cities and cities often exposed to the danger of a siege, the inhabitants were sometimes assigned to the defense of a particular section of the city wall, according to their residence. In Smyrna and Stratonikeia, for example, the town was divided into wards (*amphoda*), each assigned to the defense of a section of the wall, thus linking citizenship and residence with the fortification of the city. Each unit had its own recognition sign, an *episemon* (Garlan 1973: 20–2; Ma 2000c: 340). Service in the same military unit was an important factor of social life and created a feeling of solidarity (see chapter 5, section 5). In Tanagra (Boiotia), for example, the corps of archers (*pharetritai*) paid the expenses for the burial of Sosikles, a member or officer of the unit (*SEG* XXXII 487, ca. 150–100 BC). In Rhodes, military and naval divisions existed within private clubs (Gabrielsen 1997: 123–30).

Unfortunately, our sources often raise questions that cannot be answered. Do the contingents sent by Boiotia (10,500 men), Phokis (3,500), Aitolia (7,000), Lokroi (700), and Megara (400 men) to Thermopylai in order to stop the Galatian invasion in 279 BC represent the maximum traditional Greek states could mobilize in critical times (Launey 1987: 12)? Were the cavalrymen of Tabai in Karia, who attacked Roman troops in 189 BC (Ma 2000c: 339), a unit that had always existed, or were they a troop newly built, as soon as Tabai felt that Antiochos' III control of that region was over and aspirations of autonomy were revived?

In general, military training in the Hellenistic period retained its importance as one of the duties of the citizen. It started at a young age (see chapter 3), but continued in later years as well (Beston 2000: 317–21). One of the ideal citizens of this period was Philopoimen, the general of Megalopolis, who is praised by Polybios (*apud* Livy 35.28.1–7) as a statesman for continuing to train his mind in peace-time in order to be a military leader. He was a reader of military manuals, who tested the theories of their authors in practice (Plut., *Philop.* 4.4). Even hunting, one of the pleasant activities of wealthy men in their leisure, was practiced by Philopoimen – and in general – as part of military training (Plut., *Philop.* 3.2–4; Beston 2000: 320–1).

The close connection between a citizen's identity and military service can also be seen in the fact that people who were not born citizens, but were naturalized later, were not trusted enough to fulfill the particularly sensitive duty of serving in forts. In Miletos, service as guards or commanders of garrisons was possible for naturalized citizens only 10 (and in the case of Cretan immigrants, 20) years after naturalization (*Staatsverträge* 539, lines 39–40; *Syll.*[3] 633, lines 50–3; *Milet* I.3 37d).

Nevertheless, the native manpower was not always sufficient, and in such a situation it seemed preferable to award citizenship to potential defenders than to just hire mercenaries for money. In 219 BC, envoys of Larisa to King Philip V explained that "because of the wars our city needs more inhabitants"; Philip advised them to enfranchise the Thessalians and the other Greeks in the city (Austin 1981: no. 60; Bagnall and Derow 2004: no. 32). When, in the late second century, the Pergamenes awarded citizenship to the free population of their territory, which included garrison troops and military settlers, the justification was "for the sake of common security" (*I.Pergamon* 249 = *OGIS* 338; Brun 2004: 44–5). They expected that citizenship would made a soldier a dedicated defender, especially in the context of Aristonikos' revolt.

In desperate situations, cities might choose to increase military manpower by increasing the citizen body, not through the enfranchisment of foreigners, who might still feel strong allegiance to their city of origin, but through the liberation and naturalization of slaves, who of course lacked this and any other allegiance and would fight to protect their new status. Both Kings Kleomenes III and Nabis of Sparta implemented this measure in critical situations (in 223 and after 207 BC), and similar measures are reported in many other cases in Hellenistic history (and earlier). In this way, war occasionally became a motor of social change. Needless to say, the new citizens willingly adopted the ideology of their ex-masters.

The existence of an army was a basic constituent of civic pride. Many cities and leagues chose weapons as the symbols that decorated their coins or their official seals (see figure 2.1), thus alluding to the specific military

Figure 2.1 Golden stater of the Aitolian League with the personification of Aitolia as a seated woman, stepping on the shields of the defeated Gauls. Numismatic Museum of Athens (courtesy of the Museum).

skills of their citizens. Slingers are represented, for example, on the coins of the Thessalian League, Nysa in Karia, and Aspendos and Selge in Pamphylia (Pritchett 1991: 37). In addition, individual citizens regarded their military activity – not as professional soldiers, but in the service of their city – as the most important constituent of their identity. For example, Apollonios of Tymnos, who did not fall in combat, but died of old age (ca. 250 BC), chose to decorate his grave with the same symbol that had decorated his shield: a snake (Bean and Fraser 1954: 41, no. 27 a; *SGO* I 01/02/01; Ma 2004: 209). His grave epigram recalls the battles he had fought "for the fatherland," the great number of enemies he had killed in person, and the innumerable spears which he "firmly stuck into the flesh of the enemies."

Those who gave their life or their fortune in fulfillment of civic duties expected not only a war memorial (see chapter 11, section 6), but also that their community would take care of their families. At least in Athens this expectation could be satisfied. The laws demanded that those who set up trophies, helped to restore freedom, or consumed their property for the salvation of the community, should be assisted by the people financially, including the provision of an appropriate dowry for their daughters (*IG* II² 832, lines 12–21).

In the rhetoric of praise for the good citizen, we find virtues such as justice, zeal, love of the fatherland, courage, benevolence, prudence, moderation, and piety. At first sight, none of these require wealth, but the reality of civic life teaches us otherwise. Military service, service in office, education, rhetorical skills, and statemanship have always been the privilege of the man of independent means, and the short period of radical democracy in Athens (ca. 460–ca. 410 BC) should not deceive us about this. For this reason, the civic duties discussed in this chapter relate to the minority of the civic population that possessed citizenship, and could afford to devote themselves to public service at the expense of their private, professional interests or needs. Not all citizens owned weapons, and although tacticians such as Philon of Byzantion recommend the purchase of weapons at public expense and their distribution to those who could not afford them (Garlan 1974: 310, 383), this was by no means the general practice.

Generosity is the cardinal citizen virtue, both in a material sense (spending private money for the public good) and in a metaphorical sense (investing energy and ideas, and sacrificing oneself if necessary) (see section 2.5).

2.3. City and Land: Structure and Hierarchy

Military symbols on coins were not the only, and not the most spectacular, visible evidence for the military efforts of Hellenistic cities. Monumental buildings and structures visible from a long distance, such as city walls, long fortification walls (see figure 2.2), and forts located along the frontier of a polis and on the coast, were a source of civic pride and an expression of freedom (Garlan 1974: 244–69; Ma 2000c: 339–43). Both literary sources – especially handbooks on "poliorcetics" (the art of siege) – and inscriptions provide abundant evidence about the significance cities attributed to their city walls and forts, but also about the difficulties they had in funding such projects (see chapter 7). Only a few cities had the expertise to continually supervise and maintain their city walls, or the resources necessary for this task (see section 2.5 on the *teichopoioi* in various cities). Nevertheless, the importance of fortifications in the Hellenistic period is also confirmed by the archaeological material. In the context of this study, fortifications are significant for three reasons: they are a visible expression of the connection between civic freedom and military effort; they show the interest given by Hellenistic cities to their countryside; and they reflect hierarchical structures.

A subscription list from Chios, which records the amount of money voluntarily donated by the citizens for the fortification wall (ca. 201 BC), links fortification and freedom: "These men, wishing that their fatherland always stay free and autonomous, promised of their free will to donate money and gave it for the fortification of the walls" (Maier 1959: no. 52, lines 1–5). A public oath in Chersonesos in Tauris (*DGE* 173) invokes "the heroes who possess the city and the territory and the walls of the Chersonesitai," placing the fortification walls on the same level as the city and the country. In art, city walls symbolically crowned personifications of the Fortune of a city (Pollitt 1986: 2–3). Several epigrams apply the same

Figure 2.2 Graphic reconstruction of part of the walls of Herakleia-under-Latmos by Fritz Krischen (1922: fig. 39). One recognizes the battlement walkway with a parapet pierced by loopholes. Square towers equipped with shooting apertures protected the flanks of the curtain walls.

imagery to describe the city's fortifications – for example, "this roomy city placed on its head a high crown of towers" (Maier 1959: no. 58, Paphos, ca. 320–306 BC), and "Dorian Korinth, where is your admired beauty, where are the crowns of your towers?" (*Anthologia Graeca* 9.151). In real life, city walls effectively offered protection, resisted the sophisticated new artillery devices, or simply deterred invading barbarians or passing armies from attacking. A man from Smyrna was so closely associated with the tower he had protected in wars that he had himself buried near it in order to offer his protection even after his death (Robert 1944: 44–6; *I.Smyrna* 516). These pieces of evidence clearly reflect the symbolic significance of city walls for civic ideology. They should not, however, create the impression of a one-sided focus on the urban center of the community.

If the citadel and the fortified city were the heart of a civic community, the countryside was its economic basis (Will 1975: 312–15). One of the clauses in Cretan treaties of alliance explicitly incorporates the countryside and its population of non-citizen status to the defense of the city. For example, a treaty between Eleutherna and Lato in the early second century (Chaniotis 1996a: no. 37) states that: "If an enemy invades the territory of the Eleutherneans or cuts off parts hereof, or occupies forts or harbors, or destroys the lots of the serfs, or wages war, the Latian shall help in land and on sea without any pretext with all his might" (cf. the treaty between Gortyn and Lappa: "if someone wages war against the Gortynians or occupies a fort or harbors or cuts off part of the territory, the Lappaians shall help the Gortynians on land and on sea, with all their might, to the best of their abilities"; Chaniotis 1996a: no. 31; cf. Ma 2000c: 342 with n. 23). The land and its inhabitants were to be defended with the same zeal as the town, and many of the honorary decrees for "local heroes" (see section 2.5) concern persons who exposed themselves to dangers in order to defend the countryside. The territory was not only regularly patrolled, usually by units of young men, but was also defended with fortification works. Forts (*choria*, *peripolia*) were located near strategic routes, natural harbors, and roads, on the top of hills and mountains, near the natural frontiers or near agricultural settlements. They were usually manned by young men, sometimes by mercenaries, but also by soldiers from their environs. The forts imposed unity within the territory of a city, linking its most remote sites with the center (cf. Ma 2000c: 341–2 with n. 24). At the same time, systems of forts articulated more visibly than natural landmarks (e.g., rocks, rivers, springs, caves, mountain peaks, woods) the frontiers that separated cities. Forts thus became the visible proof of the integrity, independence, and identity of a community. If the citadel was the place where old men, children, and women retreated, the forts were the realm of the young men, who proved their ability to become citizens through military service. The Athenian *ephebes* regularly patrolled the frontier; in Boiotia, units of the cavalry were assigned to this service; and in Crete young men manned the frontier forts.

Service in the garrison of a frontier fort exposed young men to dangers and taught them discipline, togetherness, and responsibility (see chapter 3, section 2).

Forts made the boundary between a community and the next neighbor, and potential enemy, visible; sometimes they also expressed hierarchical relationships (cf. Ma 2000c: 341). A dependent community often served as a fort of a sovereign city and had to accept a garrison. We know of such dependent forts in many areas. In Crete, the island of Kaudos was a dependent community of Gortyn and the Artemitai a dependent community of Eleutherna (Chaniotis 1996a: 404–6); Teos in Asia Minor annexed the territory of Kyrbissos, preserving the citadel of this former city as a fort (Robert and Robert 1976); and Miletos did the same with Pidasa.

2.4. The Defense of the City as the Stage of Civic Elites

In the late first century AD, the Greek philosopher Plutarch remarked in his work *Political Precepts* (*mor.* 805 a): "In our times, when the affairs of the cities do not offer the opportunity to undertake military leadership in wars, or to overthrow tyrannies, or to conclude alliances, how can one start a prominent and splendid political career?" The civic elites of Plutarch's time did not have the opportunity to prove their abilities in the leadership of their communities through activities that were intrinsically connected with war (see section 2.7). The Hellenistic statesmen, on the other hand, did (Ma 2000c: 362), whether in cities as large as Athens or Rhodes or as small as Cretan Lato.

An honorary decree for the Athenian statesman Eurykleides, who dominated Athenian political life in the second half of the third century BC together with his brother Mikion, in some ways epitomizes what a Hellenistic city expected from an efficient, dedicated – and preferably wealthy – leader. Although no translation can be presented, since part of the text is not preserved, the content of this eulogy is more or less clear (*IG* II² 834): Eurykleides served as a treasurer for the military, spending a lot of his own money while in this office. As an organizer of contests he spent the enormous amount of seven talents, and "when the land was lying fallow and unsown because of the wars," he procured the necessary money for cultivation. He also "restored freedom to the city together with his brother Mikion" by procuring the necessary money for the withdrawal of the foreign garrison from Piraeus. Not only this, he also managed to fortify "the harbors and repaired the walls of the city and of Piraeus, together with his brother Mikion," he made alliances with other Greek cities, made sure that loans were repaid to Athens, proposed new laws, organized spectacles to honor the gods, and introduced an athletic competition of armed men in order to commemorate the restoration of freedom. Finally, he excelled in his building activities.

From another inscription we know that he had already served as a hoplite general (*IG* II^2 1705). Almost all of Eurykleides' services are directly or indirectly connected with war and with the defense of his city. His political and military activity may be extreme in duration, intensity, and breadth, but on a smaller scale one will find men like Eurykleides in every Hellenistic city with a substantial epigraphic record.

The innumerable honorary decrees of the Hellenistic period present an impressively wide range of activities with which a citizen could earn the official admiration, gratitude, and praise of his community – and also, naturally, the envy of his competitors. For example, a man in the small town of Moryllos (Macedonia) was honoured with an annual festival on the anniversary of his election because he had donated a cow which had proven to be so fertile that with her offspring the city was able to celebrate sacrificial festivals for many years (*SEG* XXXIX 605, ca. 204 BC). Honors were repeatedly bestowed upon a woman in Kyme for her building activities and other donations (*SEG* XXXIII 1035–1040, late second century BC). Men and women were honored for their contributions to education and culture, for the performance of religious rites, for spending money on the gymnasium, for providing funds for a theater, a stadium, a magistrates' office, or a sacred building, for buying cheap grain or theater tickets, for athletic victories, or just for remaining uncorrupted and without malice (*katharos kai misoponeros*) during their service in office.

However, it would be misleading to connect service for the well-being of a community with war, because the noble competition for public acknowledgment took place in many arenas. With this warning against generalizations in mind, I should stress that in the Hellenistic period – no less than in earlier periods of Greek history – war remained the privileged stage for the performance of a conscientious citizen, a good leader, and a generous benefactor. In a quantitative sense this is due to the fact that numerous services to the community directly or indirectly are connected with war: killing enemies with one's own hands, dying in battle, contributing to the defense of the city with funds or ideas, ransoming captives, serving as an envoy to a king, making arrangements for new alliances, contributing to military training, occupying a military office, effectively protecting the farmers with troops, participating in a voluntary raising of funds for the fortification walls (Quass 1993: 84–125). When donors provided money so that theatrical performances could take place in Iasos (*I.Iasos* 160–218), their funds allowed the city's life go on in a normal way despite the fiscal gaps caused by continual wars; and when benefactors guaranteed that cheap grain could be bought by their city, they thus covered shortages caused by wars. As the fiscal misery of Greek communities was to a great extent the result of wars, almost any financial contribution by a citizen, a foreigner, or a king can be seen in the context of war. In a qualitative sense, the services offered by citizens and statesmen to their communities in times of war, in order to avert wars, or in order to compensate the losses caused by wars, were more important than any other service. Numerous decrees explicitly state that "the protection of the city and the territory" tops the hierarchy of civic norms and duties (Gschnitzer 1981b).

2.5. Local Hero: The Statesman as a Military Leader

An honorary decree of Athens for the prominent citizen Kallias of Sphettos (*SEG* XXVIII 60; Austin 1981: no. 44; see also below) describes one of his heroic deeds (287 BC): "When Demetrios arrived, encamped around the city and besieged it, Kallias in defense of the people attacked with his soldiers and was wounded, but refused to avoid any risk at any time for the sake of the people's safety" (lines 30–2). The description of Kallias' response to this danger corresponds to the expectations Greek cities had of military commanders. Although military theorists, such as Polybios (10.32.1–7; 16.19.7), demanded that a commander take an active role on the battlefield, but at the same time criticized those who recklessly exposed themselves to danger (cf. Philon of Byzantion 4.20, 28, and 68, ed. Garlan 1974: 318–19, 323, 386), the *communis opinio* expected the military leader to fight in the front row. Philopoimen killed Sparta's king or regent, Machanidas, in person at the Battle of Mantineia in 207 BC (see chapter 10, section 2) and one of the prominent citizens of Aphrodisias was praised in the first century precisely for disregarding dangers and killing 60 enemies (Reynolds 1982: no. 28). Several other inscriptions honor commanders who killed enemies in person (*en cheiron nomais*; Robert 1937: 313–14).

The critical conditions caused by wars required political leadeship. For the Greek cities, this was certainly not a new experience. There is no essential difference between the need for political leadership in democratic Athens during the Peloponnesian War and the need for it in any small Hellenistic polis exposed to the dangers of war for a long period of time. Differences existed, however, in the general historical context: the existence of monarchies which provided models of behavior, the decline of democratic institutions, and the more prominent position of individuals. These developments will be explored here, focusing on essential aspects of the life and work of Hellenistic public figures in the context of war: military leadership, serving as a model for youth, benefaction, and the monopolization of public life by a wealthy elite.

The importance of war for the life and existence of civic communities made the defense of the city, along with warfare, one of the central duties of a Hellenistic statesman. Many important civic offices are directly connected with war – for example, the office of the *strategos* (general) in many cities (Bengtson 1937–52); the office of the *kosmoi* in Crete (see section 2.2), and of *tagoi* in Thessaly ("those who set the army in array"); that of the *polemarchos* ("commander in war") in Argos, Tritaia, Eretria, Boiotia, and

Samos (*IG* XII.6.1 262; XII.9 192; *SEG* XXIX 440; XXXVII 280; XL 400); or the various offices and commissions responsible for construction and maintainance of the city walls (Maier 1961: 43–6), such as the *teichopoioi* ("the constructors of walls") in Athens, Oropos, Demetrias, Chersonesos, Histria, Kyzikos, Miletos, and Priene, the *epistatai teichon* ("supervisors of the walls") in Teos and Erythrai, and the *epimeletai tou teichous* ("in charge of the city wall") in Olbia. Priene is perhaps a representative case for the various magistracies connected with military matters in a middle-sized, free Hellenistic polis. The "generals" (*strategoi*) were the most important officials and regularly proposed decrees to the council and the assembly. They were assisted by the *hipparchai* (commanders of the cavalry) and the *phrourarchos*, the commander of the citadel at Teloneia. The "constructors of the walls" (*teichopoioi*) administered the money and the works connected with the maintenance of the fortifications. On a smaller scale, we may see a similar specialization in the city of Plarasa/Aphrodisias, where the most important civic offices in the Hellenistic period were those of the *strategoi*; they probably constituted a board, the members of which were assigned particular duties, such as the general who commanded the troops which defended the territory (*strategos ton epi tes choras*), the general responsible for the city (*strategos tes poleos*), and possibly the *paraphylax*, responsible for the frontier.

A civic statesman was sooner or later confronted with the problem of war. Some showed their skills in the organization of defense, others on the battlefield, some in both areas. For this reason, military training, expertise, and interest in military matters characterize the statesmen of civic communities no less than the Hellenistic kings (see chapter 4; see also Beston 2000). A statesman who is often presented as a model, Philopoimen (see section 2.2), is said to have adopted new and more effective weapons for the Achaian army while serving as commander of the cavalry and then as general (Plut., *Philop.* 9.1–2 and 9.8). He showed his education in tactical matters in the meticulous planning of attacks (see Polyb. 11.10.8–9; 16.36) and in keeping his plans secret. His interest in military matters inspired the youth of his day (see chapter 3), and even foreign communities in Crete were keen on having him as a military adviser (Paus. 8.49.7; Plut., *Philop.* 7.1–2; Errington 1969: 28, 32–3).

Philopoimen was a figure of international politics, who inspired one of Plutarch's *Lives*, but hundreds of other statesmen were the "local heroes" of big and small cities. What they accomplished during local wars mattered to their population more than the distant victories of great kings. Olympiodoros of Athens was remembered as the man who liberated Piraeus and the fort of Mounychia in 287 BC (Paus. 1.26.3; Habicht 1997: 95–6; see Dreyer 1999: 257–78); Onesas gained glory in Tenos for ridding the city of "enemies" (possibly pirates) who had occupied its lower part (*IG* XII Suppl. 315; first century); Kallikratides of Aphrodisias was honored for killing 60 enemies

(Reynolds 1982: no. 28; first century); and Theokritos and Amphalkes of Tegea were lauded for their courage in fighting the Spartans after they had seized the city walls (218 BC; *IG* V.2 16; Walbank 1957: 552). Men like Kallias of Athens (Shear 1978), the general Epichares who saved the coastal population of Attika and their agricultural products during the Chremonidean War (ca. 268–262 BC; *SEG* XXIV 154; Austin 1981: no. 50), Diokles and Leodamas of Kos (see below), Sotas of Priene, who saved his city during the Galatian invasion (*I.Priene* 17, ca. 278 BC), Stasias of Perge, and Apollodoros of Berenike (see below), are known from honorary decrees of their communities.

The case of Kallias of Sphettos, a prominent Athenian from a wealthy family who served for a long time as an officer of Ptolemy I and II, is one of the best documented examples. An honorary decree describes, among his many and different contributions to the safety and well-being of his fellow citizens, his military achievements during the revolt of the Athenians against Demetrios the Besieger in 287 BC, when Kallias was stationed with Ptolemaic mercenaries on the island of Andros (*SEG* XXVIII 60; Austin 1981: no. 44):

> At the time of the uprising of the people against those who were occupying the city, when the people expelled the soldiers from the city, but the fort on the Mouseion hill was still occupied, and war raged in the countryside because of the soldiers from Piraeus, and Demetrios was coming with his army from the Peloponnese against the city, Kallias, on hearing of the danger theatening the city, selected a thousand of soldiers who were posted with him at Andros, gave them their wages and food rations, and immediately came to the rescue of the people in the city, acting in accordance with the goodwill of king Ptolemy [I] towards the people; and leading out into the countryside the soldiers who were following him, he protected the gathering of the corn, making every effort to ensure that as much corn as possible should be brought into the city. And when Demetrios arrived, encamped around the city and besieged it, Kallias in defense of the people attacked with his soldiers and was wounded, but refused to avoid any risk at any time for the sake of the people's safety.
>
> (lines 12–32)

Not blind patriotism, but the qualities of a leader distinguish Kallias: initiative in the mobilization of troops, strategic thinking in the collection of corn, heroism and self-sacrifice in battle. These – along with foresight (*pronoein, pronoia*) – are typical qualities in many other honorary decrees of a similar character.

The career of Diokles of Kos, described in an honorary decree of his district (Halasarna; *SEG* XLVIII 1104; ca. 200 BC) was perhaps more intense than that of other statesmen, since he lived in a period in which his island was under attack from Cretan pirates and then from Philip V (ca. 209–200 BC), but his activities are nevertheless not unusual:

Diokles, son of Leodamas, acting in accordance with the virtue which has been handed down to him by his ancestors, has continually shown every zeal and care for the district of the Halasarnitai, and during the wars, aimed at securing the fort and those who inhabit the territory, showing the best consideration and engaging himself in every danger for its sake. For during the Cretan War, when it was announced that the site was threatened, he arrived with many men and making inspections together with those who had been assigned to guard (the fort) he asked the inhabitants to come together to the fort and to join its defense, until it occurred that the enemies abandoned their plan to attack; and in the present war, as the enemies were often threatening [the fort], when many naval and land forces were gathered in Astypalaia, in order to keep the fort safe he brought weapons and catapult missiles; and choosing as *toparchs* [local commanders], in accordance with a decree, those who would be most capable in taking care of the protection and placing under their command enough (or capable) men who would keep guard by day [---] he also arrived in order to protect the site [---]; when he anticipated the enemy threat and the size of the dangers [--- the most suitable?] place of the fort, when the attack occurred, he followed and confined the enemies under the fort; he notified Nikostratos, son of Nikostratos, to take the light-armed among those who had come out with him and to come to assist; when due to this foresight the latter arrived zealously, it so occured that the site was not occupied and the invaders left without doing any injustice against the territory.

Diokles showed not only initiative and leadership, but also tactical thinking. A second honorary decree of Halasarna for the same man (*Syll.*[3] 569 = Maier 1959: no. 46) describes similar achievements during the Cretan War: taking care of the construction of fortifications, procuring the necessary funds, arranging for guards and their wages, and lending money, whenever necessary.

Diokles' achievements are quite comparable with those of Apollodoros of Berenike (early first century; *SEG* XXVII 1540). When King Ptolemy IX died in 80 BC and the lack of a central authority had encouraged bandits to attack the city and to terrorize the countryside, Apollodoros was appointed as commander of the young men, "and taking upon himself every danger he established the greatest peace." The city had been without a city wall and had already twice been the victim of pirates. In this critical situation, the city entrusted Apollodoros with full authority over the city and the countryside – a unique position which he held with such prudence that his fellow citizens praised him for safeguarding concord in the city and demonstrating just judgment. These are kingly qualities: peace and security, unlimited authority, justice, and good judgment. The person who demonstrated them filled a gap left by the absence of a king; in many a small city, such a "local hero" might have resembled a king.

Not unlike Philopoimen, Apollodoros inspired the youth of his city, and this seems to be another constituent of the virtuous statesman in times of war. Stasias, son of Bokios of Perge, combined the defense of the territory as a general (*strategos*) with the training of young men, as a director of the gymnasium (*gymnasiarchos*). "He made great efforts to preserve for the people peace and security under all conditions," and as the praise of his bravery (*aristeion*) shows, his services were given in times of war (*I.Perge* 14, late second century; cf. the praise of Menas in *OGIS* 339).

What is the background of these people? Some of them had served in royal armies, gaining not only military experience, but also connections: men like Kallias of Athens or the Ptolemaic admiral Boiskos of Samos, who were honored for these reasons in their fatherland (*IG* XII.6.1 282–3; Gauthier 1985: 59), or men like Antigonos of Miletos, whose family had a great reputation (Herrmann 1987). After their retirement from royal service, such men often returned to their city, where they sometimes became influential. Kallias, who served under Ptolemy I and II, was repeatedly sent as an envoy of the Athenians to the Ptolemies and represented his city's interests, arranging, for example, for donations of corn and money (*SEG* XXVIII 60; Austin 1981: no. 44). Diogenes of Kos used his friendship with the kings of Egypt to help his fatherland and avert a Cretan attack (*epipolemotatois kairois*) against the Cretans (*IscrCos* ED 231 + *SEG* L 765, ca. 155 BC; Buraselis 2000: 6–24). Antileon of Kaunos was honored by his city for his conduct in public life (*SEG* XII 472 = *SGO* I 01/09/07; late third century).

Wealth was an important requirement for military training, and in some cities only people with certain property qualifications could occupy high military offices. In Teos, only people with an estimated real property amounting to at least four talents (24,000 drachmai) – i.e., what the physician Asklepiades of Perge would earn in 24 years (*I.Perge* 12), or the equivalent of the lifetime income of a mercenary soldier – had the right to be appointed to the office of the commander of the garrison in the fort of Kyrbissos (*SEG* XXVI 1306, lines 8–11). The same regulation shows how a military office confirmed and expressed social hierarchy and order: the commander was paid four times the salary of the soldier. Officers always get higher pay than ordinary soldiers; however, in mercenary regulations the pay of an officer is only twice as high as that of a soldier, at the most (e.g., Ducrey 1970: 653–4). That the commander had to feed four dogs, in addition to his other duties, alone does not explain the difference, which is one not of needs, but of status.

The qualities expected from these local military leaders did not differ from those attributed to the great generals of the Hellenistic age: they should gather information about the enemy, carefully observe the development of things and react accordingly, expose themselves to danger, and be ready to commit themselves at crucial moments. Success was possible only if they could win the trust and respect of their troops (Beston 2000: 325, 328; cf. Polyb. 5.30; Plut., *Philop.* 12.1). A victory should be regarded as *their* victory, as in the case of the Achaian general Kyliadas, who won a victory in Elis in 209 BC (*SEG* XXXVI 397). We know of his victory thanks to his dedication in Aigion. Exactly as in the dedication of Alexander the Great to Athens after the battle at Granikos ("Alexander, son of Philip, and the Greeks"), Kyliadas appears as dedicator on the same level as the Achaian League. His individual contribution is explicitly stressed in the inscription, which presents the victory as *his* accomplishment: "the Achaians and general Kyliadas, son of Damaretos from Pharai, to the gods after he won a victory together with the Macedonians." The focus on the protagonist of a battle is entirely in accordance with battle descriptions in contemporary historiography, which show a strong interest in heroic single combats (see chapter 10, section 2). Here, art imitates life – which in its turn was inspired by art.

If war made kings (see chapter 4), military success might inspire even a local general to attempt his own small monarchical rule – in the form of tyranny over a city or as the dynast of a fort. The secession of a fort of Alabanda in the early second century BC may have been the result of an ambitious commander (see Ma 2000c: 339).

War raised individuals above their fellow citizens in life and sometimes even after death, making a mortal (not only a king) a god. Both Aratos and Philopoimen were posthumously honored with a cult (Leschhorn 1984: 326–31). A certain Mogetes, general of Maionia, is a typical "local hero" of the Hellenistic Age. He was probably killed during a war, most likely during Aristonikos' War (ca. 129 BC):

> Mogetes, Athena herself, the virgin mistress with the many weapons, gave you conspicuous prudence. She also gave you the glory of wisdom, twice making you shine to all as blameless leader of the fatherland. She alone placed you, the selected one and defender of the fatherland in all times, among the most glorious of Rome's generals. But you have left your pitiable wife and an unfinished term of office and run to the chambers of Persephone. Your mother and the fatherland lament you, as well as your brothers, now that the seventh star among them has died. Farewell. You are the selected one from a glorious family. Hades will place you, the third one, on a throne next to the other pious men.
>
> (*TAM* V.1 468b; cf. *SEG* XXVIII 891; *SGO* I 04/19/01)

Through the mention of Mogetes' brothers, the gratitude for his individual achievements is indirectly transmitted to his family. The epigram ends with the expectation that he will be placed next to the pious men, in the privileged section of the Underworld, probably the third of his family (after his grandfather and father). Military achievement justified a better afterlife.

2.6. Euergetism in War and the Ideology of Inequality

It did not only take blind courage to be a local hero; sometimes money would do. An honorary decree for the Athenian benefactor Philippides, a celebrated comic poet and friend of King Lysimachos (283/2 BC), gives an impression of the ways in which a wealthy individual could help his community without risking his life:

> When King Lysimachos won the battle which was fought at Ipsos against Antigonos and Demetrios, he had those of the citizens who were killed in this danger buried at his own expense; as for those who were taken prisoner, he presented their case to the king and achieved their release; he also arranged for the enrollment in military units of those of them who wanted to serve in the army, and to those who preferred to leave he gave clothes and supplies from his own funds and sent them to whichever place each of them wished, more than three hundred men altogether. He also requested the release of those of our citizens who were found in Asia placed in custody by Demetrios and Antigonos.
>
> (IG II^2 657, lines 16–29; Austin 1981: no. 43; Bielman 1994: no. 20; Derow and Bagnall 2004: no. 13)

The Hellenistic Age brought forth a series of public figures that monopolized public life to a larger extent than in earlier periods; the benefactor (*euergetes*) dominated the scene together with the monarch (Gauthier 1985; Quass 1993). The modern term "euergetism," derived from the word *euergetes* (benefactor), characterizes the activity of benefactors, the expectations of civic communities of their elite, and the relationship between a wealthy individual and his city. Most forms of public service presupposed a man (or a woman) of some means. Euergetism was rooted in the fact that rhetorical skills and military expertise required education, which in most Hellenistic cities was a privilege of the few. And of course, the provision of funds (as a donation or as a loan) for building or repairing fortification walls, buying cheap corn, liberating prisoners, or hiring mercenaries was a service to the community that only the wealthy could provide. Some of these benefactors – not all – also occupied political offices and influenced political life. However, in spite of the prominent position of these representatives of a wealthy elite, the institutions of the moderate democracies which characterize the Hellenistic period were not violated by their activities and their initiatives were subject to the approval and the control of the citizens (see Habicht 1995). And of course, the power and influence of an ambitious political leader was always checked by that of the next rival.

Despite the persistence of democratic institutions and citizens' sovereignty in Hellenistic cities, the weight of a wealthy elite was not less heavily felt than that of monarchs (see section 2.5). And not unlike the relations between cities and kings, the relations between the elite and the citizens were also dominated by the principle of reciprocity. We have already seen what the members of the elite offered for the defense of their cities. How was their service rewarded by their communities? In addition to respect for their leadership, their election to offices, and the acceptance of their proposals in the council and the assembly, the honors bestowed upon the members of the elite were of great symbolic value. Their statues decorated public places as eternal memorials of their services and as a point of reference for their descendants. The benefactors themselves – or members of their families – often covered the expenses as a further expression of their munificence (Gauthier 2000a), but also because of the ideological value of honorary statues. Attacks against the statues of prominent men by their adversaries (e.g., Paus. 6.11.6–8; *I.Mylasa* 2) leave little doubt about the emblematic importance of these monuments, their continual perception by the citizens, and their ideological exploitation. The most interesting piece of evidence concerns the bronze statue of the tyrannicide Philitos in Erythrai (*I.Erythrai* 503; Gauthier 1982: 215–21, early third century BC). The supporters of an oligarchical regime removed the sword from the statue, "believing that his posture/attitude was against them/threatening them." After the collapse of this regime the city decreed that the statue should be restored to its earlier completeness. Measures were also taken to keep the statue clean and to crown it on the first day of each month and on all festival days. It is clear that statues stood for ideals and values; the statues of benefactors conveyed the message that service for the community in war justified an elevated status.

The crown awarded to benefactors, and often proclaimed year after year, was another means of commemoration of personal achievement. A particular type of crown, the "crown of valor" (*stephanos aristeios*), was given especially (but not exclusively) for military achievements (e.g., *I.Perge* 14 lines 48–9; *I.Perge* 23 line 18; Chaniotis 2004 b: no. 1). Finally, two other honors, the seat of honor in theatrical performances and athletic contests, and the free meal in the seat of the magistrates, symbolically placed the honored individual above the "normal" citizens and put them on the same level as the elected political leaders of the community. Thus communities factually accepted the existence of a group of individuals who had an elevated position in exchange for their services.

The thousands of honorary decrees of the Hellenistic period have a stereotypical structure. One of the common elements is the *hortatory formula*, in which the community explains why it honors a benefactor. The Pergean decree for the statesman Stasias presents a characteristic example. He was honored with a crown of gold and a bronze statue, "so that, when the others see that the people give to the best men the appropriate honors, they also make efforts to follow their example" (*I.Perge* 14). This practice had two consequences, which should be briefly discussed.

On one level, this model worked. In Kos, for example, hundreds of citizens participated in the subscriptions initiated around 200 BC for the defense of the island. The citizens were invited to provide funds for the construction and restoration of the fortification walls and the forts, but also for the provision of troops (citizens, not mercenaries) engaged in war (Baker 1991; Migeotte 2000a). The names of the contributors were inscribed on three stelae which were set up in the most prominent public places for everyone to see: near the altar of Dionysos in the agora, near the theater, and in the Asklepieion. From the surviving fragments we may infer that more than 25 talents (roughly 152,332 drachmas) were contributed by about 400 contributors, usually the heads of families. The subscription had the character of a patriotic mobilization of the citizens. Nevertheless, what the modern reader observes, and the ancient reader also immediately saw, is the inequality of the contributions. The names of the contributors are not randomly or alphabetically inscribed, as a democratic society demands, in which any contribution made to the best of a man's means is respectfully acknowledged. Instead, they are inscribed according to the oligarchical model known to the visitors of the Metropolitan Opera or other similar institutions: according to the size of the contribution. A small number of very wealthy families, which perhaps did not show greater generosity than others, but could afford larger amounts, head the list. These lists were a monument of inequality (see Gabrielsen 1997: 31–6, for Rhodes). In 243 BC the Athenians regarded it appropriate to limit the donations for the safe transportation of agricultural products to 50–200 drachmas (*IG* II² 791; Migeotte 1992: no. 17), and this only confirms the fact that too large a donation could threaten the internal coherence of a community and make inequalities more obvious.

The second implication is also significant. By stressing their dependence on the support of generous citizens and by inviting future generations to show generosity, *in order to receive honors*, the Hellenistic communities established a privileged position for the elite and perpetuated an interdependence between benefaction and status.

2.7. From Individual Services to the Heredity of Leadership

The honorary decree for Apollodoros of Berenike, who had saved his city from its enemies in the first century BC and was given full authority over the city and the countryside (see section 2.5), begins with a reference to the fact that he belonged to one of the old citizen families. Such references to the forefathers are stereotypical in honorary decrees and reflect the fact that men not only inherited their father's property, legal and social status, but also his moral obligations and ambitions – and this did not occur for the first time in the Hellenistic period (see Gschnitzer 1981a: 149–60; cf. Ober 1989).

We have already seen how important military expertise was for political leadership. To a great extent, military expertise and political experience were transmitted within the family or within a circle of friends – and this applies in general to other forms of professional knowledge as well. The Athenian statesman Eurykleides (see section 2.4) not only worked closely with his brother Mikion, he also introduced his son to political life (*IG* II² 844, lines 1–6; Maier 1959: 79). After serving as "treasurer of military funds" (*tamias stratiotikon*) himself, and facing the prohibition against occupying this office for a second time, "he performed this office (*ten ton strati[otikon tamieian? die]xegagen*) through his son" (*dia tou hyiou*), thus involving his son in his political activities. With regard to the liturgy *agonothesia* (the financial responsibility for the organization of a contest), the same decree states that "he provided again his son for this charge" (*kai palin ton hyion dous [eis tauten] ten epimeleian*). Mikion is known to have later served as a member of a commission for the purchase of grain, and as a donor of money (Habicht 1982: 179–82). Of course, the limited data do not allow us to present statistics or to determine how frequent this phenomenon was, but Mikion is certainly not an isolated case. A further example is Helikon, commander of the guard in Priene, who was assisted by his son during his term of office (*I.Priene* 19, late third century).

If the heredity of status was established directly through the heredity of wealth, the heredity of political position was indirectly implemented through the example of fathers and forefathers and through the honors offered to benefactors by their grateful cities. This interplay can be seen in an honorary decree for Harpalos, a prominent citizen of Beroia in the late Hellenistic period (late second/early first century BC); only part of it can be translated, but Harpalos, we are told:

> renewed the glory inherited by his forefathers, even though their glory was smaller (than what they deserved) due to the (hard) times in which they lived, and he zealously tried not to be left behind with regard to virtue. As soon as he reached the age of citizenship he did not stay behind the older men in making requests or serving as an ambassador for the fatherland; and remembering that his grandfathers had served as generals and having in mind the expenses which they had undertaken and what they had constructed for the adornment and the protection of the city, he courageously (*eutharsos*) accepted the greatest priesthood which involves the largest expenses.
>
> (*I.Beroia* 2 = *SEG* XLVII 891, lines 5–17)

Harpalos felt the obligation to follow the ancestral example. While his forefathers had served their community as generals and sponsors of fortifications, a young man living under Roman rule did not have the opportunity to show his courage in war (see Plutarch's observation in section 2.4). Harpalos showed his by accepting the challenge of a costly office. His fellow citizens were still grateful and perpetuated his example by deciding that the decree to his honor should be read every year during the elections.

Sometimes the honors bestowed upon a prominent citizen were inherited by the descendant. The Athenians decreed, for example, that Philippides (see section 2.6) and the eldest of his descendants were to receive, for all time, free meals in the *prytaneion* (the seat of the excutive committee of the council), and a seat of honor in all the contests organized by the city (*IG* II² 657, lines 64–6; Austin 1981: no. 43). Such measures perpetuated the prominent position of the benefactor's family.

There was only a very small step from inherited status, inherited wealth, inherited leadership, and inherited gratitude to the institutionalization of a class of privileged citizens. From the late Hellenistic period (first century) onwards, prominent citizens are characterized as the "first citizens," the "first class," or the "leading families" (Quass 1993: 51–6). An honorary decree of Plarasa/Aphrodisias for one of the political leaders and benefactors of the community during the wars of the Late Republic is very eloquent with regard to the heredity of social position (Chaniotis 2004b: no. 1). The text begins with praise of the man's ancestors:

> Hermogenes Theodotos, son of Hephaistion, one of the first and most illustrious citizens, a man who has as his ancestors the greatest men, who were among those who built together the community and have lived in virtue, love of glory, many promises [of benefactions], and the fairest deeds for the fatherland; a man who has been himself good and virtuous, a lover of the fatherland, a constructor, a benefactor of the polis, and a saviour . . .

This aristocracy, to which Hermogenes and other "first citizens" belonged, owed its existence to a great extent to the critical situations caused by the continual wars. Not unlike kings (see chapter 4), the members of the elite to which Hermogenes belonged had established their position with their services as military leaders, peace-makers, and benefactors; not unlike kings, they exploited their personal achievements in order to set themselves apart from the rest of their community. The differences between royal and non-royal images were not fundamental, but ones of degree (Beston 2000: 315, 328).

When Octavian put an end to the civil wars of the Late Republic and established the *Pax Augustea*, this aristocracy was so deeply rooted in the economy, the society and the institutions of the Greek cities, that it continued its existence within the Imperial period. The Hellenistic wars had contributed to its genesis, but they were not needed for its survival.

Further Reading

2.1. Fighting Against a Neighbor: A Privilege of the Polis. *Fighting poleis in the Hellenistic period*: Ma 2000c; cf. Beston 2000: 317–21; Baker 2001, 2003: 381–5. *Treaties of alliance*: Crete: Chaniotis 1996a: nos. 1–2, 7, 10–13, 17, 19, 23–7, 29, 31–4, 37–8, 46, 51–3, 58–61; *SEG* L 936; for offensive wars: Chaniotis 1996a: nos. 11, 26, 28, 38, 46, 59, 60, 61; in Asia Minor: Fernoux 2004. *Hegemonial treaties of alliance*: Baltrusch 1994: 23–30 (in the Classical period); Chaniotis 1996a: 89–90 (in Hellenistic Crete). *Aphrouresia as a guarantee of authonomy*. e.g., *Staatsverträge* 442 and 489; *I.Ilion* 45 (= *SEG* XXXVIII 1252); Polyb. 15.24.2; *I.Iasos* 2; *Sardis* VII.1 2 (= *SEG* XXXVII 1003).

2.2. Warfare as a Citizen Duty. *Military organization in general*: Hamilton 1999 (overview) Baker 2001 (Asia Minor). *Types of troops*: Foulon 1996. *Exemption of priests* *from military service*: Gauthier 1991; e.g., Sokolowski 1955: no. 1; *SEG* XXVI 1334; XXIX 1088. *Personal names related to war*: *LGPN* I-IIIb; Masson 1965 (for Crete); cf. Launey 1987: 797–8. *Military society in Crete*: Petropoulou 1985: 15–46; Chaniotis 1996a. *The military reforms of Agis and Kleomenes in Sparta*: Plut., *Agis* esp. 7; *Kleomenes*, esp. 10–13; Austin 1981: nos. 55–6; Cartledge and Spawforth 1989: 38–58; Kennell 1995: 11–12. *Military organization in Boiotia:* Feyel 1942b: 187–218; military catalogs: e.g., *IG* VII 2809–32 (= *SEG* XXVI 501–23), 2817; *SEG* III 351–3; XXVI 498–500, 550; XXX 447–52; XXXVII 385; Étienne and Knoepfler 1976: 67–112, 202–10; Roesch 1982: 340–3; Hennig 1985; cf. the military catalogs from Eretria: *IG* XII.9 241, 243 and 249 (cf. Chankowski 1993); competitions of military teams: e.g., *SEG* III 354–5; XXVI 551. *Athens*: Bugh 1988. *Rhodes*: Berthold 1984: 42–7; Gabrielsen 1997: 123–30; cf. *IG* XII.1 75 B, 127, 155, and 163; *SEG* XXI 734; XXXIX 737; *I.Lindos* 251 and 264. *Kyrene*: Laronde 1987: 131–4. *Evidence for citizen militias*: Launey 1987; e.g., citizen guards in forts in Mopsion (Jeffery 1966: 18–24), Gonnoi (*Gonnoi* 146–50), and Atrax (*ISE* 100); citizen guards (*phrouroi*) in the cities of Asia Minor: Labarre 2004; cf. *I.Priene* 19 (citizen guards in the fort of Teloneia, third century); Robert 1926: 501–10; Ricl 1997: 40–2 (garison of Alexandreia Troas in Chryse); Robert and Robert 1976 (citizen guards in Kyrbissos); cf. *SEG* XLVIII 1404 (Kolophon) and *Delphinion* 146 lines 39–40 and 149 lines 15–18; *Syll.*³ 633 lines 50–3 (Miletos). Livy 38.13.11–13 (cavalry in Tabai, second century); *IG* IV 478–9 = *SEG* XI 293 (Charneux 1991: 315–16; cavalry in Argos). *Naturalization of foreigners in Larisa*: *Syll.*³ 543; Austin 1981: no. 60; Bagnall and Derow 2004: no. 32; cf. Hatzopoulos 1996: I 402–3 (on the date); Oetjen 2004 (on the identity of the naturalized foreigners: soldiers?). *Liberation and naturalization of slaves for military reasons*: e.g., Diod. 20.100.1 (Rhodes, 304 BC); Polyb. 16.31.1 (Abydos, 201 BC); *I.Ephesos* 8 (Ephesos, 86 BC); Philon of Byzantion C13, ed. Garlan 1974: 317 and 395; Garlan 1972: 33–5.

2.3. City and Land: Structure and Hierarchy. *Fortifications and freedom*: Robert 1970; Will 1975; Ma 2000c: 339–43 (with bibliography); cf. Winter 1994. *Hellenistic fortifications*: Maier 1959 and 1961; cf. Robert 1970; Debord and Descat 1994 (Asia Minor); McNicoll 1997; e.g., Ricl 1997: 23–38 (Alexandreia Troas); Allegro and Ricciardi 1999 (Gortyn, Crete); Pimouguet-Pédarros 2000 (Karia); Loots, Waelkens and Depuydt 2000 (Sagalassos); Krischen 1922; Hülden 2000 (Herakleia-under-Latmos); Kohl 2004 (Pergamon). *Wards in towns (amphoda)*: *I.Smyrna* 613; *SEG* XLIV 917 (Stratonikeia); cf. Robert 1937: 529–38; Garlan 1973: 20–2. *Forts and the defense of the territory*: Robert 1970; Ober 1985 (Classical Athens); Pritchett 1991: 352–8 (towers in rural areas); Baker 2000a and 2000b; Chandezon 2003: 341–2 (protection of pasture zones). Examples, Athens: Petrakos 1997 and 1999; Couvenhes 1999; Oetjen 2004; Phokis: Rousset 1999; Ambrakia: *SEG* XXXV 665 (+ XLIX 635); Crete: van Effenterre 1949; Ephesos: Robert 1967: 36–40; Jobst 1978; Miletos: Pimouguet 1995 (main sources: *Milet* I.3 146, 149–50); Mylasa: *Labraunda* 4; Robert 1945: 8; Rumscheid 1999; Priene: *I.Priene* 37, lines 125–31; Smyrna: Bean 1955; Bean 1966: 63–6. *Patrols in the countryside*: see chapter 3, section 2.

2.4. The Defense of the City as the Stage of Civic Elites. *Military mentality in Asia Minor*: Ma 2004. *Eurykleides of Athens*: Habicht 1982: 118–27; Gauthier 1985: 83; Habicht 1997: 155, 173–6, 191–4. *Honorary decrees for services connected with wars*: see below, 2.5.

2.5. Local Hero: The Statesman as Military Leader. *Active role of the commander in battle*: Eckstein 1995: 28–40; Beston 2000: 321. *Military achievements of citizens and officers in honorary inscriptions*: e.g., *IG* II² 682, 1209, 1299; *IG* V.2 16; *IG* XII.1 1033; *IG* XII.5 1030; *IG* XII.7 387; *IG* XII Suppl. 315; *SEG* XXXIV 1198; *OGIS* 765; *Syll.*³ 459, 567, 569; *IGR* III 34; IV 134; Amyzon 25, 37; *I.Erythrai* 24, 28–9; *I.Mylasa* 106, 612; *Milet* I.2 12 (*SGO* I 01/20/33); *Syll.*³ 459; Maier 1959: no. 80. *Military offices in Priene*: *strategoi*: *I.Priene* 14, 18, 53–4, 61, 69, 83, 99, 104, 108–9, 111, 202; *phrourarchoi*: *I.Priene* 4, 19, 21–2, 251–2; *hipparchai*: *I.Priene* 44; *teichopoioi*: *I.Priene* 70. *Aphrodisias*: Reynolds 1982: 13 and nos. 2 and 41; *CIG* 2837; *MAMA* VIII 408, 410, 414, 448; Paton 1900: 73–4 no. I; *LBW* 1611; Chaniotis 2004b: no. 1. *Cult of military commanders*: Plut., *Aratos* 53; *IG* V.2 432; Diod. 29.18 (Philopoimen); *I.Laodikeia* 1 (Achaios, Lachares, and Banabelos).

2.6. Euergetism in War and the Ideology of Inequality. *Persistence of democratic institutions and citizens' sovereignty*: Gauthier 2000b. *Hellenistic benefactors*: Gauthier 1985; Quass 1993; Shipley 2000: 96–102; Sevalli-Lestrade 2003. *Examples of benefactors*: Boulagoras of Samos (*IG* XII.6.1 11; Austin 1981: no. 113; Bagnall and Derow 2004: no. 76; mid-third century); Menas of Sestos (*OGIS* 339 = *I.Sestos* 1 = Austin 1981: no. 215; late second century); Aleximachos of Arsinoe (*SEG* XXVI 1817; ca. 100 BC); see also *OGIS* 4. *Honorary statues*: Raeck 1995. *The Koan subscriptions (205–201 BC)*: Sources: *PH* 10; *IscrCos* ED 37, 122, 206, 212, and 227. Baker 1991; Migeotte 2000a. *Awards for valor (aristeia)*: Pritchett 1974: 276–90. *"Crown of valor" (stephanos aristeios)*: e.g., Amyzon 24–5; *I.Perge* 14, lines 48–9; *I.Perge* 23 line 18; Chaniotis 2004 b: no. 1. *Hortatory formula*: e.g., Austin 1981: nos. 43–4.

2.7. From Individual Services to the Heredity of Leadership. *Development of a class of political leaders*: Quass 1993 (cf. the remarks of Habicht 1995); Lehmann 2000. *Heriditary honors in honorary decrees*: e.g., *I.Priene* 104, lines 3–5; Austin 1981: no. 51.

3

THE AGE OF WAR:
FIGHTING YOUNG MEN

3.1. Restless Warriors

In his narrative of the Lyttian War (221–220 BC), the greatest war in Cretan
history, Polybios reports an incident in Gortyn which has puzzled modern
historians (Polyb. 4.53.5–7):

> At first all the members of the Cretan alliance (*Kretaieis*) took part in the war
> against the Lyttians, but jealousy having sprung up from some trifling cause, as
> is the custom of the Cretans, they quarrelled with each other . . . Gortyn was
> in a state of civil war, the elder citizens (*presbyteroi*) taking the part of Knossos
> and the younger (*neoteroi*) that of Lyttos.

Such a conflict between young and old is unusual, but not unheard of. The
Cretans were again divided 150 years later, over the prospect of a war against
Rome. The Cretans had been terrorizing the Eastern Mediterranean with
their raids, and a first attempt by the Romans to eliminate Cretan piracy had
ended with a disaster in 74 BC. A few years later, in 70 BC, when the Cretans
sent envoys to Rome requesting a peace treaty, they were confronted with
immense demands. The Romans asked the Cretans to pay the enormous
amount of 4,000 talents, to deliver their warships, and to hand over 300
hostages, including their military leaders. The "older" men were inclined
to accept these demands (Diod. 40.1.1), but the view of those who preferred to fight prevailed. Velleius Paterculus (2.34.1) described the 24,000
Cretans who fought under the leadership of Lasthenes and Panares as "young
men" (*quattuor et viginti milibus iuvenes coactis*). The new war ultimately
led to the conquest of Crete. One may speculate whether these opposing
views may have had a socio-economic background: the young men, who
had not yet inherited the property of their fathers, saw in booty and slave
trade a profitable source of income. The elderly men preferred peace,
because the acceptance of the Roman demands did not really threaten the
foundations of their economic existence. One may wish to recognize in this

44

conflict of generations – not unparalleled in Greek history (e.g., Bertman 1976) – the universal anthropological opposition between restless youth and mature old men. But there may be another explanation, which does not necessarily exclude the other two. The young Cretans had been trained to fight; with solemn oaths (see sections 3.2, 3.3) they had obliged themselves to defend the fatherland, to assist its allies, and to fight any enemies with all their might. Making war and excelling in battle were the ultimate ideals of their education. Should we be surprised then if they opposed a peace treaty that would forbid them to behave in the way their entire education had conditioned them to behave?

Conflicts between young and old are by no means a particular phenomenon of Hellenistic Crete. A similar story is narrated about another warlike region, Pisidia. The Macedonian officer Alketas, a brother of Perdikkas and enemy of Antigonos the One-Eyed, one of the Successors, sought refuge in Termessos in Pisidia in 319 BC, organized raids, and became popular because of his generous distribution of booty. When Antigonos approached the city and demanded Alketas' surrender, the "old men," who wished to accept this demand in order to save the city came into conflict with the "young men" who were willing to risk everything in order to save their hero. While the "young men" were engaged by Antigonos in a battle, the "old men" tried to seize Alketas and hand him over to Antigonos. When Alketas committed suicide, his heroic death impressed the young Termessians so much that they recovered his body and provided for a memorable burial (Diod. 18.46.1–47.3).

It is difficult to establish whether the narratives of these events were fashioned by historians in such a way as to correspond to widespread clichés about the impulsive, restless, heroic nature of young men. What can nevertheless be established with certainty is that young men were enthusiastically engaged in battles, and were often the initiators of military operations. Aratos of Sikyon was only 20 years old when he liberated his fatherland from a tyrant, and was a mere 28 when – already in his second term of office as general of the Achaians – he led a surprise attack and captured the citadel of Akrokorinthos (Polyb. 2.43.3–4). The two most warlike kings of the Hellenistic period, Philip V of Macedon and the Seleukid Antiochos III, ascended the throne as teenagers and immediately engaged themselves in military operations which initiated three decades of continual wars. Philip was 18 when he started the war against the Aitolians, Sparta, and Elis (220 BC), and Antiochos was 21 when, already in his third regnal year, he suppressed the rebellion of Molon and started his eastern campaign. Ptolemy III, his opponent in one of the greatest battles of Hellenistic history, the Battle at Raphia (217 BC), was 22 at the most.

If in the case of these warrior kings one might detect an imitation of Alexander the Great, we have to look for other factors to explain the martial enthusiasm of the young Achaians, inspired by Philipoimen's interest in military matters (shortly before 207 BC). Young men, we are told, started spending their money on arms and armor, neglecting luxuries (Plut., *Philop.* 9.3–4). And if a mistrust in the narratives of literary sources is justified, such narratives can be confirmed by documentary sources about restless young men. When King Ptolemy died (probably King Ptolemy IX, 80 BC), and the repeated attacks of bandidts (*kakourgoi*) were threatening life in the countryside of Berenike in Kyrenaika, Apollodoros, offspring of a good family, was asked to command the "young men" *neaniskoi* in order to avert this danger. His troops were between 20 and 30 years of age (cf. Sacco 1979; Gauthier and Hatzopoulos 1993: 77–8) and with their support Apollodoros "established the greatest peace, taking upon himself every danger" (*SEG* XXVIII 1540, 62/61 BC; see chapter 2, section 5). It was a rule that when a surprise attack occured, the young men were sent to repel it. For example, when Antigonos Doson invaded Phokis in 228 BC, contigents of young men (*neoteroi*) from the cities of Doris hurried to Delphi to defend the sanctuary of Apollo (e.g., *SEG* XXXVIII 1476, lines 96–7), and Metropolis (Ionia) mobilized her young warriors (*neaniskoi*) at the beginning of Aristonikos' revolt in 133 (Dreyer and Engelmann 2003: 34–40).

Military service in the countryside and in the forts of the frontier was a typical duty of young men, deeply rooted in their training. Military education and military rituals for young men are also the key for understanding the historical background of narratives about their enthusiasm for war.

3.2. Training Fighters

What did one expect from a young man in the Hellenistic Age? The oath of the young men in Dreros on Crete (*I.Cret.* I ix 1; Austin 1981: no. 91) gives us one answer: it is the answer of the collective, not of an individual thinker, the answer of a community surrounded by enemies during a war, not that of a philosopher discussing the matter over Chian wine in a symposium:

> In the year in which the tribe of the Aithaleis provided the *kosmoi* [officials] who were in office together with Kyias and Kephalos, Pyros, Pios, Bision, and in the year in which Philippos was scribe, 180 members of the "herds" [units of *ephebes*] took the following oath, not girded. "I swear by Hestia ['Hearth'], who is in the magistrates' hall, and by Zeus, the patron of the assembly, and by Zeus of the Tallaian Mountains, and by Apollo Delphinios, and by Athena, the patron of the citadel, and by Apollo Pythios, and by Lato, and by Artemis, and by Ares, and by Aphrodite, and by Hermes, and by the Sun, and by Britomarpis, and by Phoinix, and by Amphione, and by the Earth, and by the Sky, and by the male and female heroes, and by the water sources, and by the rivers, and by all gods and goddesses; truly, I will never be benevolent towards the Lyttians, in no way and through no pretension, neither by day nor by night; and I will try, to the best of my capacity, to harm the city of the Lyttians. And neither a trial nor an execution of verdicts will be protected by

this oath; and I will be friendly towards the Drerians and the Knossians; and I will neither betray the city or the forts of the Drerians nor the forts of the Knossians; and I will betray no men to the enemies, neither men of Dreros, nor men of Knossos . . . I will not start a revolt, and I will always be an opponent of those who do; I will not participate in the organization of a conspiracy, neither in the city not outside of the city, nor I will help someone else . . .

This oath was taken under exceptional circumstances: Knossos and her allies were in war against Lyttos (the "Lyttian War"; see chapter 1, section 2), and as we may infer from several sources, this war had caused desertions and civil strife among the allies of Knossos (Chaniotis 1999c). In Gortyn, a civil war had broken out, confronting the young men with the old men (see section 3.1), and the same danger threatened Dreros. The oath of the young Drerians (180 men between 18 and 20) was taken in a solemn ceremony, probably during a ritual of transition, in which the young men took off the typical garment of the young man, and received the garment (and the armor) of the warrior (see section 3.3). Their oath is an obligation to obedience towards the authorities and to a never-ending war against Lyttos. All the elements of nature (sky, earth, water, sun), all the gods, and all the heroes are invoked as witnesses of the oath and as potential vindicators of those who would break it. No possibility of peace is left, not even through a sophistical interpretation of the oath. We know the outcome of this oath. The city of Lyttos was destroyed during an attack; the Lyttians rebuilt their city and subsequently razed Dreros to the ground.

In many Greek communities, to educate young men meant training them as warriors. This is not only reflected in the myths and traditions of initiatory rituals (Vidal-Naquet 1981; Waldner 2000), and it is not only the ritual substrate of literary narratives (e.g., Ma 1994); it is also the reality of many Hellenistic cities, which retained or revived the institution of the *ephebeia* – i.e., the training of age-classes of young men (usually between 18 and 20) under the supervision of the state authorities. It should be noted, however, that the existence of ephebic institutions in the Hellenistic period should not be taken as evidence for continuities. In many cases (e.g., Athens, Sparta, possibly Eretria) ephebic institutions declined during the Classical period and were artificially revived in the Hellenistic period, as a response of the Hellenistic communities to the need to take their defense into their own hands, and also as an expression of their sovereignty (see Chankowski 2004b). A characteristic example is Sparta, the ancient example of military training *par excellence* for its youth. The strict training (*agoge*), which started in the seventh year and was one of the requirements for citizenship, had lost its importance by the fourth century BC; it was revived by king Kleomenes III as one of the foundations of his reforms, and was abolished again in 188 by Philopoimen (Kennell 1995: 20; see chapter 2, section 2).

In the Cretan cities the young men were organized into groups (*agelai*, the "herds") under the leadership of a young man of high social status. In the *agelai* they exercised in fighting, wrestling, boxing, and running. Essential elements of their military education were also hunting – a traditional element of military training (Schnapp 1997a, 1997b; Beston 2000: 320) – and dances in full armor, which impressed a sense of harmony and rhythmic joint movement on the young soldiers. Such dances had a very long tradition in Crete (e.g., Diod. 5.65.4; Strabo 10.4.16 C 480), and dances were also performed by young men in the Arkadian cities in the Hellenistic period, as Polybios asserts (4.20.12–21.1), stressing their educational value: "the young men train in marching and battle order to the music of the flute and perfect themselves in dances and give annual performances for the citizens in the theaters, all under the supervision of the community and at the public expense." Running competitions, for which the Cretans were famous, were another essential element of training, as in Macedonia and Boiotia. The military background of Cretan runners is exemplified by the *hemerodromos* Philonides of Crete, a famous long-distance courier in the military personnel of Alexander the Great, known from his dedications to Zeus Olympios in Olympia (*IvO* 276; Tzifopoulos 1998).

At the end of the ephebeia the young men exchanged a belt, a typical clothing accessory of a young man, for the armor of the warrior. Between the ages of 20 and 30, the Cretans belonged to the age-class of the "runners" (*dromeis*; Tzifopoulos 1998). The occupation with war continued in later years, not only for the defense of the fatherland, but also in the form of raids and mercenary service (see chapter 5, section 2; chapter 7, section 3).

In Boiotia, military training was obligatory, as we can infer from the numbers of soldiers registered in the military catalogs upon completion of this training at the age of 20 (Feyel 1942 b: 215; Roesch 1982: 307–54; see chapter 2, section 2). Ephebic rituals and institutions also survived in Macedonia right up to the Hellenistic period (Hatzopoulos 1994). Some archaic practices (e.g., ritual transvestism, initiatory homoerotic relations) may have declined or disappeared, but other institutions, especially the importance of hunting for the military preparation of young men, in connection with the cult of Herakles Kynagidas, retained their importance under royal patronage (Hatzopoulos 1994: 87–111). Horse-races (*hippon dromos*) and races of men (*andron dromos, pezon dromos*), attested in fourth- and third-century inscriptions, may also be connected, as in Crete, with military training and with the end of the ephebeia (Hatzopoulos 1994: 55–61), or with funerary rituals (Manakidou 1996).

In Athens, the political turbulence of the late fourth century led to a decline of the ephebeia as obligatory military training for young men of citizen status (18–19 years). During the regime of Demetrios of Phaleron (317–307 BC), the ephebic training was a privilege of the sons of citizens with a minimum property amounting more than 1,000 drachmas. Between ca. 306 and 268 BC, participation in the ephebeia was not obligatory, and the training lasted only a year, instead of two (Pélékidis 1962: 167–72; Reinmuth 1971: 123–38). The numbers of ephebes increased (to around 100–180 men) after the end of Macedonian monarchy (167 BC), when Athens regained some of its overseas possessions and foreign residents were allowed to register (Pélékidis 1962: 184–96). The great interest shown by the community in the training of the offspring of the elite can be seen in the large number of honorary decrees, which year after year praised those volunteers who had successfully finished their education, demonstrating the virtues the Athenians expected from their future citizens and soldiers: diligence, endurance, obedience, discipline, piety, and respect towards ancestral traditions.

The content of the Athenian ephebeia was a combination of athletic activities, participation in customary rituals, military training, and preparation for civic duties (Pélékides 1962: 257–64; Launey 1987: 834). At its core were physical competition (races, boxing, wrestling, etc.) and military exercises. The ephebes learned the use of weapons (bow, javelin, lance, shield), patrolled the frontier of Attika, and manned the forts and the ships. From the third century BC onwards, more disciplines were added to the educational program of the ephebes – for example, lectures in philosophy and literature (Pélékides 1962: 197, 266–7).

An ephebic decree of the late third century (*SEG* XXVI 98; Reinmuth 1974) provides both a representative list of activities and a characteristic example of the expectations of the city: the ephebes offered sacrifices at the beginning of the year, attended the processions to Eleusis ("keeping good order following the custom of the fathers"), and looked for the pious fulfillment of the cult. They visited the gymnasia on a regular basis and participated in athletic competitions, especially in the characteristic contests of the gymnasium such as the torch race, "in a beautiful and decent manner." On the festival of the Epitaphia, in which the Athenians honored their war dead, the ephebes appeared in their armor and were reviewed (*en tois hoplois apodeixin epoiesanto*). They also did service in the temple of Hephaistos (widely known to visitors of modern Athens under the erroneous designation "Theseion"). At the end of the year they returned their weapons and their ephebic cloaks with "good order" (see *SEG* XXXV 96). The young men would then be praised for their discipline (*eutaxia*) and piety, so that future generations would compete with their achievement, knowing that those who showed such discipline would be honored.

Other activities of the ephebes included participation in many festivals, some of which have a specific ideological weight. For example, the festival of Artemis Agrotera, which was also the commemorative anniversary of the Battle of Marathon (see chapter 11, section 5 on *IG* II² 1006); the festivals connected with Theseus – the archetypical ephebe; the agons which honoured the local hero Aias in Salamis and the sacrifice to Zeus Tropaios in

Salamis, which commemorated the famous sea battle of the Persian Wars (Pélékidis 1962: 211–56).

The program of competitions at the Theseia (*IG* II² 956–7, mid-second century) reveals the originally military nature of this institution. The ephebes competed in javelin (*akontizein*), in combat with small shield and lance (*hoplomachein en aspidioi kai dorati*), and in combat with *thyreos*, a shield of the Galatian type (*hoplomachein en thyreoi*). Other disciplines included *euandria* (manliness), *euhoplia* (good maintenance and use of arms), races of armed men (*hoplites, en hoplois diaulos*), races of war-horses (*hippos polemistes*), and chariot races (*harma polemisterion*), in addition to the "classical" competitions (wrestling, races, and boxing).

The institution of the ephebeia continued to exist in many other cities and regions, as we may infer either from ephebic catalogs or from references to ephebes in, for example, grave inscriptions. The Macedonian army and the Greek settlers brought these institutions to the "New World," to Anatolia, the Near East, and to Egypt (Legras 1999: 133–54, 195–236).

For many boys, military training started earlier than their registration as ephebes and continued after the end of ephebeia. It began in the gymnasium, as it had long been established that athletic excersises and competitions were good conditioning for war (Pritchett 1974: 213–19; see also Reed 1998; Poliakoff 1987; Golden 1998: 23–8). The gymnasium is one of the best documented institutions of the Hellenistic city (see e.g., Gauthier 1995a). A lengthy law from Beroia – 173 lines are preserved – which regulates in detail the function of the gymnasium of the Macedonian city, is our best source both for the organization of Hellenistic gymnasia and for their military aspects (Gauthier and Hatzopoulos 1993; *SEG* XLIII 381; *I.Beroia* 1; Bagnall and Derow 2004: no. 78).

At the festival of the Hermaia, young men (probably between 18 and 30) competed in four disciplines: good physical condition (*euexia*); discipline (*eutaxia*) – one of the cardinal virtues of soldiers (see chapter 5, sections 4 and 5); endurance (*philoponia*); and (probably) the "long race." The prizes (*hopla*, "weapons," usually shields), which were financed from the revenues of the gymnasium, were dedicated in the gymnasium by the winners. The younger members of the gymnasium (*neaniskoi* and *paides*) competed in torch-races. The training offered in Beroia, exclusively dedicated to the athletic and military education of youth, seems to correspond to local, Macedonian traditions. Military aspects are nevertheless also evident in other gymnasia. The program of competitions in the gymnasium of Samos (*IG* XII.6.1 179–184), for example, includes disciplines of a military nature, such as the use of the catapult (*katapaltes*) and an engine used for hurling stones (*lithobolos*; see Polyb. 8.5.2), along with javelin (*akontion*), archery (*toxon*), fighting with shield and lance (*hoplomachia*), and fighting with the small shields of the Galatian type (*thyreomachia*). Overseeing such excersises was one of the duties of the *gymnasiarchos* (director of the gymnasium) in Koresia on Keos

(*IG* XII.5 647). Exactly as in Beroia, we also find prizes for *euexia*, *eutaxia*, and *philoponia* in Samos (*IG* XII.6.1 179–84).

The same selection of disciplines is found, for example, in Sestos (Thrace), where Menas, a local benefactor who served as *gymnasiarchos*, organized races, javelin and archery contests, and competitions in "good physical condition" and "manly behavior" (*OGIS* 339 = *I.Sestos* 1 = Austin 1981: no. 215; Gauthier 1982). As this short overview makes clear, military training had a more or less uniform structure in most areas, the result of mutual influence rather than common origins.

After the end of military training (usually at 20), young men were assigned military and paramilitary duties. In Gortyn, on Crete, the board of *neotas* ("the youth") exercised "police" duties, especially in the countryside, and controlled the frontier of the city (*SEG* XLVIII 1209; Magnelli 1992/3), and in other cities (e.g., Dreros and Olous) young men manned the forts on the frontier (see *I.Cret.* I,ix 1; van Effenterre 1949). This duty was exercised in Akarnania and Epeiros by the *peripoloi* ("patrolers"; Robert 1955; Cabanes 1991; e.g., *SEG* XXXII 626; *IG* IX I².4 1614), and similar troops are known from Athens (Taylor 1997: 235–7), the Korykean Cave on Parnassos (Robert 1937: 108–9), and Asia Minor (Chankowski 2004: 64–70).

In Athens, the *kryptoi* ("the secret ones") protected the fertile country-side, for example, in Rhamnous (*SEG* XLI 87; XLIV 59; Knoepfler 1993; Petrakos 1999: nos 3 and 20), in the plain of Tabai (Karia), a group of *neaniskoi* served as a mounted "patrol of the mountains" (*orophylakesantes*; Robert 1937: 106–8), and mounted guards were assigned the patrol of the border of Boiotia (Étienne and Roesch 1978: 363).

It has often been observed that the presence of young men in the periphery of the organized urban space, in the usually mountainous *eschatia* ("edge of the land"), in the realm of the wild animals and the forests, corresponds to the conception of young people – not yet citizens – as belonging to the world of unrestrained natural powers and to the periphery of the citizen body, together with other liminal groups, such as foreign mercenaries (Vidal-Naquet 1981; cf. Ma 2002: 115). It is perhaps for this reason that the cardinal virtue of ephebic education is *eutaxia*, "discipline," the virtue that permits the introduction of young people to ordered life. Transitions are marked in traditional societies through transitory rituals, some of which unexpectedly appear in ancient literary narratives (Ma 1994).

3.3. Rituals for Young Warriors

One of the honorary decrees for the Athenian ephebes describes an excursion to the sanctuary of Amphiaraos in Oropos (122 BC):

> and they made an excursion to the border of Attika carrying their weapons, acquiring knowledge of the territory and the roads [*lacuna*] and they visited

the sanctuaries in the countryside, offering sacrifices on behalf of the people. When they arrived at the grave at Marathon, they offered a wreath and a sacrifice to those who died in war for freedom; they also came to the sanctuary of Amphiaraos. And there they demonstrated the legitimate possession of the sanctuary which had been occupied by the ancestors in old times. And after they had offered a sacrifice, they returned on the same day to our own territory.

(*IG* II^2 1006, lines 65–71)

What at first sight seems like a harmless excursion acquires another dimension when we take into consideration the fact that in this period the sanctuary of Amphiaraos was *not* part of the Athenian territory, but belonged to the city of Oropos. In 156 BC, the Athenians had attacked Oropos and temporarily occupied the sanctuary and the territory (until ca. 150 BC; Paus. 7.11.4–12.3; cf. Plut., *Cato maior* 22). One generation later, the Athenian ephebes marched under arms into foreign territory, using speeches to provocatively remind the pilgrims present in the sanctuary (and themseves) that the Athenians had been the legitimate owners of the sanctuary. This done, they withdrew behind the Athenian border. Whether one still accepts the tripartite structure of rites of transition established by A. van Gennep and modified by V. Turner (rites of separation, rites of marginality, rites of reintegration) or not, this provocative and aggressive action looks very much like the survival of a rite of passage. The young Athenians were separated from urban life, they lived in the marginal area on the edge of the territory, they exposed themselves to danger by intruding into contested territory in arms, they achieved an important deed by provocatively demonstrating the claims of their city on the contested territory, and finally returned to Athens and were incorporated into the citizen body.

In modern research on rituals, more attention has been paid to questions of origins – to the reconstruction of the original form and meaning of rituals – than to their transformation and survival in later periods, notably in the Hellenistic and Imperial periods. When late evidence is studied, this is usually done with the perspective of understanding earlier forms through the late evidence, and not with the aim of placing that evidence in its historical context. Consequently, the performance of rituals in Hellenistic contexts is a subject to which little attention has been paid. This is not the place for an exhaustive study of this subject, but a few selected examples may show the importance that tratidional rituals retained in the Hellenistic period in the context of the training of young warriors.

We have already seen that in Athens religious rituals played an important role during the ephebeia, especially processions and sacrifices in festivals with a patriotic nature (Theseia, Epitaphia, the Panathenaic festival, commemorative anniversaries of great battles, etc.). Both the procession and the sacrifice are of great significance for the construction of identities. Processions – whether religious, military or ethnic, or demonstrations by people with common aims and ideals – bring together the members of a community in a common physical action, strengthening their solidarity, and distinguishing the participants from the "others." Ancient processions, especially Hellenistic ones, also expressed hierarchy and structure (Chaniotis 1995: 156–61). A characteristic example is provided by the procession established in Antioch near Pyramos in Asia Minor (ca. 160 BC) in order to commemorate the end of a conflict between this city and the neighboring city of Antioch near Kydnos. An altar dedicated to *Homonoia* (Concord) was set up, and every year the following celebration took place:

> On the day, on which the altar was founded, a procession will be held every year, a procession so beautiful and glamorous, as it is possible, from the altar of the council to the sanctuary of Athena. The procession will be led by the *demiourgos* (the highest official of the city) and the *prytaneis* (the members of the council). They will offer a sacrifice of a cow with gilded horns to Athena and Homonoia. The priests, all the other magistrates, the winners of the athletic contests, the supervisor of the gymnasium with all the ephebes and the young men, and the supervisor of the boys with all the boys, shall participate in the procession. This day will be a holiday; all the citizens shall wear garlands; all shall be released from work, the slaves shall be released from chains. The magistrates and the winners of the contests shall gather in the sanctuary of Athena, all the other citizens will gather in groups according to the divisions (the tribes). The *hieromnemon* (a sacred official) and the presidents of the tribes will be responsible for order on this day.
>
> (Sokolowski 1955: no. 81)

The position each individual takes in this festival depended on status: office, legal status (free or slave), achievement, civic subdivision, and age (young men, ephebes, boys). The participation of young people in these processions was obligatory (cf. Plut., *Aratos* 53.5) and through it they were incorporated into the group in a way that impressed on them the importance of social hierarchy and discipline. The cardinal virtue of military training, *eutaxia* (good order and discipline), is one of the recurring themes in decrees concerning processions (*IG* II^2 1006, lines 12–15; *I.Ilion* 52, line 28; Sokolowski 1962: no. 15, lines 24 and 27; no. 44, lines 2–3, 11–12; Sokolowski 1969: no. 65, line 62).

The importance of sacrifice for the strenghthening of solidarity has also frequently been stressed (e.g., Burkert 1983: 37). In the context of warfare (see chapter 9) and military training, sacrifice fulfilled an additional important function: it enacted aggression and violence (Parker 2000: 307–9), and thus brought young men into contact with killing and blood. Sacrifices structured the year of the Athenian ephebe. The ephebes offered sacrifices at the beginning and at the end of the year, and in all important festivals and commemorative anniversaries of battles. In Eleusis, they raised the sacrificial oxen high with their arms, according to an old sacrificial custom.

The sacrifices to the heroes and the war dead in Marathon and Plataia visualized the ideal of heroic death in combat, the bloody ritual re-enacting both battle and burial (Burkert 1983: 57).

All these rituals are body-centered, and special attention is given to the physical state of the body, to hair, and to garments. Long hair was a typical external feature of ephebes, and the cutting and offering of hair was a widely diffused transition rite, well attested until the Imperial period (Girone 2003). The importance of such *public* rituals, observed not by individuals but by communities, can be best seen in the treaty between the Akarnanian League and the city of Anaktorion concerning the sanctuary of Apollo Aktios (ca. 216 BC; *Staatsverträge* 523). Anaktorion was not in a position to provide the necessary funds for the sanctuary and its festivals, and agreed to let it become a sanctuary of the League, while retaining a few privileges. One of the regulations concerning the procession for Apollo, unfortunately only mentioned in a fragmentary passage (line 43), recognizes the right of the Anaktorians (rather than the obligation of all the participants) "to let their hair grow long" (*tan koman trephein*). This certainly refers to the young participants.

Elements of ritual transvestism, which had a fundamental significance in early ephebic rites of passage (Leitao 1995; Waldner 2000), can still be seen in the procession of the Oschophoria – the "historical" anniversary of Theseus' return from his adventures in Crete – in which two young men participated, dressed as girls, even in Imperial times (Plut., *Theseus* 23.3). A typical garment, the "cloak of the ephebe" (*chlamys ephebike*), was the distinguishing feature of such a person, not only in Athens (Arist., *Ath.Polit.* 42.5), but in the Greek world in general (e.g., *I.Kalchedon* 32; *SEG* XXXV 1300; Hatzopoulos 1994: 102, 2001: 138; for the Imperial period see *SEG* XL 1568, line 2). An inventory of a temple in Miletos (late second century) lists among the dedications that were to be removed because of their bad condition, "four ephebic cloaks, old, unfit" (*SEG* XXXVIII 1210, lines 11–12), which had been dedicated by ephebes during a ritual at the end of the ephebeia. The oath of Dreros (see section 3.2) was taken in 220 BC by 180 young Cretans who were "not girded" (*panazostoi*), i.e., had removed the belt of youth.

In Crete there is more evidence concerning the significance of clothes in the Hellenistic rituals of young warriors. Although it is sometimes assumed that the Hellenistic ephebic institutions in Crete were the result of an artificial revival (Bile 1992: 15), archaeological evidence from the sanctuary of Hermes Kedrites in Simi Biannou (Lebessi 1985, 1991, 2002), corroborated through literary sources – especially the report of the fourth-century historian Ephoros (*apud* Strabo 10.4.21 ca. 483.4 = *FgrHist* 70 F 149) – and Hellenistic inscriptions, suggests a strong continuity. A combination of all the evidence allows a reconstruction of the rituals. Towards the end of the period of ephebeia, a young man was kidnapped, in accordance with very strict rules, by an older man of the same social position. This ritual reflected social hierarchy (see Gehrke 1997: 63–5). The two men spent two months together, hunting on the mountains, and at the end of this period the older man gave his younger companion symbolic presents: a cup (an allusion to his ability to take meals in the men's house); an ox (as a sacrificial animal); and the "garment of war" (*stole polemike*). The young man was designated as "the one who stands at the side" (i.e., in battle, *parastatheis*), and this designation reveals the military context of this ritual.

Hellenistic inscriptions, which refer to the sub-military groups of young men (*agelai*), to the men's houses, to athletic and musical competitions of young men, and to the relevant festivals, show that these rituals continued to be practiced at least by some communities, possibly in a reduced form, until the end of the Hellenistic period (Chaniotis 1996a: 123–30). These rituals culminated in festivals in which the young men put off the garments of ephebic age and received the garments of the citizen (*Ekdysia, Periblemaia*). On the occasion of these festivals, which marked the transition of the ephebes to the status of the citizen warrior, young Cretans would take solemn oaths, promising to protect their city, defend their allies, and fight against their enemies.

With all of this in mind, we should not be surprised at the enthusiasm of these young men for war, and the resultant conflicts with their elders (see section 3.1). Only the Roman conquest put an end to this tradition, giving the Roman authorities a monopoly of violence.

Further Reading

3.1. Restless warriors. *Hellenistic youth, in general*: Kleijwegt 1991; Legras 1999: 13–29, 65–95, 109–44, 195, 236 (Ptolemaic Egypt); see also Forbes 1933 (on associations of young men, but also on the tendency to underestimate the importance of military training). *The civil war in Gortyn*: Chaniotis 1996a: 14–15, 37; see also Willetts 1977: 73–5. *Generation conflicts in Greek history*: Forrest 1975; Bertman 1976; Strauss 1993: 136–48, 179–81; Legras 1999: 228–31; Menu 2000. *Engagement of young soldiers in battle*: e.g., Livy 42.63.3 (Koroneia, 171 BC); *I.Ilion* 73 (80 BC). *Interest of young men in raids and booty*: e.g., Polyb. 5.25.1–3.

3.2. Training fighters. *Ancient military training*: Pritchett 1974: 208–31 (primarily on the Classical period); Chankowski 2004b; Lendon 2004. *The oath of Dreros*: *I.Cret.* I,ix 1; Detienne 1973; Chaniotis 1996a: 195–201. *The Spartan agoge*: Kennell 1995. *Cretan military education*: Lebessi 1985; Chaniotis 1991b; Gehrke 1997: 63–5; see also Willetts 1977. *Importance of hunting*: e.g., *I.Cret.* III.iv 36–7, 39, 59. *Macedonian institutions*: Hatzopoulos 1994, 2001: 133–40. *The Athenian ephebeia*: Pélékidis 1962: 155–277; Reinmuth 1971, 1974: 258–9; e.g., *IG* II² 665, 994b (+ *SEG* XXVI 98), 1006; *SEG* XIX 96–97, 108; XXXII 129. *Ephebes in Hellenistic cities*: e.g., Mykenai: *IG* IV 497 = Bielman 1994: no. 44 (brought to Sparta by king Nabis); Boiotia: Roesch 1982: 307–54; Delphi: *F.Delphes* III.1 457 = Bielman 1994: no. 50 (abducted and brought to the mountains); Eretria:

IG XII.9 240 (*SEG* XXXVI 797), *IG* XII Suppl. 555 (*SEG* XXXVI 799); Amathous on Cyprus: *SEG* XXXIX 1523; Asia Minor: Chankowski 2004a; Iasos: *SEG* XLV 1520; Kalchedon: *I.Kalchedon* 32 (cf. *SEG* XXXV 1300); Metropolis: *SEG* XXXII 1172 (ephebes honor an ephebe); Miletos: *SEG* XXXVIII 1210, lines 11–12; Teos: *SEG* XLI 1003, line 39; cf. Kleijwegt 1991: 89–116; Kyrene: Legras 1999: 143–8; Cordiano 2001; Pto Pemaic Egypt: Legras 1999: 133–42. *Hellenistic gymnasia*: Gauthier and Hatzopoulos 1993; Gauthier 1995a; Legras 1999: 208–17; Migeotte 2000b: 152–4 (expenses); Dreyer and Engelmann 2003: 57–65; Chankowski 2004a: 58–61.

3.3. Rituals for young warriors. *The excursion of the Athenian ephebes to Oropos*: see Knoepfler 1991: 279. *Theory of rites of passage*: van Gennep 1960; Turner 1967: 93–111 and 1974; Versnel 1994: 48–74. *Military initiatory rituals*: Brelich 1961, 1969; Vidal-Naquet 1981; Waldner 2000. *Structure and hierarchy in processions*: Rudhardt 1958: 257–8; Burkert 1983: 26, 37–40, 1985: 99; Calame 1982/3. *Hellenistic processions*: Dunand 1978: 203–4, 207–9; Chaniotis 1991a: 139–42, 1995: 156–61. *Participation of the youth in processions*: e.g., *I.Lampsakos* 9, lines 17–18; Sokolowski 1955: no. 32, lines 38–9, 1962: no. 61, line 47, 1969: no. 93; *I.Pergamon* 246, lines 35–6; *SEG* XXXIII 675, lines 10–11; Plut., *Aratos* 53.5; see also Ziebarth 1914: 147–62. *Oschophoria*: Calame 1990: 324–48; Waldner 2000: 102–75. *Clothes (and nudity) in transition rites of young men*: Leitao 1995; Bonfante 1989, 2000. *Cretan festivals of the ephebeia*: Willetts 1962: 175–8; Brelich 1969: 200–2; Chaniotis 1996a: 123–30. *The oath of Dreros*: Chaniotis 1996a: 200–1. According to a different interpretation, the short narrative of a war is a reference to a rite of passage which included a ritual battle at the border of the territory: Detienne 1973: 305–6; van Effenterre and Ruzé 1994: 200.

4

THE INTERACTIVE KING: WAR AND THE IDEOLOGY OF HELLENISTIC MONARCHY

4.1. War and the Acceptance of Monarchical Rule

One of the few definitions of monarchy that survive from the Hellenistic period is found in the lexicon *Suda* (s.v. *basileia*; Austin 1981: no. 37; Sage 1996: no. 271): "Monarchical power [*basileiai*] is given to men neither by nature nor by law; it is given to those who are able of commanding troops and dealing prudently with [political] matters". This statement summarizes the experience of the Greeks during the period of the Successors of Alexander the Great: Antigonos the One-Eyed and his son Demetrios, Ptolemy I, Seleukos, Lysimachos, and Kassandros did not acquire the title of "king" on the basis of dynastic legitimacy – as a matter of fact, Kassandros liquidated Alexander's son, who *did* have this legitimacy – but on the basis of their success in wars. Antigonos the One-Eyed initiated this practice with his carefully staged proclamation to kingship upon the announcement of the naval victory of his son Demetrios in Cyprus (306 BC; Plut., *Demetr.* 17–18). As soon as the messenger announced the victory, the "multitude" (*plethos*) acclaimed Antigonos and Demetrios as kings, and Antigonos' friends bound a diadem around his head. The proclamation of the other Successors to kingship followed soon after and gave the year 306 BC its designation as the "year of the kings."

The fact that the title *basileus* was not accompanied by an ethnic name (e.g., *basileus ton Makedonon*, "king of the Macedonians"), is plausibly taken to imply that the Successors were the kings of whichever land they could conquer (see Gruen 1985). This intentional vagueness was an invitation to conquest.

The imperialist impulse, which can be observed in the major Hellenistic monarchies of the Antigonids, the Ptolemies, and the Seleukids, and which is one of the causes of the never-ending wars, is intrinsically connected with the fact that the acceptance of monarchical rule was founded on war and military power: on the defense of patrimony, the reclamation of lost land, and the conquest of new territories (see Bikerman 1938: 15–16; see also chapter 9, section 5). As the court poet, Theokritos, put it (referring to Ptolemy II): "as a good king he cares deeply for the preservation of his fatherly inheritance and adds something thereto himself" (17.105–6). Precisely these aspects are underlined in the *res gestae* of Ptolemy III, an epigraphic account of his achievements during the Third Syrian War (Adulis, ca. 241 BC):

> King Ptolemy the Great . . . *having taken over* from his father the kingship over Egypt, Libya, Syria, Phoinike, Cyprus, Lykia, Karia, and the islands of the Cyclades, marched out into Asia with infantry, cavalry, a fleet, and elephants from the land of the Troglodytes and from Ethiopia, which his father and he himself were the first to hunt from these lands, and after bringing them to Egypt they equipped them for military use. *Having gained possession* (*kyrieusas*) of all the land on this side of the Euphrates, of Kilikia, Pamphylia, Ionia, the Hellespont, Thrace, and of all the forces in these countries and of the Indian elephants, and having made all the rulers of these areas to his subjects, he crossed the river Euphrates, and *having subdued* Mesopotamia, Babylonia, Sousiane, Persis, Media and the rest of the land as far as Baktria, and *having sought out* all the sacred objects that had been carried out of Egypt by the Persians, and *having brought them back* to Egypt together with the rest of the treasures from these areas, he sent his forces across the rivers (canals) that were dug out . . .
>
> (*OGIS* 54; cf. Austin 1981: no. 221; Sage 1996: no. 275; Bagnall and Derow 2004: no. 26)

"Conquer or perish" is a motto that guided monarchs long before the beginning of the Hellenistic Age; it is also one of the lessons one learns from Herodotus' history (Evans 1991: 9–40). But the models upon which the Successors founded their rule were not the early empires, but the conquests of Alexander the Great, in which they themselves had participated. The *imitatio Alexandri* remained a source of inspiration for Hellenistic kings many generations later, and as far west as Sicily the coins of monarchs in the late fourth and early third centuries exploited the image of Alexander and the representation of Victory (Stewart 1993: 264–9, 313–21).

The youthful Pyrrhos of Epeiros, a relative of Alexander, also resembled him in appearance (Plut., *Pyrrhos* 8.1; Stewart 1993: 284–5). His campaigns brought him to Italy and his purported intentions concided (coincidentally?) precisely with the purported last plans of his hero: the conquest of Carthage. His discussion with the philosopher Kineas not only reveals the importance of war in the ideology of a Hellenistic king, but is also one of the best ancient comments on the constraints and absurdities of the imperialist impulse:

> When Kineas saw that Pyrrhos was at this time eager to sail to Italy, and found him at leisure, he drew him into the following conversation. "Pyrrhos, the

Romans are said to be good soldiers and rulers of many warlike peoples; if, then, a god should permit us to defeat them, how should we use our victory?" Pyrrhos said: "Your question, Kineas, really needs no answer; the Romans once defeated, there is neither barbarian nor Greek city there which would resist us, but we shall immediately possess all Italy – and no man should know better than yourself how large, rich, and powerful she is." After a little pause, then, Kineas said: "And after taking Italy, O King, what are we to do?" Pyrrhos, not yet perceiving his intention, answered: "Sicily is near, and stretches out her hands to us, an island abounding in wealth and men, and very easy to conquer, for there is nothing there, Kineas, but faction, anarchy in her cities and excitable demagogues, now that Agathokles is gone." "What you say," replied Kineas, "is probably true; but will our expedition stop with the capture of Sicily?" "May god grant us victory and success," said Pyrrhos, "and we will use this as a preliminary to great enterprises. For who could keep us away from Libya or Carthage, when they get within our reach, when Agathokles nearly captured them, secretly escaping from Syracuse and crossing over with a few ships? And when we have conquered these, none of our enemies, who are now treating us with scorn, will offer resistance; no one can dispute this." "None whatever," said Kineas, "for it is clear that with such a power behind us we shall be able to recover Macedonia and rule Greece securely. But when we have got everything subject to us, what shall we do?" Then Pyrrhos laughed and said: "We shall be much at ease, and we'll drink bumpers, my good man, every day, and we will entertain each other with conversations." Now that Kineas had brought Pyrrhos to this point, he said: "Well then, what prevents us now from drinking bumpers and enjoying leisure among ourselves if we so wish? Surely this possibility is ours already and we can have it without taking any trouble; so why try to attain the same thing by bloodshed and great toils and perils, after inflicting on others and suffering ourselves great harm?"

(Plut., *Pyrrhos* 14; trans. B. Perrin, modified; cf. Austin 1981: no. 47b)

Kings were supposed to drink bumpers only when there was nothing more to conquer, or when they were conquered themselves (e.g., Demetrios the Besieger). Among the later Hellenistic kings, the best example of the exploitation of war as a fundamental part of kingship is provided by Antiochos III and the campaigns with which he established his rule (Ma 2000a: 53–63). He was 20 when his brother, King Seleukos III, was murdered during a campaign in Asia Minor (221 BC). Molon, the governor of the upper satrapies, proclaimed himself king in Media and before his revolt was subdued, Antiochos' uncle Achaios had overcome his original hesitation and also proclaimed himself king in Asia Minor. Antiochos' reaction was a large-scale reconquest, which started with an effort to conquer south Syria (Fourth Syrian War, 219–217 BC), continued with a war against the usurper Achaios, in which Antiochos re-established control of the largest part of Asia Minor (216–213 BC), and culminated in a new *anabasis* that brought his troops to Armenia, Parthia, Baktria, and beyond the Hindu Kush (212–205 BC), where the local kings recognized his supremacy. The last campaign echoed those of Alexander and of the founder of the dynasty, Seleukos I, and consolidated Antiochos' rule. The royal nickname "the Great," which was adopted immediately after his return (204 BC?; earliest attestation in 202 BC; *Amyzon* 14), and his later title, "the Great King," stem from success in war (see Ma 2000a: 272–6). Many other royal epithets among the Seleukids and the Ptolemies stress victory and protective power (see section 4.5): *Nikator* (the Victorious), *Nikephoros* (the one who brings victory), *Soter* (the Rescuer), *Kallinikos* (the one with the fair victories), *Keraunos* (the Thunderbolt), and *Epiphanes* (the one with the manifest power).

That victory made kings could still be observed by the Hellenistic Greeks long after Alexander's conquest and the Wars of the Successors. Antigonos Gonatas owed his kingship to his victory over the Galatians (see chapter 11, section 3). And it was only after a great victory over the Galatians, probably in a battle in Mysia (ca. 238 BC) that the dynast of Pergamon, Attalos I, assumed the title of king (Walbank 1967: 604; Allen 1983: 31–2). In an appraisal of his personality, Polybios (18.41) continually stresses the military context of his achievements: he secured his position and assumed the royal title by defeating the Galatians; he died during a glorious campaign for the freedom of the Greeks (in reality he had a stroke while delivering a speech in Thebes); and he handed down to his grandchildren a secured kingdom. Achievements in war are the beginning of Attalos' kingship, the end of his life, and the warrant of a safe succession.

Power and authority were the rewards that awaited the charismatic and victorious military commander. As long as his actions remained successful, his power was unquestioned. It is not surprising then if military failure was the beginning of many a ruler's end (see Bikerman 1938: 13) or had to be compensated with a successful demonstration of military power. One of the most impressive military parades of the Hellenistic period was organized by Antiochos IV in Daphne, immediately after his shameful failure to take control of Egypt (Athen. V 194 c–195 f; Bunge 1976). More than 50,000 men participated in this parade, which was, at the same time, a demonstration of wealth and exotic weapons.

Even the masculinity of the king, another pillar of monarchical self-representation (Roy 1998), was questioned after a military disaster (see chapter 6, section 1 on Polyb. 28.21.3). The failure of a king to offer the protection expected from him would generally revive local conflicts and encourage renegade dynasts (see section 4.4). The independent Greek-Baktrian kingdoms in the Seleukid upper satrapies (in northern Iran and Afghanistan), which were continually confronted with attacks from nomadic tribes, broke away when the attention of the Seleukids was diverted to other affairs (Tarn 1951; Narain 1989). It is also possible that Philotas founded his own dynasty in Gadara/Seleukeia by taking advantage of the vacuum left by the defeat of the Seleukid king, Alexandros Iannaios, in the Goan by Obedas I (ca. 93/2 BC; Wörrle 2000a: 267–71).

Although little is known about the education of the sons and potential successors of kings or of the offspring of their courtiers, there can be little doubt that training in weapons, in horsemanship, and in hunting took the lion's share of their preparation for their future activities. Physical and military training was one of the foundations of the education of Hellenistic youths in general (see chapter 3, section 2). In antiquity, the transmission of professional expertise was primarily a family concern, and the education of the future king relied to a great extent on his experiences accompanying his father and his father's friends on campaigns. Not unlike Alexander and the Sucessors, kings were expected to launch attacks at the head of their troops (see e.g., Polyb. 10.49; Livy 37.42.7–8), and they were criticized when they did not (see chapter 6, section 1). However, they were also open to criticism when they exposed themselves to dangers without good reason (Eckstein 1995: 28–40; Beston 2000: 321). Kings were often wounded, and many were killed in action. Numerous Successor kings died in battle (e.g., Antigonos the One-Eyed, Ptolemaios Keraunos, Lysimachos, and Pyrrhos), and the later Hellenistic kings – with the notable exception of the Ptolemies – usually died a violent death, being either murdered or killed in battle (e.g., Areus II of Sparta, Zaielas I of Bithynia, Demetrios II of Macedon, the Seleukids Demetrios I, Alexandros Balas, Antiochos X, Antiochos XII, Ptolemy VI, and Ptolemy X). Antigonos Doson of Macedonia died as a result of wounds, and other kings such as Molon, Achaios, Antiochos V, Diodotos Tryphon, Antiochos VII, Demetrios II, and Alexandros Zabinas were either executed or committed suicide. The death of Seleukos II during a campaign was less heroic: he accidentally fell off his horse.

Death in battle was not an act of heroism, or just part of the job, but a risk a king had to take in order to safeguard the continuation of his rule. If a king killed an oponent with his own hand in battle – as Seleukos I killed the satrap of Media, Nikanor (Appian, *Syr.* 55), so much the better. Most kings of the third and early second century spent the majority of their reign on campaign (again, the Ptolemies are an exception), and this corresponds with the expectation of their troops and of their subjects.

Naturally, some Hellenistic monarchs were more interested in military matters than others, and some were better generals than others. Expertise in war characterizes Demetrios the Besieger, who owes his nickname to the new mechanical devices he used during the siege of Rhodes (305–304 BC), and many other kings promoted what we today would call "applied science" for the sake of warfare (Garlan 1974: 209–10; Will 1975: 311; Green 1990: 474–8; Austin 2001: 98; Pimouguet-Pedarros 2003). The Ptolemies were particularly keen on ballistic research, and their engineers included the famous scientist Ktesibios of Alexandria (see chapter 5, section 7). Archimedes applied his knowledge to solve problems of siege warfare under Hieron II of Syracuse, and some of the greatest military writings of Aineas the Tactician were composed in the court of Pyrrhos (*FgrHist* 603). Pyrrhos himself, along with his son Alexandros, were the authors of works on military tactics (Ailianos, *Taktika* 1.2).

The demonstration of innovative military techniques was as much a part of a ruler's image as the promotion of culture. One of the achievements narrated by Ptolemy III in his aforementioned *res gestae* is that he and his father had been the first to equip elephants from the land of the Troglodytes and from Ethiopia for military use.

The Hellenistic king is in many respects a warrior king: the helmet was as much a standard attribute of his portrait as the diadem; he was often assimilated with Herakles; he took the initiative for new wars, either encouraged by victories or eager to compensate defeats with new enterprises; he took an interest in military equipment, and martial parades were a standard component of the festivals he celebrated; his epithets stressed military success – even if in some cases the discrepancy between the wishful thinking of an epithet and the reality cannot have escaped the notice of a king's contemporaries. For example, Seleukos VI Epiphanes Nikator ("the one with the manifest power, the victorious") ruled for less than a year, was defeated, and roasted in his palace by an angry mob.

The Hellenistic king was, however, more than a warrior in a world of continual wars. The acceptance of his rule depended on the successful conduct of delicate negotiations with other kings (and their daughters), with his "friends," with his army, with the population of his cities, and with the gods (see Ma 2000a: 179–242, 2003: 179–86). This complex field of interactions with the "others," a play of promises and expectations, requests and offers, achievements and threats, power and tolerance, constitutes Hellenistic kingship. In the following pages we will explore the part played by war in the life of the interactive king.

4.2.   The King and his Army

Hellenistic kingship is in part rooted in Macedonian traditions, and in part in the traditions of Egypt and the Persian Empire. One of the primary functions of the king in all these traditions is the leadership of the army and active participation in war. In the Macedonian traditions, this function is expressed by the acclamation of the new king by the army. This is not the place to discuss the question of whether the acclamation of a king by the Macedonian army corresponded to the election of military commanders in other Greek communities by the popular assembly, which originally was an assembly of warriors. The problem is that the proclamation of the king by the army in pre-Hellenistic Macedonia is only known from late sources (Hatzopoulos 1996: 276–9). There is no reliable evidence for a formal election by the army assembly, but it is probable that after the death of a king either his legitimate heir or the person whom the "first of the Macedonians" had agreed should succeed him – sometimes the most powerful pretender or the only survivor of the bloodshed that regularly followed a king's death – was presented to the army and recognized as king through acclamation. We have several references to this practice, both in connection with the events following Alexander's death and in connection with the Successors. For instance, when Demetrios the Besieger had King Alexander V, Kassandros' son, murdered in Larisa (294 BC), the army "acclaimed him [Demetrios] king of the Macedonians . . . and this development was not against the will of the Macedonians at home" (Plut., *Demetr.* 37.2–3; cf. Just. 16.1.9 and 18). It was also the army that acclaimed Pyrrhos king of the Macedonians in 288 BC. Although the legal or "constitutional" aspect of these acts is a matter of controversy, the ritual of acclamation clearly denotes the acceptance of the new king as a military commander by his troops. There is hardly any evidence for this practice after the period of the Successors; the sources are usually late and vague, and if an acclamation by the army did take place, it only happened in connection with usurpations or conflicts of succession (Bikerman 1938: 8–9; Ritter 1965: 129–32, 136, 139–40). The men to whom the army offered the diadem or proclaimed king include: Achaios, after the murder of Seleukos III by one of his officers; the king of Egypt, Ptolemy VI Philometor, who was proclaimed king by the Seleukid troops; Tryphon, after the murder on Antiochos VI; possibly Demetrios I Soter, after the army had executed Antiochos V; and Antigonos Doson, when the legitimate heir was still a child.

Evidence for the survival of this ritual of acclamation can be found in the announcement of the death of Ptolemy IV to the army in 204 BC. The most influential member of the court, Agathokles, summoned a meeting of the "Macedonians," probably the guards camped near the palace, as a substitute for the army assembly. He announced the king's death and presented the new king, the 6-year-old Ptolemy V, in a carefully staged scene (Polyb. 15.26.1–4):

> Agathokles first summoned the Macedonians and appeared together with the king and Agathoklea [his sister and lover of the deceased king]. At first he pretended that he could not say what he wished because of the abundance of tears; but after wiping his eyes many times with his cloak he subdued the outburst, took the child in his arms and said: "Take the child whom his dying father placed in the arms of this woman," pointing to his sister, "and confided to your faith, Macedonians. Her affection indeed can hardly ensure his safety, but his fate depends on you and your actions."
>
> (trans. W. R. Paton, modified)

Agathokles went on to explain that a pretender was already making preparations to assume the diadem; altars were being erected and sacrificial victims prepared in the presence of the populace for the proclamation ceremony. At this point he must have expected a spontaneous acclamation in favor of the child king. He was wrong: "When the Macedonians heard this, not only did they feel no pity for Agathokles but paid absolutely no attention to what he said, and showed such a contemptuous [or silly] behaviour by hooting and murmuring to each other that he did not know himself how he got away from the assembly. The same kind of thing took place at the assembly of the other units." Instead of acclamation, disapprobation. The anticipated ritualized communication spectacularly failed to take place (see chapter 11, section 1 on Plut., *Sulla* 13).

But even if the army was not the source of a monarch's legitimacy, as it had been in Macedonia, it remained a very important factor of power, especially in periods of crisis, defeat, or unclear succession. When Achaios proclaimed himself king in 220 BC, his army refused to follow him in his war against the legitimate king (Polyb. 5.57.6: "against the king which they had from the beginning in accordance to nature"); when Demetrios I, the legitimate heir of Seleukos Epiphanes, reclaimed the throne (162 BC), it was the army in Antioch that seized and executed the pretender (Polyb. 31.12.4).

The absence of a "constitutional" part played by the army was fully compensated by the personal relationship of the monarch to the military commanders, and to a lesser extent to the troops. For the administration of their kingdoms, the Hellenistic kings relied on a circle of "friends" (*philoi*), who were advisers, teachers of the princes, good company in hunting and drinking parties, governors of districts and provinces, envoys, and – above all – commanders of important army units (Savalli-Lestrade 1998: 355–61). When in the early second century the honorary titles of the members of the highest administration of the Ptolemaic kingdom were standardized, these revealed the personal character of government, but also the military origin of the kings' collaborators (Mooren 1975, 1977; Austin 2001: 91). The ranks began with those of the bodyguards (*somatophylakes*) and the "followers" (*diadochoi*), and reached the higher levels of "friends" (*philoi*), chief body-guards (*archisomatophylakes*), "first friends" (*protoi philoi*), and "relatives" (*syngeneis*). The career of Demodamas of Miletos (Savalli-Lestrade 1998: 4–5) may give an insight into of the activities of a *philos*. Demodamas served as a general under Seleukos I and later under Antiochos I. He participated in campaigns in the eastern parts of the Seleukid empire and while in his native city of Miletos he mediated between the city and the kings, proposed honors for Antiochos I and Queen Apame, and used his influence for the benefit of the local sanctuary of Apollo Didymaios.

The relationship between a king and his officers was based on trust and reciprocity. The innumerable private dedications by military commanders, and sometimes by associations of soldiers, to and for the well-being of kings express gratitude and expectations: gratitude for the promotion and protection hitherto given by the king and the expectation of future rewards and patronage. This idea is expressed, for example, in an epigram from Pergamon (ca. 250–220 BC; Müller 1989; *SEG* XXXVII 1020), written on the base of a statue of the satyr Skirtos. The statue was dedicated by an admiral of the Attalid fleet, Dionysodoros, to both Dionysos and King Attalos I. In the last line, the dedicator expresses his expectations: "may both of you take care of the dedicator." King and god are associated in their function as protectors of Dionysodoros. He had a close personal relationship with both: he was in the service of Attalos, but was also the "gift" of Dionysos (*Dionysos + doron*), the patron god of the Attalids.

Kings rewarded faithful and effective service with honors and promotion, but also with material gains, usually land (Savalli-Lestrade 1998: 335, 362–4, 378–80; Virgilio 2003: 150–6). The Thessalian military settlers in Larissa (Syria) received their land from the Seleukid kings "because of their bravery" (*ep andreia*; Diod. 33.4a). The commander of the Ptolemaic garrison at Philai proudly mentions in a dedication he made that he was given a distinction during the visit of Ptolemy IX (*SEG* XXVIII 1429). Aristodikides of Assos was one of the "friends" of Antiochos I, to whom the king gave land in the Hellespontine satrapy (ca. 275 BC; Savalli-Lestrade 1998: 11–12; Bagnall and Derow 2004: no. 18). The king explains his motivation in his letters to the governor: "because being our friend he has rendered his services with all goodwill and zeal" (*RC* 11); "seeing that he is benevolent and zealous in our interest we are anxious to favor the man highly" (*RC* 12). Such phrases not only honor the recipient of the gift, but also encourage other officers to demonstrate analogous zeal and goodwill. A letter sent by Seleukos IV to Seleukeia in Pieria concerning honors for one of his father's veterans (*RC* 45, 186 BC) reinforces this point: "Aristolochos, one of the 'honored friends,' has rendered his services with all good-will to our father and our brother and ourself, and has at the most critical times given splendid demonstrations of his attitude towards our affairs"; the "critical times" (*anankaiotatoi kairoi*) are the uninterrupted wars of Antiochos III, who had recently died before he had a chance to reward Aristolochos. His son inherited this obligation and honored Aristolochos with a statue in the city of Skepsis, where the veteran had chosen to spend the rest of his life.

The ability of a king to reward past services and at the same time inspire service in the future very much depended on his wealth. Although "royal economy" cannot be reduced to a model of the seizure of the goods of others and their redistribution among faithful collaborators, the revenues of war – captured slaves and manpower, conquered territory, captured valuables and cash – were of enormous importance for any monarchy (Austin 1986). The regular payment of mercenary soldiers and standing troops, the settlement of military colonists in strategic sities on conquered territories, the giving of gifts for important services and permission given to soldiers to loot enemy territory (alas, sometimes more than that), all contributed to the popularity of a monarch and strengthened the relationship of trust.

Incompetence and defeat occasionally disturbed the relationship between a king and his officers, and some officers might choose to seek another "employer" as a result. A general of Ptolemy IV provides an instructive example. Ptolemaios, son of Thraseas, served the king of Egypt as his general in 219 BC but deserted to Antiochos III some time between 204 and 201. The king's death in 205, the succession by the 6-year-old Ptolemy V, and the Egyptian defeat in the Fifth Syrian War may be why Ptolemaios decided to leave, while other members of his family stayed in Egypt (Jones and Habicht 1989; cf. *SEG* XXXIX 1426). Some officers did not hesitate to take more radical measures. Seleukos III, who had been given the nickname *Keraunos* by his soldiers ("the Thunderbolt"; Porphyrios, *FgrHist* 260 F 32.9), was murdered by one of his own officers (or by his friends) during an unsuccessful campaign against Attalos I (Walbank 1957: 502; Will 1979: 313–14).

Most kings would be likely to interact more with their officers or elite units (such as their personal bodyguard) than directly with the common soldiers. However, the fact that Seleukos III was nicknamed by his *troops* suggests a certain amount of familiarity. The soldiers themselves would have been quite familiar with their king: his face was represented on the coins with which they were paid, and they saw him in person at military parades, at meetings of the army assembly (e.g., Polyb. 5.25.4–5), during daily military training (Just. 37.4.2; Polyb. 5.2.4–5), and in action (see sections 4.1, 4.5). At a critical moment during the Battle of Raphia (217 BC), one of the greatest battles of Hellenistic history, Ptolemy V – who is known to have drilled and exercised with his men on a regular basis (Polyb. 16.21.6–7) – appeared amid a phalanx, inspiring his men and leading them to victory (Polyb. 5.82.5–86.6).

A king's army owed him a great deal, not least the expectation of land and privileges on retirement (e.g., *RC* 51; see chapter 5, section 3). However, if their expectations were not met, there was always the risk of a mutiny. Even Alexander the Great experienced this. The best documented mutiny is that of the troops of Eumenes I in Philetaireia and in Attaleia (ca. 263–241 BC), which forced the king to make extensive concessions with regard to provisions, pay, a winter rest period, and the testamentary rights of soldiers' children and relatives (*Staatsverträge* 481; see chapter 5, section 3). Eumenes presented his concessions as grants from a superior authority and he made sure that the soldiers swore a long oath which obliged them never to abandon him, but rather to die, and to serve him faithfully. All this may have been helpful for saving face, but hardly conceals the fact that the ruler had to succumb to his soldiers' demands or, potentially, lose his power.

The inscribed results of negotiations often gloss over the concessions a king had to make. A dossier of letters of Eumenes II concerning the status of Tyriaion after the peace of Apameia presents a nice example of the developed skill of saving face when a king interacted with demanding subjects who could prove useful or dangerous in a war (*SEG* XLVII 1745; Bagnall and Derow 2004: no. 43). Tyriaion was a settlement in Phrygia, its population consisting of both natives (*enchorioi*) and settlers – probably military settlers or soldiers serving in a garrison. The settlement did not have polis status or any recognized form of self-administration. The area passed under Eumenes' control after the defeat of Antiochos III and the peace of Apameia (ca. 187 BC), and an embassy of three men with names untypical for this region (Antigenes, Heliades, and a man with the characteristic Galatian name Brennos), who can plausibly be identified as (active or retired) soldiers, appeared before the king, expressed sentiments of joy for what their (new) king had accomplished, informed him that the inhabitants of Tyriaion had offered sacrifices to the gods for these tidings, and requested that their settlement be given its own laws, a council, and a gymnasium. In essence they were requesting the status of a self-governed polis. Their arguments are summarized in Eumenes' answer: "because of the goodwill which you show with regard to our affairs . . . ; they explained the zeal, with which you honestly support everything that pertains to our advantage; . . . they said that the people will always show the appropriate gratitude, never abandoning what is advantageous or necessary to me" (lines 4–17). Hardly any other text documents so clearly the principle of reciprocity and the theatricality that governed the negotiations between a king and his subjects. What this part of the document does not state is that the Tyriatai had already been given these privileges by another authority, presumably Antiochos III, the previous lord of the area, in a desperate effort to safeguard the support of this community in his war. Innumerable rejected requests are unknown to us, because they were never written on stone. In this case, Eumenes accepted the request of Tyriaion, but very unwillingly. As a matter of fact, his indignation can be seen in the use of the first person singular (*ego*) in his response:

> I reckoned that the grant of what you request is a matter of great importance to me and is also relevant for many and much more significant issues; this grant might only now become valid, if it is given by me, for I hold lawful possession [*ektemenou kyrios*, sc. of this land], since I received [it] from the Romans, who had won both in war and through treaties, and unlike the grant which was written by those who were not the lawful owners (*hypo ton me kyrieuonton*).
>
> (lines 17–23)

After putting this straight, the king (now in the first person plural) "nevertheless" (*homos*) accepted the request, "because of the goodwill which you have towards us and which you demonstrated in the present critical time [*kairos*]" (lines 24–6). The principle of *do ut des* is once again stressed at the end of the letter: "since you have been granted by me such a great privilege, you should make efforts to truly demonstrate through your deeds your goodwill at all times [or, critical situations, *kairois*]" (lines 36–8). The words "truly" (*alethos*) and "through deeds" (*dia ton ergon*) were not pure rhetoric. Eumenes had recognized that the Tyriatai had turned their back on a benefactor once before, the unnamed "unlawful owner" who had granted them privileges, probably when his defeat became likely. It must have been frustrating for the less shortsighted among the Hellenistic kings to recognize how fragile the construction was on which their power rested: an unstable mixture of legality and power, benefactions and expectations, threat and trust.

4.3. The King and the City

The Stoa of Attalos in the Athenian Agora is one of the buildings that impresses modern tourists the most, especially those who do not know that they actually see only the modern reconstruction of a sumptuous two-story *porticus* donated by King Attalos II of Pergamon (ca. 159–146 BC). It is one of more than 200 donations hitherto known to have been made by Hellenistic kings to Greek cities (Ameling et al. 1995). These donations ranged from vases, jewelry, and cult utensils, to money, land, corn, olive oil for gymnasia, statues, trophies, and representative buildings. A large part of the evidence concerns royal contributions to the defense of cities: donations of weapons, timber, funds for the construction or repair of city walls. Demetrios the Besieger gave 1,200 pieces of armor to the Athenians after the great victory near Salamis in Cyprus in 306 BC (Plut., *Demetr.* 17.1). Ptolemy V donated armor for 6,000 peltasts to the Achaian League (Polyb. 22.9.1–4; 24.6.3; ca. 182 BC), and Hieron II and Gelon of Syracuse gave the Rhodians 50 catapults (Polyb. 5.88.7; 227/6 BC). Parts or the entire city walls of Megalopolis (Livy 41.20.6), Melitaia (*ISE* 94; *IG* IX.2 208), Rhodes (Polyb. 5.88.5), Chios (Maier 1959: no. 51), Gortyn (Strabo 10.4.11 C 478), and Alexandreia Troas (Strabo 13.1.26 C 593), plus fortresses such as Elaos in Kalydonia (Polyb. 4.65.6), were built with the financial support of kings.

Royal donations also included warships (e.g., Polyb. 5.89.8, 24.6.1; 22.7.4; Diod. 29.17), or timber for their construction (Polyb. 25.4.10; Diod. 20.46.4; cf. *Syll.*[3] 645), horses for the cavalry which patrolled the frontiers (*OGIS* 748), and mercenary soldiers (Diod. 20.88.9, 98.1). These donations were made for particular wars or as a sign of goodwill, both to cities within the realm of a king and to independent allies.

A new inscription from Kyme (Manganaro 2000) is of particular interest, because it presents the perspective of the recipient of such a benefaction. Around 270 BC the Kymeans sent envoys to Philetairos, the ruler of Pergamon, requesting 600 shields. Philetairos' offer surpassed all their expectations, for he donated 1,000 shields. Kyme's response was equally magnanimous: the Kymeans could not bestow upon Philetairos the greatest honor a Hellenistic city could give (i.e., a divine cult), because Philetairos had already received divine honors in their city. Instead, they decreed new honors which aimed at perpetuating the memory of his benefaction. His statue was erected in the sacred house of the Philetaireion (the precinct dedicated to Philetairos); the crowning of the benefactor with a golden crown was to be announced at the most important public festivals, and Philetairos' name was inscribed on the shields which were carried in processions – thus continually reminding the Kymeans how much they owed the ruler of Pergamon. Both the offer and its appraisal are part of the ideology of *do ut des* that characterizes the "interactive kingship" of the Hellenistic world.

The occasional refusal of a donation is even more revealing than its acceptance. When Eumenes II offered to provide to the Achaian League the funds to pay the council on the occasion of federal meetings (185 BC), the Achaians rejected the offer when a member of the assembly reminded them how the Aiginetans had suffered because of Eumenes' actions (Polyb. 22.7.3; Ameling et al. 1995: no. 68). The refusal freed the Achaians from obligation, exactly as the acceptance of gifts was connected with a commitment to goodwill in the future.

Many cities faced acute financial problems due to war (see chapter 7). Time and again envoys lamented in front of kings the state of their cities after a long conflict and appealed to their generosity. Sometimes they were successful. The representatives of an anonymous city in Asia Minor presented their sufferings to Antiochos III (*Sardis* VII.1 2; *SEG* XXXVII 1003, ca. 197 BC?): their city had been burned down during a war, and most of the citizens had lost their property. By cancelling the tribute that this city had to pay for a certain period of time, the king demonstrated consideration and kindness, without losing his claim on tribute in the future. The publication of documents relating to this offer demonstrated the gratitude of the city, but also the expectations of the ruler.

Such expectations are often clearly formulated in letters (see section 4.2). The admonishing and "educational" purpose of royal letters can be observed, for example, in a letter from Attalos II (not yet a king) to the Pisidian city of Amlada. Its inhabitants, part Greek, part native, had taken advantage of the Pergamene involvement during the Third Macedonian War and of a Galatian invasion in 168 BC, and had overthrown the Pergamene garrison. When their revolt was subdued, they had to provide hostages and pay substantial sums for reparations. A few years later (160 BC?) Amlada was in a desparate financial situation. When the city appealed to the king's benevolence, Attalos, acting on behalf of his brother Eumenes II, explained why he accepted their request, released the hostages and reduced the tribute (*RC* 54): "because I saw that you have repented of your former offenses and that you zealously carry out our orders." Through the publication of this letter on stone, the principle of *do ut des* became an example for future generations.

Finally, the beneficent nature of Hellenistic kingship could be propagated through the dispatch of troops (*phylake*) to protect cities from enemies in wartime, from pirate attacks or from barbarian invasions (Chaniotis 2002: 107–8; Ma 2002: 116–17). The detachment sent by Attalos I to Lilaia in Phokis during the First Macedonian War (208 BC) was so warmly welcomed that some of its members were later awarded citizenship (Launey 1987: 654–5). In addition, the establishment of a permanent garrison (*phroura*) was sometimes justified as an act of benefaction which aimed at protecting the place in question. When king Philip V, notorious for his cunning, was asked by the Aitolian statesman Alexandros why he kept a garrison at Lysimacheia in Thrace (198 BC), thus undermining the city's freedom, he pointed out the distinction between *phrourein* (garrison) and *phylattein* (protect): his troops were present not as a garrison (*ou tous phrourountas*), but as protectors of the city (*alla tous paraphylattontas*) against the Thracians (Polyb. 18.4.6). A fragment of a contemporary treaty between Philip and Lysimacheia (ca. 202–197 BC) refers to the restoration of the forts (*Staatsverträge* 549 A 11; cf. *SEG* XXXI 628; XXXVIII 603). Similarly, the Ptolemaic garrison at Itanos on Crete, possibly established at the initiative of the Itanians but certainly very advantageous for the control of the sea routes in the southern Aegean, was officially represented as "helping and protecting the Itanians" (*I.Cret.* III iv 9, line 40: *charin boetheias kai phylakes*; line 97: *eis prostasian kai phylaken*). Garrisons on islands and in coastal sites are known to have defended local populations from marauding pirates (see chapter 6, section 2). For example, the commander of the Macedonian garrison in Piraeus was honored by the Salaminians for defending them from pirates (*IG* II^2 1225, ca. 250 BC); the Ptolemaic troops in Thrace protected, upon request, the mainland possessions of Samothrake (Bagnall 1976: 160, 221); a Ptolemaic commander of the garrison in Thera saved more than 400 people from an attack by pirates (*IG* XII.3 1291, ca. 250 BC); and another Ptolemaic naval commander was honored by the Athenians in ca. 286 BC for escorting grain ships coming to Athens (*IG* II^2 650, lines 15–16; de Souza 1999: 53).

By rendering such services, a Hellenistic monarch could justify his claim to the title of *Soter* ("Savior"). Of course in many cases the king had to save a city from its protectors, especially from soldiers camping in disorder. The rebuke given by an anonymous king to his commander for his behavior and that of his troops in Soloi shows the dimensions of the problem (*RC* 30, late third century). The population complained that "not only the outer but the inner city as well was occupied by the soldiers camping in disorder, although the inner city had never been subject to billeting, not even in the time of king Alexander, and the burden was due particularly to the supernumeraries, for it was they who ocupied the greater part of the houses." The king made sure that he shifted all the responsibility to his commander: "now I think that when you were with me I gave you an order on this matter; even if I did not, it was your duty to take all care . . ."; the rest of the text is unfortunately not preserved. However, this royal letter was certainly inscribed at the initiative of Soloi, as a protective measure against similar encroachments in the future, and at the same time glorifyng the protective king.

4.4. The Wolf as a Sheep: Royal Peace-makers

Eumenes II paraphrases in a letter to the Ionian League a decree voted to his honor by the Ionians (167/6 BC): "I had from the start chosen the finest actions and had shown myself a common benefactor of the Greeks; consequently I had undertaken many great struggles against the barbarians, exercising all zeal and forethought that the inhabitants of the Greek cities might always dwell in peace and the outmost prosperity" (*RC* 52; Bagnall and Derow 2004: no. 47).

Most of the sufferings that Hellenistic populations had to endure in Greece, Asia Minor, and Syria were the result of the campaigns of kings. It is, nevertheless, questionable whether anyone perceived this praise of Eumenes, the main cause of the Third Macedonian War, as irony, although a modern observer cannot help but think of the Nobel Peace Prizes given to statesmen who have invested most of their energy in provoking military conflicts.

A Hellenistic Greek might best define "peace" as the short break between wars. Hence, a period of peace usually began with the victory of one king over another – or over a barbarian (see chapter 9, section 3). In this sense, the royal ideology of victory is entirely compatible with the royal ideology of peace. That military power is a warrant of prosperity, security, and peace is an idea expressed, for example, by the court poet Theokritos in Alexandria, in his poem in praise of Ptolemy II, the "skilled spearman" (17.98–101, 103; Austin 1981: no. 217): "No enemy by land has crossed the teeming Nile to raise the cry of battle in villages that do not belong to him, nor has he leaped in arms upon the shore from a swift ship with hostile intent to seize the herds of Egypt." On the other hand, a king keen on peace for its own sake was regarded as idle (Polyb. 5.34.1–10; Beston 2000: 318).

Many Hellenistic kings contributed to peace simply by eliminating an opponent and ending a war (see *I.Ilion* 32; *I.Iasos* 4). Others contributed to peace, at the local level, by suppressing local conflicts. As soon as royal power declined, the autonomy of cities revived and with it the autonomy to fight wars (see chapter 3, section 1). The unpacified landscape encountered by Cnaeus Manlius Vulso during his campaign against the Galatians in 189 BC (Ma 2000c: 338–9), with the Alabandians fighting against a renegade fort, the Termessians occupying the city of Isinda and besieging the Isindians in their citadel, and Aspendos and other Pamphylian towns being involved in wars, was probably the result of the defeat of Antiochos III and the absence of royal control in the region. We saw a similar phenomenon in the former Yugoslavia and in the former Soviet Union in the 1990s. Strong monarchical power may have been unpopular among communities with strong feelings of freedom, precisely because it curtailed their freedom to fight against each other.

Royal ideology, in particular the self-representation of kings as protectors of cities, obliged the Hellenistic kings to play an active part in the establishment of peace. Based on prestige and power, kings could arbitrate in local conflicts between cities, which were a major cause of wars (Ager 1996: 20–2). One of the best documented territorial conflicts of the Hellenistic period is that between Priene and Samos, which lasted for centuries. The verdict given in 283/2 BC by Lysimachos (Ager 1996: no. 26), after scrutiny of the evidence (including the study of historiographical works), seems to have been objective, but did not settle the matter. The conflict flared up again and again in the following centuries, keeping two other kings (Antigonos Doson and Antiochos III?) and the city of Rhodes busy with the issue of arbitration.

Not all kings could be as neutral as Lysimachos. The Cretan city of Gortyn suggested, in at least two of its wars against Knossos, the arbitration of a Ptolemaic king (Chaniotis 1996a: nos. 40 and 43; cf. Ager 1996: no. 128; Magnetto 1997: no. 43) – not because of the objectivity of the Ptolemies, but because of their alliance with Gortyn.

As arbitrators and peace-makers, the Hellenistic kings protected their interests, earning at the same time the gratitude of cities, especially those that profited from their verdict (see Ager 1996: no. 24).

4.5. War and Mortal Divinity

In the Hellenistic period, military success did not only compensate for the lack of dynastic legitimacy (see section 4.1) – it could also make a mortal "godlike" (*isotheos*). This idea is expressed very eloquently in a hymn sung by the Athenians for Demetrios the Besieger around 291 BC:

> How the greatest and dearest of the gods have arrived to the city! For the hour has brought together Demeter and Demetrios; she comes to celebrate the solemn mysteries of the Kore, while he is here full of joy, as befits the god, fair and laughing. His appearance is majestic, his friends all around him and he in their midst, as though they were stars and he the sun. Hail son of the most powerful god Poseidon and Aphrodite! For the other gods are either far away, or they do not have ears, or they do not exist, or do not take any notice of us, but you we can see present here, not made of wood or stone, but real. So we pray to you: first make peace, dearest; for you have the power. And then, the sphinx that rules not only over Thebes but over the whole of Greece, the Aitolian sphinx sitting on a rock like the ancient one, who seizes and carries away all our people, and I cannot fight against her (for it is an Aitolian custom to seize the property of neighbors and now even what is far afield), most of all punish [or stop] her yourself; if not, find an Oedipus who will either hurl down that sphinx from the rocks or reduce her to ashes.
>
> (Douris, *FgrHist* 76 F 13; Athen. VI 253 D-F; cf. Austin 1981: no. 35)

Power and protection made Demetrios' rule acceptable and even gave the ruler divine properties.

Long before the beginning of the Hellenistic period, the Greeks had been bestowing divine honors upon extraordinary individuals after their death, but the first mortal known to have received godlike honors during his own lifitime was the Spartan general Lysandros (Douris, *FgrHist* 76 F 71, 26). His achievement was his military victory over the Athenians and the return of the Samian oligarchs. In the Hellenistic cities, the cult of kings and members of dynasties was usually introduced to honor past achievements and benefactions, but also to express the expectation of similar benefactions in the future. A military background – i.e., a victory, the repulse of danger, or the liberation of a city from foreign troops of occupation – is evident in many cases (Habicht 1970). The cult of Antiochos III in Teos (ca. 204 BC), for example, was the response of its grateful citizens for the consideration the king had shown when he observed how much the continual wars had weakened the city (*SEG* XLI 1003, lines 12–15). In Pergamon, the cult of Attalos III in the temple of Asklepios was introduced after a victorious campaign (*I.Pergamon* 246; *SEG* XXXIV 1251; Virgilio 1993: 23–7): a statue was dedicated, representing the victorious king standing on war booty in the temple of Asklepios Soter, "so that he may be sharing the temple with the god" (*synnaos toi theoi*). Another statue representing the king on a horse was to be erected next to the altar of Zeus Soter, and on this altar the eponymous magistrate, the king's priest, and the official responsible for competitions were to burn, every day, incense "for the king." An annual procession and sacrifice celebrated the anniversary of the king's return to Pergamon, reserving for this victory a place in the city's cultural memory (see chapter 11).

The protective and charismatic nature of monarchy is also expressed by the epithets attributed to kings (see section 4.1). When Antigonos the One-Eyed and Demetrios the Besieger expelled Kassandros' garrison from Athens (Plut., *Demetr.* 8–9; Diod. 20.45.2–5; Polyainos, *Strategemata* 4.7.6; Habicht 1970: 44–8), they were regarded as saviors (*Soteres*) and liberators of the city. A decree introduced the office of the "priest of the Saviors," an altar was erected, the names of the benefactors were given to two new tribes (Antigonis and Demetrias), and an annual festival, with procession, sacrifice, and *agon*, was founded.

The notion of victory is even more clear in Herakles' epithet *Kallinikos* ("the winner of fair victories"), which was also used for Seleukos II and Mithridates I. What placed the kings on the same level with the gods is the security they offered, and the past or potential recipients of this protection acknowledged this by establishing a cult.

Royal processions are an effective means of promoting the charisma of a ruler (Stewart 1993: 254–5). The best documented royal procession is that organized by Ptolemy II in honor of his father – the founder of the dynasty

– in Alexandria (275/4 BC?). It is described in great detail by Kallixenos of Rhodes (*apud* Athen. V 196 a–203 b). Highlighting the royal family's affinity to the gods, this procession demonstrated the king's political and military supremacy as it progressed through the streets of Alexandria. The population witnessed a lavishly-staged spectacle, and this celebration was a very complex propagandistic enterprise conveying more than one message: legitimacy of rule, divine protection, affluence, and power. It would be misleading to stress too much the military aspects, since the sacred elements (a focus on Dionysos, Zeus, and other gods) prevailed. Kallixenos' description also makes it clear that the procession propagated legitimacy of rule through subtle, multiple allusions – for example, to the king's parents (197 d), to the association of the Ptolemies with Alexander the Great (202 a–f), to the divine protection of Dionysos (197 a–202 a), to the freedom of the Greeks, and to military strength. An essential and extremely impressive part of the celebrations was the military parade of 57,600 infantry and 23,200 cavalry, accompanied by the presentation of military equipment (202 f–203 a). Besides this evidently warlike element, military aspects can be recognized in a number of details. For example, in the procession of Dionysos, an army of satyrs marched in silver, gold, and bronze panoplies; Silenoi, boys and girls, represented Dionysos' triumphal return from India (200 d–f), accompanied by women prisoners (201 a); women represented the cities liberated by Alexander in his war against the Persians (201 e); Alexander's golden statue, carried on a chariot, was flanked by statues of Athena and Nike (Victory), and further statues of victory were carried in the Dionysiac section (202 a). The procession of Alexander also included vast quantities of gold and silver weapons (breastplates, shields, and panoplies; 202 d–f). A plausible date for this procession is the winter of 275/4 BC; if we accept this date, then it was not just a celebration of a triumph, but also a response to the dangers that had just been overcome – an invasion by Magas of Kyrene, a revolt of mercenaries in Egypt – and an acknowledgment of the challenges that still lay ahead: the First Syrian War that started in 274 and the question of succession (Stewart 1993: 255–6).

A common theme of this chapter has been the interaction between the king and other people or groups. War, or the threat of war, are central to this interaction. In all its aspects one can recognize the principle of reciprocity: the authority of the king was primarily based on whether he could fulfill the expectations of others – cities, leagues, friends, officers, soldiers – and not on a legally defined position. Conversely, the king offered privileges, material gains, protection, and peace to those who supported his rule. Reciprocity is clear also in the assimilation of kings with gods. The principle of *do ut des* underlies the relationship between mortals and gods (Grotanelli 1991) and the same mentality is revealed by the relevant correspondence between cities and kings. A decree of the League of Islanders explains: "the Islanders were the first to have honored Ptolemy Soter with godlike honors because of his services to individuals" (*IG* XII.7 506 = Austin 1981: no. 218). Similarly, kings and queens responded to these honors by promising to consider the interests of the cities concerned. Eumenes II writes, for example, to the Ionian League: "the honors I accept kindly and having never failed, as far as it lay in my power, to confer always something of glory and honor jointly upon you all and individually upon your cities, I shall now try not to diverge from such a precedent" (*RC* 52). In the same letter, Eumenes explains what his services had been: "I had undertaken many great struggles against the barbarians, exercising all zeal and forethought that the inhabitants of the Greek cities might always dwell in peace and the utmost prosperity." Could any (other) god offer more?

Further Reading

4.1. War and the acceptance of monarchical rule. *Hellenistic kings*: Bikerman 1938: 11–30 (still an invaluable and brilliantly short characterization of the personal and charismatic nature of Hellenistic kingship); Leveque 1968: 276–81; Gehrke 1982; Walbank 1984: 62–100; Austin 1986; Sherwin-White and Kuhrt 1993: 114–40; Billows 1995: 56–80; Bilde et al. 1996; Roy 1998; Bringmann 2000: 108–25; Shipley 2000: 59–86; Bosworth 2002: 246–66; Ma 2003; Virgilio 2003. *The Wars of the Successors*: Will 1984; Shipley 2000: 40–52; Bosworth 2002. *The year of the kings*: Diod. 20.47; Plut., *Demetr.* 17–18; App., *Syr.* 54; see Ritter 1965: 79–91; Müller 1972: 56–9; Briant 1973: 303–10; Errington 1978: 124–5; Gruen 1985; Wheatley 2001: 151–6; Braund 2003: 29. *Imitatio Alexandri*: Stewart 1993: 229–340. *The anabasis of Antiochos III*: Will 1962; Schmitt 1964; Sherwin-White and Kuhrt 1993: 197–201; Ma 2000a: 63–5. *Royal nicknames. Seleukids*: Seleukos I Nikator, Antiochos I Soter, Seleukos II Kallinikos, Seleukos III Soter Keraunos, Antiochos III Megas, Antiochos IV Epiphanes, Demetrios I Soter, Demetrios II Nikator, Antiochos VI Epiphanes, Seleukos VI Epiphanes Nikator, Antiochos XI Epiphanes, Philippos I Epiphanes, Demetrios III Soter. *Ptolemies*: Ptolemy I Soter (see Hazzard 2000), Ptolemy IV Soter and Nikephoros (*OGIS* 89), Ptolemy V Epiphanes, Ptolemy IX Soter; see also Eumenes Soter (*I.Tralleis* 23); on Soter see also Jung 2001. *Death of kings in battle*: Landucci Gattinoni 1990 (Antigonos the One-Eyed and Lysimachos). *Wounded kings. Alexander the Great*: Chandezon 2000: 184–208; *Antiochos I*: OGIS 220; Bagnall and Derow 2004: no. 79; *Antiochos III* (Polyb. 10.49.14; Plut., *Cato major* 14.1); see Sherwin-White and Kuhrt 1993: 129. *The king as military leader*: Beston 2000; Austin 2001: 92–3; Pimouguet-Pedarros 2003. *Assimilation of kings with Herakles*: Huttner 1997; see also Queyrel 2003: 16–18 (Attalids). *Royal portraits and iconography*: Pollitt 1986: 19–46; Smith 1988; Ashton 2001 (Ptolemies); Fleischer 1991 (Seleukids); Queyrel 2003 (Attalids; esp. 41–8 on statues of kings with cuirasses; 200–34 on the "Hellenistic ruler" in the Museo dei Terme).

4.2. The King and his Army. *Acclamation of the king by the army*: Granier 1931: 52–4, 58–103, 130–2 (but see the criticism and modifications esp. by Ritter, Errington, Lévy, and Hatzopoulos); Bikerman 1938: 8–11; Ritter 1965: 79–94, 108–13, 121–4, see also 129–32, 136, 139–40, 151–3, 160; Müller 1972: 35–9; Briant 1973: 235–350, esp. 303–22; Errington 1978: 115–31; Lévy 1978: 218–22;

Gehrke 2003: 159–62, 170–1; Hatzopoulos 1996: 276–9; Bosworth 2002: 29–63. *Examples*: Demetrios the Besieger: Plut., *Demetr.* 37.2–3; see also Just. 16.1.9, 18; Errington 1978: 126–8; Pyrrhos: Plut., *Pyrrhos* 11.6; see also Just. 16.2.3; Achaios: Polyb. 4.48.10; Ptolemy VI Philometor: Jos., *Ant. Iud.* 13.113; Tryphon: Jos., *Ant. Iud.* 13. 219–20; *Maccab.* 12.39 + 13.32; Bikerman 1938: 10; Ritter 1965: 140; Demetrios I Soter: Ritter 1965: 136; Antigonos Doson: Briant 1973: 314–5. *The presentation of Ptolemy V to the army (204 BC)*: Granier 1931: 140–2; Ritter 1965: 151–3; Walbank 1957: 488–9; Chaniotis 1997: 229–30; Mittag 2000. *The "friends" of Hellenistic kings*: Sherwin-White and Kuhrt 1993: 133; Savalli-Lestrade 1996 (Attalids); Le Bohec 1985 (Antigonids); Mooren 1975, 1977 (Ptolemies); Savalli-Lestrade 1998 (Seleukids, Attalids); Virgilio 2003: 131–91. *Dedications of soldiers for kings*: e.g., *IG* XII.3 464, 1389; *SEG* XXXI 1521, 1359, 1574; *SEG* XXXIII 942; *SEG* XXXVIII 1526; *OGIS* 17–18, 20 (= *SEG* XXXI 1348), 86; *Syll.*[3] 595 B (= Bagnall and Derow 2004: no. 38); Bernand 1987: nos. 70 and 86; Dietze 2000 (Ptolemaic Egypt). *The mutiny of Eumenes' troops*: Schalles 1985: 32; Allen 1983: 23–5; Virgilio 1988: 111–51. *The negotiations between Eumenes II and Tyriaion*: Jonnes and Ricl 1997; *BE* 1999: no. 509 (Ph. Gauthier); Schuler 1999; Ma 2000b: 79; Chaniotis 2002: 105; Virgilio 2003: 162–3.

4.3. The King and the City. *Contacts and negotiations between kings and cities*: Bertrand 1990; Kralli 2000; Kotsidu 2000. *Royal benefactions, in general*: Gauthier 1985: 39–53; Bringmann 1993, 2000. *Royal donations for the defense of cities*: Ameling et al. 1995: nos. 11, 52, 54, 66–7, 82, 103, 202–3, 207, 210, 215, 231, 238–9, 245. Examples: Demetrios and Athens: Plut., *Demetr.* 17.1; Philetairos and Kyme: Manganaro 2000 [with *BE* 2001: no. 373 (Ph. Gauthier) and *EBGR* 2000: no. 126 (A. Chaniotis)]; Ptolemy V and the Achaian League: Polyb. 22.9.1–4; 24.6.3; Hieron II, Gelon and Rhodes: Polyb. 5.88.7. Fortifications of Megalopolis: Livy 41.20.6; Melitaia: *ISE* 94; *IG* IX.2 208; Rhodes: Polyb. 5.88.5; Chios: Maier 1959: no. 51; Gortyn: Strabo 10.4.11 C 478; Alexandreia Troas: Strabo 13.1.26 C 593; Elaos: Polyb. 4.65.6. Warships: Polyb. 5.89.8, 24.6.1; 22.7.4; Diod. 29.17; timber: Polyb. 25.4.10; Diod. 20.46.4; cf. *Syll.*[3] 645; mercenary soldiers: Diod. 20.88.9, 98.1. *Cancellation of taxes for a city that was destroyed during a war*: Sardis VII.1 2; *SEG* XXXVII 1003; Gauthier 1989: 171–8; cf. *SEG* XLI 1003 (Teos). *SEG* XXIX 1516 (Termessos) may have a similar background. *Protection offered by the king (phylake, phroura)*: Amyzon 19; cf. *IG* XII.3 328; *OGIS* 9 (*I.Ephesos* 1452); Bikerman 1938: 53; Robert and Robert 1954: 301 n. 3; Launey 1987: 644–5; Bagnall 1976: 128, 160, 132–3, 221; Chaniotis 2002: 107–8; Ma 2002: 116–17. *The Ptolemaic garrison in Itanos*: Kreuter 1992: 18–34; Viviers 1999: 222–4.

4.4. Royal Peace-makers. *Arbitrations of kings*: Ager 1996: nos 11 (Antigonos the One-Eyed, concerning the Lokrian maidens), 13 (Antigonos the One-Eyed, between Teos and Lebedos), 24 (Lysimachos, concerning a sacred precinct in Samothrake), 25 (Lysimachos, between Magnesia and Priene), 26 (Lysimachos, between Priene and Samos; see Magnetto 1997: no. 20; *RC* 7; Bagnall and Derow 2004: no. 12), 50 (Antigonos Doson, between Sparta and Messene), 54 (officials of Philip V, between Gonnoi and Herakleion), 128 (Ptolemy VI?, between Knossos and Gortyn), 138 (officials of Ptolemy VI, between Arsinoe and Troizen); see Magnetto 1997: nos 10, 20, 25, 31, 43 (Antigonos Doson?, between Priene and Samos), 44, 48, 49, 57, 58 (Antiochos III, in a Cretan War), 75 (Antiochos III?, between Samos and Priene).

4.5. War and Mortal Divinity. *Hellenistic ruler cult*: Habicht 1970; Price 1984: 23–53; Walbank 1984: 87–99, 1987; Chaniotis 2003b; Virgilio 2003: 87–130. Antiochos III and Teos: Herrmann 1965; Ma 2000a: 71–2, 206–10, 210–23, 228–30, 260–5. *Royal processions*: Walbank 1996; Stewart 1993: 252–60. *The procession of Alexandria*: Kallixenos, *FgrHist* 627 F 2 (Athen. V 196 a–203 b); Rice 1983; Hazzard 2000: 60–79; Thompson 2000. *Reciprocity in ruler cult*: e.g., *IG* XII.5 1008; *I.Cret.* III.iv 4; *RC* 22; *SEG* XXXIX 1284 B.

5

WAR AS A PROFESSION: OFFICERS, TRAINERS, DOCTORS, ENGINEERS

5.1. The Professionalization of Hellenistic Warfare: Definitions and Modifications

The Hellenistic age was in many respects an age of professional specialists. We observe this in the performing arts, in politics, in the economy, and in warfare. Professional specialization presupposes that a person has been educated and trained in a specific and well-defined art, skill, or discipline; that he commands this discipline or skill so well that others rely on his knowledge and employ him; and that he makes his living through this employment. Ancient professionalism often presupposed the transmission of skills within the family, and specialization was occasionally reflected by "professional names" or nicknames. On the other hand, unlike in most modern societies, ancient professional specialization did not necessarily mean exclusiveness – i.e., an occupation with only one specific skill. For example, a mercenary soldier could be – and often hoped to become again – a farmer.

In Hellenistic warfare, and also in other areas of economy and culture, a clear indicator of specialization was the use of specific terminology. A wide range of specific military terms had a tradition going back to the fourth century BC, culminating in the Hellenistic period. The specific designations for different kinds of troops – beyond the generic designations for the cavalry, the phalanx of the hoplites, the light-armed, and the fleet – reflect the existence of specific weapons, special training, and special skills. Specialization was by no means limited to professional armies. We find it, for example, in the Boiotian citizen army (see chapter 3, section 1: *peltophoroi, thyreaphoroi, epilektoi, hippotai, pharetritai, sphendonitai*), and aboard any Rhodian ship there would be up to 46 people with specific duties (Gabrielsen 2001a: 73). In some cases, special skills were a matter of local tradition – for example, the Cretans were famous as archers, the Achaians as slingers, and the Thessalians as cavalry-men.

Besides these traditional forms of specialization, the development of new weapons, complex fortifications (see chapter 2, section 3), and artillery devices, along with sophisticated tactics in the fourth century BC, produced professional soldiers and officers who recruited and trained mercenary troops, and then offered them into the service of whoever was in need of them and willing to pay (Pritchett 1974: 59–116).

It is possible to distinguish two groups of mercenaries: those who temporarily agreed to serve a king or a city during a war, for an agreed period of time, or on the basis of a treaty, after which they had to look for their next employment, and those who served in the large royal armies, especially those of the Ptolemies and the Seleukids, more or less permanently.

The most important innovations in warfare had already occurred in the course of the fourth century and, therefore, antedate the Hellenistic period: the introduction of the oblique phalanx by Epameinondas of Thebes; the new role given to the specialized light-armed soldiers (peltasts, archers, slingers), especially by Iphikrates of Athens; the new weapons introduced to the Macedonian army by Philip II; the tactical innovations of Alexander the Great; and the tremendous developments in artillery, fortifications, and the organization of the siege of a city (*poliorketike*). These developments made Hellenistic warfare a highly professional matter.

In the main, the tendency towards specialization was enhanced in the Hellenistic period by the needs of kings, but to some extent by the requirements of cities and leagues. An area in which specialization was clearly combined with professionalism was the Hellenistic artillery (Marsden 1969, 1971; see also section 5.7). In addition to the specialized personnel that used catapults and other artillery devices (e.g., *katapaltaphetai* in *Staatsverträge* 429), we encounter specific designations for military engineers, such as *mechanopoioi* (e.g., Diod. 17.41.3; Polyainos, *Strategemata* 4.2.20), *organopoioi* (e.g., Diod. 17.43.7), and *mechanikoi* (Garlan 1974: 207; see also Will 1975: 309), which were introduced in order to distinguish these professionals from other types of engineer (*technitai, architektones*).

One should, as ever, avoid generalizations. Hellenistic war is not only the Battle of Raphia, in which 140,000 men fought, but also the surprise attack of the Knossians against Lyttos during the absence of the men (220 BC), and that of Kleomenes against Argos in 225/4 (Polyb. 2.52.2), or the incursion of cavalry-men from Tabai against Roman troops (189 BC); not only the highly sophisticated siege of Rhodes by Demetrios the Besieger and the two-year siege of Baktra by Antiochos III (Will 1982: 50–1), but also the sieges in Gortyn (220 BC) involving blockades aimed at starving the besieged into capitulation. The majority of the Hellenistic male population experienced warfare not in great tactical battles, but in the form of temporary raids, incursions into the territory of the enemy, surprise attacks against cities, and occasional street fights (see Will 1975: 298–301, 317). Therefore, professionalism did not diminish the importance of the citizen militias (see chapter 2).

5.2. The Social Context of Mercenary Service

Theokritos describes in his 14th idyll the sufferings of Aischinas, a lovesick young man, abandoned by his lover Kyniska for another man (lines 50–6, trans. A. E. F. Gow):

> If only I could fall out of love all would go as it should; but as it is, how can I? I'm like the mouse in the pitch-pot, as they say, Thyonikos, and what may be the cure for helpless love, I do not know. Except that Simos, who fell in love with that brazen girl, went abroad and came back heart-whole – a man of my age. I too will cross the sea. Your soldier is not the worst of men, not yet the first, maybe, but as good as another.

Aischinas' friend does not disagree with the suggested remedy for a broken heart, and gives instead practical advice: Ptolemy II of Egypt is the best paymaster for a free man. Theokritos may have been speaking from personal experience, since most of his poetry was written in Ptolemy's court.

Disappointment in affairs of the heart and fear of the revenge of cuckolded husbands have always caused men, young and old, to turn their back on home and devote themselves to martial occupations. However, the explosion of mercenary service in the Hellenistic period had a less erotic origin; it was more an issue of supply and demand. The demand had increased immediately after the conquests of Alexander the Great. The Successors mobilized large numbers of troops in their wars for the division of Alexander's empire (for numbers see Launey 1987: 8–11), and the kingdoms that emerged out of this process needed trained military manpower in order to man garrisons, avert barbarian invasions, control native populations, and fight against other kingdoms. In addition, cities with declining populations or those often exposed to attack required additional troops (Launey 1987: 7).

The supply of mercenaries was not a problem. The Peloponnesian War and the subsequent wars and civil wars of the fourth century had left thousands of men without land to cultivate, and often without a homeland. The problems of those who had lost their land during the process of concentration of landed property, which characterized the fourth century BC, were only to some extent solved through the foundation of new cities in the conquered areas. The problem of the exiles was not solved at all; on the contrary, the political conflicts and the continual wars created new masses of fugitives and exiles, who were more than willing to offer their services as mercenaries.

Of course, every mercenary might have a different story to tell. The Spartan King Leonidas II spent part of his adult life as a mercenary (Cartledge and Spawforth 1989: 44), and Charmadas of Anopolis on Crete joined the Ptolemaic army, probably because his city had been destroyed (*SEG* VIII 269). Generalizations should be avoided, and regional studies of the context of mercenary service tend to lead to different conclusions (Launey 1987: 104–615).

The complexity of this phenomenon and local peculiarities can be best recognized if we focus on a particular case, and the Cretan mercenaries offer without any doubt the best example (Ducrey 1985: 130–2; Petropoulou 1985: 15–31; Launey 1987: 248–86). In Crete, the origins of mercenary service are to be found in a conglomerate of factors that range from demographic developments and military traditions to a socio-economic crisis (Chaniotis 1999a: 182–6, 210–11). A central aspect of Cretan history before the Roman conquest was the division of the island between about 60 independent poleis. Citizenship depended on military training, on the rule over a dependent population of various legal positions, and on the participation of the citizens in common meals. This social organization promoted a subsistence economy based on farming and animal husbandry. The stability of such a system requires that the land can produce enough food for the support of the population; that the small, privileged group of citizen-warriors owns enough landed property to maintain its status; and that the dependent population cultivates the land and pays its tribute. These conditions can hardly be met for long periods of time: demographic developments, a bad harvest, short-term climate changes, the concentration of landed property in a few large estates, the destruction or the loss of cultivated land during wars, the escape of slaves, and the uprising of serfs are some of the factors which may – and did – disturb a very unstable equilibrium. When food and land shortages occurred, solutions were not sought in reforms, but in the conquest of a neighbor's territory and in migration. The archaic military education of Cretan youth and the traditional ideal of the citizen-warrior continued unchanged into the Hellenistic period, as did the old division of land into private lots, private land cultivated by serfs, and communal land cultivated by a dependent population. An important change was the concentration of landed property in a few large estates, leaving part of the citizen population without land. This, combined with the preoccupation of free men with military training and the rise in population (which can be inferred by the large numbers of Cretan mercenaries in foreign armies), the massive immigration to Asia Minor and Egypt, and the evidence for migration within the island, led to continual wars of conquest, raids, and mercenary service. The Cretan expansion wars, the efforts to colonize abandoned or uninhabited areas in the island, and the economic clauses of interstate agreements can best be interpreted as efforts to solve the social and economic problems generated by the fact that many citizens had lost their land. Although the strategic position of the island on the trade routes of the eastern Mediterranean increased transit trade in Hellenistic Crete, this did not substantially change the traditional social and economic order and did not set aside the traditional ideal of economic status based on land ownership; the instability and the orientation towards subsistence and not towards trade hindered the formation of a strong group of manufacturers. Citizens without land, along with young men who could not wait for their inheritance, saw in warfare a profitable profession. The fact that many of these mercenaries settled abroad, for example, in Kretopolis in Pisidia in the late fourth century (Cohen 1995: 345–6; Sekunda 1997), in Miletos in the late third century (see section 5.3), and in Egypt, where a community of Cretans (*Kreton politeuma*) is attested (Launey 1987: 1068–72), leaves little doubt about the fact that what forced them to leave their island was the desire for land ownership and the lack of prospects for this.

In the case of Crete, the sources allow us to see socio-economic factors that explain the large numbers of mercenaries, many of which migrated permanently to the areas of their service. In instances in which we may observe similar effects – large numbers of mercenaries in different armies and large numbers of military settlers – we may assume similar causes, but certainty is not possible. It is plausible that poverty or the expectation of wealth, in addition to military traditions, motivated the populations of other mountainous areas to seek employment as mercenaries – for example, the warlike Lykians, Pamphylians (especially soldiers from Aspendos), and Pisidians (Launey 1987: 461–76). In general, in areas in which neither colonization could be practiced nor was conquest unlimited, part of the population lived by means of war: on raids and/or on mercenary service. Aitolia was another region which provided large numbers of mercenaries, but was also notorious for raids. The Athenian hymn for Demetrios (see chapter 4, section 5) refers to the "Aitolian custom to seize the property of neighbors," and Polybios had spiteful remarks to make on this subject (4.3.1: the Aitolians "are accustomed to live on their neighbors and required many funds because of their inherent greed, enslaved by which they always lead a life of greed resembling wild beasts, regarding no one as a friend and everyone as their enemy"). In Aitolia, again, the ideology of violence and seizure, combined with a surplus of population (see Paus. 1.4.4.), made warfare a profitable occupation (Launey 1987: 176–201; cf. Scholten 2000). The conditions of service, which are discussed below, also suggest that the main motivation of mercenaries was not to heal a broken heart, but to make a living.

5.3.   The Conditions of Service

Cape Tainaron, south of Sparta, was traditionally one of the gates of Hades in Greek myth; in Hellenistic reality it was the most important gateway for mercenaries anxious to find employment in a foreign army. No less than 8,000 men, left unemployed in the aftermath of Alexander's conquests, were gathered there in 323 BC (Diod. 18.9.1; cf. Launey 1987: 105 n. 1) and were hired by the Athenians as part of their war for freedom. In most cases, mercenaries were not hired as individuals but joined a foreign army either on the basis of a treaty between their city and a potential employer or as groups under the leadership of an experienced officer or general. Several members of the Spartan royal families are known to have served in foreign armies as *condottieri* (e.g., Akrotatos and Kleonymos), but in most cases we know only the name, not the social background, of such men. The huge demand for mercenaries created one of those parasitic occupations which often occur under similar conditions: the *xenologos*, the recruiter of mercenaries (Launey 1987: 30–2; Couvenhes 2004: 88–9). These "soldier brokers" were given large amounts of money by kings, cities, or ambitious generals, visited the areas where they expected to find potential mercenaries (e.g., Tainaron, Crete, Lykia, Pisidia, Thrace), and recruited the necessary manpower. Pyrgopolynikes, the protagonist of Plautus' comedy *Miles gloriosus*, had his recruiting agency in Ephesos, an important harbor in Asia Minor (Bikerman 1938: 69). Defeat offered the opportunity to change employer, and in many cases the mercenaries of a defeated army were offered the opportunity to serve the victors (e.g., *IG* II^2 657; *Staatsverträge* 429; Diod. 18.45.4).

The best sources for the conditions of service of mercenaries are the surviving treaties between employers and the cities providing the necessary manpower. Of course, it is difficult to estimate if the conditions were worse for people who were employed individually and without the mediation of their city or a *condottiere*. A treaty between Rhodes and the Cretan city of Hierapytna (*Staatsverträge* 551; Austin 1981: no. 95), gives us an impression of the aspects covered by such agreements: numbers and status of the soldiers, weapons, transportation, deadlines, and wages:

> If the Rhodians demand an auxiliary force from the Hierapytnians, the Hierapytnians shall provide the force within 30 days of the request of the Rhodians, consisting of 200 men with their own weapons, unless the Rhodians need less; at least half of the men sent shall be Hierapytnians [i.e., citizens]. And if the Hierapytnians find themselves at war, they shall send as many men as they are able. To the men sent by the Hierapytnians the Rhodians shall provide transport for the journey from Crete to Rhodes. And if the Rhodians demand an auxiliary force within the first four years (after the signing of the treaty), from the day of the allies' arrival at Rhodes the Rhodians shall pay to every man a daily wage of nine Rhodian obols [= 1 drachma and 3 obols], and to every officer who commands at least 50 men a daily wage of two drachmas each.

The Hierapytnians were also obliged to assist the Rhodians whenever they wanted to recruit a mercenary army in Crete. The Hierapytnian "allies" were in fact mercenaries (see Launey 1987: 38). Only after the first four years were the Hierapytnians obliged to send auxiliary troops at their own expense, for the first 30 days of service; but not many Cretan treaties lasted that long.

Depending on the conditions agreed between mercenaries and employer, the soldiers received a rather good salary, which depended on rank and weapons, but at least in the third century was above the average pay of other professionals (Launey 1987: 763–4). In addition to this, a mercenary could expect a ration of grain and other food, and sometimes clothes, plus, after a victorious battle, a share of booty (Launey 1987: 725–80). There are several indications about the relative wealth of mercenaries, such as the ownership of slaves and the quality of their funerary documents (Launey 1987: 781–94), but in these cases our sources may be deceiving, since they may refer to a visible minority.

One of the best sources for the life of mercenaries is a treaty between the ruler of Karia Eupolemos and the besieged city of Theangela (ca. 310 BC; *Staatsverträge* 429 = Austin 1981: no. 33 = Couvenhes 2004: 107–9). After a siege, the city capitulated, and the treaty is concerned (among other things) with the foreign soldiers (*stratiotai*, mercenaries rather than troops of a foreign garrison). The treaty makes provisions for the soldiers under the command of three men (Philippos, Demagathos, and Aristodemos = *I.Iasos* 33), who were probably *condottieri*. The soldiers and the artillery-men (*katapaltaphetai*), who are mentioned separately, were to be given "the four months' salary [*opsonia*] that was due to them"; Aristodemos and those of his soldiers who decided to serve under Eupolemos were given, in addition to the salary, a gift (*doma*) corresponding to two months' salary – perhaps a reward for their willingness to be hired by Eupolemos (or for having forced the Theangeleis to capitulate). They were probably to man the garrison of the two citadels. Eupolemos' deserters were given amnesty. The mercenaries in Theangela could choose between departing and marching through the territory of Eupolemos with their property, paying no customs duty, or joining Eupolemos' army. The latter became military settlers and were given Pentachora ("the five villages"). The last stipulation again re-veals the vital need of many mercenaries to receive what they lacked in their homeland: land (see Couvenhes 2004: 90).

The area where mercenaries could acquire land often became their new home: *ubi bene, ibi patria*. The right to own land (*enktesis*) was restricted to citizens and privileged foreigners. The cities which enfranchised mercenaries proceded to this measure because they needed manpower; the award of citizenship was attractive for new citizens because it satisfied their desire for the ownership of land, which in all periods of Greek history was the most important basis for wealth and status. In the late third century (234/33 and 229/28 BC), Miletos enfranchised more than 1,000 Cretan mercenaries, some under the leadership of *condottieri* (*Milet* I.3 33 g: Philanor and So[---]).They were settled with their families (ca. 3,000–4,000 people) in the newly-acquired territory of Hybandis, which was contested by Magnesia on the Maeander (*Milet* I.3 33–38 = Herrmann 1997: 160–4). In Athens, foreign soldiers serving at Rhamnous were honored with the privileged status of the *isoteleis* (mid-third century). Citizenship was also given to groups of mercenaries serving in Lillaia (208 BC) and in Aspendos (ca. 300 BC), to mention only a few examples (Launey 1987: 653–6). Individual mercenaries acquired this privileged status (e.g., Kryton, an officer from Aptara on Crete in the service of Miletos, who was naturalized on the grounds of his successful service) (*Milet* I.3 39; ca. 200 BC). Not only with booty but also with citizenship and status in mind, mercenaries were willing to risk their lives and accept all the hardships of military service. They would often have to spent the winter in the countryside, in makeshift barracks (*stegna*), and in the worse cases in tents (Launey 1987: 693–5).

Hellenistic kingdoms had not only a great need for mercenaries, but also the best opportunity to provide them with land in the numerous new cities and military colonies. The original population of Alexandria, the greatest Hellenistic city, consisted of soldiers, and this holds true for the largest part of the population of the new Hellenistic colonies. Of course, most of them can be dated to the early Hellenistic period: Kretopolis was founded with Cretan mercenaries in the late fourth century in Pisidia, and soldiers were settled by Seleukos I at Thyatteira in Lydia around 281 BC, to mention only two of the innumerable early military settlements. This process of colonization did not stop until the second century BC. As late as 192, Antiochos III brought Greeks from Euboia, Crete and Aitolia to Antioch, and 2,000 Jewish families from Mesopotamia and Babylonia were settled by the same king in strongholds, especially in Asia Minor, and were given land. Attalos II founded Eukarpeia in Phrygia ("the fruitful city") with *klerouchs* in the mid-second century, and a newly-discovered Hellenistic settlement at Bucak (ancient Syneta?), a fort probably with the status of a polis on the border between Karia and Phrygia, was founded with settlers (probably mercenaries) from the coast of Asia Minor in the early second century.

Sometimes we can only indirectly infer the presence of military settlers. In Sagalassos, funerary monuments (*osteothekai*), and buildings in the agora, decorated with Macedonian shields in relief (third–first century), are connected with the settlement of Macedonian soldiers from the third century onwards (possibly under Antiochos III), which had a lasting impact on the Hellenization of this city. Macedonian shields decorate the coins of several cities in Asia Minor in which Macedonian settlers lived (e.g., Philadelphia, Stratonikeia, Apollonis, Blaundos, Hyrkanis, and Peltai).

The system of military settlement is best known in Egypt, where experienced soldiers and officers were given a lot (*kleros*) in exchange for military service, whenever needed. The soldiers owned their weapons and armor, which they could bequeath in their wills (e.g., *Select Papyri* I 83; 126 BC). Their families kept the original designation of ethnic origin or citizenship generations after the original settlement, even though they did not retain any contact with their city of origin – and even if that city had ceased to exist (Bickermann 1927; Launey 1987: 676–8). Philippos, a high officer in the Polemaic army, was still called "the Korinthian" in 70 BC, 76 years after the destruction of his ancestral city (*SB* 6236). The four daughters of

Ptolemaios of Kyrene, who lived in Pathyris (ca. 147–127 BC), adopted Egyptian names *next to* their Greek name (Apollonia, also called Semmonthis; Ammonia, also called Semminis; Herakleia, also called Senapathis; Herais, also called Tasris; *SB* 4638).

In the kindom of the Seleukids, mercenaries were usually settled in colonies of an urban character, which at some point could acquire the status of a polis (Launey 1987: 335–6; Cohen 1995). In the Seleukid military colonies, the lot could be inherited by the colonist's close relatives and was only returned to the king when its transmission to a person who could serve as a soldier was not possible. An analogous system of military settlers is not known with certainty from mainland Greece, but it is quite possible that the *paroikoi* mentioned in inscriptions of Rhamnous were soldiers in the service of King Antigonos Gonatas of Macedonia, who were given land there in exchange for military service at the king's initiative (Oetjen 2004). This has also been suggested for the enfranchised foreigners who were given land in Larisa (*IG* IX.2 517), Pharsalos (*IG* IX.2 234), and Phalanna (*IG* IX.2 1228) in Thessaly, and in Dyme in Achaia after the Social War (*IG* IX.2 517).

For mercenaries, who were only temporarily employed, land ownership was a less realistic perspective than death in a battle, captivity, invalidity, or unemployment. A sacred regulation of the sanctuary of Hera in Samos (ca. 245/4 BC) considers the possibility of unemployed mercenary soldiers (*apergoi*) illegally occupying themselves in the sacred precinct as traders (*IG* XII.6.1 169; Couvenhes 2004: 98). What they sold was probably booty gained during their service. War booty was an investment for "retirement," and this, of course, contributed to the brutality of Hellenistic warfare (see chapter 7).

Realistic mercenaries had to consider the possibility of death in combat. For this reason they needed to be sure that their employer would take care of their widows and orphans. Philon of Byzantion (C 47, ed. Garlan 1974: 312, 387) recommends such measures (without providing any details), in addition to a public burial, expecting that the care of widows and orphans would increase the dedication of mercenaries to their employer. The Athenian decree for Euphron of Sikyon – not a mercenary, but an ally in their war for freedom against the Macedonians (323–318 BC) – corresponds to this recommendation: not only Euphron was honored, but his orphans were put under the care of the generals and were given precedence of access to the council. The Athenians also sent an embassy to Sikyon, when a child of Euphron was in need (*IG* II² 448 = Austin 1981: no. 26; see figure 1.2).

The issue of orphans was part of the negotiations between Eumenes I and his merceneries, who served at Phileteraia and Attaleia, after a mutiny (ca. 263–241 BC; *OGIS* 266; *Staatsverträge* 481; Austin 1981: no. 196; Bagnall and Derow 2004: no. 23). Despite the fact that the interpretation of most of the clauses of the final agreement between ruler and mercenaries is the object of controversial discussions and different interpretations, the

86

importance of this document as a source of information for the social aspects of mercenary service justifies the presentation of a tentative translation of the relevant clauses here:

> (i) For grain the price of four drachmas a medimnus will be paid [by the soldiers?], for wine four drachmas a measure. (ii) Concerning the [campaigning] year: it will be reckoned as having ten months; and [Eumenes] will not insert an intercalary month. (iii) Concerning those who have fulfilled the agreed/valid/appointed (*kyrios*) number of years [or months?] of service and have become idle [*apergos*]; they shall receive the wages [*opsonion*] for the time for which they have already served. (iv) Concerning the property [or rights or money or affairs] of orphans [*orphanika*]; the next of kin shall receive it [or them?] or the person to whom he [the soldier?] has bequeathed it. (v) Concerning taxes: the freedom of taxation granted in the 44th year [269/8 BC?] shall be valid; if someone goes out of service or requests discharge, he shall be discharged and he shall pay no customs when he exports his belongings. (vi) Concerning the wages [*opsonion*] which he [Eumenes] agreed to pay for the four months: the agreed sum shall be paid and it will not be deducted from the wages. (vii) Concerning the soldiers decorated with wreaths of white poplar: they shall receive the grain [i.e., ration of grain] for the same period, for which they received the crown.

The clauses represent the demands of the mercenaries and, therefore, reflect their main concerns and problems that often arose. The first clause gave the soldiers the right to buy grain and wine at a fixed (low) price (rather than to sell their provisions at a fixed price, as an alternative interpretation suggests). The soldiers were given two months of leisure (with or without pay?) and made sure that Eumenes would not prolong the year by inserting an intercalary month; this issue had to be clarified in a world in which sophistic interpretations of agreements were not uncommon (see Wheeler 1984; Chaniotis 1996a: 77).

The next clause implies that some mercenaries who had already served for an agreed period of time and had been discharged (voluntarily or because of invalidity?) had not received their pay for their previous service. If we are dealing with soldiers who had voluntarily quit service, the Pergamene ruler may have refused to pay, in order to force them to stay in his army. Some scholars interpret this clause in an entirely different way, as evidence for a pension: "they shall receive the wages as in the time in which they used to work." But the formulation used in the text does not justify this view.

The clause concerning the orphans is far from clear. The word *orphanika* is attested in the meaning "property of orphans" (Arist., *Polit.* 1 1268 a 14), but it is conceivable that in the army of Eumenes it had a particular meaning (e.g., financial support for the orphans). The main issue of this clause is to determine the person who had the right of guardianship – and thus the right to administer the inheritance of the soldier until his orphans came of age, or who would receive the inheritance if the orphans died prematurely (*SEG* XXVII 806). The mercenaries wanted to make sure that this person would be the next relative or a person designated by the soldier in his will, and not, for example, an officer. It should be noted that in Ptolemaic Egypt measures were taken in order to protect the family members of soldiers during their absence in wars (see chapter 6, section 2).

Soldiers who wished to leave Pergamene territory were allowed to do so, without paying high export duties for their property. The next clause refers to an agreed wage for a period of four months. It is usually assumed that the mutiny lasted for four months and Eumenes agreed to give the mercenaries their wages for this period. There are two problems with this interpretation. First, the term *he tetramenos* (exactly as the term *dekamenos* = a period of ten months, in the same text) can only designate a standard period of four months. The second problem is that in the aforementioned agreement between Eupolemos and Theangela, an agreement between ruler and besieged soldiers, we find again a reference to "the four months' salary that was due to them." Rather than assuming that the conflict (mutiny/siege) coincidentally lasted in both cases for four months, it seems more plausible to assume that the wages of the mercenaries were agreed and payable for a period of four months. It should be noted that the commander of the garrison at Kyrbissos served for four months (*SEG* XXVI 1306). The mercenaries perhaps wanted to make sure that they received the agreed pay for the *coming* four months, and that this pay would not be set off against other sums owed to them by Eumenes.

The last clause concerns soldiers who were decorated for bravery and good service and received a higher ration of grain.

Mercenary soldiers did not have to deal only with the dangers of battle, but also with the risk of a bad employer, who might attempt to cheat them. We recall that Theokritos praised Ptolemy II as the best paymaster of mercenaries (see section 5.2); this presupposes that other employers had a bad reputation. Eumenes may have been one of them.

5.4. Garrisons and Foreign Troops in Hellenistic Cities

Many mercenaries came to Hellenistic cities uninvited, as garrison troops. For many cities, foreign garrisons were part of everyday life, usually an annoyance and a burden, an unpleasant instrument of subordination to a foreign power, a cause of disorder, and a significant factor in social, economic, and religious life. Garrisons were usually established by a king who wanted to impose control over a city. Macedonian garrisons were established in various forts in Athens after the defeat of Greek cities in the "Hellenic War" (322 BC) and, with the exception of a short period (307?–295 BC), remained there until 229 BC. Foreign troops garrisoned, for different periods, the Long Walls, the Mouseion Hill, Piraeus, Mounychia, Salamis, Panakton, Phyle, Eleusis,

Sounion, and Rhamnous. To give but a few examples from mainland Greece, the Aegean islands, and Asia Minor, Ptolemaic garrisons were placed in and around the major cities of Cyprus, in several cities in Asia Minor (e.g., Ephesos and Xanthos), in Cretan Itanos, in Thera, in Thrace, and probably on Lesbos (Bagnall 1976: 220–4). The Antigonid control of southern Greece relied on garrisons, especially in Athens, Akrokorinthos, Chalkis, and Eretria (Hatzopoulos 2001: 29–32). Sometimes garrisons were only temporarily dispatched in order to protect a strategic area during a war, and cities would occasionally hire mercenaries to garrison a citadel or a fortress.

However, garrisons were not the only foreign troops in the territory of a city. Soldiers having their barracks in the countryside (*hypaithroi*) are often mentioned in Hellenistic texts (Launey 1987: 693–4). The "Macedonians near Thyateira" or "in Thyateira" (*OGIS* 211; Launey 1987: 338, 685) were military settlers in the countryside and soldiers in the city. In the late second century, after the death of the last Attalid king (133 BC) the Pergamenes, now a sovereign polis, faced the dangers of Aristonikos' War. As a result, they awarded citizenship to the free population living in the city and its environs, and the recipients included several different military groups (*I.Pergamon* 249 = *OGIS* 338; Launey 1987: 664–9). First there were mercenaries and auxiliary troops serving in the city in 133 BC. Then there were the old Seleukid military settlers of the early third century ("the Macedonians"). There were also indigenous military settlers ("the Mysians"), and active soldiers in the citadel and the old town. Added to these groups were the military settlers in Masdye, and mobile troops who protected the countryside (*paraphylakitai*).

The mention of "foreign troops" or "garrison soldiers" in our literary sources is usually impersonal. Historians refer to a garrison as a whole and not to its individual members – and if so, only to the commander. Some insights on the interaction between the native population and military personnel (officers and garrison soldiers) are, nevertheless, given by the numerous honorary decrees for the commanders of garrisons (*phrourarchoi*), or for other foreign officers decreed by the communities in which the garrisons served (Launey 1987: 642–50). Despite their formulaic language, these inscriptions do indicate – rather vaguely – some kind of interaction, as for example in the honorific decree of Xanthos in Lykia for Pandaros, commander of the garrison sent by Ptolemy II (*SEG* XXXV 1183): "Pandaros, son of Nikias from Herakleia, was sent by king Ptolemy as commander of the garrison at Xanthos; he has shown good and meritorious behavior, worthy of the king, providing no reasons for complaint to the polis of the Xanthians and doing many and great services both to the entire community and to each one individually."

An anonymous commander, who served in the garrison at Philai, the sacred island of Isis in the Nile, is described with similar words (*SEG* XXVIII 1429, after 115 BC):

[---]aios, son of Ammonios, one of the "followers" [an elite troop], who has been commander of the garrison of this site for thirty-two years without causing any reason for complaint either to those who inhabit this place nor to the foreign visitors, a man who was praised when the generals were present and who was given a distinction [*episemasia*] during the visit of our lord, King and God Philometor Soter [Ptolemy IX], on the second year.

To say that a commander had not given reasons for complaints (*anenkletos*), a formulaic expression often attested in such decrees (e.g., *Amyzon* 4), suggests that garrison commanders often *did* behave in a way that provoked negative reactions. Of course it lies in the nature of the honorific decrees that we only hear of commanders who have been righteous, well disposed, and disciplined (e.g., *SEG* XXXV 926); but even these sources, with their trivial phraseology, reveal that some commanders were better than others. Otherwise, it would be difficult to understand why the Aiginetans repeatedly sent envoys to the Attalid kings, asking them to maintain Kleon of Pergamon as the commander of their island – obviously with some success, since he remained in this office for 16 years (*OGIS* 329).

Some historians would be inclined to see the phrase "services, both to the entire community and to each one individually" in the aforementioned decree of Xanthos as a stereotypical formula which does not really imply any kind of relations between the commander and individual citizens. However, the fact that the formulaic language of Hellenistic decrees displays many individual variants makes it probable that Pandaros did in fact interact with individual citizens. This is directly attested in the case of Hieron of Syracuse, commander of the Ptolemaic troops in Arsinoe (Koresia) on Keos. A decree of Karthaia in his honor (*IG* XII.5 1061) gives a very concrete narrative of his zealous intervention to save the property of a citizen (lines 8–11): "and now, when Epiteles was deprived of movables from his house on the field, he has shown every zeal and care; he has recovered them, returning to Epiteles whatever items he had received personally and giving the price for the rest, wishing to do the city a favor."

It is also known that Dikaiarchos, commander of the Macedonian garrison in Eretria, protected the shepherds of Rhamnous who had brought their flocks to Euboia in order to save them from the pirates (Roussel 1930; Petrakos 1999: no. 17).

Naturally, many honors were decreed for services offered by foreign officers and their troops when a city was attacked by an enemy (e.g., *IG* II^2 469) or by pirates (e.g., *IG* II^2 1225). Archestratos of Macedon, an officer of Demetrios the Besieger and governor of Klazomenai, was honored in Ephesos for protecting ships that transported corn to the city (*OGIS* 9 = *I.Ephesos* 1452). Neoptolemos, a Ptolemaic general, was honored in Tlos for saving the city from a barbarian attack of Pisidians, Agrians, and Galatians in the 270s (*SGO* IV 17/11/02; Vandorpe 2000: 497–8). A Ptolemaic commander from Crete saved the citizens of Thera from a raid by pirates (*IG* XII.3 1291), and Achaios, a member of the Seleukid family, and his officers were honored by the inhabitants of Neon Teichos and Kiddiou Kome with the establishment of their cult because of their services during a war against the Galatians (ca. 267).

By rendering such benefactions officers contributed to the popularity of the king whom they served (see chapter 4, section 3). Officers with high ranks could offer great services to a city, acting as intermediaries between the city and a king (e.g., *Syll.*[3] 333). Most of the numerous Samian decrees issued after the return of the Samians from exile in 322 BC, for people who had helped them during their exile and continued intervening for the well-being of Samos, were for officers in the service of Antigonos the One-Eyed (*IG* XII.6.1 17–41, especially 30–1). Some time later, Pelops and Aristolaos of Macedon, officers of another king, Ptolemy II, were honored in Samos as benefactors (IG XII.6.1 119–20).

More rare, but nonetheless attested, is the cooperation between the natives and a foreign garrison against the power that had established it (Launey 1987: 650; Chaniotis 2002). Such cooperation presupposes intensive inter-action between the foreign soldiers and the inhabitants of the garrisoned settlement. Strombichos, an officer in the service of Demetrios the Besieger in Athens, when the Athenians revolted against the Macedonian garrison in 289/8 BC, took the side of the Athenians (*IG* II[2] 666, lines 8–14): "when the people took up the weapons to fight for freedom and asked the [garri-son] soldiers to take the part of the polis, he accepted the call of the demos for freedom and he placed his arms in the service of the polis, in the belief that he should not oppose the polis' benefit, but that he should contribute to its rescue." If Strombichos had been just one of the many opportunists who served as mercenaries in the Hellenistic armies, and changed fronts to save his life, the gratitude of the Athenians would probably have been less eloquently expressed.

We have more information about officers, since due to their elevated status they were more likely to receive honors. And yet, sometimes, we catch glimpses of good relations between the citizens and ordinary foreign soldiers. In the opening lines of Theokritos' 14th idyll (see section 5.2), Aischinas describes a drinking party in the countryside (lines 12–17):

> The Argive, and I, and Agis, the Thessalian horse rider [or trainer, *hippodioktas*], and Kleonikos, the mercenary soldier [*stratiotas*] were making merry at my place in the country. I had killed two chickens and a sucking pig, and opened a fragrant, four years old wine from Byblos, almost as sweet-scented as the day it was pressed. Some onion or so was found, and snails. A jolly drinking-party.

Aischinas was a native – an owner of land in the countryside – celebrating with his foreign friends. One of them was a Thessalian, the name of the other (Argeios) reveals an Argive descent, and the third was a mercenary. For two of them, a military occupation is certain. Leaving the world of idyllic poetry and coming to the reality of our documentary sources, we may assume that when foreign soldiers were granted citizenship in the city where they served, this presupposed personal contacts with the natives, especially with influential men. Members of the troops sent by Attalos I to protect Lillaia in Phokis during the First Macedonian War (ca. 208 BC) were granted citizenship after their service, and similar measures are known in several other cities, usually after a dangerous war – for example, Messene, Aspendos, Dyme, and Pharsalos (Launey 1987: 654–9).

Of course, the allusions to the possibility of complaints in honorary decrees remind us that, usually, foreign soldiers were a burden on a community (Launey 1987: 690–1). Garrisons established more or less permanently, in a citadel or a fort, did not cause problems with respect to billeting, but their soldiers could still be an element of disorder, or even of insecurity. The treaty between the city of Iasos, Ptolemy I, and the commanders of his garrison at Iasos (ca. 309 BC) includes an amnesty clause for legal disputes between the foreign troops and the Iaseis (*I.Iasos* 2, lines 21–4). The charter of the shopkeepers in the sanctuary of Hera in Samos (ca. 245 BC) refers to four potential violators of order: *stratiotai* (obviously soldiers of the Ptolemaic garrison); unemployed mercenaries (*apergoi*); suppliants; and runaway slaves (*IG* XII.6.1 169; cf. *I.Labraunda* 46). A great (and justified) preoccupation with discipline, order, and good behavior (*eutaxia*) is clear in the few surviving Hellenistic military regulations, as it is in the honorific decrees for troops and their commanders (see section 5.5).

Despite these ideals of conduct, foreign soldiers caused many problems for local inhabitants. Billeting in private houses was not just an intrusion of privacy (Plut., *Demetr.* 23.6), but also an economic burden, and foreign soldiers often damaged agricultural production (see chapter 7, section 2). The burden imposed by the presence of troops on the population of the countryside was so heavy that the royal administation had to take measures to prevent it (e.g., *SEG* XXIX 1613).

A treaty of *sympolity* between Teos and Kyrbissos points to further problems (*SEG* XXVI 1306; Robert and Robert 1976: 188–228; Fernández Nieto 1997: 244). In the third century BC, Teos absorbed Kyrbissos and granted its inhabitants Teian citizenship. The "citizens in the polis" swore an oath that they would not destroy the dependent settlement at Kyrbissos, and "the citizens who inhabit Kyrbissos" swore that they would not abandon the foreign commander, that they would follow whatever he commanded (*parangeilei*), and that they would defend the fort and reveal any plans against the fort or the garrison. Although this agreement does not concern "foreign troups" in a narrow sense, since Kyrbissos was incorporated into the state of Teos, this does not change the fact that the Teian garrison was a foreign body in Kyrbissos. The mutual oaths suggest obvious tensions between the two groups. The Teians were also concerned that the garrison might revolt against the polis; this fear was not only felt in Teos but was typical of concerns over Hellenistic garrisons in general (Robert and Robert 1976: 199, 210–14). For example, the Cretans enfranchised in Miletos swore to defend the city and its forts, but the limited faith the Milesians had in the trustworthiness of the Cretans can be seen in the fact that they allowed them to occupy the office of the commander of the garrison (*phrourarchos*) only 20 years after their naturalization in Miletos (see chapter 2, section 2). This fear was not imaginary, but fully justified. In the early Hellenistic period, soldiers seized (or, rather, were expected to seize) the citadel at Sagalassos (Vandorpe 2000). It is generally assumed that the troops in Magnesia-by-Sipylos, which concluded a treaty of *sympoliteia* with Smyrna (ca. 243 BC), constituted the Seleukid garrison in that city which had betrayed Seleukos II during the War of Laodike and taken over Magnesia (*Staatsverträge* 492; Bagnall and Derow 2004: no. 29; Launey 1987: 671–4). A mutiny of the Attalid garrisons at Philetaireia and Attaleia could only be settled after hard negotiations between Eumenes I and his troops (ca. 263–241 BC; see section 5.3).

Garrisons were not only an instrument of subordination, but also a factor of anxiety and trouble in a city, since they could revolt or become the object of attacks. Mounychia, the garrisoned site in Piraeus, was under attack by the troops of Demetrios the Besieger for two days in June 305 BC (Diod. 20.45.2–4; Plut., *Demetr.* 9.4; Polyainos, *Strategemata* 4.7.6); the garrison in the Mouseion Hill was attacked by Athenian citizens in 287 BC (Paus. 1.26.1–2; 1.29.13; *IG* II² 666–7), and this attack was followed by one against the garrison in Piraeus (Polyainos, *Strategemata* 5.17; Paus. 1.29.10), resulting the death of more than 400 Athenians.

5.5. Professional Ideals: Discipline, Solidarity, Masculinity

A fragmentary letter sent by an official in the service of Antiochos III (probably Zeuxis) to the Seleukid army at Labraunda urges the soldiers to "Be well disciplined [*eutakteite*] in all other matters as is fitting, and do not camp [---] in Labraunda and do not live in the sacred places and do not bring in pack animals" (*Labraunda* 46; Ma 2000a: 304–5, no. 15).

From the fourth century BC onwards, discipline (*eutaxia*) is continually praised as one of the cardinal virtues of armies. Generals who effectively implement it were as equally acclaimed as the soldiers and ephebes who practiced it. One of the first duties of the *phrourarchos* sent by Teos every four months was to establish discipline and *eutaxia* (*SEG* XXVI 1306, lines 31–33). A certain maturity was required for this office, since its holder had to be older than 30 (lines 8–11).

The Macedonian royal regulations (*diagrammata*) concerning military service pay particular attention to discipline. One of these texts, found in

Amphipolis (*ISE* 114; Hatzopoulos 2001: 161–4, no. 3), concerns the proper conduct of soldiers during campaigns, and one clause is dedicated to order in the distribution of war booty (B I, lines 10–18: *eutaxias tes ek ton ophelion*). Discipline means obedience towards the officers, respect in the conduct of soldiers towards (foreign) civilians, and justice and solidarity in the relations between soldiers.

The motivation of soldiers (not only mercenaries, but also citizens) could be enhanced with rewards for good service and bravery in the form of promotion, a military command, honors, booty, and gifts. The honors were often connected with material advantages. For example, the agreement between Eumenes I and his soldiers (see section 5.3) stipulates that those soldiers who had been "decorated with wreath of white poplar"– i.e., distinguished for good service – were to receive a specific ration of grain. A similar stipulation can be seen in the Macedonian military regulations from Amphipolis (Hatzopoulos 2001: 161–4, no. 3 A III, lines 2–4). In a fragmentary context, after mention of a wreath (as a distinction?), we are told that a person (the recipient of the distinction?) "shall receive a double share of the booty." Such distinctions presuppose a close observation of the behavior of soldiers by their officers. Archelaos, a general of Mithridates VI, gave as a distinction (*aristeion*) a silver bracelet to Apollonios, a soldier who served in Piraeus during the siege by Sulla, because of a particular service (*SEG* XXXI 1590).

Serving in a fort, or aboard the same ship, and facing the same dangers, brings people together. The successful and safe end of an assignment motivated soldiers to thank those who had contributed to their safe return: their commander and the gods. In the Hellenistic period, honorary inscriptions for officers and dedications by soldiers who served together abound. We have, for example, numerous honorific decrees of soldiers serving in the Athenian garrisons – especially in Rhamnous (Petrakos 1999; Oetjen 2004), and dedications made by crews of the Rhodian ships. An association of Cretan mercenaries serving in Cyprus (*to koinon ton en tei nesoi tassomenon Kreton*) honored, for example, the governor Seleukos (*SEG* XXX 1640, ca. 142–131), for his benevolence, but also for his benefactions towards their *ethnos*, i.e. Crete. The crew of a warship of Kyzikos, which probably fought during the Third Mithridatic War, made a joint dedication to Poseidon (*SEG* XXIX 1272), and many dedications with a similar background are known from Rhodes (e.g., *IG* XII.1 43, 75B; *I.Lindos* 88). Such actions presuppose initiatives and interactions among the soldiers: collecting the necessary money, discussing the divinity that should receive the thanksgiving dedication, determining the type of dedication, formulating the text of the decree, engaging a poet who would compose the honorary or dedicatory epigram, and so on. Such inscriptions are, therefore, indirect evidence for close interaction between soldiers and for a feeling of solidarity among them.

Very often, mercenaries organized themselves into associations (*koina*), normally composed of those belonging to the same ethnic group (especially in the Ptolemaic army). For example, there were associations of Achaians, Thracians, Cretans, Kilikians, and Lykians serving in Cyprus, and of soldiers serving in the same place or under the same officer (e.g., "those who jointly participated in the campaign and were assigned to the general in this fort" in Smyrna – Cohen 1978: 75). Within such associations, soldiers could fulfill their cultural obligations, honoring the gods of their homeland or their place of service (see chapter 9), establishing good relations with the king and his representatives (e.g., by setting up honorary inscriptions), celebrating festivals, cultivating a feeling of solidarity, and creating a new framework of social life in foreign lands.

Professionals often develop their own language, and soldiers are no exception. The names given to warships, sometimes indicating military pride (*"Brave," "Strife," "Victory," "Saviour of the City," "The One that Sets up Trophies," "Lover of Victory"*), sometimes a competitive spirit (*"The Best," "The Greatest," "The First"*), sometimes hope (*"Help," "Blessed"*), sometimes an almost erotic affection (*"Sunshine," "Beloved," "Charming," "Joy for the Eyes," "Sweet as Honey"*), reflect the close relationship between a crew and their ship.

An unexpected source of information for military vocabulary is inscriptions engarved on sling bullets, before they were thrown to the enemy – a practice that reminds us of the graffiti on bombs in World War II. A large number of inscribed sling bullets were found at Olynthos, the city in the Chalkidike that was destroyed after a siege in 348 BC, but similar material has been found in numerous Hellenistic cities and forts (Pritchett 1991: 45–8; Anochin and Rolle 1998). These inscriptions are one of our best sources of soldiers' humor in battle. The texts are addressed to the potential victims of the bullets, playfully associating the bullet with a gift: "get this" (*dexai, labe*), "all yours" (*sou*), "eat this idle bullet" (*troge halion*), "it rains (bullets)" (*hyse*). The opponent is ironically warned: "watch it" (*proseche*), and a dialogue with the bullet can also take place: "go" (addressed to the bullet, *baske an*). Of course, feelings of violence cannot be concealed (see chapter 10, section 2): "blood" (*haima*), "ouch" (*papai*), "to hell (to the fire)" (*pyri*). The most interesting text, especially as an expression of masculinity (see chapter 6), consists of a single word: "get pregnant (with this)" (*kye*). This black humor helped soldiers to overcome the anxiety of battle and verbally reassured them, giving them a feeling of superiority.

If one may judge the reputation of mercenaries and officers by reference to the representatives of this group in Hellenistic comedy (Launey 1987: 794–812), what characterized them was a constant boasting about their exploits, whether in conquering cities or (defenseless) girls. A dedicatory epigram composed by the great Hellenistic poet Kallimachos for a Cretan mercenary, who had fought in a campaign of Ptolemy III in Kyrenaika (ca. 246–221 BC), reveals this attitude of superiority (*epigr.* 37 ed. Pfeiffer): "Menitas from Lyttos dedicated these arches proudly saying: To you, Sarapis, I offer this bone arch and the quiver; as for the arrows, the Esperitai have got them." Such boasting sometimes continued even after a soldier's death, through the medium of funerary inscriptions, as in the case of Apollonios of Tymnos (ca. 250 BC; see chapter 2, section 2), whose grave epigram recalls the great number of enemies he killed in person, and the innumerable spears which he "firmly stuck into the flesh of the enemies."

5.6. Professional Risks: Doctors and Patients

One of the "healing miracles" of Asklepios, narrated in inscriptions set up in his sanctuary at Epidauros (fourth century), concerns a war victim: "Euhippos bore a spearhead in his jaw for six years. While he was spleeping here, the god drew the spearhead from him and gave it to him in his hands. When day came, he walked out well, having the spearhead in his hands" (*IG* IV 1² 121; LiDonnici 1995: 94, no. A12; see chapter 1, section 1).

The greatest risk in war is death in battle. The greatest suffering is to survive but be disabled. Although numbers of casualties are often given by Hellenistic historians, we get no information about their treatment or about their future life. There is no way to estimate the percentage of crippled soldiers who lived as a burden on their families, and the fact that our sources are silent on this point does not necessarily mean that the relevant social and economic problems did not exist (Grassl 1986). Of course, not only professional soldiers were wounded in wars, but if I discuss this subject in this context it is because their case presents particular problems and significant differences from the situation of wounded civilians. In the case of the latter, we may safely assume that they were taken care of by their families, and although their life and work were inevitably affected, they often possessed landed property or workshops and could employ others to replace them. Certainly they suffered a financial loss, but they did not (or at least rarely so) lose their livelihoods. In the case of professional soldiers, (i.e., those employed as soldiers because they did not have an alternative), a wound that seriously affected their performance clearly had more dramatic consequences.

The problem was certainly recognized in antiquity, not least by the specialists of warfare. Philon of Byzantion gives the following recommendation in his *Mechanics* (C 45, ed. Garlan 1974: 312, 386): "One should attend with great care the wounded among the mercenary soldiers [*xenoi*], making all the necessary provisions. And those who do not have persons who would treat them, should be placed in the houses of the citizens." Some mercenaries were accompanied by their families (see section 5.3), and it seems that those who were not would be cared for by citizen families. This system was also intended to increase the solidarity between mercenaries and locals and decrease the likelihood of desertion (see C 48). However, recommendations do not always represent the reality.

The treatment of wounds was given a lot of attention in Hellenistic cities. One of the recommendations given by Philon of Byzantion to cities that might face the danger of war and siege was to employ in the city suitable doctors, experienced in the treatment of wounds and in the removal of arrowheads, with adequate medical equipment (C 72, ed. Garlan 1974: 315, 392). Indeed, many cities did employ public doctors – not only in times of war, but also when they faced epidemics or earthquakes (Massar 2001). Hermias of Kos is one of the best documented cases (*I.Cret.* IV 168 and I,xviii 7; Massar 2001: 192–3; Samama 2003: 231–4). He was invited by the Cretan city of Gortyn to serve as a public doctor arround 225 BC and stayed there for five years. During his stay, the greatest war of Cretan history – the Lyttian War (ca. 222–220 BC) – broke out. During the war, Hermias treated not only the Gortynians, but also their allies, saving many lives. As a result, he was honored by the Gortynians and the Knossians.

Another doctor, called Apollonios, was praised for not abandoning Tenos to escape the dangers of a war (*IG* XII.5 824 = *SEG* XXXVI 765, 190/89 BC; Samama 2003: 284–8). Diodoros of Samos did not spare costs and disregarded all dangers during the attack of Ptolemaic troops against the Macedonian garrison (ca. 200 BC), "when many men were wounded during the siege of the citadels and the close struggles which took place day-by-day" (*IG* XII.6.1 12; Samama 2003: 289–91).

Such services made some physicians of the Hellenistic period important public figures and benefactors. Asklepiades of Perge (second century BC) was honored in Seleukeia (one of the many cities of this name, possibly the one in Pamphylia) for serving as a public doctor for the rather modest salary of 1,000 drachmas per annum, for giving public lectures, and for "accomplishing many and unexpected [*paradoxa*] cures in the practice of surgery (*en tois kata ten cheirourgian*)" (*I.Perge* 12 lines 32–3; Samama 2003: 439–42). Athletes are usually characterized as *paradoxoi* because of unbelievable achievements. Many a doctor, who defeated death, must have acquired a similar reputation and won the admiration of cities and concomitant privileges. Those of them who happened to cure wounded kings (e.g., Metrodoros of Amphipolis, who successfully treated a wound of Antiochos I) also acquired political influence and power (*OGIS* 220 = *I.Ilion* 34; Bagnall and Derow 2004: no. 79, ca. 276–269 BC; Samama 2003: 303–5).

5.7. War as a Science: Trainers, Tacticians, and Inventors

Commanders of troops were expected to have their men regularly exercise in the use of the spear and the bow (*akontismos, toxeia*; see *SEG* XXVIII 107). Training in the use of weapons often started at a very young age (see chapter 3, section 2) and required specialists such as the *hoplomachos* (master-at-arms). A decree of the Boiotian city of Thespiai (ca. 240 BC) concerns the appointment of an Athenian military instructor:

> Since the Boiotian League has a law according to which the cities should provide for teachers, who will instruct the young men [*neaniskoi*] in archery, in throwing the javelin, and in making formation in order of battle, and since Sostratos is zealously taking care of both the boys and the young men, the city should assign him to this duty, as he wishes, so that he may take care of the boys and the young men and instruct them according to the provisions of the law; his annual salary will be four mnai.
>
> (Roesch 1982: 307–54; *SEG* XXXII 496)

The law in question may have been introduced after a Boiotian defeat by the Aitolians in 245 BC, which made the Boiotians realize the importance of specialized military instruction. We know of the existence of military trainers primarily from the honorary decrees for the Athenian ephebes (see chapter 3, section 1), which mention, among other educators, teachers in archery (*toxotes*), in throwing the javelin (*akontistes*), in the use of the catapult (*katapaltaphetes*), and in the use of lance and shield (*hoplomachos*) (Pélékides 1962: 207). In several cases, the trainers were foreign; exactly as the Athenian Sopatros trained the young Boiotians, the *toxotes* Aristokles came from the island of Crete, which was famous for its archers, to teach the Athenian youths his skill (Pélékides 1962: 173, n. 5; 231 BC).

The science of Hellenistic warfare went beyond the skills of trainers in traditional weapons. Military tactics was a specialty which was enormously valued, particularly in royal courts, since the kings were both in a position, and had a need, to mobilize large numbers of troops. Such kings and generals recognized the value of studying the exploits of their predecessors on the battlefield, and this was in part achieved by reading historiographical narratives. By the fourth century (and possibly earlier), compilations of examples of great generalship had begun to appear (*strategemata*; cf. Xenophon, *Memorabilia* 3.5.22), and from the mid-fourth century onwards, authors with military experience began to publish their own works on tactical matters.

The treatise on the defense of a besieged city by Aineias the Tactician (possibly an Arkadian general) is the earliest work of this genre. An epitome of his military writings was later composed in the court of Pyrrhos (*FgrHist* 603), and the king himself, as well as his son Alexandros, were the authors of works on *Tactics* (Ailianos, *Taktika* 1.2). The author of another work on the art of siege (*Poliorketika hypomnemata*), Daimachos, was probably in the service of Antiochos I (*FgrHist* 65; Garlan 1974: 210).

The science of warfare also played an important part in the works and inventions of engineers, who were frequently to be found in royal courts. There they found the financial means, the practical help, and the ideological motivation for their work. For instance, a particular type of sling, the *kestros*, was invented during the Third Macedonian War (Polyb. 27.11.1–7; Livy 42.65.9–11; Pritchett 1991: 37). One of the few areas in which applied science advanced in the Hellenistic period was the invention of new siege equipment, such as the torsion catapult (ca. 270 BC), the repeating catapult, the ram, the tower, and the flame-thrower (Marsden 1969, 1971; Garlan 1984).

Specialized military engineers were responsible for the construction and transportation of artillery and other siege equipment (Garlan 1974: 207–11). Demetrios the Besieger brought special engineers (*technitai*) from Asia Minor for the siege of Salamis on Cyprus in 306 (Diod. 20.48.1), and the inventiveness of such men (e.g., Epimachos of Athens, Zoilos, and Kallias of Arados) was demonstrated during the siege of Rhodes by the same king (305–4 BC; Garlan 1974: 209). Even Archimedes, who was not particularly interested in applied science, put his genius in the service of his city during the siege of Syracuse in 218 BC.

A reasonable insight into the content of military treatises is provided by the works of Philon of Byzantion (third or second century) on engineering (*Mechanike syntaxis*), in which many military subjects were covered, in particular the construction of artillery and missiles (*Belopoiika*), harbor-building (*Limenopoiika*), and the construction of defensive (*Paraskeuastika*) and offensive siege-works (*Poliorketika*). In the chapters on military architecture, Philon explains the construction of towers, gates, and ditches (1.1–87), but also gives practical advice about the storage of food (2.1–10, 25–9), plus recipes for the preparation of nutritious bread (2.35–40), advice on planting gardens in sacred precincts (2.48), instructions for the safe storage of water (2.54), and guidance on the best material with which to write letters.

Philon was by no means the only author of such treatises. One should mention the work on war machines by Biton (*Kataskeuai polemikon organon*), the *Belopoiika* and *Cheirobalistras kataskeue*, dedicated to the construction of artillery by Heron of Alexandria, and the *Poliorcetics* of Apollodoros (Garlan 1974: 285).

Further Reading

5.1. The Professionalization of Hellenistic Warfare: Definitions and Modifications. *Personal names of soldiers related to war*: Launey 1987: 797–8; ch. 2.2 (further reading). *Military developments of the fourth century*: Garlan 1974: 183–200, 244–69 (fortifications), 155–83, 202–44 (poliorcetics) (cf. the criticism of Will 1975); Pritchett 1974: 59–116 (*condottieri* and mercenaries); Müller 1999: 22–33 (defense of the territory); Baker 1999 (mercenaries); Pimouguet-Pedarros 2003 (poliorcetics); Gaebel 2003: 199–209 (cavalry); for a selection of sources see Sage 1996: 135–61.

5.2. The Social Context of Mercenary Service. *Hellenistic mercenaries:* Launey 1987; Lévêque 1968: 262–6; Foulon 1996: 317–22; Sion-Jenkis 2001; Couvenhes 2004; Lendon 2004. *The case of Crete:* Cretan mercenaries: Ducrey 1970, 1985: 130–2; Petropoulou 1985: 15–31; Launey 1987: 248–86, 1068–72; Foulon 1996: 334–6; socio-economic crisis in Hellenistic Crete: Chaniotis 1996a: 179–85, 1999b: 182–6, 210–11, 2004a.

5.3. The Conditions of Service. *Mercenary treaties:* e.g., *Staatsverträge* 551; see also Ducrey 1970; Petropoulou 1985: 23–6. *Enfranchisment of Cretan mercenaries in Miletos:* Launey 1987: 660–4; Brulé 1990. *Military settlers:* Cohen 1978, 1995; Billows 1995. Examples: Kretopolis: Cohen 1995: 345–6; Sekunda 1997; Thyatteira: Cohen 1995: 238–42; Antioch: Libanios, *oratio* 11.119 (309); Jews in Asia Minor: Jos., *Ant. Iud.* 12.149–53; Austin 1981: no. 167; Cohen 1978: 5–9; cf. Trebilco 1991: 7, 124; Eukarpeia: Cohen 1995: 299–300; Bucak/Syneta: Chaniotis 1998a; Amyzon: Robert and Robert 1983: 231, 233; Sagalassos: Kosmetatou and Waelkens 1997. *The Ptolemaic klerouchoi:* Préaux 1939: 400–3, 463–77; Uebel 1968; van t' Dack 1977; cf. Bagnall and Derow 2004: nos 123, 148; see also Manning 2003 on land tenure in Ptolemaic Egypt. Honigman 2003 on the nature of the *politeumata* in Egypt. *The Seleukid klerouchoi:* Cohen 1978: 45–71. *The Seleukid army:* Bar-Kochva 1976. *Measures for the orphans of war dead:* Stroud 1971: 287–8 (Athens). *The treaty between Eumenes and his mercenaries:* I.Pergamon 13 = *Staatsverträge* 481 = OGIS 266; Launey 1987: 738–46; Schalles 1985: 32; Allen 1983: 23–5; Virgilio 1988: 111–51.

5.4. Garrisons and Foreign Troops in Hellenistic Cities. *Garrisons, in general:* Launey 1987: 633–75; Baker 2000a; Chaniotis 2002; Ma 2002; Labarre 2004. Ptolemaic: Bagnall 1976. Seleukid: Bikerman 1938: 53–5. Antigonid: Holleaux 1938a: 261–8. Hatzopoulos 2001: 29–32. *Selection of sources:* Launey 1987: 633–75; e.g., Athens: Diod. 18.18.1–6; Plut., *Phokion* 28.2; Plut., *Demosthenes* 28.1; see Launey 1987: 634–41; Habicht 1997: 36–172; Taylor 1998; Dreyer 1999; Oetjen 2004. Sikyon: *IG* II² 448. Chalkis: *IG* II² 469. Eretria: *IG* XII.9 192. Argos: Vollgraff 1908. Elateia: *Syll.*³ 361. Troizen: *IG* IV 769. Methana: *IG* IV 854; *IG* XII.3 466. *Honors for commanders:* Roussel 1939; Robert 1967: 36–40; *SEG* XXXV 926; Amyzon 14; *I.Ephesos* 1408; *I.Iasos* 33–4; *I.Stratonileia* 4, 9. *Honors for soldiers:* Robert and Robert 1954: 289 n. 1; Launey 1987: 652–75; Pritchett 1974: 276–90. *Attacks against garrisons:* e.g., Polyainos, *Strategemata* 5.17; Paus. 1.29.10 (Athens, 286 BC); Polyb. 2.41.13 (Aigion, 275 BC), 2.43.4 (Akrokorinthos, 243 BC).

5.5. Professional Ideals: Discipline, Solidarity, Masculinity. *Praise of discipline (eutaxia):* e.g., *IG* VII 1; *SEG* XXVI 1306, lines 31–33; *SEG* XXXV 926; *I.Iasos* 33; *ISE* 114 (Hatzopoulos 2001: 161–4, no. 3); *Labraunda* 46; *eutaxia* in processions: e.g., *IG* II² 1006, lines 12–15; *I.Ilion* 52, line 28; Sokolowski 1962: no. 15, lines 24 and 27; no. 44, lines 2–3, 11–12; Sokolowski 1969: no. 65, line 62; see also Robert 1927: 121; Robert and Robert 1954: 289; Pritchett 1974: 236–8; Launey 1987: 692–3; Gauthier and Hatzopoulos 1993: 104–5; Hatzopoulos 2001: 141–5. *Rewards for good service:* Philon C 46, ed. Garlan 1974: 312, 386–7; Pritchett 1974: 289–90. *Dedications by groups of soldiers:* *IG* II² 1995; *IG* IX.2 1057; *SEG* XXXIII 640, 684; Dietze 2000 (Ptolemaic Egypt). *Military regulations:* Fernández Nieto 1997; Hatzopoulos 2001: 29–32, 152–3., nos. 1 I/II. *Honorary inscriptions of*

100

soldiers for their commander. e.g., *IG* II² 2854, 2971, 3206 I, 3209, 3460 VI/VII; *IG* IV² 244; *IG* XII.1 75 B; *I.Smyrna* 609–12; *OGIS* 445, 447; *SEG* XLV 1825; cf. Petrakos 1999; Oetjen 2004. *Associations of soldiers.* Launey 1987: 1001–36; Cohen 1978: 73–83; Crawford 1984. *Names of ships in Athens* (*SEG* XLV 145, ca. 358–352 BC); *Aigle* (Sunshine), *Akryptate and Akrypton* (Unhidden), *Ariste* (the best), *Boetheia* (Help), *Gennaia* (Brave), *Dorkas* (roe), *Dramosyne* (ceremony), *Eris* (strife), *Eromene* (the beloved), *Euneos* (well disposed), *Eutyches* (fortunate), *Eucharis* (gracious, charming), *Theamosyne* (joy for the eyes), *Hikane* (able), *Makaria* (blessed), *Megiste* (the greatest), *Melitta* (sweet as honey), *Nike* (Victory), *Nikephoros* (the one that brings victory), *Orthopolis* (the one that saves the city), *Prote* (the first), *Tropaia* (the one that sets up trophies), *Philonike* (the lover of victory).

5.6. Professional Risks: Doctors and Patients. *War wounds.* Salazar 2000; Samama 2003: 33. *Medical services in armies.* Sternberg 1999; Salazar 2000: 72–4; Samama 2003: 33–4, 47–51. *Public doctors.* Cohn-Haft 1956; Samama 2003: 38–45. *Royal doctors.* Marasco 1996. *Taxes for public doctors (iatrikon):* Samama 2003: 50–1.

5.7. War as a Science: Trainers, Tacticians, and Inventors. *Regular training.* Beston 2000: 317–21; Lendon 2004; cf. the ironical remarks of Theophrastos, *Characters* 27. *Hoplomachos* (master-at-arms): Theophrastos, *Characters* 21; *I.Callatis* 5. *War machines:* Shipley 2000: 334–41; Irby-Massie and Keyser 2002: 157–63. *Warships.* Morrison and Coates 1994. *Philon of Byzantion.* Garlan 1974: 281–5.

6

THE GENDER OF WAR: MASCULINE WARRIORS, DEFENSELESS WOMEN, AND BEYOND

6.1. War and Masculinity

A lead sling bullet found in Cyprus, probably intended to be thrown by Ptolemaic soldiers at the enemy, is inscribed with the laconic text: "get pregnant (with this)" (*kye*) (Pritchett 1991: 46) (see chapter 5, section 5). The text associates success in battle (i.e., hitting the opponent with the sling bullet) with success in sexual intercourse. The bullet penetrates the body of the enemy warrior exactly as the slinger's penis penetrates a woman's vagina. The underlying idea has, however, less to do with sexuality than with subordination. In a society in which Nike, the goddess of victory, is represented on vases with wedding scenes as a symbol of the victory of the bridegroom over the bride (Oakley and Sinos 1993: 20), the victory of the male warrior over his enemy can easily be associated with the subordination of the female by the male through the act of sexual intercourse. One can think of insults in many languages – not only in modern Greek and Italian – which use vulgar variations of the word for sexual intercourse in order to express the superiority and victory of one male over another.

That wars are presented as an intrinsically male activity has been observed in the work of Hellenistic historians (Roy 1998: 120; Beston 2000: 316–17). Polybios underlines the unmanly behavior of King Prousias II of Bithynia in connection with his disastrous war against Pergamon: "After doing nothing worthy of a man in his attacks on the town, but behaving in a cowardly and womanish manner both to gods and men, he marched his army back to Elaia" (32.15.9; cf. 36.15.1–3; 28.21.3). Similarly, the brave – but unfortunately not always victorious – king is a man with a strong masculine sex drive and potency. Demetrios the Besieger is said to have visited his mistress Lamia in armor, and it is perhaps not the wild imagination of a modern historian that can associate the impressive *helepolis*, a mobile siege machine with a long, projecting beam ending in a cone decorated with a ram's head, with which the Besieger attempted to penetrate city walls, with the male sex organ.

Greek cities usually have female names. If the personification of the citizen body in art is a bearded mature man (the *Demos*), the personification of the polis and her fortune (*Tyche*) is a woman wearing the city walls as a crown (see chapter 2, section 3). The walls surround the city like a belt, and when they fall because of an earthquake, or are destroyed by the enemy, they leave the city, and the most defenseless of its inhabitants, open to the enemy. Men are to be killed, women are desired booty to be taken by the winner. In Phylarchos' account of the war in Sparta in 272 BC, the fight between the exiled Spartan King Kleonymos and the defender of Sparta, Akrotatos, is styled as one for the possession both of Sparta and of Chilonis, former wife of Kleonymos and new lover of Akrotatos (Beston 2000: 316–17). In the imagination of the Hellenistic Greeks, war and sexual desire were associated – one may remark in passing that in myth, the god of war is the lover of the most beautiful goddess.

Among the immortals, two virgin goddesses, Athena and Artemis, are the female patrons of war and victory *par excellence* (see chapter 9). They drive away from cities and territories (in Greek, both words are female: *polis* and *chora*) the male intruders with the same effective violence with which in the myths they drive back the men who attempt to violate their own virginity.

In the great Ptolemaic procession of Alexandria (see chapter 4, section 5), women prisoners (Athen. V 201 a) represented the booty of Dionysos' mythical campaign in India, followed in the next section by women who represented the cities liberated by another mortal god, Alexander, in his Persian war (201 e). The two contrasting images – both staged by men – stress the dependence of passive women on successful men.

Of course, reality and imagination do not always overlap. It is true that women were victimized in many ways during wars, primarily as prisoners, and as the mothers and wives of dead warriors. But as they were exposed to the imminent perils of war, women, at least in some cities, also took an interest in war. They were eye-witnesses of fights and the judges of valorous deeds, and in some cases they were also actively engaged in battle, without, however, changing the impression that Hellenistic wars remained a manly activity, where men showed their character (see chapter 9, section 2): a business for kings, generals, mercenaries, diplomats, statesmen, and pirates.

Despite a reassessment of the social roles of women in the Hellenistic world, it should be stressed that even wealthy women of good families were only able to participate in public life to a limited extent (van Bremen 1996). Consequently, and with a few notable exceptions, women are almost absent in Hellenistic historiography in connection with war. This is not the place to discuss the social and legal conditions of Hellenistic women, but a survey of the social aspects of Hellenistic wars cannot possibly be complete without an effort to estimate the ways in which the lives of women were affected by war.

6.2. In the Shadow of Soldiers: Women in Garrisons and Forts

Soldiers of citizen militias (see chapter 2) had families, and when not serving in a fort or participating in a campaign they lived a family life. The life of professional soldiers (see chapter 5) was different. Whether serving in the army of a king or manning a garrison or a fort, they may have left behind their native city but not their sexual desires or their hope of marital life. The sexual desires could be satisfied through visits to the local brothel – and perhaps, occasionally, through the rape of a native girl. Many Hellenistic comedies – known from Latin adaptations – introduce into their plot the intimate relations of a mercenary soldier with a prostitute (e.g., Menander's *The Samian Woman*; Plautus' *Bacchides, Curculio, Epidicus, Pseudolus,* and *Truculentus*; and Terence's *Eunuchus*), and this stereotype must have been inspired by reality (see Launey 1987: 801–3). On the other hand, the obligation to produce legitimate heirs required a legitimate marriage. A long funerary epigram from Palestine (late third or early second century BC) narrates the adventurous life of a certain Charmadas from Anopolis (Crete), who joined the Ptolemaic army and served in a garrison somewhere in Koile Syria. There his daughter Archagatha married a fellow soldier called Machaios, an Aitolian (*SEG* VIII 269; *SGO* IV 21/05/01). We do not know whether Charmadas created a family in the place where he served or whether he brought his family there from Crete. But he did have a family in the Ptolemaic garrison where he lived and died, and his daughter also married, lived, and died there.

The story of Charmadas is the story of a man, narrated by a man, and is not unusual. The thousands of mercenary soldiers meticulously counted by recruiters and officers, and mentioned by historians, were often accompanied by women. Women were part of the "baggage" (*aposkeue*; Pomeroy 1984: 100–1), and we only know of their existence thanks to inscriptions and papyri. In addition to honorary inscriptions, dedications, and epitaphs, there are many grave inscriptions relating to foreign women and young people in garrisoned cities, who must have been the relatives of soldiers. In a few cases, we get more information about the massive migration of women who accompanied their men and fathers to the forts they were hired to man.

Many mercenary soldiers – not unlike modern immigrants – hoped to return to their native cities one day. This hope was connected with a serious legal problem: the legitimacy of their marriage and, consequently, the legitimacy of their children. In many Hellenistic cities (e.g., on Crete) a marriage was only legitimate if husband and wife were both citizens, or if there was an appropriate interstate agreement (*epigamia*) in place. In some cities, the legal restrictions were loosened in the course of the Hellenistic period (Ogden 1996: 291), but in many others they remained valid. Legal barriers were often stronger than physical attraction, or the wish to create a family.

When we study particular ethnic groups, we can observe the effect of legal considerations on marriage patterns, especially the effort to avoid mixed marriages. The Cretans present a good case. Their island was one of the main sources of mercenaries in the Hellenistic period (see chapter 5, section 2), and consequently the Cretans attested to in the inscriptions of garrisoned areas can easily be recognized as soldiers. In the late third century, Miletos recruited a huge number of Cretans, in order to settle them in the newly-acquired territory of Hybandis, which was contested by Magnesia on the Maeander. More than 1,000 Cretans soldiers migrated to Miletos in two waves (234/3 and 229/8 BC) and were enfranchised there. The enfranchisement list shows that they came to Miletos together with their families, a total of around 3,000–4,000 people (*Milet* I.3 33–8; Herrmann 1997: 160–4). Although these men were naturalized in Miletos, they retained their original civic identity, and attempted to return to their native cities some time later. If unmarried Cretan mercenaries wanted to marry women from Crete, they could find a bride among the other immigrants.

Although the Cretans in Miletos are a particular case, we find Cretan women present in other places with Cretan garrisons such as in the Antigonid garrisons of Attika, Euboia, and Thessaly (Chaniotis 1996a: 27, n. 118). This kind of evidence is not, however, limited to Cretan women. In many garrisoned sites we find evidence for women from areas which supplied the Hellenistic armies with mercenaries; it is therefore reasonable to assume that they were dependents (wives, daughters, or sisters) of members of the garrison. We encounter women from Aspendos, Euboia, Byzantion, Crete, and Arabia in Cypriot cities with Ptolemaic garrisons (Bagnall 1976: 263–6), and with the exception of Arabia, these were the very areas where the male soldiers of the garrisons were recruited.

Ptolemy I encouraged the settlement of mercenaries with their families in Egypt, thus increasing the loyalty of his soldiers, and measures were also taken from time to time to protect soldiers' families during their absence in wars (Pomeroy 1984: 100–3). For example, cases could not be brought to court against them (*Select Papyri* II 201), and Ptolemy VI exempted soldiers' wives from compulsory cultivation of the land.

Mixed marriages were, however, often unavoidable. They were very common in Egypt (Mélèze-Modrzejewski 1984; Launey 1987: 714), where the crossing of ethnic boundaries was less significant, since most merceneries had migrated there permanently. But in some cases we observe a preference for mixed marriages between representatives of cities which had signed an agreement of *epigamia* (legitimate mixed marriage). The Cretans again offer instructive examples. In addition to Archagatha of Crete, who married the Aitolian Machaios, in another Ptolemaic garrison, at Kition on Cyprus,

Aristo, the daughter of the Cretan Dion, married the Aitolian Melankomas (ca. 146–116 BC). Both her husband and his homonymous father were highly-ranked officers of the Ptolemaic garrisons (*OGIS* 134; Bagnall 1976: 52).

The legal status of a woman was a matter of great importance. Even in Plautus' *Miles Gloriosus*, Pyrgopolynices asks more questions about the legal status of a woman (lines 961–4: *ingenuan an festuca facta e serva liberast?... Nuptan est an vidua?*) than about her looks.

The case of Dryton, a man of Cretan descent, exemplifies how the conservative marriage pattern, in which origin and legal status were of great importance, was gradually abandoned within the same generation (Winnicki 1972; Pomeroy 1984: 103–24). We know of Dryton's family relations thanks to a large group of documents that include his wills. He was born around 195 BC as a citizen of the Greek city of Ptolemais, and his father (and his ancestors?) must have been Cretan mercenaries. As we can infer from the name of his father-in-law (Esthladas), his first wife, Sarapias, was also of Cretan descent and a member of a citizen family. In this respect Dryton confirms the pattern of marriage within the same ethnic group and of persons of the same legal status. After Sarapias' death or divorce, Dryton married a second time (around 150 BC) and his second wife, Apollonia, also called Senmouthis, was much younger, did not have citizen status, and was not Cretan. Her family probably emigrated to Egypt in the mid-third century (or earlier) from Kyrene. After three or four generations of living in the Egyptian countryside, the members of this family had to a great extent adopted Egyptian culture and names. Apollonia, her four sisters, and her five daughters all had double names, Greek and Egyptian. Such "Egyptianization" is even more evident in the generation of Dryton's children, and three of his daughters are known to have married Egyptian men (Kames, son of Pates; Psenesis; Erienupis).

6.3. Spectators, Judges, and Defenders: Women's Share of War

Polyainos (*Strategemata* 7.30) narrates an obscure incident of early Hellenistic history. In a war between Arhibaios (possibly the Macedonian officer Arrhidaios) and Mempsis, the latter prevented the siege of a city by bringing out and arraying before the walls everything the men might lose, should the city be taken: "women, children, and property." Arhibaios realized that the men, who had retreated behind the walls and barricaded the gates, would fight to the death, and withdrew. The historicity of this event is questionable, but we also find the mention of "women, children, and property" in a similar context in a documentary source. In a letter sent by the city of Plarasa/Aphrodisias to the Roman proconsul Q. Oppius during the Mithridatic War (Reynolds 1982: no. 2), the authorities declare: "our entire people, together with the women and the children and the entire property, are willing to risk everything for Quintus and for the Roman interests, for we do not wish to live without the leadership of the Romans." Both in Polyainos' narrative and the letter, "women, children, and property" represent a passive, potential booty, manipulated by men or included in a rhetoric of self-sacrifice.

This may have been the role of women in the male imagination, but in real life, when war reached a town, women did not remain inactive.

Let us consider another episode of early Hellenistic history. Pyrrhos of Epeiros attacked Sparta with the help of its exiled King Kleonymos (272 BC). Phylarchos (*apud* Plut., *Pyrrhos* 28.4–5) gives a very dramatic description of a critical moment, when Pyrrhos' son, with 2,000 men, tried to force a passage into the city:

> The young Akrotatos saw the danger, and running through the city with three hundred men got round behind Ptolemy without being seen . . . The elderly men and the host of women watched his deeds of bravery . . . And when he went back again through the city to his allotted post, covered with blood and triumphant, elated with his victory, the Spartan women thought that he had become taller and more beautiful than ever and envied Chilonis her lover.

This passage demonstrates two parts played by women in war: as spectators of battle scenes near and in the town (rarely in Sparta), and as judges of military valor – an important public role for Spartan women.

One of the typical images of besieged cities in ancient art and literarure – for example, in the *Iliad* or in the Nereid Monument at Xanthos (ca. 400 BC; Boardman 1995: fig. 218i) – represents women anxiously watching from behind the city walls a battle that might determine their fate. When young men fight, elderly men, women, and children seek refuge behind the fortification wall. Their role is, nevertheless, not just that of the passive spectator. Very often they pass judgment upon the warriors. Again, this goes back to a very early tradition. In a famous scene in the *Iliad* (3.161–242), Priam and Helena – an old man and the propective booty of the besiegers – watch the battle and Helena recognizes the Achaian warriors and gives information about them. Later, when Paris retreats, she is the one who castigates his behavior as cowardly (3.426–36).

According to Spartan tradition, which is certainly reflected in the passage cited above, the Spartan women used to sing the praise of those who had shown themselves worthy (Plut., *Lykourgos* 14.5–6). The contemporary images of Palestinian women hailing the warriors of the *intifada* may give us an impression of such scenes. The proverbial "sayings of Spartan women" (*apophthegmata*) collected by Plutarch (*mor.* 240 c–242 d) consist of comments on the proper behavior of the warrior; it is conceivable that in the aforementioned narrative concerning Akrotatos, the admiration of the Spartan women of the beauty that accompanies the valiant warrior, their collective sexual desire, and their collective envy for the one woman who has won his heart, were expressed in spontaneous song. Admittedly, Sparta is a particular case, and we can expect such a role primarily in communities dominated by a warrior spirit. This may have been the case in Cretan cities. According to the literary sources on the Cretan "men's houses" (*andreia*) of the citizen-warriors, which still existed in the Hellenistic period (Chaniotis 1996a: 123, 133), women were responsible for the organization of common meals, and had the privilege of distributing the food according to valor and military achievement (Dosiadas, *FgrHist* 458 F 2).

The praise of heroic death in battle is, however, not limited to Sparta and Crete. A few grave epigrams written by Anyte and Nossis, Hellenistic women poets, praise the heroic death of men in battle (*Greek Anthology* 6.132; 7.208, 232, 724; Loman 2004: 34–5).

Aineias the Tactician (mid-fourth-century BC) describes a trick used by the people of Sinope during a war (ca. 370 BC), in order to create the impression that their army was bigger: they dressed women like men and placed them on the walls, in full view of the enemy (Aeneias Tacticus 40.4). When Pyrrhos attacked Sparta in 272 BC, the women refused to be transported to Crete, completed one third of the trench that was built in a hurry (Phylarchos, *FgrHist* 81 F 48), and urged the young men to defend it, "saying that it is sweet to be victorious before the eyes of the fatherland and glorious to die in the hands of mothers and wives" (Plut., *Pyrrhos* 27.9). One should remark here that the Spartan women were led by Archidamia, widow of a king and one of the richest women in Sparta (Schaps 1982: 194; Cartledge and Spawforth 1989: 33–4); wealth and status for women was no less important than for men with regard to participation in public life.

Women and slaves frequently participated in street battles, throwing clay tiles from the roofs of their houses (Aeneias Tacticus 2.6; Polyainos, *Strategemata* 8.69; Schaps 1982: 195–6; Barry 1996; Loman 2004: 42), and the women of Chios are said to have saved their city from an attack in this way (Plut., *mor.* 245). Philon of Byzantion explicitly recommends this practice: "the children, the female slaves, the women, and the virgins should hit from the roofs and everyone in the city should be active" (C 31, ed. Garlan 1974: 311, 384). This is – we are told – the way King Pyrrhos was killed while invading the city of Argos in 272 BC: "the Argive men ran to the market place with their arms, while their women occupied in advance the roofs and forced the Epeirotans to withdraw by throwing objects from above, so that even Pyrrhos, the most skillful of generals, was killed when a roof-tile fell on his head" (Plut., *Pyrrhos* 34; Polyainos, *Strategemata* 8.68; Paus. 1.13.8). It should be remarked that the Argive women are said to have saved their city as early as the fifth century BC, after Kleomenes of Sparta had defeated the men and was attacking Argos (Sokrates, *FgrHist* 310 F 6 = Plut., *mor.* 245; Polyainos, *Strategemata* 8.33). The women armed themselves, defended the walls, and pushed the enemy back. The

Hellenistic historian Sokrates reports that a festival commemorated this achievement, where the women dressed themselves in male tunics and cloaks and the men in female garments. This celebration (*Hybristika*, the "festival of insolence" or "insults") belongs to a widespread category of rituals of reversal and is presumably older than Kleomenes' war, being associated with it later (Graf 1984). Nevertheless, the celebration of this festival, and the collective memory transmitted to Argive women through such a celebration, may have contributed to their heroism, just as similar traditions inspired Spartan women and their behavior.

So we can see that in desperate situations, when even the slaves were mobilized, women did not fail to contribute to the defense of their cities, not only by giving encouragement and moral support, but by actively taking part in combat. During the Galatian invasion (278 BC), the Aitolian women are said to have participated, along with all the men, young and old, in the campaign and the fighting against the invaders, showing more courage (*thymos*) than the men (Paus. 10.22.5–7; Antonetti 1990: 126–31).

A recent archaeological discovery in Messene may be associated with the active participation of women in battles (perhaps street fights). In the late third century, a grave monument was erected in this city of the Peloponnese for the burial of six men and four women (*SEG* XLVII 428; Themelis 2001). The burial, *intra muros* and in such a prominent place, is an extraordinary honor, probably awarded to dead heroes, possibly killed in the war against Demetrios of Pharos (214 BC) or Nabis of Sparta (201 BC).

Financial contributions to the defense of a city were primarily expected from men. However, as the degrees of participation of women in the public life of their cities very much depended on status and means, some wealthy women occasionally offered money not only for peaceful building works, to which most of the evidence refers (e.g., temples), but also for the construction of fortifications. Examples of this practice come from Kos (*PH* 10; Migeotte 1992: no. 50) and Naxos (*IG* XII Suppl. 92; Migeotte 1992: no. 54). The Koan decree concerning a subscription for the defense of the city explicitly appeals to the generosity of all: "male and female citizens, illegitimate children, foreign residents and foreigners." At least 23 women responded, although only men responded to a similar appeal in Ioulis on Keos (*SEG* XIV 532; Maier 1959: no. 38, late fourth or early third century BC). Kourasio, a wealthy woman in Aspendos, who occupied the office of a *demiourgos*, financed the construction of a tower (Bielman 2002: 92–5; second century); Timessa, a woman of Arkesine on Amorgos, saved citizens captured by pirates or enemies, probably with her financial aid (*IG* XII.7 36 = Bielman 1994: no. 39; late third or early second century). Perhaps not surprisingly, women were by no means excluded from the financial contributions imposed upon the wealthy citizens of the Achaian League before its last battle against the Romans in 146 BC (Polyb. 38.15.6–11).

When the enthusiasm for military preparations pervaded a city, women were certainly not excluded. Plutarch's Hellenistic source on the life of the Achaian general Philopoimen describes the frantic preparations for war in the Achaian cities, in which women played their part (Plut., *Philop.* 9.5–6):

> ... in the stadia colts were being broken in and young men were learning the use of heavy armor, and in the hands of women there were helmets and plumes for dyeing, and horsemen's tunics or soldier's cloaks for embroidering. The sight of this increased men's courage, called forth their energies and made them venturesome and ready to incur dangers.
>
> (trans. Beston 2000: 320)

The highest position in Hellenistic society was occupied by the "warrior-kings," but several queens and mistresses directly instigated wars, indirectly caused them, or actively participated in them by leading armies (Loman 2004: 45–8). For instance, Olympias, Alexander's mother, had an ominous part in the Wars of the Successors, allying herself with Polyperchon and arranging the murder of another very energetic queen, Eurydike, granddaughter of Philip II and wife of Alexander's brother, King Philip III Arrhidaios. She was finally killed by Kassandros after her defeat. Arsinoe Philadelphos, daughter of Ptolemy I and Berenike, had a far more adventurous and succesful life. She first married King Lysimachos, but when she arranged for the assassination of his son Agathokles, who was very popular in Asia Minor, she caused a war in this part of Lysimachos' kingdom (283/2). Agathokles' widow Lysandra (Arsinoe's half-sister) sought refuge, together with her brother Ptolemaios Keraunos, in Seleukos' court, and instigated Seleukos' campaign against Lysimachos. This war ended with the defeat and death of Lysimachos at Kouropedion (281 BC). Ptolemaios Keraunos murdered Seleukos immediately after the battle, but Arsinoe managed to escape to Egypt in 279, where she married her brother, Ptolemy II. She was the driving force behind his policy to create a Greek alliance against King Antigonos Gonatas, which led to the Chremonidean War (268–261 BC).

One of the greatest "world wars" of the Hellenistic Age is named after another Hellenistic queen. Laodike was divorced by Antiochos II when Ptolemy II offered him his daughter Berenike as his wife. The death of Ptolemy II (246 BC) brought the two kingdoms back to the warpath. In unclear conditions, and after Ptolemy III had already started operations against Antiochos II, the Seleukid king left Berenike in the capital and joined his ex-wife in Ephesos, where he died. It is quite possible that, despite their reconciliation, Laodike murdered him. From that point onwards the war became "her" war. She arranged for the murder of Berenike and her son, and made her own son, Seleukos (II), king. The war then continued until 241 BC and ended with the defeat of the Seleukids.

To the Hellenistic queens who caused wars (and civil wars) through their actions and intrigues, one may add Deidameia, Pyrrhos' daughter, Apama of Kyrene, Kleopatra II (Ptolemy VI's widow), and her daughter Kleopatra Thea, the wife of the Seleukid King Demetrios II. Of course, none of them is a match for the last Hellenistic queen, Kleopatra VII, who was also present on the battlefield. If only she hadn't been! Her ships abandoned Mark Antony at a crucial point during the sea battle at Actium and sealed the fate of the last Hellenistic kingdom.

These queens usually acted in an underhand manner; they were neither Amazons nor warrior-princesses, but conspirators in, and instigators of, murder. Their wars were family matters, and they were driven by personal motives of hate, envy, revenge, love, and care for their children. These are to a great extent clichés generated by the exclusion of women, even of queens, from public life. The most important asset of those who had to live in the shadow of men was not heroism in an open conflict, but cunning intelligence. In the imagination of the Greeks, heroic death in battle was primarily a virtue of barbarian women: the Amazons of myth. If in the historical narratives – written by men – women were killed during the sack of a city, they were killed by their own men, who destroyed all their other possessions as well, so that nothing would be left for the enemy to capture, as in the case of Abydos and Xanthos (see chapter 10, section 2). In their death, women were passive – or rather, they were portrayed as passive. However, the grave monument in Messene (see above) seems to tell a different story, and one of Anyte's poems glorifies three women of Miletos who committed suicide when attacked by the Galatians (Loman 2004: 43).

How could the Greeks reconcile themselves with the active role of women in war? We are told, for example, that during the street fights in an Akarnanian city, the women so closely embraced the defeated men that the victorious Aitolians had to kill them, as they were unable to drag them away from their fathers, brothers, and husbands. When King Nikokles of Paphos was forced by Ptolemy I to commit suicide together with all his brothers, his wife Axiothea persuaded all the female family members to kill themselves as well (310 BC). In the Laodikeian War, most of the female attendants of Queen Berenike died defending her.

6.4. Anonymous Victims

Around 220 BC the Knossians attacked the city of Lyttos, which had been left defenseless, since the armed men were participating in a campaign. As Polybios reports (4.54) the city was taken and destroyed completely, and the women and children were taken captive. Their fate is unknown. It is the fate of their men that Polybios describes in detail. They marched to the city of Lappa, about 100 kilometers as the crow flies, and continued from there the war against Knossos. A few years later they founded their city again. Conceivably, the captured women may have been returned to Lyttos by the Knossians when the war ended, but only if they had not already been sold as slaves abroad.

This incident of Cretan history confronts us with the basic features of mobility during wartime (Chaniotis 2004a): it is massive, impersonal, involuntary, and, above all, gendered. There is an enormous difference between the Lyttian warriors who marched through enemy territory, continued the war, and returned to their destroyed city and rebuilt it, and the Lyttian women, who were taken prisoner and disappeared in the brutal anonymity of history.

We encounter such anonymity elsewhere. From a letter of the Cretan city of Axos we learn about the history of Eraton, a citizen of Axos, and his son (*Syll.*³ 622 B = *I.Cret.* II v 19): Eraton had come as a mercenary to Cyprus, where he married a woman; her name is not given. This anonymous woman gave birth to two sons, Epikles and Euagoras. After Eraton's death in Cyprus, his widow and his older son, Epikles, were captured (probably by pirates). Epikles was sold as a slave in the Aitolian city of Amphissa, where he was somehow able to pay the necessary ransom, was liberated, settled in Amphissa and took a wife (again of unknown name and origin); his mother's fate is not mentioned.

There are many such stories of female anonymity in a world dominated by wars fought by men. However, it would be misleading to interpret such documents as evidence for a lack of interest in the fate of female captives. Female anonymity should be seen in context: in the first instance, Polybios, as a historian of war, was interested in military operations; in the second case, the Axian magistrates were interested in proving the status of a fellow citizen, and not in narrating a moving story of adventure and loss. But still, these two texts show to what extent war and citizenship were male issues, and this is not irrelevant for the social conditions of Hellenistic women. A late third-century inscription from Aigiale (on the island of Amorgos) contains an honorary decree for two courageous citizens (*IG* XII.7 386 = Bielman 1994: no. 38): "During the night pirates landed in our territory and virgins and [married] women and other persons, both free and slaves, were captured – a total of more than thirty persons." This text also stresses legal status: unmarried and married women, free and slaves. The text goes on to narrate how the efforts of two citizens led to the liberation of the prisoners. It is one of many inscriptions that concern themselves with captivity and with the efforts of Hellenistic cities to liberate captured people, the victims of enemies and pirates. These texts show how much legal status mattered, but also that the efforts of communities to liberate captives were equally intense, whether the people concerned were men or women, citizens or citizens' property (Bielman 1994: 236–7, 324–5; Ducrey 1999: 283–8).

Two important factors determined the fate of captives in general, and of women in captivity: status and the cause of their captivity (Chaniotis 2004a). The women and children who were carried away from sacked and destroyed cities to be sold in distant places were usually lost for ever (see Ducrey 1999: 80–92). This anonymity of captivity is opposed to the eponymous victims of pirates who had the hope of being ransomed, especially when they were kept in places where they could be recognized (or make themselves recognized) by private individuals. The realistic expectation of a ransom for people of wealth and high social status meant that their captors were more likely to desire the ransom than the captive, and that such a ransom would exceed any amount they were likely to receive for such a captive were they sold as a slave (see e.g., *IG* IX.4 1054 + a; *IG* XII.7 386 = Bielman 1994: nos. 32 and 38). References to ransom negotiations suggest that the captives' cities received lists with the numbers and names of the persons that had to be ransomed. Private initiative was extremely important for the safe return of captives; the foreigners who were honored by a city for saving its citizens were usually people who already had close contacts with the city and its citizens, were engaged in trade, or had even inherited specific relations from their forefathers.

We observe another form of female anonymity when we take war dead into consideration. The names of soldiers were often inscribed on their graves, and some were honored with funerary epigrams that praised them for their heroic death in defense of their homeland. Eponymous heroic deaths are a privilege of women in Greek myths and legends – the beautiful kings' daughters who sacrifice themselves to save their cities – or of women of royal status and their entourage (see chapter 6.3), but in real Hellenistic wars the women who lost their lives or were raped during the sack of cities are as anonymous as the mothers and widows of the dead warriors.

It may seem surprising that the social problems we would expect continual war and the consequent production of widows and orphans to have caused are hardly reflected by our sources. For example, Philon of Byzantion recommends the civic authorities of cities under siege not to neglect the orphans and widows of mercenaries (C 47, ed. Garlan 1974: 312). Again, as in other cases of female victims of war, the question of status is of fundamental importance. Most warriors were men of some means (see chapter 2), and consequently the widows of war dead usually belonged to the better-off families and were taken care by their next of kin. In the case of the widows of mercenaries, Philon recommended that they should be looked after in order to increase the loyalty of other mercenary families – especially in besieged cities (Philon 5.94.26–9 ed. Schoene; Pomeroy 1984: 102).

A photograph published in the *International Herald Tribune* (4 January 2001) shows a Lebanese woman crying in despair after Israeli shelling in a disputed area. She is not crying for the destruction of a house or the death of a relative, but for the killing of her goats. Women in the Hellenistic world were also engaged in agricultural activities, and the destruction caused by wars to crops, livestock, olives, and gardens (see chapter 7, section 2) must have affected them dramatically. I know of no source which addresses this problem, and I can only attribute this to the anonymity of female suffering in the Hellenistic Age.

Further Reading

6.1. War and Masculinity. *War and masculinity in Hellenistic historians*: Beston 2000: 316–17. *The social and public roles of Hellenistic women*: van Bremen 1996; cf. Vatin 1970; Pomeroy 1984.

6.2. In the Shadow of Soldiers: Women in Garrisons and Forts. *Soldiers' wives*: Pomeroy 1984: 98–124. *Marriage in the Hellenistic period*: Vérilhac and Vial 1998; cf. Pomeroy 1984: 83–98. *Mixed marriages in garrisoned sites*: Chaniotis 2002. *Cretan migration to Miletos*: Launey 1987: 660–4; Brulé 1990: 238–42; Herrmann 1997: 160–4. *Epitaphs of mercenaries' relatives*: e.g., *SGO* IV 17/01/07 (Cretan from Rhaukos in Kibyra). *Wives of soldiers in Egypt*: Pomeroy 1984: 98–124. *Dryton and his family*: Winnicki 1972; Mélèze-Modrzejewski 1984; Scholl 1988.

6.3. Spectators, Judges, and Defenders: Women's Share of War. *Spartan women*: Cartledge and Spawforth 1989; Mossé 1991. *Women in battle*: Schaps 1982; Whitehead 1990: 103, 205–6 (on Aineias the Tactician); Barry 1996; Mauritsch 2003: 316–19 (in Polybios); Loman 2004. *Argive women and the festival of the Hybristika*: Graf 1984; Chaniotis 1991a: 137–8. *Financial contributions by women*: Migeotte 1992: 371–6; Bielman 2002: 92–5, 133–41, 158–60. *Hellenistic queens and war*: Pomeroy 1984: 20; Loman 2004: 45–8; e.g., Olympias: Carney 1987, 2000: 138–44; Arsinoe II: Hauben 1983; Hazzard 2000: 81–100; Laodike: Holleaux 1942: 281–310. Deidameia: Polyainos, *Strategemata* 8.52. *Suicide of women in the face of defeat*: Loman 2004: 42–4; *Greek Anthology* 7.492 (Anyte), 7.493 (women kill themselves during the sack of Korinthos); Polyainos, *Strategemata* 8.69 (Akarnanian women); *Strategemata* 8.48; Diod. 20.21.2 (Axiothea); *Strategemata* 8.50 (Berenike's slaves); cf. *SEG* XXXIV 1271 (suicide of a girl, captured by brigands, third century AD).

6.4. Anonymous Victims. *Enslavement of women*: Schaps 1982: 202–6; e.g., Plut., *Aratos* 31–2; Bagnall and Derow 2004: no. 34; *Anth. Gr.* 7.368.

7

THE COST AND PROFIT OF WAR:
ECONOMIC ASPECTS OF
HELLENISTIC WARFARE

7.1. The Budget of War: Fiscal Aspects of Hellenistic Warfare

Direct income taxes were unknown in most Hellenistic cities. Contemporary conservative politicians may rejoice at hearing this, but not so fast. There were many indirect ways for communities to get funds from wealthy – and less wealthy – citizens and foreigners. The main revenues of cities were customs duties for imports and exports, revenues from the leasing of public land or other communal resources (e.g., fees for fishing permits), fines payable to the city's treasury, and occasionally war booty. Regular expenses (e.g., for the upkeep of buildings, for religious activities, for the gymnasium, for festivals and athletic contests) were often imposed on the wealthier citizens in the form of "liturgies": the financial responsibility for a particular public work or activity was assigned to a wealthy citizen.

An inscription from Priene (*I.Priene* 174; Sokolowski 1955: no. 37, second century BC), gives an impression of the multitide of such liturgies in a medium-sized city. The text concerns the sale of the priesthood of Dionysos; the purchaser, who would have the office of the priest for life, was freed from a series of liturgies depending on the amount he was willing to pay (12,000, 6,000 drachmas, or less). The long list of liturgies includes expenses for the organization of torch races and athletic contests, for the raising of horses (perhaps for war), for the funding of a sacred embassy, for the administration of the gymnasium, along with responsibility for triremes (*trierarchia*). This list is of course anything but complete.

Only two of the liturgies mentioned in the inscription from Priene seem to concern military matters (horses and warships); the exemption from irregular poll taxes (*ateleia somatos*), usually imposed upon citizens in times of war, is explicitly excluded from these privileges (see Gauthier 1991). The public expenses of a community were complex and varied; only a few items in the annual budget can be regarded as war expenses, but these few tended to absorb a large percentage of the total public purse (Migeotte 2000b; de

Callataÿ 2000) – certainly a larger percentage than any "hawk" in a contemporary government would ever dream of achieving. This section focuses on the budget for war in Hellenistic cities. The situation in monarchies, which could finance their military organization and expeditions from direct tribute and the royal treasury, was very different, and the challenges were far more complex. The fiscal system of the Ptolemies of Egypt enabled them, for example, to maintain specialized troops for the control of the desert frontier and the routes of the caravans (Hennig 2003) in a way which would have been impossible in any city.

Substantial amounts were spent by civic communities to pay soldiers for their service in campaigns, on patrol duties (*hypaithroi, kryptoi, paraphylakitai, periploi, orophylakes*), and in forts. Such soldiers included citizens and mercenaries, although the latter were more often employed by kings than by civic communities (see chapter 5, section 3). The information on the payment of citizen troops is rather limited. We do know that each of the 20 soldiers serving in the garrison which the city of Teos established in the citadel of Kyrbissos (*SEG* XXVI 1306; Robert and Robert 1976) received the more or less standard *per diem* payment of one drachma. The salary of the commander amounted to four drachmas, and the annual expenses of Teos for manning just this one fort amounted 8,760 drachmas. More than 35,000 drachmas were collected by the Athenians in 243 BC, in order to fund troops to protect the transportation of the agricultural products of Attika to the city (Migeotte 1992: 340–1). If we estimate wages and provisions of two drachmas for each soldier *per diem*, with this amount the Athenians could pay a substantial troop of 200 men for three months.

During campaigns, the cities were also obliged to supply the soldiers with provisions, and the duty of a good commander was to seek out cheap grain. During the wars of the late third century BC, first against the Cretans and then against Philip V, Kos organized public subscriptions for its defense. The surviving lists of donors give the names of men who committed themselves to providing wages for soldiers (*misthophora*) and provisions for troops (*siteresion*) for two, four, or six months, and sometimes for a whole year (*PH* 10, D lines 64–5; *IscrCos* ED 212; Migeotte 2000a: 167–9).

In most cities, citizens were expected to supply their own weapons. However, extraordinary situations might oblige a city to call on the less well off and provide them with weapons (a shield, a lance or sword, and a helmet). Sometimes weapons would be donated; otherwise they had to be obtained using public funds (e.g., *Syll.*[3] 569, lines 31–2).

The construction and repair of fortification walls was one of the heaviest burdens on the public finances (Maier 1961: 55–68; Baker 2000a). For the enlargement of thir city walls, the Kolophonians collected, via private contributions, more than 200,000 drachmas (Migeotte 1992: 337). It has been estimated that the construction of a tower alone cost more than 20,000 drachmas (Maier 1961: 66; Migeotte 1992: 106, n. 11; see also Ducrey

1985: 135). In some cities (e.g., Athens, Miletos) funds for "the construction of walls" (*teichopoika*) were placed under the responsibility of commissions (*teichopoioi*, etc.; see chapter 2, section 5). In Miletos, these funds were occasionally used for other purposes, and from this we may infer that they were collected as a reserve for unexpected expenses, rather than collected for a specific project (*Milet* I.3 139, lines 56–7; 146, lines 46–50).

Fortifications continued to cost money even after they had been constructed. Damage was caused not only by enemy artillery or earthquakes, but in some cases by the native population. For example, in Selymbria, the generals punished someone either for stealing or for illegally using timber from a fortification and a watch tower (*I.Byzantion* S 3).

Most cities do not seem to have had regular funds for city walls and, unable to cope on their own with the enormous expense of maintaining existing fortifications and building new ones, they either received loans from citizens and foreigners, or let their hopes rest upon donations from friends, most often from kings (Maier 1961: 60–6; Migeotte 1984: chapter 4.3). In the early third century BC, Oropos undertook a dramatic effort to procure money for the construction of a city wall and decided to use the entire public purse for the building works and the repayment of debts (*SEG* XVI 295; *I.Oropos* 302; Maier 1961: 118, no. 26 *bis*). A letter sent by the inhabitants of Kytenion, a small polis in Doris in central Greece, to Xanthos in Asia Minor, eloquently describes the dimensions of the problem in the case of this small community (206 BC):

> it so occurred that at the time when Antigonos [Doson] invaded Phokis [228 BC] part of the walls of all our cities had collapsed because of the earthquakes and the young men had gone to defend the sanctuary of Apollo in Delphi; when the king came to Doris, he destroyed the walls of all our cities and burned the houses; we now implore you to remember the ancestry that exists between us and you and not allow the greatest of the cities in Metropolis ["the mother city"], Kytenion, to vanish, but help us in the construction of walls for our city, as best as you think you can help.
>
> (*SEG* XXXVIII 1476, lines 93–104)

The Kytenians soon found that they were not the only community in such a terrible situation. The Xanthians gave them the very modest amount of 500 drachmas (the amount given by many private donors in Kos), but in order to provide this they had to take out a loan themselves. In their letter they explain at length that their situation is not much better than that of Kytenion, as ever due to the expense of war (lines 49–57):

> if the public finances had not been in a weak state, we would have demonstrated our benevolence, surpassing all the others in benefaction; however, not only have we spent the entire public money and taken many loans, but because of a decree regulating the financial administration it is also impossible

to impose upon the citizens any additional requisition for a period of nine years; and the wealthiest of the citizens have recently made great extraordinary contributions due to the calamities that have occurred.

Given that 20,000 drachmas were needed for the construction of a single tower, the Kytenians did not make a great progress in their endeavor with the donation of the Xanthians.

Some cities were proud of their city walls, others of their fleet, which was an equally costly contribution to their defense. Because of the limited space for provisions on board a ship, long naval operations away from land were not possible, and consequently the basic aim of Hellenistic naval warfare was not to control the sea, but to avert attacks and raids by enemy or pirate ships against merchant ships or coastal sites. Such a limited radius of action obliged a city with maritime interests to maintain harbors, naval bases, and headquarters with the necessary infrastructure for the logistical support of the ships – i.e., to provide materials, food, and manpower (Gabrielsen 2001a: 73–6). Locations offering such facilities were frequently subjugated, and both Antigonid Macedonia (Buraselis 1982) and Ptolemaic Egypt (Bagnall 1976) were extremely active in the subjugation of coastal towns on the islands (especially in Euboia, Thera, Samothrake, Samos, and Cyprus, in part also in Crete), and along the coast of Asia Minor and Syria-Palestine. This subjugation took different forms, from indirect control by means of an alliance to direct control through the establishment of a garrison.

A recognizable increase in the number of coastal sites in Hellenistic Crete is also connected with the maritime interests of many Cretan cities, which were actively involved in piracy and trade with booty (especially with slaves, see section 7.3). Important cities, such as Gortyn, Lyttos, and Knossos, acquired harbors and naval bases, either through conquest, by founding harbors, or by incorporating independent communities by means of inter-state agreements (*sympolity*). Alternatively, they might reduce a previously free city to the status of a dependent community. Praisos, for example, conquered the coastal cities of Setaia and Stalai and later gave them certain privileges as an exchange for naval services offered by these dependent communities (Chaniotis 1996a: nos. 64–5).

The expenses connected with the construction and maintainance of an ancient warship were manifold and high, ranging from iron and lead for the metal parts, to timber and sail-cloth, to tow, pitch and tar (Morrison and Coates 1994; Gabrielsen 2001a: 81). In one instance (ca. 200 BC) it is reported that the daily cost of keeping a trireme in commission was 330 drachmas – which corresponds to the annual salary of a mercenary soldier – but unfortunately we do not know whether this amount corresponds to the avarage, is exceptionally high, or extremely low (Gabrielsen 2001a: 75). The main problem of financing a fleet was the constant flow of resources for manning and maintaining the ships (see below).

To the more or less regular expenses (wages and provisions for soldiers, funds for the fleet and the city walls) one should add the expenses incurred during a war: employing public doctors for the wounded (see chapter 5, section 6), burying the dead, and ransoming war prisoners or the victims of pirates. These costs were also substantial, and a community rejoiced whenever a benefactor volunteered to cover them. The Athenian benefactor Philippides (see chapter 2, section 6; *IG* II^2 657) had the Athenian citizens who were killed in the Hellespont buried at his own expense (283/2 BC); he also gave clothes and supplies to 100 prisoners, enabling them to return home. An honorary decree for the Athenian general Epichares praises him for making a deal with pirates so that the citizens who had been captured were freed on a payment of 120 drachmas each (an amount that corresponds to four months' wages for a mercenary soldier). The mention of the amount in the context of praise suggests that this was a bargain (*SEG* XXIV 154; Austin 1981: no. 50; Bielman 1994: no. 24, p. 99; Ducrey 1999: 252; see also below). More than 20 talents (120,000 drachmas) were needed in 229 BC to liberate the Athenians who had been captured by Aitolian raiders during the War of Demetrios and sold in Crete (*IG* II^2 844; Bielman 1994: no. 31). When Teos (Ionia) was attacked in the late third century by pirates (possibly Cretan), who occupied part of the territory and seized women and children, the city was able to ransom the captives only after a dramatic appeal to the citizens to lend money. The situation was so desperate that, as a fragmentary section of the relevant inscription implies, all precious objects (gold and silver goblets, clothes embroidered with gold and purple) had to be registered (*SEG* XLIV 949; Sahin 1994; Merkelbach 2000).

The range of expenses related to warfare, which exhausted the budget of cities, does not end here. Extraordinary conditions confronted many a city with extraordinary burdens. In the early third century, cities in Asia Minor had to pay a contribution to a royal war fund established by Antiochos I for the war against the Galatians (e.g., *I. Erythrai* 30–1). Athens had to pay the enormous amount of 150 talents (900,000 drachmas) in order to get rid of the Macedonian garrison in 229 BC; in order to collect this amount the Athenians received loans from citizens, foreigners, and Boiotian cities (Feyel 1942a: 19–37; Maier 1959: 79; Habicht 1982: 79–93).

For a city, a foreign attack and a long siege not only meant the temporary loss of its countryside with all it resources (see section 7.2), but also the substantial destruction of the urban center, especially as artillery devices became increasingly effective. After the siege of Rhodes by Demetrios the Besieger (304 BC), the Rhodians had to rebuilt parts of the city wall that had collapsed and many other buildings that had been destroyed, including the theater (Diod. 20.100.4). Battles often took place in the inhabited areas of a city, for example in Sikyon (302 BC), when Demetrios forced his way inside the fortifications and occupied the area between the citadel and the private houses (Diod. 20.102.2).

When a city was actually taken (*dorialotos*) – and this occurred quite often – the damage was more substantial. An inscription from Xanthos refers to the burning of the houses in Kytenion, and this was the fate of many Hellenistic cities. Some were rebuilt (e.g., Mantineia, Lyttos on Crete, Aphrodisias in Karia, Xanthos in Lykia), but others vanished for ever.

In order to solve the budgetary problems caused by the preparation for war (cf. *IG* II² 505; Maier 1959: no. 13, lines 29–30: *paraskeue tou polemou*) and by warfare itself, the Hellenistic cities could not rely on their regular revenues and the liturgies. This is particularly evident in terms of fortifications and fleets, for which a regular flow of resources was not guaranteed (Gabrielsen 2001a). Sometimes we are informed about contributions for military purposes (*tele*) only when someone is exempted from them (e.g., *SEG* XXVI 1334: *ateles . . . [phy]la[kes? s]trateias*). For the funding of a fleet, many cities introduced the liturgy of *trierarchy* (providing the funds for a trireme; e.g., *RC* 3, section 9; Bagnall and Derow 2004: no. 7). In the case of Rhodes, the trierarch was not obliged to command the ship he funded, but was substituted by a captain (*epiplous*). The Rhodian state also put private ships to its service in return for a fixed sum of money (Gabrielsen 2001a: 81–3).

Extraordinary taxes (*eisphorai*) were imposed from time to time, but more often, citizens and foreigners, men and women, were invited to contribute to voluntary subscriptions (*epidoseis*), which provided the funds for all kinds of projects, from the organization of festivals, the purchase of grain, the delivery of olive oil to a gymnasium, the celebration of a banquet, to the creation of a library (Migeotte 1992; 2000b: 164–6). However, defense expenses always had the lion's share. Sometimes the aim is described in general terms as the "protection of the city" (*phylake tes poleos*) or the "salvation of the city" (*soteria tes poleos*), but in most cases a specific project is explicitly stated: the protection of the agricultural produce of Attika during a war (Migeotte 1992: no. 17); the fortification of the harbor of Zea (no. 18); the construction or reconstruction of fortifications in Troizen (no. 21), Megalopolis (nos. 23–4), Rhodes (no. 37), Naxos (no. 54), Ioulis in Keos (no. 56), Chios (no. 60), Erythrai (no. 68), and Kolophon (no. 69); and of course garrison duty (*SEG* XXVI 1817, lines 22–3: *eis tan paraphylakan tes polios* during a war in Arsinoe/Tokra). The amounts varied from a few drachmas, which represent the earnings of a worker in roughly ten days (e.g., no. 56: mostly 5–20 drachmas), to extremely high amounts (e.g., more than 20,000 drachmas in no. 37; 1,000–7,000 drachmas in no. 50).

It does not come as a surprise to a modern reader that a frequent solution to such budgetary problems was to take a loan (Migeotte 1984). Argos, for example, received a loan of 100 talents (600,000 drachmas) from Rhodes for repairs of fortifications and additional cavalry (Maier 1959: no. 33, ca. 300–250 BC). The Rhodians did not demand interest, and this explains why we are informed about this loan: the Rhodians were honored for this extraordinary service to Argos. Most cities had great difficulty finding lenders, and in repaying the resulting debts. When obliged to offer securities against loans, cities sometimes had no other choice than to mortgage their entire territory (Hennig 1995). A decree of Krannon in Thessaly (ca. 179–142 BC) describes the state of the public finances: "the city is in numerous debts because of the war that it had to endure, and these debts are dragged about already for many years" (Migeotte 1992: no. 34). Krannon had been conquered by Antiochos III in 191 BC and was later occupied by the Romans; during the Third Macedonian War, agricultural production was taken over by Roman troops (171 BC). With a subscription and private donations, the city hoped to repay its debts. In some cases the ultimate solution was to appeal for donations from wealthy citizens or kings (see chapter 4, section 3).

The lack of sufficient representative material on Hellenistic war budgets makes quantitative studies in this area meaningless. Nevertheless, the existing sources give us an impressive picture of the variety of expenses a Hellenistic community had to cover due to wars. These high costs on the one hand and fiscal weakness on the other made Hellenistic cities increasingly dependent either on local benefactors (see chapter 2, sections 4, 6) or on monarchs (see chapter 4, section 3). Any contribution was welcome, even that of an anonymous general in Athens who was honored for feeding the watchdogs in Rhamnous (SEG XLI 76, third century; cf. SEG XXIV 154, lines 14–15).

7.2. War and Agriculture

One of the longest and more detailed honorary decrees of the Hellenistic period is the Athenian decree honoring Kallias of Sphettos (see chapter 3, section 2). One of his services during a war against Demetrios the Besieger (287 BC) was an initiative to protect the farmers: "leading out into the countryside the soldiers who were following him, he protected the gathering of the grain, making every effort to ensure that as much grain as possible should be brought into the city" (SEG XXVIII 60, lines 23–7; Austin 1981: no. 44).

Twenty years later, during the Chremonidean War, general Epichares offered similar services to the coastal population of Attika, and these are described in detail in an honorary decree:

> He gathered in the crops and fruits within a range of thirty stadia [ca. 5 km] ... set up covered silos [?] in the land, kept guard himself with the soldiers at the look-outs to enable the farmers to gather in their crops safely; and he also protected the vines as far as he was master of the land; and he constructed at his private expense a portico to provide shelter for all in any emergency, and to make it possible for help to come quickly ...
>
> (SEG XXIV 154; trans. Austin 1981: no. 50)

Many other inscriptions show that the collection, transportation, and safe storage of agricultural products and the protection of farmers was a major concern of Hellenistic Athens. More than 35,000 drachmas in donations were collected by the Athenians in 243 BC, in order to fund troops that would protect the transportation of agricultural products to the city (see section 7.1). One of the central functions of forts and towers in the countryside was the protection of agricultural production and produce, and of other resources (Ma 2000c: 342–3; see also Pritchett 1991: 352–8).

The countryside and its economic activities were the greatest victims of wars (Harvey 1986; Foxhall 1993; Chandezon 1999 and 2000). The countryside was the place where battles and skirmishes usually took place; it fed invading armies; it was abandoned by its population in times of threat; and it was intentionally devastated by the enemy, not as an act of revenge, but as a planned destruction of the most important economic resource of the opponent. The season of war, from late spring to late summer, was the same period in which the harvest of crops took place, the grapes ripened in the vineyards, and the olive trees needed care. During a war, the manpower needed for agricultural activities was lacking, either because the men had to fight, defending their land or devastating the land of a neighbor, or because they sought security behind the city walls. In additoin, agricultural slave labor may have had an opportunity to escape.

Even if we take into consideration the exaggerations of ancient sources – in their rhetoric of praise, complaint, and pity – the financial and fiscal misery that is often lamented was not imaginary. One of its most serious causes was the destructive effect of warfare on farming and pastoral activities. A characteristic example is provided by the city of Kios in Asia Minor. As a colony of Miletos, Kios had the religious obligation to dedicate a (silver) bowl to Apollo of Didyma every year, as a "first-fruit offering." In the late third century BC, Kios was unable to fulfill this act of piety for several years, presenting as an excuse the wars which had devastated its territory, and expenses caused by them. The Kians asked Miletos to waive as many of the owed bowls as possible. The response of Miletos is extremely telling:

> If we had not suffered ourselves because of the wars and the loss of the harvest and if it was not impossible for the people to waive the first-fruit offerings on which the god [Apollo] has a claim, since the relevant law forbids this, the people would have done everything in their power to accept the request of the Kians in this matter; but now the people allows to deliver the bowls, which they owe, when this seems appropriate to them.
> (*Milet* I.3 141; Günther 1971: 125–7; Herrmann 1997: 175–6)

The winner in the conflict between rituals and material needs was, on this occasion, the ritual, but this was by no means always the case, and religious duties were often neglected because of fiscal difficulties (e.g., *I.Beroia* 2 =

SEG XLVII 891). Analogous complaints abound in the Hellenistic period. The honorary decree for Menas of Sestos (late second century) presents a very similar picture to that in Miletos and Kios a century earlier:

> when he was invited a second time to act as supervisor of the gymnasium, he accepted this duty in difficult circumstances; for we had been worn out for many years because of the incursions of the Thracians and the wars which were engulfing the city, in the course of which everything in the fields had been carried off, most of the land was not sown, and the dearth of crops which recurred continuously reduced the people publicly and every individual citizen privately to penury, and Menas was one of the many to be afflicted; but he put aside all this, as he could observe that the people was grateful and knew how to honor good men, and he surpassed himself in the expenses he incurred and in his zeal; for when he entered office on new year he celebrated sacrifices for Hermes and Herakles, the gods consecrated in the gymnasium . . .
>
> (*OGIS* 339, lines 54–64; trans. Austin 1981: no. 215)

References to a decline of the productivity of land because of wars are found in literary and documentary sources throughout the Hellenistic period and in every region. The following selection of incidents and sources will give an idea of the variety and complexity of the problems.

An invading army destroyed the corn, burned the fields and the farms, and stole the gathered surplus, which was needed as fodder for the horses and the draft animals (see *SEG* XXIX 1516). To mention but a few examples, the territory of Argos was devastated by Kleomenes III in 223 BC (Polyb. 2.64), that of Alabanda by the army of Philip V in 201–200 BC (Polyb. 16.24.8), and in the same year the Athenian countryside faced raids by the Akarnanians and the Macedonians (Polyb. 16.27.1; Livy 31.14.9–10). During a dispute between Magnesia and Priene in the early second century, claims were made that buildings (*stegna*, farms or silos) were burned down and livestock stolen (*I.Magnesia* 93 III).

Prohibitions presuppose the practices they intend to limit. We therefore have to assume that the advice given by tacticians to generals not to allow their soldiers to devastate the fields of the enemy only confirms that this was often the case. Philon of Byzantion (see chapter 5, section 7) gave generals the advice to prevent their soldiers from burning the fields or taking the fodder of a besieged city, in order to encourage the population to capitulate while their fields were still intact. He also advised that the generals should ensure that agricultural produce was distributed in an orderly manner to the units of the invading army (D 6–7, ed. Garlan 1974: 316, 394). Similar prohibitions (taking fodder, burning corn, destroying vineyards on enemy territory) are also included in a military regulation of a Macedonian king in Amphipolis (Hatzopoulos 2001: 161–4, no. 3 B II 15–18). Only if a siege proved to be unsuccessful did Philon recommend that the fields be destroyed (D 87 and 90–1, ed. Garlan 1974: 325).

The destructive effect of wars on agriculture was to some extent limited by the fact that fragmented holdings were the norm in ancient Greece – and this applies to the Hellenistic period as well – especially in cities with a large territory (Foxhall 1993: 136–8). A landowner usually owned rather small fields, widely distributed over the territory; therefore, an invasion usually affected the holdings of a particular area, causing many farmers to lose part of their produce, but not all of it, since they would normally have some property in another area. It has also been observed (Hanson 1983; Foxhall 1993: 138–42) that the burning of grain on a large scale is not very easy, and that the destruction of other crops (e.g., olive trees, which are usually on hills) requires a lot of effort. But even if "attacks on crops would almost never actually threaten a city's food supply," unless they were repeated and intensive (Foxhall 1993: 141–2), the destruction of crops should not be considered in isolation, but in combination with other "collateral damage," in particular damage to agricultural infrastructure and manpower.

To begin with, the invading army needed to be fed, and since the possibilities for carrying food during a campaign were limited, these troops subsisted on the surplus of the invaded state. War meant the presence of an additional number of men and animals that did not contribute to the economy, but had to be fed instead by the production of others. The inhabitants of Krannon, for example, fed Roman troops and were afterwards left financially ruined (Livy 42.64–5; Migeotte 1992: no. 34), and Antiochos III ravaged the territory of Pergamon in 190 BC, in order to supply his troops (Polyb. 21.10.14). Allies and mercenaries were no less of a burden for a city in times of war. Treaties of alliance and agreements that concern the service of mercenaries include clauses according to which the state that invited the allies or hired the mercenaries was responsible for providing them with food. A contract for the leasing of a piece of land in Attika mentions "an invasion of enemies or the camping of friendly troops" as possible troubles in its exploitation (*IG* II² 1241, lines 15–16: *polemion eisboles kai philiou stratopedou*; cf. Launey 1987: 692). This fear was not purely imaginary. If the Athenian ephebes of 107/6 BC were honored for patrolling the Athenian border without causing any harm to the farmers (*IG* II² 1011, lines 15–16), it is clear that damage to the fields by a city's own troops was not unusual (cf. Fernández Nieto 1997: 226–7).

The settlements of the countryside also had to face the burden of the billeting of soldiers. When a Hellenistic king awarded a community near Termessos (or Termessos herself) a temporary exemption from the burden of billeting (*epistathmeia*) for ten years, he used the verb *parenochlein* (*oudeis parenochlesei*, "no one will be for you the cause of great annoyance"; *SEG* XXIX 1516, early second century). Military leaders knew well how much damage their troops caused. During the Chremonidean War allied troops served in Attika, in Rhamnous among other places. The Athenian general Epichares was praised by the population because he constructed camp installations (*stegai*), thus alleviating the citizens and forcing no one to offer billeting (*SEG* XXIV 154 = Austin 1981: no. 50). However, such foresight and care was rather unusual. One of the rulings of Antiochos III concerns these problems in Skythopolis/Bethshean in Palaestine (*SEG* XXIX 1613, ca. 199–195 BC): the king forbade billeting and abuses on the part of the soldiers, which damaged the land and the farmers, and imposed heavy penalties for such acts. But, interestingly enough, this particular land happened to belong to his general, Ptolemy. One can infer that ordinary farmers in other places could not count on similar beneficence.

Wars also caused loss of manpower and disrupted regular cultivation, although massacres of the population of sacked cities seem to have been less common in Hellenistic Greece than during the Peloponnesian War (see the list in Pritchett 1991: 218–19; see also Ducrey 1999: 56–74). During an attack against the Macedonian garrison in Mounychia in 286 BC (?), 420 Athenians lost their lives (Polyainos, *Strategemata* 5.17; Paus. 1.29.10); if they were citizens, this may correspond with 2 per cent of the citizen body. Around 219 BC, the city of Larisa lacked manpower "because of the wars" and the fields were not fully cultivated (*Syll.*[3] 543; Austin 1981: no. 60; Bagnall and Derow 2004: no. 32). In addition to the casualties of battles, slaves and free persons were frequently captured in the countryside (see section 7.3), and when they were ransomed or freed (e.g., Bielman 1994: nos. 16, 22, 24–5; *Syll.*[3] 588; Ager 1996: no. 109) they were a financial burden. If they were sold abroad, as frequently happened (especially in the wars against the Romans), they were lost for ever. If we can trust the numbers given by Plutarch; (*Kleomenes* 18.3), 50,000 *perioikoi* (i.e., free, non-citizen inhabitants of Lakonia) were enslaved by the Aitolians during a single campaign in 240 BC. A decree of Hyettos (ca. 150 BC) describes the situation in Boiotia in a turbulent period: "great deeds of injustice occur in the countryside, because due to the arrival of a mob, which has come with the purpose of stealing and seizing the property of others, farms are devastated, murders take place as well as seizures of men and animals" (Étienne and Knoepfler 1976: 163–6, 244–5; Bielman 1994: 49).

When Selge was engaged in a war, some of the troops holding a pass withrew "because the grain harvest was imminent" (Polyb. 5.72.7; 218 BC); other farmers who did not have the luxury of this choice often lost their harvest, i.e., last year's toilsome work and next year's income, because they were away from their fields. It is therefore not surprising that the population of the countryside often sought protection either in a nearby fortress, or behind the city walls. The result was that if a conflict turned out to be lengthy, the fields were completely abandoned. The inhabitants of Megalopolis fled to Messene during the war of Kleomenes (223 BC; Plut., *Kleomenes* 45.6), more than 5,000 Eleians sought refuge in the fort of Thalamai in 219 BC, together with their livestock (Polyb. 4.75.2–8), and during the war between Miletos and Magnesia over disputed land (Hybandis), part of the population of the countryside had to seek refuge in other areas. After the establishment of peace, they were given the right, for two months, to move through foreign territory with their property without paying customs (*Syll.*[3] 588; Ager 1996: no. 109; ca. 184 BC). Because they failed to ally themselves with the Romans during the Second Macedonian War, the defeated Elateians had to abandon their city and live for eight years as fugitives in Stymphalos (ca. 198–190; *SEG* XI 1107; Maier 1959: no. 30).

The references to abandoned landscapes in our sources are in many cases the result of continual war, and indirectly that of demographic decline. A letter of Eumenes II sent to the village of the Kardakoi, a military settlement in the territory of Termessos, after the end of the war between Rome and Antiochos III (181 BC), sketches a gloomy picture; the population had left the settlement "because the produce of trees was scant and the land poor." In order to encourage the return of the population, Eumenes cancelled the debts for the purchase of land and for unpaid taxes, reduced the taxes for a year, and awarded new settlers and repatriated fugitives exemption from taxes for three and two years respectively (Maier 1959: no. 76). Similar measures after wars in the kingdoms of the Seleukids and the Attalids are not unknown (Holleaux 1938b: 111–12; Maier 1959: 249; e.g., *Sardis* VII.1 2; *SEG* II 663).

The correspondence of Herakleia-under-Latmos with the Seleukid official Zeuxis (ca. 196–193 BC) suggests that the population had left the countryside, and the city requested exemption from taxes so that "the villages and the dwellers be gathered, as they used before" (*SEG* XXXVII 859 C, lines 9–10; cf. Ma 2000a: 340–5 no. 31). Samothrake was facing a similar problem in the late third century, when part of its territory on the Thracian coast remained uncultivated, obviously because of the attacks of Thracian tribes; the Samothrakians asked a Ptolemaic commander to assist them in the construction of a fort (*ochyroma*), so that the citizens would be able to receive land lots there and cultivate them (*IG* XII.8 156 B, lines 17–23, late third century). They promised at the same time that part of the revenue raised would be spent on sacrifices for the well-being of the royal family.

As previously mentioned, war often presented slaves with a chance to escape, and the treaty between Theangela and the ruler of Karia Eupolemos (ca. 310 BC) refers to this problem (*Staatsverträge* 429; Austin 1981: no. 33). Slaves had come to Theangela both during the war and during the siege of the city, some of them in order to find safety, others escaping from their masters, some perhaps hoping to be rewarded if they fought for the city. Unfortunately, the vague formulation of the treaty does not allow any certainty on this matter ("for all the slaves who came to the city in peace the clauses of the treaty between Eupolemos and Peukestas shall apply; for those who came in war there shall be an amnesty"). When some ships under the command of the Ptolemaic naval commander Zenon visited Ios, a number of slaves escaped on his ships and were returned to their owners only after investigations (*OGIS* 773; Heinen 1976: 146; Bagnall 1976: 147; see also Launey 1987: 648).

If, in the short term, warfare meant the destruction or loss of part of the harvest, the long-term economic impact was more severe. Agriculture in Greece, in the islands, and in many parts of Asia Minor, required the exploitation of the slopes of hills by means of the construction of terraces, which provided additional terrain for olive trees, vineyards, gardens, and to some extent the cultivation of cereals and the keeping of a few animals. Although the textual and archaeological evidence for terraces is rather limited, analogies with modern agricultural practices and some direct evidence leaves little doubt about the importance of terraces in ancient agriculture. Terraces require the attention of farmers, especially in the periods in which other agricultural activities are less intensive. They need to be continually maintained, and additional terraces built, to expand the cultivated territory. A description of the frontier of the Cretan cities of Hierapytna and Lato (*SEG* XXVI 1049; Chaniotis 1996a: no. 59; 111/10 BC) gives us an idea of the agricultural and other activities in the mountainous border. The points of orientation used in this text presuppose habitation and farming: we find a reference to the estate of a certain Exakon, which was cultivated by his serfs; next to it lies land which "used to be waste," i.e., which had been taken under cultivation recently; ruins are described at some distance ("from the east side of Mt. Benkasos to the cliff, all round, to the other cliff, all along the 'band'; and from there all round to the peak at Mitoi; and straight on to the summit of the previously wasteland, which is adjacent to the estate of Exakon; and from there to the summits of the wooded valley, near the ruins").

The word *tainia* – literally a band or stripe – in the same delimitation is of particular interest. This word is used by modern farmers in eastern Crete to describe a strip of cultivated land along the rock which separates the cultivated land from the rocky terrain. Such a strip can be best understood as the result of terracing. The impact of war on terraces may be indirectly inferred from a passage of Theophrastos (early third century), which has survived in Pliny's *Natural History* (31.53) and Seneca's *Natural Enquiries* (3.11.5). When the (or a) settlement of the Arkadians of Crete – on the western foothills of the Lasithi mountains – was destroyed, their land remained uncultivated for six years. Consequently, the springs and streams, which used to abound in the region, ceased to carry water. Water returned only after the farmers were able to resume their work. This story probably alludes to the erosion which inevitably occurs when agricultural activities are interrupted and terraces are not being attended to by the farmers.

The destruction of olive trees, vineyards, and orchards due to war meant more than the loss of important staple products for a year – it also meant the loss of an important investment of manpower and had a long-term effect. Olive trees need seven years to bear fruit; vineyards need two years.

In addition to this, vineyards require intensive care for at least 35 days each year (Amouretti 1986). Even if the extensive destruction of olive groves required a lot of energy, since the trees were usually on hills, the cutting down or burning of just two grown trees meant for a farmer the permanent loss of a yield of at least 10–20 kilograms of olive oil, and this corresponds to the annual consumption of one person (see Amouretti 1986: 183).

Finally, military constructions affected agricultural activities. When Ephesos constructed a city wall around 290 BC, those who leased public land were obliged to leave 15 meters outside and 12 inside the wall unexploited, and in addition to this they endured the exploitation of these areas as quarries, for water supplies, and for highways (Maier 1959: no. 71).

Farmers were not the only victims of war in the countryside. Livestock was a very welcome form of booty for invaders, raiders, and pirates, since it required minimal manpower for its movement or transportation (e.g., Polyb. 4.29.6; Pritchett 1991: 84; Chandezon 2003: 50–4, 339–40). This problem was particularly acute in areas where the geographical conditions made a seasonal movement of herds to and from pasture land necessary (e.g., Asia Minor, Crete, Central Greece). In Hellenistic Crete, the problems of animal theft are addressed in interstate agreements between cities. Cases of theft were investigated by an authority responsible for keeping peace and order in the mountainous pasture. Theft on the roads regularly used by foreigners and leading beyond the border (*xenike hodos*) was subject to very severe punishment (Chaniotis 1999b: 201–2). The dangers faced by shepherds in the countryside are also evident in the case of the inhabitants of Rhamnous, in Attika, who brought their flocks to Euboia, in order to protect them from the dangers of a war (Bielman 1994: no. 30; Chandezon 2003: 25–8, 235–6). During a war in 279 BC, the inhabitants of Kyzikos brought their flocks to the territory of Pergamon for security (*OGIS* 748). This phenomenon seems to have been quite common, as we may infer from regulations which concern themselves with the citizens of a community who brought their possessions in safety into the territory of a neighbor; these persons were often exempted from the dues for import and export (Müller 1975; Chandezon 2003: 185). In one of these treaties (between the Cretan cities of Hierapytna and Priansos, ca. 200 BC) we find a reference to the "produce" or "offspring" (*karpos*) of the possession in question, and this suggests that we are dealing with livestock (*I.Cret.* III,iii 4 = Chaniotis 1996a: no. 28, lines 27–30).

Given all these problems, shortages of food, especially of the most important staple product, grain, were not uncommon in the Hellenistic period. Usually, we are informed about them indirectly. Philon of Byzantion discusses in detail the storage of food because of the permanent danger of a siege, recommending the purchase of cheap grain in advance (2.30); the same recommendation is given by king Antigonos the One-Eyed to Teos and Lebedos (*RC* 3, section 10 = Austin 1981: no. 40; Bagnall and Derow

2004: no. 7). When a king or a citizen made a donation of grain or when a citizen or a magistrate is praised for making provisions for the supply of grain at reasonable prices, we may assume that a city was facing a shortage either of grain or of *cheap* grain; also the measures taken by Hellenistic cities for collecting funds in order to buy grain in advance or to successfully face raised prices (*sitonia*) show that grain shortages were one of the most serious problems facing Hellenistic cities from the early fourth century onwards (Stroud 1998).

The historical context of food shortages cannot always be identified and the causes are rarely explicitly stated, although they can be inferred without difficulty. The destruction or collection of crops by invading troops and the absence of farmers during the critical days of harvest could easily and rapidly have detrimental effects. Entella, a Sicilian city which was destroyed during a war by the Carthaginians (early third century BC), faced a shortage of grain when the citizens returned from Enna, where they had found refuge; they were only saved when other cities made generous contributions of grain (*SEG* XXX 1121 and 1123). "During the war against the Libyans, when there was a shortage of grain" in Arsinoe (Tokra, Kyrenaika, ca. 100 BC) and the prices were rising, the donation of a citizen made the purchase of cheap grain and its transportation from Leptis to Arsinoe possible (*SEG* XXVI 1817, lines 33–54).

To these problems one should add the interruption of trade because of naval warfare and the raids of pirates, which frequently occurred during wars – for example, Archestratos of Macedon, an officer of Demetrios the Besieger, was honored in Ephesos for protecting ships that transported grain to the city during a war (*OGIS* 9 = *I.Ephesos* 1452, ca. 302 BC). An inscription at Erythrai (*I.Erythrai* 28; Bielman 1994: no. 21, ca. 277 BC) explicitly regards the abundance of food as the result of the efforts of a wealthy citizen to provide safety to traders. At the beginning of the war between the Romans and Antiochos III (191 BC), the Achaian League forbade exports of grain, because of shortages (*SEG* XI 1107; Maier 1959: no. 30).

Food shortages and loss of income caused serious collateral damage: the dissatisfaction of part of the population and, consequently, conflicts that threatened social unity (Foxhall 1993: 142–3). The devastation of the Argolid by King Kleomenes III of Sparta (222 BC) aimed precisely to create popular indignation and dissent (Polyb. 2.64). That social dissent did not occur very frequently and on a large scale was to a great extent due to wealthy citizens who had the foresight to sacrifice part of their property in donations (see chapter 2, section 6).

7.3. The Economy of Booty

Philon of Byzantion urges generals to regard the money spent on a siege and for bribing potential traitors as a good investment (D 65, ed. Garlan

1974: 322): "do not spare money for bribery or for other expenses; for when you take the city you will get a multiple of this money." Capturing booty was always a strong motive for Greek warfare, and in this respect the Greeks did not behave any differently to, for example, the Assyrians. The aquisition of booty was of fundamental importance, especially for Hellenistic monarchies, since it enriched the royal treasury and gave the king the opportunity not only to pay his troops, but also to reward his friends and strengthen their loyalty (Austin 1986).

In a more general sense, the most important "booty" was the conquest of land and the acquisition of its resources. The wars between Hellenistic kingdoms were wars of conquest or wars over the control of territory. Most of the conflicts that arose between cities and leagues were generated by the wish (and need) for territorial expansion (see chapter 1, section 3). The most frequent issue that Hellenistic interstate arbitration had to face was disputes over the ownership of territory (Ager 1996). In many cases we only have the result of the arbitrations, i.e., the delimitation, but vague references to accusations (*enklemata*; e.g., *IG* IV² 71; *IG* IX.2 7; *F.Delphes* III.4 42) and direct references to killings, devastations, and seizures (e.g., *RC* 8) leave little doubt about the violent form of these disputes. For example, Magnesia and Miletos fought a war over the Hybandis (ca. 185 BC), in which their allies (Priene and Herakleia) were also involved (*Syll.*³ 588; Ager 1996: no. 109). Analogous wars between cities over disputed territories were not uncommon. It is not known whether a war between Kimolos and Melos (Cyclades) was the result of a dispute over the three islets of Polyaiga, Heteireia, and Libeia (*IG* XII.3 1259; Ager 1996: no. 3), which were probably only suitable for the raising of livestock (Polyaiga = "the island with many goats"; see Robert 1949), but a similar conflict between Lato and Olous (Crete) over the islet of Pyrrha was certainly one of the causes of a war that lasted for almost a decade and led to repeated arbitrations of the Romans and the Knossians in the late second century (see chapter 1, section 3).

In some cases the disputed land had a strategic or religious significance (Ager 1996: no. 45), but in numerous others the economic background of the disputes can be seen when the information about the disputed territory permits its exact location and, thus, a close study of the resources it provided. This has been done, for example, in the case of disputes between the cities of the Argolis (Epidauros, Troizen, Arsinoe/Methana, and Hermione) in the third century, over mountainous regions which offered excellent pasture and timber, but also over stone quarries, salt works, and tuna fisheries (Jameson et al. 1994), or in the case of the dispute between two Thessalian cities over arable land and pasture, but also over the use of the River Peneios for fishing (Helly 1999; ca. 189 BC). Halos and Phthiotic Thebes, Priene and Samos, Magnesia on the Maeander and Miletos, Mytilene, and Pitane, plus Nagidos and Arsinoe in Kilikia count among the many cities

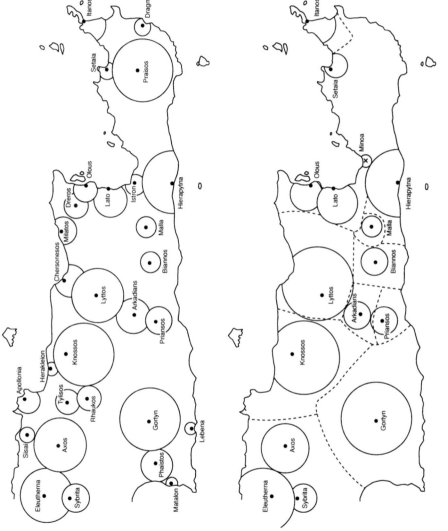

Map 3 The expansion of Cretan cities in the Hellenistic period

which engaged in disputes over fertile plains. Unfortunately, in many other cases we only have vague references to the economic significance of a disputed territory – for example, references to agricultural products, farming, pasture, timber, harbors, brickworks, and water sources.

One can best see the causes and effects of expansion when studying individual cases. The Cretan city of Hierapytna (today's Ierapetra) offers one of the best (and best documented) examples (Chaniotis 1996a: 173–4; fig. 6). Hierapytna lies on the south coast of Crete, near a relatively extensive coastal plain, but in the narrowest part of the island. In addition to this, Hierapytna has the lowest rainfall in Greece and the highest temperatures. To make things worse, Hierapytna's territory was enclosed by those of many other independent cities, which were only a short distance (12–35 kilometers) away: Malla (14 kilometers) and Biannos (35 kilometers) in the west, Lato in the north (20 kilometers), Istron (14 kilometers) and the Lyttian excalve Minoa (12 kilometers) in the northeast, plus Praisos in the east (32 kilometers). Hierapytna was evidently not in a position to provide all its citizens with land. The solutions in such a situation are many: migration, other economic activities (trade, piracy, mercenary service), and conquest. The Hierapytnians are in fact known as mercenaries and sailors, and a series of treaties with other Cretan states enabled them to settle on the land of the partner cities. Nothing makes the need for land as clear as Hierapytna's wars against its neighbors (Priansos, Malla, Praisos, and Itanos) and her conquests from the late third century to the late second century BC (see map 3). In 145 BC the Hierapytnians conquered the entire territory of Praisos, and by 110 BC they had tripled their territory.

An analogous territorial expansion can be seen in the cases of Knossos, Gortyn, and Lyttos (see chapter 1, section 2). One of the most eloquent documents of these efforts is a treaty between Gortyn and Knossos concerning their neighbor Rhaukos. In 167 BC, Knossos and Gortyn agreed not to stop their war against Rhaukos until they had defeated it (Polyb. 30.23.1). They jointly sacked Rhaukos in 166 BC and divided the territory into two. An inscription describes the line which divided the territory and the town between the conquerors (Chaniotis 1996a: no. 44). This line follows the course of a street that goes through the center of the lower town, passes in front of the town hall, and leads on through one of the gates to the citadel and from there to the countryside. Everything south of the line belonged to Gortyn, the rest to Knossos; the "movables" (*epipola*), i.e., captives, livestock, money, and valuables, were divided into two.

In a narrower sense, the booty collected during wars consisted of prisoners, who were either sold or ransomed, livestock, and movables. We have information primarily about the booty gained following the sack of a city. Although the numbers given by literary sources are sometimes exaggerated, they give an impression of the extent and type of booty that an invading army could expect if they were successful in their campaign. For example, the plunder of Mantineia in 223 BC is given by Phylarchos (*FgrHist* 81 F 56) as 6,000 talents – which is implausible (it corresponds to the price of more than 150,000 slaves). However, Polybios corrects the amount to 300 talents (Polyb. 2.62.11–12), which is still huge, and suggests that at least 9,000 people were sold as slaves (Volkmann 1990: 18). Some 50,000 people were enslaved by the Aitolians during a campaign in Lakonia in 240 BC, and 5,000 Eleians were captured by Philip V in a single fort in 219 BC. In some other instances we are only informed that the "entire population" was enslaved (Pritchett 1991: 232–4) – for example, all the free men of Mantineia (227 BC), all the women and children of Lyttos (220 BC), the entire population of Phthiotic Thebes (217 BC), Antikyra (211 BC), Aigina (210 BC), Thasos (202 BC), and Kios (210 BC). The same is said of Kephallenia (188 BC), Apollonia on Crete (170 BC), and Siphnos (153 BC).

The involvement of the Romans in the Hellenistic wars resulted in increased brutality, more frequent destruction of cities, and higher numbers of prisoners, who were sold as slaves (Volkmann 1990: 20–34). This process culminated during the Third Macedonian War when in Molossis (Epeiros) alone, 70 sites were destroyed and 150,000 people sold as slaves. This figure is only topped by the sacking and plundering of Korinth in 146 BC.

The chaotic scenes which took place during the plundering of a city are described, for example, by Plutarch (partly based on Aratos' memoirs) in his narrative of an attack by the Aitolians against Pellene in 241 BC:

> as soon as they had entered the city, the common soldiers had scattered themselves among the houses, jostling and fighting with one another over the booty, while the leaders and captains were going about and seizing the wives and daughters of the Pellenians, on whose heads they put their own helmets, that no one else might seize them; the helmet would show to whom each woman belonged.
>
> (Plut., *Aratos* 31–2; cf. Aratos, *FgrHist* 231 F 2; trans. B. Perrin)

The Antigonids formulated regulations concerning discipline and order in the distribution of war booty (*eutaxias tes ek ton ophelion*; *ISE* 114; Hatzopoulos 2001: 161–4, no. 3 B I, lines 10–18), and the division of booty was often the subject of treaties of alliance (see below).

Booty was brought to places where one could expect potential purchasers, and this is evident in Philip V's movements during his campaign in the Peloponnese (219–218 BC). After the plundering of Eleia he brought his booty to Olympia and from there to Heraia, where it was sold (*elaphyropolei*; Polyb. 4.77.5). After a campaign in Lakonia, he went to the next major city of Arkadia, Tegea, to sell his booty (Polyb. 5.24.10).

The division of booty often led to conflicts, one of which is described by Polybios (5.25.1–3) in the same context:

Leontios, Megaleas, and Ptolemaios [opponents of Philip V], still hoping to intimidate Philip and thus retrieve their former errors, disseminated among the light soldiers and the body of the troops which the Macedonians call the *agema* suggesting that they were in risk of losing all their privileges, that they were unfairly treated and did not get in full the customary booty. By these means, they excited the young soldiers [*neaniskoi*] to collect in a body, and attempt to plunder the tents of the king's most prominent friends.

(trans. W. R. Paton, modified)

It is interesting to note that the *neaniskoi* (soldiers between the ages of 20 and 30) were those who could be most excited about this issue (see chapter 3, section 1).

If raids and piracy deserve a place in a discussion of warfare it is because a very thin line – if any – separated war from maritime and land expeditions aimed at collecting booty. Grievances, so frequent among neighbors with an overdeveloped sense of honor, often caused acts of reprisal (*rhysia*), exercised both by communities and by individuals. They usually took the form of raids and the seizure of people, livestock, and other property. Certain regions of the Hellenistic world, in particular regions in its periphery, such as Illyria in the northwest, Aitolia in western Greece, the island of Crete, and Kilikia in southeast Asia Minor, were notorious for regular raids. Those participating in such raids are commonly described in ancient sources as "pirates" (*peiratai, leistai*), but this term conceals a variety of groups (de Souza 1999: 2–13, 43–96; Gabrielsen 2001a: 84–5; 2003: 398–404), especially individuals who organized raids, part-time merchants and part-time privateers who exploited the chaotic conditions during wars, accompanied an allied army (often a royal army), and supported its operations by attacking ships and coastal sites, plundering, and making maritime communications insecure. "Pirates" supported, for example, the military operations of Antigonos Gonatas (Buraselis 1982: 158), and Philip V paid the Illyrian ruler Skerdilaidas, notorious for his raids, 20 talents per annum in exchange for his services: Skerdilaidas was to attack the Aitolians with 30 light ships (Polyb. 4.29.7).

The Cretans were also known for such practices, and their activity is well documented through epigraphical sources (Brulé 1978). These sources are, primarily, treaties of alliance that concern themselves *inter alia* with the division of booty and the taxation of the participating soldiers. A treaty between Lyttos and Malla (Chaniotis 1996a: no. 11, late third century) provides a characteristic example: "if the Lyttians and the Mallaians start a campaign [*exhodousanton*] and if we, so the gods will, capture something from the enemies in a joint military action [*koinai stratouomenoi*], let each party receive by lot a share that corresponds to the number of the men that had come [i.e., had participated in the campaign]." The verb *exhodeuo* ("to march out") makes clear that this clause did not concern booty gained during a defensive war, but campaigns initiated by the two cities (and as the word *hekastos* suggests, by other partners as well).

Of course, booty could also be gained in an offensive war which started with a motivation other than plunder (e.g., revenge or preemption), but such a clause encouraged campaigns which aimed exactly at the capture of movables: slaves, money, livestock, and other valuables. We need not speculate about this, because there are even clearer formulations in the Cretan treaties about the organization of raids for the purpose of booty. A treaty between Hierapytna and Priansos (Chaniotis 1996a: no. 28) is the most eloquent evidence: "if with the will of the gods we capture something good from the enemies, either jointly starting a campaign or if some individuals from each city march out, either by land or by sea, let them divide the booty by lot proportionally to the men that have come and let each part bring the tithes to its own city."

When studying such treaties, one immediately observes the use of stereotypical formulations, despite the fact that the treaties were concluded by different cities. Such formulations presuppose not only the existence of rules, but also of intensive contacts between cities; they are evidence for a widespread phenomenon. We have only nine such treaties from Crete (Chaniotis 1996a: nos. 11, 26, 28, 38, 46, 59–61; *SEG* L 936), in which at least 11 cities are involved (Aptera, Eleutherna, Gortyn, Hierapytna, Lato, Lyttos, Malla, Olous, Phalasarna, Polyrhenia, Priansos), but this is only a small surviving portion of agreements that were concluded in the third and second centuries BC. In the Cretan treaties, the main principles in the division of booty are the use of lots, proportional division corresponding to the number of soldiers that each party had contributed (presumably including the casualties), payment of a contribution (a tithe) to the city's treasury, and the dedication of part of the booty to the gods.

The booty was probably divided according to the following procedure: each city received its share, according to the aforementioned principles, and then, after a tithe had been paid to the treasury, the rest was distributed among the soldiers.

A treaty between Gortyn and another anonymous city, describes a different procedure: the city which had taken the initiative for the joint raid and had provided the commanders received the entire booty. The soldiers of the partner who participated in the campaign probably received wages as mercenaries (Chaniotis 1996a: no. 46: "with regard to the profit from enemy territory, whatever they capture in joint campaigns in which one of the magistrates has the command, this should belong to the part that invited the allied troops"). One of the treaties explicitly refers to expeditions by sea, which can safely be connected with Cretan piracy.

It is with the aforementioned tithes from booty that the common meals (*syssitia*) in the men's houses (*andreia*) were funded in Crete until the end of the Hellenistic period, and the stability and maintenance of the social structure of Cretan cities relied to a great extent on capturing booty. On the one hand it was an important source of revenue for the city's treasury, and on the other it was a source of income for men who did not have a substantial (or any) income from land, either because their family did not possess enough (or any) or because these men were still young and had not received their inheritance. With this income, the soldiers could pay their contribution to the *syssitia* and maintain their social status. This explains why the Cretans, especially the masses (*plethos*) and the young citizens (*iuvenes*, cf. Diod. 40.3; Vell. Paterc. 2.34.1), zealously dedicated themselves to this activity until the conquest of their island in 67 BC (see chapter 3, section 2).

The profit from piracy and raids consisted primarily of prisoners, who were sold as slaves or ransomed to their families or their city, thus generating a substantial gain; sometimes the profit consisted of livestock, otherwise in valuables. As soon as a raid was over, the "pirates" transformed themselves into merchants, approached the next important harbor or returned to their home, and sold their booty. The main slave markets of the Aegean (Rhodes, Delos, and Crete) were regularly supplied by such pirates (de Souza 1999: 60–5).

With the exception of the slave trade, for which we have more evidence, it is difficult to estimate the contribution of booty to the economy of a region. Around 114 BC, two small Cretan cities, Lato and Olous, were engaged in a long dispute over a ship – probably jetsam on their coast, rather than the victim of pirates (see chapter 1, section 2). Its content consisted of two free men and a slave, some silverware, some bronzeware, and some coins – certainly not a great treasure. The capture of people was more profitable, since a slave could achieve a price of 100–300 drachmas (Bielman 1994: 99; Ducrey 1999: 246–54; see also Pritchett 1991: 244–5) and a *free* person could be ransomed for a much higher price (300–600 drachmas; Gabrielsen 2003: 393). The ransoming of Athenians who had been captured by Aitolian raiders and brought to Crete in 229 BC cost the city 20 talents (Brulé 1978: 19; Petropoulou 1985: 73). The Aitolian raid in Naxos, which brought them 280 prisoners (*IG* XII.5 36; Bielman 1994: no. 26), could have easily generated for each of the participants a profit corresponding to the annual earnings of a mercenary soldier. No surprise then that Cretans and Aitolians were willing to risk their lives by engaging in raids.

The Hellenistic poet, Leonidas of Tarent, presents in an epigram the clichés connected with Cretan piracy: "ever brigands and pirates, not righteous, are the Cretans" (*Anth.Gr.* 7.654). Polybios' deleterious remarks against the Aitolians (4.3.1: the Aitolians "are accustomed to live on their neighbors and required many funds because of their inherent greed, enslaved by which they always lead a life of greed resembling wild beasts, regarding no one as a friend and everyone as their enemy"; cf. Antonetti 1990: 13–19) reflect not only the historian's hatred of the traditional enemies of his own people, but also reality. The proverbial saying "the three worst *kappas* are Kappadokia, Crete, and Kilikia" (Suda, s.v. *tria kappa kakista*) is certainly evidence for ethnic stereotyping (see Perlman 1999), but this should not lead us to the wrong conclusion that Cretan and Kilikian pirates were the product of the ancient imagination.

Although Hellenistic sources usually attribute such raids to greed and other ethnic stereotypes, a socio-economic context similar to that discussed in connection with mercenary service offers a further explanation – albeit not the only one – for this activity. One should add two further substantial factors: first, piracy was encouraged by monarchs (e.g., Demetrios the Besieger, Philip V), who directed the attacks of the pirates against their enemies. Second, in some regions military training was connected with regular raids against those who were not protected by a treaty of inviolability. The gaining of booty – not unlike conquest – was not regarded as theft, but as the result of military superiority and divine assistance. The Cretans often chose names which allude to the gaining of booty – i.e., names related to the word *syle* ("spoils") such as Syladas, Sylichos, Solos, Sotosylos, and Damaisylos (Masson 1965), and the dedication of a Kilikian, who plundered Xanthos in 42 BC (App., *b.civ.* 4.76–82) shows the mentality of Kilikian raiders (*IGR* III 852; *SGO* IV 19/07/01): "After I had destroyed the city of Xanthos with dark fire, I, Mongidris, son of Teukros, dedicated to the pure goddess a golden crown. And you, Athena, who sacks the cities, always arm the man, from whose booty you receive a tithe."

Raids were nourished by the mentality of superiority based on military strength, but also by the idea that success was a gift of the gods.

7.4. Winners and Losers: The Impact of War on the Hellenistic Economy

Some time in the late third or early second century (ca. 197 BC) the envoys of an unknown city appealed to a functionary of Antiochos III (*SEG* XXXVII 1003; Gauthier 1989: 171–8; Ma 2000a: 352–3, no. 36): their city had been burned down during a war, and most of the citizens had lost their fortunes. They requested a cancellation of taxation and the sending of new settlers. The functionary agreed not to tax the city for seven years and to demand a reduced tax after this period; the city would also be free of garrisons, billeting and the payment of other contributions. Another document of the same period (196 BC) describes the desolate situation in Herakleia-under-Latmos (*SEG* XXXVII 859; Ma 2000a: 340–5, no. 31; Chandezon 2003: 232–40). In this case, the envoys of the city explained to a royal functionary that war had resulted in poverty for its people.

Fragmentary though these documents are, they are not isolated (cf. *I.Prusa* 1001); they clearly show the substantial impact of war on economic activities. Trade became insecure and the movement of itinerant artists (e.g., those of the performing arts – *Dionysiakoi technitai*) was connected with the risk of captivity and death (Aneziri 2003: 248–9). The communities continually lamented their desperate fiscal situation and the burden of debts, and the countryside was often devastated and denuded of its population.

A decrease in population is attested by Polybios for the mid-second century BC, although the causes the aged historian presents cannot be taken seriously (36.17.5–7):

> In our time childlessness and in general a decrease of the population have spread all over Greece; for this reason the cities have become deserted and dearth has occurred, although we have been befallen neither by continuous wars nor by epidemics . . . For men turned to arrogance, avarice and indolence; they did not wish to marry, and when they did marry, they did not wish to rear the children born to them, except for one or two at the most, in order to leave them wealthy and wanton; in this way the evil rapidly grew unnoticed.

It has been pointed out that Polybios possibly refers to a regional phenomenon or to the attitude of the wealthy elite, and that his remarks reflect ideology more than reality (see Davies 1984: 268; Alcock 1993: 25–7). But even if not a general phenomenon and not of the exaggerated dimensions given to it by the historian, a decrease in population has been confirmed by other sources – for example, for Boiotia (Étienne and Knoepfler 1976: 208–9). Its cause was not the egotism of landowners, but the extensive destruction of cities and the surrounding countryside, which had long-term consequences.

Nevertheless, wars produce "those who regard the misfortune of war as an opportunity for their own profits" (Diod. 20.82.5). Hellenistic wars were, of course, no exception to this universal experience. The previous pages have primarily sketched the negative consequences of warfare on the economy. Some of the winners in war are quite obvious: traders in war booty and slave traders (see section 7.3) along with all those who were professionally associated with war, such as mercenaries, trainers, doctors, historians, artists (for war memorials), weapons and warship manufacturers, constructors of fortification works, and those who supplied them with the necessary materials. The building of a fortification wall meant the cutting of stone, the purchase of timber, and the production of clay tiles (e.g., *IG* II^2 463; Maier 1959: no. 11). Specialized engineers were responsible for siege machines (e.g., Diod. 20.48.1), and even the making of such a simple weapon as a sling bullet was the object of a specialized trade.

The Hellenistic world was as close as an ancient economic system comes to our modern notion of "globalization." The creation of large kingdoms brought huge regions under more or less unified administrative structures, and the improvement of the conditions for trade by means of international treaties intensified trade activities, in spite of the difficulties caused by campaigns and raids. At the same time, the damage caused by war had to be compensated, and this was also an important motor for economic activity: the loss of production could be alleviated through the import of grain, wine, and olive oil. The creation of large networks of grain trade is connected with the efforts of communities to safeguard the supply of their population with the necessary food items at low prices, in a period in which isolation was no longer possible (or desirable). Piracy, which was a permanent danger for trade ships in the eastern Mediterranean, was at the same time one of the most important contributors to trade (Gabrielsen 2001b).

One of the most important impacts of warfare on the Hellenistic economy (and society) can be seen in the redistribution of material goods, land, and money (see Austin 2001: 90). The conquest of the Persian Empire by Alexander the Great released immense ammounts of wealth in the form of new coinage (de Callataÿ 1989), and the foundation of new cities and military colonies provided large numbers of immigrants from mainland Greece, the islands, and the coastal cities of Asia Minor with land. Economic and social mobility is not a one-way process: the profit of one party is usually the loss of another. Property changed hands due to wars in the ways described above, and the victims of war not only faced the prospect of losing property and life but were handled as property, generating profit for their conquerors. In total, for almost two centuries this redistribution of wealth within the Hellenistic world took place without creating intolerable misery for all, only for some – exactly as it had been for centuries.

The coming of Rome disturbed this balance in a dramatic way. The problem was not the fact that the wealth of the defeated Hellenistic states – and their manpower in the form of slaves – was brought to Rome. More severe was the impact of the indemnities that defeated monarchs and leagues had to pay (Gruen 1984: 291–5) and which reached unprecedented levels. The Romans demanded 1,000 talents from Philip V (196 BC), 500 from Nabis of Sparta (195 BC) and the Aitolian League (189 BC), 15,000 from Antiochos III (188 BC), and 300 from Ariarathes of Kappadokia (188 BC). The Romans intervened in the exploitation of local resources by forbidding the working of mines in Macedonia after 167 BC. Taxation and the notorious greed of the *publicani* (private businessmen) who untertook contracts on public works and were responsible for the collection of public revenues (e.g., in Boiotia and Asia Minor), were new external burdens (Badian 1972). The dynamic presence of Italian businessmen (*negotiatores*), bankers, and traders in the East was a new factor in economic life, which substantially limited the opportunities of native traders. The effects of Roman interventions were felt in a very dramatic way in Rhodes, a major trade power, when the Romans made Delos a free harbor which immediately superseded the importance of Rhodes as a trade center. In other areas the effects were less visible, but the massacre of thousands of Italian traders, tax collectors, and other foreign residents in Asia Minor on the orders of Mithridates VI

(88 BC) – allegedly 80,000 persons – leaves little doubt about the dissatisfaction of the natives with this massive intrusion (Green 1990: 561). If we add to these factors piratical activity, the presence of Roman troops, and the Roman civil wars which were fought on Greek soil, one begins to understand why the misery caused by warfare in the first century surpassed everything hitherto known (see Alcock 1993: 9–32). Under these conditions, the victory of Octavian at Actium came as a blessing, and the new era that it initiated had for some areas – especially those with an "economy of booty" (Aitolia, Crete) as dramatic an effect as the introduction of the market economy into the communist countries after 1990.

Further Reading

Hellenistic economy, in general: Rostovtzeff 1941 (albeit out of date in many respects, unsurpassed as an all-encompassing study); Davies 1984: 264–96; Reger 2003.

7.1. The Budget of War: Fiscal Aspects of Hellenistic Warfare. *Fiscality of the Hellenistic cities*: Gauthier 1991; Migeotte 1994 (Boiotia), 1995; Chandezon 2003: 309–30. *Expenses for fortification walls*: Maier 1961: 55–68; Baker 2000a; Migeotte 2000b: 147–52. *Expenses for a fleet*: Gabrielsen 2001a; Migeotte 2000b: 154–8; Rhodian naval bases and control of Karia and Lykia: Bresson 1999; Reger 1999. *Coastal settlements and harbors in Hellenistic Crete*: Kirsten 1942: 82–4; Brulé 1978: 149–56; Chaniotis 1996a: 105–6; Perlman 1999: 139–44. *Ransoming prisoners of war and victims of pirates*: Pritchett 1991: 245–97; Bielman 1994; Ducrey 1999; de Souza 1999: 65–9; Chaniotis 2004a; e.g., *IG* II^2 398a and 493; *SEG* XXXVII 82 (Bielman 1994: nos. 10, 12–13). *Battle within a city*: e.g., *IG* XII Suppl. 315; Plut., *Aratos* 31–2; Polyainos, *Strategemata* 4.6.3; cf. Garlan 1974: 207. *Destruction of urban centers in Hellenistic wars*: e.g., Pallantion: *SEG* XI 1084; XLI 277 ter (ca. 318–300 BC). Kynaitha: Polyb. 4.18, 4.19.6, 4.29.6, 9.38.8 (220 BC). Mantineia: Plut., *Aratos* 45.6–7; Polyb. 2.54.11 and 2.62.11–12 (223 BC). Megalopolis: Polyb. 2.55.7 (223 BC). Pharos: Polyb. 3.19.12; App., *Illyr*. 8; cf. *SEG* XXIII 489. Haliartos: Livy 42.63.11 (171 BC). Antipatreia: Livy 31.27.3–4 (200 BC). Lysimacheia: Livy 33.38. 10–12 (198 BC). Lyttos: Polyb. 4.54 (220 BC). Xanthos: App., *b.civ.* 4.76–82 (42 BC). Aphrodisias: Reynolds 1982: no. 13 (ca. 40 BC). *Subscriptions for defense*: Migeotte 1992: 336–41, 2000b: 164–6; see also Maier 1961: 58–60; subscriptions for the "protection of the city" (*phylake tes poleos*): Migeotte 1992: nos. 15–16; for "salvation of the city" (*soteria tes poleos*): Migeotte 1992: nos. 9, 50; cf. nos. 47, 53. *Donations by wealthy citizens*: e.g., *IOSPE* I^2 32; Maier 1959: no. 82. *Loans*: Migeotte 1984; Gabrielsen 1997: 80–3 (given by Rhodes to other states); *I.Ephesos* 4 = Bagnall and Derow 2004: no. 9 (private debts). *Contributions of foreign residents*: Adak 2003: 100–17, 133–42, 161–6, 184–93. *Watchdogs in forts*: *SEG* XXIV 154, lines 14–15; XXVI 1306, lines 19–20; XLI 76; cf. Plut., *Aratos* 24.1; Aeneas Tacticus 22.14.

7.2. War and Agriculture. *Disastrous results of war for agriculture*: Classical period: Hanson 1983: 11–63 (with a warning against overestimations); Ober 1985 (Classical Athens); Foxhall 1993 (primarily for the late fifth century, but with important methodological remarks); Thorne 2001. Hellenistic period: Holleaux 1938b: 100; Will 1975: 313, 317; Chandezon 1999, 2000. *Measures for the protection of agricultural production in Hellenistic Athens*: e.g., *IG* II² 682, lines 35–6; 1281, lines 4–6; 1299, lines 16–17; *SEG* XV 113, lines 4–5; XXXII 118, lines 10–12; XLIII 40, lines 7–9; Maier 1959: 25 *bis*, lines 6–7; cf. *I.Iasos* 34 (protection of fishermen). *Destruction of the countryside of Hellenistic cities because of war*: e.g., Polyb. 4.67.2–3 (Epeiros); 24.9.13 (Messene); Paus. 7.14.7 (Euboia, Amphissa); *I.Ephesos* 4 = Bagnall and Derow 2004: no. 9 (Ephesos); *Syll.*³ 495 (Olbia); *OGIS* 339 (Sestos); *RC* 6 and 8 (Priene); *TAM* I.1 1 (Telmessos, 240 BC); see Quass 1993: 230–3. *Casualties and loss of manpower*: Brulé 1999 (for the Classical period). *Evacuation of persons and property*: Hanson 1983: 87–101; Pritchett 1991: 350–2; Chaniotis 1999b: 200–1. *Agricultural terracing*: Isager and Skydsgaard 1992: 81–2; Schas and Spencer 1994: 424–30; Foxhall 1996: 45–53, 60–4; on Crete: Chaniotis 1999: 186–8; Rackham and Moody 1996: 140–5. *Livestock as booty*: e.g., Polyb. 4.29.6; Pritchett 1991: 84; Chaniotis 1999b: 201–2; Chandezon 2003: 50–4, 339–40. *Royal donations of grain*: Ameling et al. 1995: nos. 6, 11–12, 15–16, 27, 31–2, 34, 36, 39, 50, 76, 195–6, 203, 205, 207, 211–13, 224, 241–5, 255, 296–7, 317; see also Quass 1993: 235–8. *Measures for grain supply*: Fantasia 1989; Migeotte 1991; Quass 1993: 238–52; Reger 1993; Dirscherl 2000; selection of sources: *IG* XII.6.1 172 (Bagnall and Derow 2004: no. 75); *Samothrace* II.1 5; *RC* 3 (Bagnall and Derow 2004: no. 7); *SEG* XXIV 154 = Austin 1981: no. 50; Holleaux 1938b: 102–3; Ameling et al. 1995: no. 93. *Grain shortage in the early second century in Thessaly and Boiotia*: Walsh 2000 (favoring as explanation drought or blight, but see *SEG* L 1694); in Lesbos (during the War of Aristonikos): *IG* XII Suppl. 116 (Brun 2004: 51, no. 15); high prices in Seleukid Babylonia: van der Spek 2000. *The burden of billeting*: Launey 1987: 695–713; Habicht 1984: 213n.8; Austin 2001: 92 with n. 8; e.g., *SEG* XXIV 154 = Austin 1981: no. 50 (by native soldiers); *I.Labraunda* 46; *RC* 30; *I.Mylasa* 612; Briant, Brun and Varinlioglu 2001: 246–7; Bagnall and Derow 2004: no. 121.

7.3. The Economy of Booty: *Territorial conflicts*: e.g., Ager 1996: nos. 3, 15–18, 20, 22, 25–6, 30–4, 36, 38, 40–2, 44–6, 50, 54–6, 62–3, 65, 70, 74, 79–80, 82, 85, 88–9, 99, 108–10, 116–18, 120, 125–6, 128–31, 135–8, 141, 146, 150–4, 156–60, 162–4, 167–8; see also Daverio Rocchi 1988; Chandezon 2003: 332–6; Chaniotis 2004d; examples of wars over disputed territories: *I.Cret.* III.iv 9–10; Sherk 1969: no. 14; Polyb. 22.15. *Economic background of territorial disputes*: Argolis: *IG* IV² 71, 75–7; Thessaly: *IG* IX.2 521; Halos and Phthiotic Thebes: *F.Delphes* III.4 355; Priene and Samos: *I.Priene* 37 and 40; Ager 1996: nos. 74 and 160; Magnesia on the Maeander and Miletos: Ager 1996: no. 109; Mytilene and Pitane: *I.Pergamon* 245; Nagidos and Arsinoe: *SEG* XXXIX 1426; Ager 1996: no. 42; other references to the economic significance of a disputed territory: *IG* IV² 75; *IG* V.1 1430; *IG* V.2 443–5; Ager 1996: no. 54 (agricultural products and farming); *F.Delphes* III.3 352; Ager 1996: nos. 54 and 107 (pasture); Ager 1996: no. 107 (timber); *IG* V.1 931; Ager 1996: no. 85 (harbors); Ager 1996: no. 108 (brickworks); *IG* V.1 1430; *F.Delphes* III.2 136 (water sources). *The expansion of Hierapytna*: Baldwin Bowsky 1994; Guizzi 1997, 2001. *War booty, in general*: Ducrey 1977; Pritchett 1991: 68–541 (esp. 138–43 and 148–52, for the Hellenistic period); Ducrey 1999: 229–70. *Shares captured in the countryside*: Amyzon 14. *Plundering of cities*: e.g., Polyb.

141

4.72.1; Livy 38.29.11; 43.7.10; Pritchett 1991: 152–7. *Enslavement of the population of sacked cities:* Gruen 1984: 295–9; Volkmann 1990; Pritchett 1991: 223–45; Ducrey 1999: 83–92. Examples: Lakonia (240 BC): Polyb. 4.34.9; Elis (219 BC): Polyb. 4.75.2 and 6; Mantineia (227 BC): Polyb. 2.62.12; Plut., *Aratos* 45.4; Lyttos (220 BC): Polyb. 4.54.2; Apollonia on Crete (170 BC): Polyb. 28.14.4; Phthiotic Thebes (217 BC): Polyb. 5.100.8; Antikyra (211 BC): Polyb. 9.39.2; Aigina (210 BC): Polyb. 9.42.5; Thasos (202 BC): Polyb. 15.22.1; 18.3.12; Kios (210 BC): Polyb. 15.24.1; Same in Kephallenia (188 BC): Polyb. 21.32b; Siphnos (153 BC): Diod. 31.45; Molossis in Epeiros (170–167 BC): Polyb. 30.15; Livy 45.34.5; Korinth (146 BC): cf. Paus. 7.16.8. *Sale of booty:* Pritchett 1991: 84–5. *Raids as reprisals:* Pritchett 1991: 86–116 (with criticism on Bravo 1980); Lehmann 2003. *Raids for obtaining booty:* e.g., Diod. 18.46.1–47.3; *I.Iasos* 150; *I.Mylasa* 102. *Hellenistic piracy:* de Souza 1999: 43–96; Gabrielsen 2001b; Wiemer 2002; Gabrielsen 2003; see also Garlan 1978; Pritchett 1991: 312–63 (esp. 339–48). *Cretan piracy:* Brulé 1978; Petropoulou 1985. *Illyrian piracy:* Dell 1967. *"Pirates" as irregular troops:* e.g., Diod. 20.82.4–83.3, 20.97.5 (in the war of Demetrios the Besieger against Rhodes, 305/4 BC; de Souza 1999: 44–6; Gabrielsen 2001a: 84); Polyainos, *Strategemata* 5.19 (war of Demetrios the Besieger against Ephesos, 287 BC; de Souza 1999: 46–7); Polyainos, *Strategemata* 4.6.18 (war of Antigonos Doson against Kassandreia, 277/6 BC; see Pritchett 1991: 342); *IG* II² 1225 (Alexander against Antigonos Gonatas, 248/7 BC); see Buraselis 1982: 158. *Wars against pirates:* de Souza 1999: 76–84, 125–78; Rhodes: Wiemer 2002; Gabrielsen 2003: 395–8; Rome: Pohl 1993; Korkyra (against the Illyrian pirates): *IG* IX 1.4², 928–9. Ephesos: Robert 1967: 38–9 (*I.Ephesos* 5). *Division of booty:* in general: Bickerman 1950: 17; Aymard 1957: 236–8; Garlan 1977: 158–64; Pritchett 1991: 363–89; Ducrey 1999: 258–67; on Crete: Brulé 1978: 106–14; Petropoulou 1985: 20–1, 80–1; Chaniotis 1996a: 93–4. *Treaties of inviolability as protection from piracy:* Rigsby 1996; de Souza 1999: 69.

7.4. Winners and Losers: The Impact of War on the Hellenistic Economy. *The Roman factor:* Hatzfeld 1919; Alcock 1993; Rauh 1993; Baslez 1996; Reger 2003: 351–2.

8

AN AGE OF MIRACLES
AND SAVIORS: THE EFFECTS
OF HELLENISTIC WARS
ON RELIGION

8.1. Communicating with the Gods, Boasting to Mortals

On 25 May 2002, the German newspaper *Frankfurter Allgemeine Zeitung* published a photograph which shows a football player of Bayer Leverkusen after a game that saved his team from being relegated to the second division. He is wearing a T-shirt with the text "Thanks, Jesus" on it. Such naive belief – that Jesus takes a personal interest in whether a football team wins or loses – is, in principle, not very much different from the attitude of three men from Epeiros, who upon returning from Aristonikos' War, dedicated a statue of Herakles, their savior, "who stood beside them in all battles" (*SEG* XXXVI 555; see chapter 11, section 1), or from the conviction of a Pergamene that Athena saved him when he was captured by hostile troops (*I.Pergamon* 14 = *SGO* I 06/02/11, third century BC). These demonstrations of gratitude, not unlike prayers and dedications, are very egotistic expressions of faith; they presuppose that a divinity takes notice of the petty happenings of everyday life and takes sides in the countless, and often trivial, conflicts among humans. The hymn sung by the Athenians for Demetrios the Besieger around 291 BC connects belief in the existence of gods with such utilitarian ideas: "The other gods are either far away, or they do not have ears, or they do not exist, or do not take any notice of us, but you we can see present here, not made of wood or stone, but real. So we pray to you: first make peace, dearest; for you have the power" (Austin 1981: no. 35; see chapter 4, section 5).

To publicly thank a god by means of a dedication is of course more than a demonstration of gratitude; it is also a commemoration of a successful communication between humans and gods, and – even more important – a subtle strategy of self-representation: the dedicant presents himself not just as a thankful recipient of a divine favor, but also as the beneficiary of a privileged relationship with the divinity. And, of course, these thanksgiving dedications are also expressions of superiority. I call to mind the dedication of a Kilikian warrior, who plundered Xanthos in 42 BC (*IGR* III 852; *SGO* IV 19/07/01; see chapter 7, section 3): "After I had destroyed the city of Xanthos with dark fire, I, Mongidris, son of Teukros, dedicated to the pure [virgin] goddess a golden crown. And you, Athena, who sacks the cities, always arm the man, from whose booty you receive a tithe."

Various forms of communication overlap in Mongidris' dedication. With it he communicates with Athena, perceived here as a goddess of war, but at the same time the written text establishes a communication with the observers of his dedication, both during his lifetime and for eternity. The expression of gratitude is in the same breath a boast of superiority; the personal achievement ("I destroyed") is ultimately referred back to divine favor ("Athena, who sacks the cities, always arm the man . . ."), and the divine favor is based on the idea of *do ut des* – dedication in exchange for protection, the underlying principle of behavior which characterizes communication between mortals and gods (Grottanelli 1991), kings and cities, citizens and benefactors.

Mongidris' epigram is only one example of many. A similar combination of gratitude and boast can be seen, for example, in a dedicatory epigram composed by the great Hellenistic poet Kallimachos for a Cretan mercenary who had fought in a campaign of Ptolemy III in Kyrenaika (ca. 246–221): "Menitas from Lyttos dedicated these arches proudly saying: To you, Sarapis, I offer this bone arch and the quiver; as for the arrows, the Esperitai have them" (Kallim., *epigr.* 37, ed. Pfeiffer).

Given the ideological importance of war for the construction of hierarchical structures in the cities and for the legitimacy of power in the monarchies, the religious aspects of warfare gained great significance in the Hellenistic period. This chapter does not aim at describing the rituals and cults connected with Hellenistic warfare in their entirety. Indeed, a general discussion of the relationship between religion and warfare would have to cover such diverse phenomena as the existence of divinities worshipped as patrons of war (e.g., Ares or Athena Nike) and of cultic epithets which express precisely this role (see below); the conflation of Greek and non-Hellenic divinities in Anatolia, Egypt, and the Near East; the dedication of war booty (see chapter 11, section 6); divination in the preparation for wars and before battles; pre-battle sacrifices; the explanation of the divinity of Hellenistic rulers in view of their victories in wars (see chapter 4, section 5); the destruction and plunder of sanctuaries during wars (Pritchett 1991: 160–8); cult transfer as a result of mobility caused by wars and military colonization; cult associations of soldiers; the heroic cult of the war dead (e.g., *IG* IX 1.4², 787); narratives of miracles during battles; the participation of soldiers and ephebes in religious festivals and processions (see chapter 3, section 2; see also Launey 1987: 878–97) and so on and so on. Most of these phenomena go back to earlier periods of Greek history (Pritchett

1979; Jacquemin 2000), and I think a study of the cultural history of Hellenistic wars should focus on a selection of those phenomena which best reveal the peculiarities of Hellenistic warfare, and the specific or new part played by religion in this period (cf. Lévêque 1968: 284–5).

At first sight, little changed in the relationship between war and religion after the end of the Classical period. Patrons of war, such as Ares, Athena, and Apollo, and patrons of sailors, such as Poseidon, Aphrodite Pontia, the Dioskouroi, and the Samothrakian gods, continued to be worshipped. Dedications of war booty continued to increase the wealth and the monumental appearance of sanctuaries. Warships continued to be named after gods (e.g., Demeter, Aphrodite, Isis, Athena) and soldiers continued to ask the gods for their protection, to receive oracles, and to offer sacrifices. Athenian generals continued to employ a *mantis* for their pre-battle divinatory sacrifices (*IG* II^2 1708, early second century BC), and in the turmoil of the battlefield, people still fancied that gods and heroes fought on *their* side.

The most prominent and obvious religious aspect of warfare – in the Hellenistic world as in other periods of ancient history – is the dedication either of part of the booty or of other objects and monuments to the gods after a victory. We have already seen that this practice reflects the belief that the gods were ultimately responsible for military victory. At the same time, it reflects a dependence on divine help and the powerlessness of humans – the best-trained soldiers no less than civilians – when confronted with the calamities of war. Despite doubts, and attacks by some representatives of philosophical schools on traditional religion, individuals and communities still turned to savior gods for help, especially in periods of intensive warfare – for example, during the Galatian invasion in Greece and Asia Minor (280–277 BC), or the long and ubiquitous wars of the late third and early second century, and the wars of the Late Republic, which were carried out in the East with extreme brutality. These were the periods in which the collective belief in miraculous divine interventions (*epiphaneia*) almost acquired the dimensions of a massive delusion (see section 8.4).

The aforementioned dedication of Mongidris concerns assistance offered by a divinity in an act of aggression. The attack against Xanthos is not justified, and the help offered by Athena is interpreted as a response to the promise of a tithe. This attitude goes back to the belief that victory in a war can be attained with divine help. The justification of conquest as a legitimate means of acquiring land reflects the same idea (see chapter 9, section 5). This idea was so deeply rooted that in Cretan treaties, which concern campaigns of plunder, the booty is almost always referred to as "the good things captured with the will of the gods" (e.g., Chaniotis 1996a: no. 28: "if with the will of the gods we capture something good from the enemies"; see nos. 11, 26, 38, and 59).

The assistance of the gods was prayed for in offensive wars, no less than in defensive ones. In the late second century, a prayer for the success of

King Attalos III (*I.Pergamon* 246, line 31) expressed the wish that the gods give him victory and success not only in the defense of his kingdom (*amynomenoi*), but also in his campaigns (*archonti*). Yet, in the preserved material the gods most often appear as saviors in desperate situations. This is to some extent related to the interest in dramatic narratives which characterizes this period (see chapter 9). It can also be explained by the fact that gratitude is more strongly felt the greater the danger one escapes; but it also reflects a general interest during this period in *soteriology*, – in the discourse of rescue, both in life and (through initiation in a mystery cult) in the underworld.

Gods have always been regarded as saviors in times of need, but in no earlier period of Greek history was the cult of deities and deified mortals, worshipped as *Soteres* (saviors), so widespread as in the Hellenistic period. The epithet *Soter* may refer to protection against disease, earthquakes, or bad weather, but a military context is in many cases certain. Sometimes, rescue from danger was provided by a mortal benefactor – for example, when he paid the ransom for captured citizens – or by a king when he relieved a city from financial burdens or from the fear of a barbarian invasion. But in a period of great uncertainty and sudden and unexpected calamities, the hopes of individuals and communities usually rested upon the intervention of a savior god. Characteristic examples of this attitude can be seen in the wide diffusion of newly-introduced festivals with the name *Soteria*, in honor of gods who saved cities during wars (e.g., Delphi, Kyme, Pergamon), or in the introduction of the cult of Zeus Soter in the Hellenistic gymnasia, which were traditionally under the patronage of two other gods – Hermes and Herakles. The earliest attestation of the cult of Zeus Soter in a gymnasium is in Xanthos (Lykia), where the young men decreed in 196 BC the erection of an altar of Zeus Soter in their training area. The establishment of this cult should be seen in the context of recent wars and crises (*anankaiotatoi kairoi*), alluded to in their decree (*SEG* XLVI 1721, 196 BC; see Gauthier 1996: 23–7). A recently published inscription from Apollonia Mygdonike (Macedonia, 106 BC) mentions that this city's gymnasium was dedicated to Zeus Soter (*SEG* L 572).

Any god can be regarded a patron on the battlefield and a savior in times of need. An Attalid admiral called Dionysodoros ("the present of Dionysos") expected protection from Dionysos (ca. 250–220; *SEG* XXXVII 1020); the crew of warships in Kos was obliged to sacrifice to Aphrodite Pontia (patron of sailors) upon their return – or otherwise pay an amount to the priestess and to the treasurer of the sanctuary (*SEG* L 766; Parker and Obbink 2000, ca. 125 BC); Sulla dedicated an axe to Aphrodite of Aphrodisias, "for in a dream he saw her as she fought, full armed, leader of his troops" (App., *b. civ.* 1.97); soldiers serving in Ephesos made a sacrifice to Ptolemy II, Arsinoe and the "Saviours," whoever the latter divinities might have been (*SEG* XXXIX 1234); and the Rhodians dedicated 900 stone bullets in a sanctuary dedicated to "All the Gods" (*Pantes Theoi*; Kantzia 1999). At least they were certain that they had not mistakenly forgotten any divine helper.

And yet, certain divinities appear more frequently than others as patrons of war. Athena, often identified with *Nike* (Victory) and worshipped as *Nikephoros* ("the one who brings victory"), was traditionally the protector of citadels (*Polias, Poliouchos*). Her cult as a war goddess acquired great prominence in Pergamon, where the Attalid kings regularly offered dedications to her from their war booty (see chapter 11, section 6). One of these dedications is of particular interest, since it gives a moral justification for the war: "King Attalos, son of King Attalos, and those who campaigned together with him against Prousias and besieged him in Nikomedeia, *after he had violated the treaties which were concluded with the mediation of the Romans*, to Zeus and Athena Nikephoros in return for the advantages acquired through the fortunate outcome of the war" (ca. 154 BC; *OGIS* 327; Allen 1983: 82). It seems that the sanctuary of Athena Nikephoros, the recipient of the booty, had actually been plundered by Prousias in the first phase of the war (Polyb. 32.15.3; App. *Mithr.* 3).

The importance of dedications for the propaganda of the Hellenistic monarchies has been demonstrated through a study of the dedications and dedicants mentioned in the Delian inventories. As early as 322 BC, this sanctuary was an "international" center in which renowned statesmen made expensive dedications primarily for reasons of propaganda. A study of the dedicators and the dates of the dedications shows that the dedications of the period (ca. 322–296/95 BC) reflect important events, such as the Lamian War (322/21 BC), the war on Cyprus (315 BC), and the Aegean expedition of Ptolemy in 308 BC (Baslez 1997).

Because of the large numbers of international visitors, sanctuaries have always been the preferred place for the self-representation of rulers and communities, who erected victory monuments, made dedications, and funded festivals. Since this in not a specific Hellenistic phenomenon, a single example suffices to illustrate the exploitation of sanctuaries for war propaganda. It concerns the role played by Delphi on the eve of the Third Macedonian War for both Perseus of Macedonia and the Romans. Perseus was represented in the Amphictyonic council in 178 BC (*Syll.*[3] 636) and ordered the construction of two monuments (Polyb. 30.10.2; Plut., *Aemilius* 28.4), which must have been approved by the Amphictyony. In 174 BC, he marched peacefully, but with armed forces, to this Panhellenic sanctuary, calling to memory the traditional relationship between the Macedonian monarchy and Delphi. A little later he dedicated in the sacred precinct a pillar inscribed with documents, more than a century old, which demonstrated the energetic engagement of Demetrios the Besieger, Perseus' ancestor, on behalf of the Delphic Amphictyony, but also his collaboration with the Aitolians (*SEG* XLV 479 and XLVIII 588; Lefèvre 1998, 2002: 80–1). The pillar was at least 3 meters high, and probably carried a statue of Perseus. It stood in the proximity of similar pillars erected by King Prousias of Bithynia and Eumenes II of Pergamon. It was at this very sanctuary that the Romans chose to publish their manifesto accusing Perseus, with which they justified the war (see chapter 9, section 4). The Roman commander in this war, Aemilius Paullus, dedicated a pillar commemorating his victory over Perseus on the very spot where Perseus' pillar had once stood (Jacquemin and Laroche 1995).

Dedications to patrons of war often served as demonstration of the loyalty of officers and soldiers. Praxidemos, who "dedicated an altar to Athena Nike, the Savior (*Athena Soteira Nike*) and to king Ptolemy [I], for good fortune" (*OGIS* 17; cf. *SEG* XXXVIII 1526) in Lapethos on Cyprus and the Athenian Epikrates, who made a dedication to Artemis Soteira ("the Savior") on behalf of the same king in Egypt (Abukir; *OGIS* 18) must have been officers in the local garrisons. Hundreds of such dedications survive (see chapter 4, section 2), especially from Ptolemaic Egypt. In some cases the exact occasion is indicated, as for example in a dedication of unknown provenance (ca. 221–205 BC):

> On behalf of king Ptolemy [IV] and queen Arsinoe and their son Ptolemy [V], the Father-loving gods, the offspring of Ptolemy [III] and Berenike, the benefactor gods, Alexandros, son of Syndaios, from Oroanna, the *diadochos* [elite soldier] who was sent together with Charimortos, the general, for the hunting of elephants, and Apoasis, son of Miorbollos, from Etenna, officer [*hegemon*], and the soldiers under his command [dedicated this] to Ares, who brings victory [*Nikephoros*], the patron of good catching [*Euagros*].
>
> (*OGIS* 86)

In this dedication, we can see the evocation of quite different aspects. On one level of reading, the text commemorates a military activity of substantial importance for the Ptolemaic army and the Ptolemaic monarchy – i.e., the catching of elephants (see chapter 4, section 1); on another level, the text stresses the continuity of dynastic rule, referring both to the deceased king and to the heir. The dedication gave two mercenary officers from two small towns of Pisidia, in mountainous Asia Minor, the chance to associate themselves with their employer, and the joint act of worship, in an unknown and dangerous region, brought the officers and their soldiers together. A final point deserves attention. The dedication is addressed to a "military" god invoked with a Greek name and the Greek attributes Nikephoros and Euagros. We may assume that Ares, whom the Pisidian officers (and their possibly Pisidian soldiers) had in mind, was the god who was widely worshipped in Pisidia; however, there the Greek name concealed an indigenous god of war (Mitchell 1993: II, 28). A Pisidian god with a Greek name somewhere in the Egyptian desert is a characteristic example of the religious complexities to which Hellenistic armies contributed and to which we now turn.

8.2. War and Cult Transfer

Around the end of the third century BC, a man from Thera serving in the army of the Ptolemies set up a dedication in Koptos (Egypt) after he had survived a dangerous journey in the Red Sea: "Apollonios, son of Sosibios from Thera, officer of the external units [soldiers serving outside Egypt] made [this dedication] to the Great Samothrakian gods, in fulfillment of a vow, having been saved from great dangers after he had sailed out from the Red Sea" (*OGIS* 69; cf. *SEG* XXVI 1800). When facing a dangerous sea journey, Apollonios made his vow to gods which would have been familiar to sailors of the Aegean sea: the Samothrakian gods, who were often identified with the Dioskouroi. Setting up a dedication in a foreign place, where the name of these gods had perhaps not been heard of, does not necessarily mean the introduction of a new cult; but Apollonios' dedication is an example of how religious ideas travelled as a result of the mobility caused by wars and mercenary service.

Hellenistic warfare resulted in the temporary or permanent relocation of large numbers of people: the involuntary relocation of captives, hostages, fugitives, and slaves, and the systematically organized, controlled, and more or less voluntary relocation of troops through the foundation of military settlements, the establishment of garrisons, and the service of mercenaries. The soldiers brought the cults of their place of origin to their place of service. When they took an oath, cursed, or prayed, they most frequently invoked the gods of their homeland, exactly as Apollonios of Thera did while sailing in the Red Sea. However, the religious practices of a foreign city or country did not leave them untouched. In Greek religion, the idea prevailed that local gods inhabited and controlled a place. It was therefore advisable to respect them, to sacrifice to them, to pray to them; and should a soldier experience the protection of these foreign gods, he might be tempted to bring them back to his homeland. This is what happened time and again in the Hellenistic period, as hundreds of inscriptions demonstrate.

Such transfers of cults and rituals via military settlers and mercenaries is a very complex phenomenon, the most important aspects of which will be summarized here on the basis of a few selected examples.

Falaika is a small, but strategically important, island in the Arabian Gulf. Under the early Seleukids, a military settlement was established here and the island was given the Greek name Ikaros. An early dedication (late fourth or early third century BC) shows that Greek soldiers (*stratiotai* under the command of Soteles, probably an Athenian) worshipped Zeus Soter (the Savior), Poseidon, and Artemis Soteira (the Savior) on Ikaros. These divinities were frequently regarded by soldiers as their patrons and protectors (*SEG* XXXV 1477). A sanctuary of Artemis Soteira was either founded when the garrison was established, or converted from the sanctuary of a local goddess. At some point a Seleukid king made provisions for the relocation of the sanctuary – possibly for security reasons or in order to disassociate the cult from its indigenous roots. Still later (around 204 BC), typical Greek rituals were introduced: on the occasion of the goddess' festival, athletic and musical competitions (*agon gymnikos and mousikos*) were to take place (*SEG* XXXV 1476). In this case, the Greek cultic elements were intentionally strengthened and gave the soldiers of the fortress the possibility to continue the worship of their familiar gods, away from their Greek homeland. In other military settlements, the local influence was stronger and led sometimes to the assimilation of a local divinity with a Greek one, or to the adaptation of a local god.

Soldiers who served abroad and were continually exposed to danger were informed about the numinous power of the local gods and sought their protection. It is Egypt that provides us with abundant evidence for this phenomenon. Egyptian sanctuaries had attracted the interest of Greek visitors already in the Archaic period. Some came as "tourists," interested in the Pharaonic monuments; others interrupted their journey while on a diplomatic, military, or administrative mission; while still others came in order to specifically participate in the cult. It was a common practice to engrave their names on the walls of the temples or on the statues, occasionally providing some information about the reason for their visit – for example, "I have come to the god/goddess," "I have made a pilgrimage (*proskynema*)." In the case of pilgrimages, we can be certain that we are dealing with people who came to the sanctuary and performed the customary act of worship which is expressed by the verb *proskyneo* or the word *proskynema* (Bernand 1994). These terms probably imply that a person had kneeled in front of the god, had commemorated his or her visit by inscribing their name (or asking a professional scribe to do it for them), had participated in worship and left, possibly having acquired a closer relationship with the divinity. The stereotypical phrases *mnesthei* ("he will be remembered by the god") and *pollakis akousetai* ("he will be heard many times" – i.e., by the god) express the hope that the inscribed name will remind the god of its promise to help the pilgrim. Sometimes, pilgrims inscribed the name of a relative or a friend. Many visited sanctuaries which were famous for their healing miracles, such as the sanctuary of Imhotep/Asklepios at Deir el-Bahri or the Memnoneion of Abydos; others went to a sanctuary (e.g., the sanctuary of Bes in Abydos) in order to consult an oracle or expecting the god to appear in a dream. These forms of worship have their origin in Egyptian religion, but they were adopted by the Greek settlers and later by the Romans.

When the occupation of a pilgrim is not given (e.g., Launey 1987: 979–92) we can hardly distinguish between soldiers and civilians – or even between Greeks and natives who had adopted a Greek name. The case of the Cretans is an exception, because they can easily be recognized as foreigners – either due to their characteristic names or because of explicit mention of the ethnic name "Cretan." Although there must have been exceptions, most of the Cretans known as visitors or pilgrims to Egyptian sanctuaries must have been soldiers, since almost all the information we have about Cretans in Egypt concerns military personnel (see chapter 5, section 2).

Cretan mercenaries came into contact with the Egyptian religion in many ways. While serving in forts in the interior, they paid visits to the nearby sanctuaries. There, they heard about the power of the gods and their miracles. While they crossed the deserts they were as terrified as the natives, and they fulfilled their vows in return for safe passage in the same sanctuaries in the oases. Sometimes the gods who appeared in their dreams were the gods of the foreign country, not their native gods. For example, a Cretan mercenary from Phaistos made a dedication to Osiris upon divine command (*kata prostagma*) – i.e., after the god had appeared in his dream or via an oracle (*SEG* XX 698, ca. 200 BC).

In Alexandria, mercenary soldiers attended the impressive processions of the ruler cult and experienced the rapid diffusion of the cult of the new god, Sarapis, who promised security and prosperity in this life and serenity in the next.

How much they were impressed by these experiences can be easily seen in the inscriptions they left as pilgrims in the Egyptian sanctuaries – usually humble graffiti scratched on the walls, but sometimes elegant dedicatory epigrams. We find their graffiti in the oracle of Ammon in Siwa, in Abydos, on the royal graves of Thebes (the "Syringes"), in the temple of Isis at Philai, but most frequently in the sanctuaries of Min, who was assimilated with the Greek Pan, in the oases east of the Nile. In Koptos, a Ptolemaic officer from Gortyn on Crete made a dedication to Pan Euodos ("the one who gives a good way") and to other gods for the well-being of Ptolemy VIII and Kleopatra (130 BC; Bernand 1987: no. 86).

In the distant region of Trogodytike, on the coast of the Red Sea, where Nubian nomads still lived in conditions that resembled those of the Stone Age (Strabo 16.4.17 C 775–6), visitors were exposed to great dangers. It is here, in the Paneion of El-Kanais, that we find many graffiti in which the soldiers express their gratitude for a safe journey. Echephyllos, another Ptolemaic officer from Cretan Polyrhenia, made a dedication on behalf of Ptolemy VIII in the major city of this region, Berenike Troglodyike (ca. 124–116 BC; Bernand 1987: no. 70). The Cretan Akestimos reveals in his graffito in the Paneion of El-Kanais the precise background of many of these inscriptions: the safe return from a dangerous military mission. "Akestimos, a Cretan from Kourtolia made this dedication to Pan Euodos, having been saved from the region of the Trogodytai" (Bernand 1972: no. 13). The military context is also evident in the dedicatory epigram of Kallimachos for a Cretan mercenary who had fought in a campaign of Ptolemy III in Kyrenaika (ca. 246–221 BC; see section 8.1).

151

Some Cretans stayed in Egypt and became members of the "Cretan community" (*politeuma ton Kreton*), while others returned to their homeland, bringing with them their experiences of the legendary country and its gods. The main bearers of the cult of the Egyptian deities in Crete were mercenaries. In Gortyn, the cult of Isis was introduced by the high-ranking mercenary Pyroos, who had fought for Ptolemy VI in Cyprus (155/4 BC). In the same period, another mercenary, Philotas from Epidamnos (Illyria), who served in the Ptolemaic garrisons in Itanos (Crete), made a dedication to Zeus Soter and Tyche Protogeneia Aienaos (Isis). It is certain that the cult of Tyche Protogeneia was not native to Itanos, but introduced by foreign soldiers – either by Philotas himself or by one of his predecessors. It seems that Philotas was a man with deep religious feelings, since we know him also as a dedicant to Isis at Philai a few years later (after 139 BC). There is hardly a more eloquent testimony for the religious mobility caused by army service than the dedication to an Egyptian deity by a soldier from Epidamnos in Crete.

The wide diffusion of the Egyptian cults, especially those of Isis and Sarapis, was to some extent the result of the soldiers' mobility, but was also promoted by the Ptolemaic administration. A nice example of the indirect means by which the knowledge of foreign cults could reach distant areas is a fresco found in a room of the sanctuary of Aphrodite at Nymphaion on the north shore of the Black Sea (ca. 285–245 BC). Among other representations, one recognizes the detailed image of an Egyptian ship called *Isis*, possibly the ship of ambassadors of Ptolemy II. One of the Dioskouroi, patrons of sailors exactly like Aphrodite and Isis, is represented under the inscription with the ship's name (Grac 1987; Höckmann 1999; Vinogradov 1999).

The island of Thera, where Ptolemaic troops served for a long period, provides important evidence for the complex process of cult transfer through soldiers. Of particular interest is the introduction of cults which were closely connected with the Ptolemaic dynasty: the cult of the Egyptian deities, especially the cult of Sarapis, who was promoted by Ptolemy I; the cult of Dionysos, the patron of the Ptolemaic dynasty; and the ruler cult. The cult of the Egyptian deities is attested in numerous dedications from the early third century onwards (Vidman 1969: 88–91). The earliest was made by a member of the garrison, Diokles, and by the association of the *Basilistai* (early third century), which was devoted to the Ptolemaic dynastic cult (*IG* XII.3 443). The sanctuary of the Egyptian deities in Thera was restored by a former Ptolemaic officer (Artemidoros of Perge, who was granted citizenship in Thera; see below) on behalf of King Ptolemy III and his deified ancestors, who were probably worshipped in the same *temenos*, i.e., sacred precinct (*IG* XII.3 464).

Another member of the same garrison – a man from Myndos – made a dedication there for the well-being of Ptolemy IV and Queen Arsinoe (*IG* XII.3 1389). Some soldiers in Thera (and elsewhere) were organized in religious associations (Launey 1987: 1001–36), and one of the soldiers at Thera served as a priest (*leitoreusas*) of Dionysos Thrax, who was worshipped by a religious association of soldiers. It is tempting to assume that the choice of this particular god is connected with the fact that he was the patron god of the Ptolemies (*SEG* VIII 714); the same god was worshipped by the association of the Bakchistai which honored the Ptolemaic commander at Thera, Ladamos of Alexandria, together with his wife (*IG* XII.3 1296). The vague formulations of the decree do not reveal the exact nature of his services.

Similarly, the Attalid garrisons in Aigina and in Panion in Thrace worshipped deities particularly associated with Pergamon – i.e., Zeus Soter and Athena Nikephoros (Launey 1987: 956; *OGIS* 301). It is not necessary to assume that the promotion of these cults was guided by the royal administration. The dedicant's own religious beliefs were often the decisive factor, as in the case of Philotas from Epidamnos (above). The activities of another two Ptolemaic officers illustrate the significance of private faith for cult transfer in a military context. Apollonios, probably a citizen of Aspendos in Pamphylia, one of the main recruitment areas for mercenaries, had a successful carreer in the Ptolemaic army and reached the highest administrative position, that of the *dioiketes* in Alexandria (ca. 250 BC). Around 246 BC, he made a dedication, somewhere in Egypt (possibly Koptos), to a series of divinities which are evidently of foreign origin: Apollo Hylates was worshipped in Kourion on Cyprus, an island where thousands of Ptolemaic mercenaries (among them soldiers from Aspendos) served. It is therefore conceivable that Apollonios was acquainted with this cult while serving on Cyprus himself. A dedication of a certain Apollonios (the same Apollonios?) has been found in the sanctuary of Apollo Hylates (*I.Kourion* 57, third century). It is possible that he knew of this cult from his native city, which claimed to be – exactly like Kourion – a colony of Argos. Two other recipients of the dedication, Artemis Enodia (the patron of roads) and Artemis Phosphoros (the bringer of light), may be deities of his homeland. Leto Euteknos (the one with fair children) forms, together with Apollo and Artemis, a triad, which was widely worshipped in Pamphylia. The last divinity is Herakles Kallinikos (the patron of fair victories), a typical patron of soldiers.

The second example concerns a contemporary of Apollonios, another man from Pamphylia: Artemidoros, son of Apollonios, originally a citizen of Perge. After serving in the armies of the first three Ptolemies (ca. 285–245 BC), he settled as an old man of means on the island of Thera. He had probably served in the Ptolemaic garrison there. A large number of inscriptions record his activities: he restored the temple of the Egyptian gods (see above), and after a dream, in which the personification of Concord appeared to him and recommended the foundation of her altar, he founded a sacred precinct for her cult. It is assumed that the introduction of this cult occurred after some undetermined strife in Thera, but we cannot be certain about this. On this occasion, Artemidoros also established in the sacred precinct the cult of many other protective divinities: the cult of the Dioskouroi Soteres, the savior gods of sailors and soldiers; the Great Gods of Samothrake, perceived as protectors of individuals in need; the local deities Zeus Olympios, Apollo Stephanephoros, Poseidon, and Hekate Phosphoros; the god of fertility Priapos; Tyche (the personification of Fortune); and the heroines (*Heroissai*). Yet another altar was dedicated to the cult of Artemis of Perge, the goddess of Artemidoros' homeland, but also his personal savior. This sacred percinct assembled a series of divinities, some of which were obviously of foreign origin. The Great Gods were worshipped in Samothrake, where an old mystery cult became very popular, particularly among soldiers. During the wars of the first century BC, several Roman officers are known to have stopped at Samothrake in order to be initiated in this cult (Cole 1984: 42, 92–3), and it is almost certain that Artemidoros himself had been initiated into this cult (Cole 1984: 63). The cult of Priapos was introduced from Lampsakos, that of Artemis from Perge. In addition, Artemidoros also supported the cult of the Egyptian deities and the ruler cult of the Ptolemies. At least one of the cults he introduced, that of Artemis Pergaia, was continued after his death (*IG* XII.3 494). Besides the interest of Artemidoros' activities as an example of the wide range of cults soldiers could be acquainted with during a long period of service (Artemidoros seems to have died at the age of 94), they also testify to the possibilities religious activities offered for interaction with the natives and the incorporation of a foreign soldier into another community. After the dedication of the sanctuary of Homonoia, and possibly due to his contribution to concord in the city, the Thereans honored Artemidoros with citizenship, and after his death a Delphic oracle recommended his heroization.

Artemidoros' case shows that the social barriers facing foreign soldiers were not insurmountable. Evidence for their interaction with the native population is particularly clear in the case of commanders or soldiers who are honored for their benefactions – for example, for erecting or restoring buildings in sanctuaries (Chaniotis 2002: 109–10). It goes without saying that a military commander's position and means provided him with many opportunities to distinguish himself as a benefactor, especially when he was stationed in a poor and less prominent city. This explains why Delphi appointed as its *theorodokoi* (those responsible for receiving the sacred envoys) in three rather small poleis of Cyprus – Lapethos, Karpasia, and Tamassos – the local garrison commanders from Gortyn, Chios, and Aspendos (late third century; Bagnall 1976: 65–6).

8.3. Violence against Sanctuaries and the Discourse of War

Babrius, an author of the second century AD, narrates the fable of a peasant who came to despair when he realized that the gods failed to punish even those who had stolen sacred property (*fab.* 2):

A farmer while digging trenches in his vineyard lost his mattock and thereafter began a search to find out whether some one of the rustics present with him had stolen it. Each one denied having taken it. Not knowing what to do next, he brought all his servants into the city for the purpose of putting them under oath before the gods . . . When they had entered the gates of the city . . . a public crier began to call out that a thousand drachmas would be paid for information revealing the whereabouts of property that had been stolen from the god's temple. When the farmer heard this, he said: "How useless for me to have come! How could this god know about other thieves, when he doesn't know who those were who stole his own property? Instead, he is offering money in the hope of finding some man who knows about them."

(trans. B. E. Perry)

Many gods saw their property being stolen during Hellenistic wars or by pirates. In the second half of the third century BC alone, some of the most important sanctuaries of Greece were war victims: the Aitolians plundered the famous Heraion of Argos, the sanctuaries of Poseidon in Mantineia and at Tainaron, and the temple of Artemis at Lousoi on the Peloponnese, as well as the sanctuary of Zeus at Dion in Macedonia; Philip V avenged this attack by plundering the federal sanctuary of the Aitolians in Thermon (see below). If one considers how frequent the plundering of sanctuaries was in the Hellenistic world, one would expect very few Hellenistic Greeks to have retained their faith in the existence of divine powers, or at least of divine powers which really took notice of these earthly events. This at least is what the followers of the Epicurean philosophy and the author of the hymn for Demetrios the Besieger (see chapter 4, section 5) believed. However, the majority of Greeks reconciled themselves with the idea that the property of gods also suffered in war and found some consolation in the belief that such forms of violence only made the injustice of the attackers more obvious, and provoked, sooner or later, divine wrath and punishment. It is for this reason that acts of violence against sanctuaries are often castigated not only in later literary sources, but also in contemporary documents: these references are not only expressions of abhorrence at the sacrilegious behavior of an enemy, but also a strategy of self-representation, which underscores moral superiority – sometimes also the opposition between Greeks and impious barbarians (e.g., Polyb. 9.34.11) – and appeals to divine and human support.

In the rhetoric of Hellenistic decrees an attack against a community is very often presented as an act of injustice which was accompanied by sacrilegious deeds (see Rigsby 1996: 15). The inhabitants of Apollonia, for example, mention in a decree the undeclared war of Mesembria against their city, in the same breath as impious acts against the sanctuary of Apollo: "the Mesembrianoi started an undeclared war against us and did many and great impious deeds against the sanctuary of Apollo" (*IGBulg* I² 388 *bis*). Similarly, a decree of Priene in honor of Sotas for bravery in the war against the Galatians (*I.Priene* 17, 278 BC) castigates their unprecedented brutality (*omotes*). They not only violated customs with regard to the treatment of captives (*eis tous halontas parenomoun*), they also showed impiety towards the gods, destroying sacred precincts, altars, and temples, "falling short of no expression of shamelessness towards the gods" ([*meden elleipon*]*tes tes eis to th*[*ei*]*on anaideias*).

The many grants of *asylia* – i.e., the inviolability of a sacred space – are to some extent a reaction to the frequent attacks against sanctuaries. The term *asylia* is used with a variety of meanings, which range from the inviolability of every sanctuary to the personal inviolability of an individual against reprisals guaranteed by a foreign city and the prohibition of reprisals agreed by two communities. In a narrower sense, in the Hellenistic period, *asylia* designates the inviolabiliy of certain sanctuaries recognized by kings, cities, and confederations. This inviolability goes back to an early perception of sacred space and supplication: by coming into physical contact with a sacred place the suppliant is incorporated into the sanctity of the place and cannot be harmed or dragged away (Chaniotis 1996b; Rigsby 1996: 1–40).

In the Hellenistic period, the ubiquitous and never-ending wars presented a clear danger for the life, the personal freedom, and the property of Hellenistic cities, and also made journeys of pilgrims, athletes, and performers dangerous, thus threatening to interrupt the regular course of religious life and the celebration of festivals. Many cities officially declared their sanctuaries as inviolable, and in some cases even dedicated the entire city and its territory to a god, thus putting it under the same protection. The islands of Tenos and Anaphe and the cities of Smyrna, Kalchedon, Miletos, and Magnesia on the Maeander, and Teos, Alabanda, Xanthos, and Kyzikos in Asia Minor are among those which were declared "sacred and inviolable" (Rigsby 1996: nos. 7, 53, 63–5, 67–161, 163–5, 175). More than 200 documents attest to this practice (Rigsby 1996: 54–579), especially in Greece, on the Aegean islands, and on the coast of Asia Minor.

It would, however, be erroneous to attribute all the declarations of *asylia* to a wish to protect sanctuaries in a period of impious wars. An interplay of various expectations is closer to reality (see Rigsby 1996: 13–17). The declaration of *asylia* increased the honor of the gods and was very often connected with the organization of new festivals or with the enlargement of already existing celebrations with new athletic and musical competitions. *Asylia* gave a city the opportunity to approach old friends and make new diplomatic contacts, which could prove helpful in times of need. The economic impact was occasionally substantial, and sometimes *asylia* was also combined with a truce (*ekecheiria*; Rigsby 1996: 11–12), which made the journeys of pilgrims, performers, and traders much safer.

Asylia may have been an effective instrument of diplomacy, but it did not effectively protect sanctuaries from the violence of war. It did not save the Nikephorion of Pergamon or the sanctuary of Artemis at Hiera Kome from plunder, and in 88 BC Roman suppliants were massacred in the inviolable temple of Asklepios in Pergamon (Cic., *Flacc.* 57; App., *Mithr.* 23). Neither were such acts of violence more numerous in the Hellenistic period than in other periods of intensive warfare (e.g., during the Peloponnesian War), nor should they be regarded as evidence for a decline of religious feeling. Sanctuaries were sacred spaces, but sacred spaces attached to a particular community – a city or a confederation. In the countless conflicts between Greek communities sanctuaries fell victim to attacks which were not directed against them – even though the property of the gods was welcome booty – but against the community. What was violated was the symbolic space where the communication of the enemies with their gods took place.

For the Greeks, who were very versatile in sophistical interpretations, the plundering of a sanctuary could be interpreted as a sign that a community had been abandoned by its gods. After the Aitolians had plundered the "national" sanctuary of the Macedonians at Dion, Philip V attacked the federal center of the Aitolians at Thermon and destroyed the sanctuary of Apollo, its buildings, and the dedications, with the exception of statues with inscriptions naming or representing gods (Polyb. 5.9.2–6; Burzacchini 1999). For Philip and his officers this was not an act of sacrilege against Apollo, but a justified revenge for the sacrilege committed at Dion (Polyb. 5.9.6). If one asked the Aitolians, they would probably also make similar sophistical distinctions.

The violence against sanctuaries is very prominently represented in Hellenistic documentation, both because it offended religious feelings and because this offense against religious feelings could be exploited for the moral condamnation of an enemy – Polybios' relevant comments, for example, are always directed against the enemies of Achaia (see chapter 9, section 4). The protagonists of such sacrilegious acts – or their descendants – would sooner or later face a calamity, which could be interpreted as divine punishment, thus ultimately strengthening the belief in gods.

8.4. War and the Supernatural

In the winter of 279/8 BC, when the Gauls attacked the sanctuary of Apollo in Delphi, one of the most sacred places of the Greeks, they not only faced the resistance of the Greeks, but also that of all the elements of nature:

> The whole ground occupied by the army of the Gauls was shaken violently most of the day, and there was continuous thunder and lightning. The thunder both amazed the Gauls and prevented them hearing their orders, while the lightning from heaven set on fire not only those whom they struck but also those who were standing next to them with all their armor. Then there were seen by them ghosts of the heros Hyperochos, Laodokos, and Pyrrhos . . . The night was to bring upon them far more painful sufferings. For there came on a severe frost, and snow with it; and great rocks slipping from

Mt. Parnassos, and crags breaking away, made the barbarians their target . . . They encamped where night overtook them in their retreat, and during the night there fell on them a panic. For causeless terrors are said to come from the god Pan . . . At first only a few became mad, and these imagined that they heard the trampling of horses riding against them and the attack of enemies; but after a little time the delusion spread to all. So taking their weapons they divided into two parties, killing and being killed, neither understanding their mother tongue nor recognizing one another's forms or the shape of their shields . . .

(trans. W. H. S. Jones, modified)

This story is narrated centuries later by Pausanias (10.23.1–10; cf. Iust. 24.8), after the original nucleus had been enriched with typical elements of similar narratives. Natural phenomena, not very unusual in the region of Mount Parnassos, were interpreted as a form of divine intervention that punished the bad and saved the good. A contemporary decree of Kos (*Syll.*[3] 398; Austin 1981: no. 48; Bagnall and Derow 2004: no. 17) also refers to a miracle of Apollo, but in more general terms: "it is reported that the aggressors of the sanctuary have been punished by the god and by the men who came to defend it during the barbarian incursion, that the sanctuary has been saved and adorned with the spoils from the enemy and that of the remaining aggressors the majority have perished in combat against the Greeks." Apollo should be honored "for manifesting himself during the perils which confronted the sanctuary."

Narratives of miraculous salvation were very popular in the Hellenistic period. Collections of miracles (*epiphaneiai*), often written by professional praisers of the gods, were a popular literary genre, but no examples survive. Several narratives of miracles that occurred during wars do survive, however, in inscriptions. In 99 BC, the Lindians decided to inscribe on a stone stele a list of the most important dedications that had decorated the sanctuary of their patron goddess, Athena Lindia, and had been destroyed in the course of time, but also of the most important miracles of the goddess. It is certainly not a coincidence that this decree was proposed by the father of one of the two potential authors. The collection of the miracles is, unfortunately, not well preserved – only a miracle that had occurred when the Persians under Dareios attacked Rhodes is preserved entirely.

One of the three miracles that are still preserved to some extent narrates how the city of Lindos was saved when Demetrios the Besieger attempted to capture the island. When the city of Rhodes was under siege by Demetrios, the goddess appeared to her priest Kallikles, who was still in Lindos, in his dream, and asked him to urge Anaxipolis, one of the magistrates, to write a letter to King Ptolemy I and request his help. The goddess promised victory and power if her command was followed. Kallikles did not respond to this dream, but the goddess did not give up. She continued appearing in his dreams every night, until he finally went to the besieged city, informed the councilors, and Anaxipolis was sent to Ptolemy with the letter. Here the stone breaks, but we can imagine how proud the Lindians must have been for reminding both the inhabitants of Rhodes that the salvation of their city was the result of a miracle of Athena Lindia, and the Ptolemies that their goddess had promised them victory and power (*nike kai kratos*).

Another miracle closely connected with the self-representation of a sanctuary is known from the sanctuary of Zeus and Hekate at Panamara in Karia. This sanctuary was under attack by the troops of Labienus during one of the last wars of the Republic (42 BC). Only part of the inscription survives, but we can still recognize the essential elements: the god burned with his divine fire the weapons of the enemy; when the enemy attacked a fort during daylight, fog suddenly covered everything and "those who fought with the god" escaped without being noticed by the enemy; a sudden storm, with thunder and lightning, terrified the enemy to such an extent that "many were those who were deserting, asking for forgiveness and cried out with loud voice 'Great is Zeus Panamaros'"; in this confusion and chaos, the enemy ended up killing and wounding one another; out of their senses, as if pursued by the Furies, they met a terrible death in the nearby mountains. The god saved all the defenders of the site, fulfilling a promise he had given when he had urged them to defend it and not send the women and the children to the city. "Although many missiles were thrown, they were all seen failing their target. Not a single one of those of us that were hit during the attacks received a dangerous wound," and the 30 men who were wounded were all saved. The enemy attempted a second attack, surrounding the fort and laying a siege. But then "one heard a cry, as if help was coming from the city, although nobody was seen coming; and one heard the loud barking of dogs, as if they were mixed among those who were attacking the fort . . . And all of those, who were attacking the sanctuary of Hera, at once fell headlong down, leaving their standards and their ladders. The lamps of the god were seen burning, and they continued to burn throughout the siege."

The miracles of Delphi, Lindos, and Panamara are only the best and directly preserved narratives of "military epiphanies" in the Hellenistic period (Pritchett 1979: 29–41). Similar stories are known from Greece (Argos, Mantineia, Pellene, Lysimacheia, and Chios), the Black Sea (Chersonesos in Tauris), and Asia Minor (Kyzikos, Kelainai, Knidos, Pergamon, Bargylia, Lagina, Ilion, and Stratonikeia). It has also been suggested that Ptolemy IV's success in the Battle of Raphia (217 BC) was attributed to Isis and Sarapis (Bricault 1999).

Besides their significance as evidence for the religious attitudes of Hellenistic communities, these narratives are very interesting with regard to the self-representation of sanctuaries. The epiphanies of Lindos were inscribed on stone in order to increase the glory of the local sanctuary (*I.Lindos* 2; Higbie 2003), and in the small city of Bargylia, the citizens continually increased the size of the festival of the local goddess Artemis Kindyas and the glamor of the celebration in order to express their thanks for the many miracles of Artemis during wars (Blümel 2000; Zimmermann 2000). These efforts to increase the eminence of local sanctuaries by pointing to the military epiphanies of their gods should be seen in the context of a competition among communities. This is probably the most plausible way to explain the concentration of many narratives of miracles in the years of the Galatian invasion. In Kyzikos, Herakles was represented in a relief standing over a Galatian; in Themisonion Herakles, Apollo, and Hermes are said to have appeared in the dreams of magistrates and advised them to save the entire population in a cave; at Kelainai the barbarians were repelled by Marsyas and his music; Antigonos Gonatas attributed his victory over the Galalatians in Lysimacheia to the intervention of Pan. Such a concentration of miracles in a single year is unique in Greek history, and unless we attribute it to mass delusion – or a mass descent of the Olympians to earth – we have to assume that the narrative about the miracle in Delphi inspired the other narratives, or made the defenders of Greece more susceptible to belief in divine intervention. By bringing the gods to earth, the Greeks who experienced the invasion of the Galatians were also assimilating their battles with the Homeric narratives, in which gods and men fought side by side, but also with the miracles narrated in connection with the Persian Wars. Consequently, the defeat of the Gauls with divine assistance acquired epic dimensions and was elevated to the status of a pan-Hellenic victory over the archetypical barbarian. The representation of divine miracles turns out to be a self-asserting representation of human success.

8.5. Pragmatism Versus Tradition: War and the Dynamics of Rituals

In 192 BC, during a conference in Aigion, an Aitolian representative accused the Roman general Flamininus of having done nothing in the previous war against Philip V but "take auspices and sacrifice and pronounce vows in the front like some little sacrificial priest," while the Aitolians were risking their lives and confronting the real danger in battle (Livy 35.48.12–13; Parker 2000: 301). There are many ways to interpret this incident: one may detect here a contempt for omens, or one may suspect that Flamininus was criticized for *personally* performing the rituals. Alternatively, the criticism may have been a strategy of the Aitolian representative in order to stress the Aitolian contribution to the victory; or it may have been an attempt by Livy (or his source) to highlight the impious nature of the Aitolians. On the other hand, it may be a reflection of the ancient proverbial saying, *syn Athenai kai cheira kinei* ("in addition to Athena's help, do something yourself"), or it may be an expression of the tension between the pragmatism dictated by war and the fulfillment of a ritual imposed by tradition.

It is easy to find similar stories in ancient literature, and also in Hellenistic contexts. Hannibal, in exile in the camp of Antiochos III (or possibly Prousias), is said to have advised his host to pay more attention to the opinion of a great general than to the entrails of a dead sheep – an allusion to divinatory practices (Plut., *mor.* 606 c; Parker 2000: 303, with n. 19). This criticism reveals more than just a tension between pragmatism and traditions – it also expresses cultural tensions. The criticism, in both cases, comes from the representative of a different culture: an Aitolian criticizes a Roman, a Carthaginian criticizes a Greek king.

These two anecdotes belong to the few direct sources on the traditional rituals of Greek and Roman warfare. Pre-battle divinatory sacrifice, one of the most important rituals of war, is hardly ever mentioned in Hellenistic historiography, and this is more the result of the rather limited interest of "great historiography" in the gods and in superstition than of a change of ritual practices. The rituals primarily fulfilled a communicative function – divination served as a "a mechanism of reassurance, which helped men accustomed to the pursuits of peace to confront the terrors of the hoplite engagement" (van Wees 1996: 11–12), and sacrifice enacted aggression (Parker 2000: 307–9). Rituals were widely established, stereotypical activities, followed consistently and (at least in theory) invariably. War not only had its own rituals (e.g., pre-battle divinatory sacrifices, dedication of booty, burial of the dead, etc.), but is also a factor which in many, and sometimes unexpected, ways brings dynamics to rituals, at times subverting, interrupting, or intensifying them. A few selected examples demonstrate this multifaceted interdependence of rituals and warfare.

First, the knowledge of rituals my be strategically exploited by an enemy. Philon of Byzantion, author of military treatises, recommends generals to prepare attacks against a city on festival days when the celebrations would take place outside the city walls or in which wine consumption at public expense was likely (see Aeneas Tacticus 10.3; Garlan 1974: 293, 315). This was of course not a new practice in Greek history, as many coups or attempts to assassinate statesmen occurred during festivals, because of the possibilities large gatherings of people always offer to conceal such schemes. Harmodios and Aristogeiton murdered the Peisistratid Hipparchos in Athens during the celebration of the Panathenaia, and an attempt on the life of Mausolos, dynast of Karia, was made during a celebration in the sanctuary of Zeus Labraundos, just to mention two of the most famous examples.

Philon's advice seems to correspond to reality. We have already seen that the Milatians attacked the city of Dreros on the first day of the new year (*nea nemonia*) in ca. 220 BC (see chapter 3, section 3). In such days, respect for the worship of gods becomes a military disadvantage, and yet the subversive effect of war on rituals was rather limited. Those who respected custom and tradition could live with this discrepancy only because of the hope or faith that the gods would sooner or later punish the sacrilege.

Second, wars interrupted the practice of rituals, especially sacrifices in extra-urban sanctuaries (e.g., in the sanctuary of Nemesis in Rhamnous: *SEG* XXV 155, lines 27–30, 235/4 BC), the rites of local cult associations (e.g., *SEG* XXIV 156 + XXXII 149, Eleusis, 238/7 BC), the celebration of festivals, and the athletic competitions connected with them. The continual wars on the Peloponnese in the third century BC caused a neglect of traditional sacrifices, festivals, and rites, as Polybios asserts (5.106.1–5; Austin 1981: no. 59). Even a festival as important as the Pythian festival in Delphi was not celebrated in 86 BC because of the Mithridatic War (*Syll.*³ 738), and this has been assumed to be the case for other festivals as well – for example, the Great Elaphebolia and Laphria at Hyampolis (Pritchett 1996: 105–29 on *IG* IX.1 90; ca. 50 BC). In addition to this, the fiscal difficulties caused by war made the fulfillment of religious obligations difficult. We have already seen that Kios was unable to fulfill its religious obligation towards Apollo of Didyma (the annual dedication of a silver bowl) for many years because of wars (see chapter 7, section 2).

Third, the respect or disrespect for rituals became a criterion for the moral judgment of people. Let us take as an example one of the oldest and most awesome rituals: the burial of the dead. Any military leader, whether victorious or defeated, had a duty to bury his dead soldiers. The victorious Athenian generals at the Battle of Arginousai were condemned to death in 406 BC because they had failed to fulfill this duty (Thucydides 8.101). The unwritten military customs obliged a victorious army to give the enemy the chance to bury their dead, and a refusal was regarded either as a terrible insolence or a terrible punishment of the dead. The behavior of a person, general, benefactor, or king with regard to this custom was carefully observed and served as a criterion for the characterization of his personality or for the explanation of his motives. The Athenian benefactor Philippides was honored for taking care of the burial of his countrymen after a battle, at his own expense (283/2 BC; see chapter 2, section 6), and King Antiochos III had 8,000 Macedonians, whose bones were still lying on the battlefield of Kynos Kephalai six years after the battle, buried in a tomb, in order to gain the support of the Greeks in his war against Rome (Livy 36.8; App., *Syr.* 16).

Historical narratives exploit this element for the characterization of individuals, but also in order to underline divine punishment. Those who read in Polybios and Appian how Prousias, king of Bithynia, treacherously attacked, plundered, and destroyed the sanctuary of Athena Nikephoros, the temple of Asklepios in Pergamon, and many other sanctuaries, including the sanctuary of Artemis in Hiera Kome, which was recognized as inviolable, in 155 BC (Polyb. 32.15; App., *Mithr.* 3; Walbank 1979: 536), must have regarded his death as the punishment he deserved. He was attacked by his own son as he fled to the sanctuary of Zeus in Nikomedeia, hoping to save his life in an inviolable sacred space. The violator of sanctuaries did not find protection, but was killed by his son's soldiers (App., *Mithr.* 7; cf. Diod. 32.21).

This overview of the responses of the Hellenistic Greeks to the supernatural and to religious rituals and customs reveals an ambivalent attitude: declarations of the inviolability of sanctuaries were as frequent as their violation; rituals were criticized, but the criticism shows that they were still practiced; although mortal saviors were appreciated, the belief in divine patrons did not decline; a few years after the author of the hymn on Demetrios believed the gods to be absent and indifferent, people from Delphi to Kelainai believed they had seen the gods fighting among them. Such discrepancies and inconsistencies are not unknown in Greek religion, both in earlier and in later periods (Versnel 1994), but ambivalence may have been intensified in the Hellenistic period because of the multiplicity of philosophical schools and their influence, and also because of the coexistence of many different cultures.

An oracle given by Apollo of Klaros in the first century BC to the Pamphylian city of Syedra, continually plagued by the Kilikian pirates, epitomizes in a witty way the attitude towards the supernatural, this time spoken by a god:

> Pamphylians of Syedra, who inhabit a common land of mixed races of mortals, erect in the middle of your town an image of Ares, the blood-stained slayer of men, and flog and perform sacrifices; Hermes should hold him captured in iron chains; on the other side Justice [Dike], who declares wrong and right, will judge him; he should look [i.e., be represented] like someone who pleads [for mercy]. For thus he will be peacefully disposed to you, having driven the hostile mob far away from your fatherland he will raise up the much-prayed-for prosperity. But also you yourselves together put your hand to the hard toil, and either chase these men away or bind them in unloosable bonds; do not delay the terrible vengeance on the plunderers, for thus you will escape from impairment.
>
> (*SEG* XLI 1411)

The Syedrians needed to perform a magical ritual for the expulsion of the pirates, but this religious ritual was not enough: they should also fight against their enemies. Hence, the expectation of divine help should not abolish pragmatism altogether.

Further Reading

8.1. Communicating with the Gods, Boasting to Mortals. *Thanksgiving dedications after wars:* e.g., *SEG* XXXVI 555; Brun 2004: 45–6, no. 3. *The epigram of Menitas:* Laronde 1987: 396. *Ships named after gods:* Aphrodite: *SEG* XIV 344, XLIII 641; Athena: *SEG* XIV 339, 342; Demeter: *SEG* XXXIII 684; Hestia: *SEG* XIV 342; Isis: *SEG* XLV 997; Parthenos: *OGIS* 447. *Towers named after gods:* I.Smyrna 613. *Cult of savior gods (Soter/Soteira):* e.g., *SEG* XXX 69; Sarapis and Isis: Bricault 1999;

Herakles: *SEG* XXXVI 555; Zeus Soter and Athena Soteira in Athens (after the liberation of the city in 287 BC): Rosivach 1987; Petrakos 1999: nos. 2, 146, 148–53; for Zeus Soter, Artemis Soteira, and Athena Soteira also see below; for kings with the epithet Soter see chapter 4, section 1; see also *SEG* L 606 (Philip Soter, i.e., Philip II or V). *Festivals with the name Soteria*: Delphi: Nachtergael 1977; Kyme: Manganaro 2000; Pergamon: Wörrle 2000b. *Divine patrons of war*: e.g., Artemis Soteira: *OGIS* 18 (Egypt); *SEG* XXXV 1477 (Ikaros, Arabian Gulf); Athena Nike: *SEG* XXX 69 (Athens); Athena Soteira Nike: *OGIS* 17 (Cyprus); Athena Nikephoros: *OGIS* 248 (= Austin 1981: no. 162), 273–9 (Austin 1981: no. 17), 281, 283–5, 298, 328 (Pergamon); *OGIS* 301 (Panion, Thrace); Athena: *IGR* III 852 (Kilikia); Herakles Kallinikos ("the patron of fair victories"): *OGIS* 53 (Egypt); Hermes Hegemonios: *IG* II² 1496, 2873 (Athens); Zeus Soter: *OGIS* 301 (Panion, Thrace), 332 (Pergamon); *SEG* XXXV 1477 (Ikaros); *SEG* XLVI 1721 (Xanthos); *I.Cret.* III.iv 14 (Itanos, Crete); Pan (patron of the Antigonids): Barigazzi 1974; Laubscher 1985; Stewart 1993, 286–7; Diogenes Laerties 2.17.141; *SEG* XLVII 893; Zeus Tropaios (the patron of the turning point of a battle): Robert 1928: 438–41; *SEG* XXXV 680 (Byllis in Illyria); *OGIS* 300 (Pergamon). *Divine patrons of sailors*: e.g., Poseidon Aisios and Theoi Megaloi Samothrakes Dioskouroi Kabeiroi: *OGIS* 430; Grac 1987; Poseidon: *SEG* XXIX 1272 (dedication by the crew of a warship); Aphrodite Pontia: Parker and Obbink 2000 (Kos). *Dedications to patrons of war by soldiers on behalf of kings*: e.g., *OGIS* 18 (to Artemis Soteira for Ptolemy I), 734 (to Zeus Soter for Ptolemy VI); see also chapter 4, section 2 (further reading). *The cult of Ares in Pisidia*: e.g., *I.Selge* 17 and 20 (Selge); *SEG* XXXIII 1159; *CIG* 4377 (Sagalassos); for the identification of Ares with indigenous deities see also Engelmann 1993; Lebrun 1994; Delemen 1999: nos. 374–5.

8.2. War and Cult Transfer. *The cult of Artemis Soteira at Falaika/Ikaros*: Roueché and Sherwin-White 1985; Piejko 1988; Callot 1989; Jeppesen 1989; Potts 1990: II 183–96. *Cult transfer and Cretan mercenaries in Egypt*: Spyridakis 1969 (Itanos); Magnelli 1994/5 (Gortyn); Philotas: *SEG* XXXI 1521; cf. Cabanes and Drini 1995: 155. *Introduction of cults in Thera*: Vidman 1969: 88–91; Launey 1987: 1026–31; Bagnall 1976: 129; Chaniotis 2002: 108–9. Apollonios (of Aspendos?): *OGIS* 53; Bernand 1984: no. 47; Criscuolo 1998. Artemidoros of Perge: *IG* XII.3 421–2, 464, 863, 1333–50, 1388; *SEG* XLVII 490; Bagnall 1976: 134; Cole 1984: 62–4; Graf 1995; see also Palagia 1992. The military context of the cult of the Egyptian gods in Rhamnous: *SEG* XLI 74 = Petrakos 1999: no. 59.

8.3. Violence against Sanctuaries and the Discourse of War. *Plundering of sanctuaries*: Pritchett 1991: 160–8; e.g., Polyb. 4.25.2 (Athena Itonia); 4.62.2 (Dion); 4.67.3–4 (Dodona); 5.9–13 (Thermon); 7.14.3; 9.33.4; 9.34.8–11; 11.7.2; 31.9–11 (sanctuary of Artemis in Elam); 32.15.11 (sanctuary of Artemis at Hiera Kome); Plut., *Pompeius* 24.5. *Combination of unjust war and impious deeds of the aggressors*: e.g., Polyb. 4.25.2. *Asylia*: Chaniotis 1996b; Rigsby 1996. The following sancturies are known to have attempted, and in most cases successfully achieved, the recognition of their asylia (Rigsby 1996): Athena Itonia at Koroneia, Apollo Ptoios at Akraiphia, Dionysos Kadmeios at Thebes, Amphiaraos at Oropos, Zeus Basileus at Lebadeia, Apollo Delios at Tanagra, the Muses at Thespiai (*SEG* XLVI 536), Athena Alalkomenis, Aphrodite Stratonikis at Smyrna, Asklepios on Kos, Poseidon and Amphitrite on Tenos, Apollo Pythaios at Kalchedon, Apollon Didymeus at Miletos,

Artemis Leukophryene at Magnesia on the Maeander, Dionysos at Teos, Zeus Chrysaoreus and Apollo Isotimos at Alabanda, Artemis at Amyzon, Leto, Apollo and Artemis at Xanthos, Kore Soteira at Kyzikos, Apollo Klarios near Kolophon, Persike Thea at Bargylia, Apollo on Anaphe, Athena Nikephoros at Pergamon, Asklepios Soter at Pergamon, Artemis at Ephesos, Hera on Samos, the Samothrakian gods, Plouton and Kore at Nysa, an unknown god at Mylasa, Dionysos Bakchos at Tralleis, Hekate at Lagina, Zeus at Panamara, Aphrodite at Aphrodisias, Artemis at Sardeis, Artemis Persike at Hierakome/Hierokaisareia, Demeter at Nikomedeia, Dionysos at Nikaia, Zeus at Aizanoi, Artemis at Perge, Athena at Side, Mes at Sillyon, Ma at Komana, Isis and Sarapis at Mopsouhestia, Zeus at Seleukeia in Pieria, Zeus at Baitokaike.

8.4. War and the Supernatural. *Miracles (epiphanies) in battles:* Pritchett 1979: 11–46 (add *ISE* 152 = Bagnall and Derow 2004: no. 42); Launey 1987: 897–901; Chaniotis 1998b; see chapter 10, section 3 on *IOSPE* I² 352. *Ancient collections of miracles (epiphaneiai):* Chaniotis 1988: 39, 53, 83–4, 145–6, 163–4, 300–1.

8.5. Pragmatism Versus Tradition: War and the Dynamics of Rituals. *Financial difficulties for the fulfillment of rituals:* e.g., *I.Prusa* 1001. *The oracle of Syedra and its magic rituals:* *SEG* XLI 1411; *SGO* IV 18/19/01; Faraone 1991, 1992: 75 (with a slightly different translation of the difficult text).

9

THE DISCOURSE OF WAR

9.1. War Reflections

From 132 BC onwards, Egypt was in a state of dynastic warfare, the background of which can hardly have been topped by the script of the worst soap opera: King Ptolemy VIII, married since 145 BC to his brother's widow Kleopatra II, who was also his sister, had taken as his second wife Kleopatra's daughter, Kleopatra III. The conflict between his two wives ultimately led to a civil war which also produced uprisings of the local population in some areas (Thompson 1999, 2003: 117). The war reached the town of Hermonthis, which took the side of Kleopatra II against the king and his young wife. In 130 BC Hermonthis was threatened by forces commanded by the king's general, Paos, and it was at this point that a young soldier wrote a letter to his father, the former cavalry officer Dryton (see chapter 5, section 3):

> Esthladas to his father and mother, greeting and good health. As I keep writing to you to keep up your courage and take care of yourself until things settle down, once again please encourage yourself and our people. For news has come that Paos is sailing up in the month of Tybi with abundant forces to subdue the mobs in Hermonthis, and to deal with them as rebels. Greet my sisters also and Pelops and Stachys and Senathyris. Farewell. Year 40, Choiach 23.
> (trans. Bagnall and Derow 2004: no. 53)

Time and again, personally motivated conflicts between men and women of power have ruined family lives, and time and again soldiers – themselves in agony – have tried to conceal their own fears and console their family members with letters which very much resemble that of Esthladas.

A very different impression of war is given in a memorandum written either by King Ptolemy III or in his name, which describes the opening stages of the "Third Syrian War" (246 BC). His sister, Queen Berenike, had appealed to Ptolemy after the death (probably murder) of her husband – the Seleukid king, Antiochos II. Thereupon, Ptolemy invaded Syria, and in this fragmentary text, surviving on a papyrus, he describes an unbroken series of successful operations which culminated in a triumphant entrance to the capital city of the Seleukids:

After Aribazos [the Seleukid governor of Kilikia] had escaped and was approaching the pass of the Tauros, some of the natives in the area cut off his head and brought it to Antioch . . . From there [i.e., the harbor Posideon], early the next morning we weighed anchor and arrived at Seleukeia. The priests and the magistrates and the other citizens and the commanders and the soldiers crowned themselves [with garlands] and met us on the [road] to the harbour, and [no extravagance of] goodwill and [friendship towards us was lacking] . . . Afterwards, [we arrived] at Antioch. [And there] we saw such a preparation [for our arrival] and so [great a mass of the populace] that we were astonished. For the satraps and other commanders and the soldiers and the priests and the colleges of magistrates and all the young men from the gymnasium and the rest of the crowd, crowned [with garlands], [came to meet] us outside the gate, and they led all the sacrificial victims to the road in front [of the gate], and some welcomed us with their hands while others [greeted us] with applause and applause . . .

(trans. Bagnall and Derow 2004: no. 27)

The nature of our evidence hardly ever allows us to divine the thoughts of individuals, and the letter of Esthladas is a good example. The personal voices of mourning mothers, of captives in despair, and of timid soldiers just before their first battle, rarely reach us. The experience of war is related by collective voices: the decrees of the popular assembly, the formulaic verses of poets hired to praise heroism, and the boasting dedications of victors. The voice of a historian, for example, the voice of a Polybios, is at the cutting edge between the thoughts of an individual and the expression of collective feelings. Many historians recognized the didactic function of the history of wars. Philippos of Pergamon, a historian of the wars of the Late Republic (*FgrHist* 95 T 1; see chapter 11, section 7), explained in the preface of his history that he described the wars of the Late Republic so that people might live their lives in the "right way," by observing the sufferings of others. But in most cases the Hellenistic historians were concerned with the protagonists of history, and not with their victims. Such individuals are more often than not obscured under a veil of heroic rhetoric. For example, when the Aphrodisians declared their willingness to sacrifice themselves for the Roman cause in the first Mithridatic War, "to risk everything for Quintus and for the Roman interests, together with the women and the children and the entire property" (Reynolds 1982: no. 2), it is doubtful whether the women and the children had given their consent.

Hellenistic intellectuals and philosophers observed the impact of war no less than their contemporaries. Some of them thought that there was some utility in external war, since the threat of an enemy increased the solidarity of a community – even though contemporary experience should had taught them that an external war often instigated civil strife (Polyb. 6.18; see also Ramelli 2001: 54–60). Others saw in wars of conquest a meaningless diversion from the enjoyments of life – drinking wine and debating with friends

– as Plutarch's anecdote about the discussion between King Pyrrhos and the philosopher Kineas suggests (see chapter 4, section 1). From another perspective, a historian in Pergamon recognized in the narrative of the violent conflicts of the Late Republic an opportunity to instruct his contemporaries about the perils of war (see chapter 11, section 7).

Erratic and impressionistic as this survey of the evidence unavoidably is, it nevertheless allows us to discern several elements which we have already seen in other contexts: a taste for dramatic changes, a feeling of superiority, and a competitive spirit.

9.2. War Reveals the Character of Men and Groups

In Hellenistic public discourse, the behavior of a person during times of need was taken to reflect the most essential elements of his character. Since war was the greatest danger that might threaten a community, wars were often used as the setting for the portraiture of individuals and groups. Theophrastos, for example, describes in his *Characters* the behavior of various types of person, such as the flatterer, the garrulous, the newsmaker, etc. The settings of his descriptions are easily recognizable public spaces (e.g., the market-place, the theater, the assembly) and familiar situations: the drinking party, the theatrical performance, the court, or the assembly of the people. In some cases, the context in which his protagonists reveal their character is clearly military in nature, connected with the everyday experiences of the Athenians in the aftermath of Alexander's campaigns and during the Wars of the Successors. The "newsmaker," for example, will spread news about battles, claiming to have information from eye-witnesses who have come straight from the battlefield (Theophr., *Char.* 8). The "officious" will ask the general when he intends to give battle and what his orders will be the day after tomorrow (*Char.* 13). The man of petty pride will buy a little ladder for his pet jackdaw, make a little bronze shield for the jackdaw to wear, and have it hop up and down the ladder like a soldier taking a city; he will also invite masters-at-arms (*hoplomachoi*) to perform in his little wrestling-place (*Char.* 21). The parsimonious man will leave the assembly when voluntary contributions are asked, and when furnishing a warship for the state he will use the captain's blankets to spare his own (*Char.* 22). The pretentious will claim that he had served under Alexander the Great and had brought back from the campaigns jewelled cups (*Char.* 23). The coward, when at sea, will take the rocky capes for pirate ships; when serving on land he will find excuses to leave the battlefield, by claiming that in his haste he has forgotten to take up his sword; covered with blood from another's wound, he will tell how he has saved the life of a friend at the risk of his own (*Char.* 25). And the late-learner, already over 60 years, will have his son teach him military commands and will exercise in arrow-shooting and javelin (*Char.* 27).

In a similar manner, the public decrees in praise of individuals focus on their behavior during war. Let us take the case of Kallias of Sphettos (see chapter 2, section 5; Austin 1981: no. 44). The setting in which his services are praised is dramatically described: "the fort on the Mouseion was still occupied, and war raged in the countryside . . . and Demetrios was coming with his army from the Peloponnese against the city." The introduction of the honorary decree for Agathokles of Histria (first half of the second century BC) is very similar as regards the dramatic description of the situation: "the city was in a state of confusion and a large number of Thracian pirates were attacking the land and the city, and the harvest was imminent and the citizens were in distress . . . a heavier attack of the Thracians fell on the advance guards and they retreated across the river through fear and the land was unprotected" (*SEG* XXIV 1095; Austin 1981: no. 98). Indirectly, the proposer of this decree was comparing the behavior of others – the confusion of the citizens, the fear of the soldiers – with Agathokles' brave attitude. *He* was not paralyzed, but took the initiative and ingnored danger, "showing himself zealous in all the crises faced by the city." "Without avoiding any danger" is a formulaic expression frequently used in such decrees (e.g., Robert 1925: 426), opposing the attitude of the masses. A third example, this time not concerning bravery, but generosity, comes from Arsinoe in Kyrenaika (late second or early first century BC). The city honored Aleximachos (the "one who protects in battle"), son of Sosistratos (the "one who saves the army"), one of the city's magnates (*SEG* XXVI 1817). During a dangerous situation caused by war, Aleximachos made a voluntary donation for the protection of the city, and when the war against the Libyans had caused corn shortages and the prices were going up, he did not remain indifferent towards the sufferings (*thlipsis*) of his fellow citizens, but with his contributions enabled the city to purchase cheap grain. Another case of a citizen whose generous behavior is explicitly compared to the lack of solidarity shown by others, is that of Protogenes in Olbia (Black Sea; *IOSPE* I² 32; Austin 1981: no. 97). Among his numerous contributions, the decree in his honor highlights his behavior during a grain shortage:

> because of the danger that was threatening the people, the people thought it necessary to build a sufficient stock of grain, and invited those who had grain to do this; he was the first to come forward and promise 2,000 medimnoi at ten medimnoi for a gold coin [i.e., half the price], and whereas the others collected the price on the spot he himself showed indulgence for a year and did not charge for a year.

Protogenes repeated this service a second time, when a barbarian attack was threatening the city and "no one would volunteer for all or parts of the demands of the people." Protogenes volunteered to cover all the expenses for the fortification of the city.

These decrees, only a small selection among many, share some common features: they describe the sufferings of the community in a dramatic way, thus making the contribution of the benefactor appear all the more welcome and salutary. They compare, explicitly or implicitly, individual achievement with the passive attitude of the masses. And, by placing the achievement of the honored person in the context of competition, they aim to inspire imitators.

The idea that a man's true character is revealed through his actions in war can also be found in contemporary historiography. The Achaian historian Polybios draws a portrait of King Philip V of Macedon, in his early years an ally of the Achaians but later their enemy, focusing precisely on his behavior in his war against the Aitolians and the plundering of their federal sanctuary at Thermon (5.9–12). He compares this behavior with acts of moderation shown by other victorious kings – for example, his uncle, King Antigonos Doson, refused to hurt the Spartans who were at his mercy after the Battle of Sellasia, thus receiving undying honor, and Philip II of Macedon had demonstrated leniency (*epieikeia*), humanity (*philanthropia ton tropon*), good judgment (*eugnomosyne*), and moderation (*metriotes*) after his victories. Philip V was, according to Polybios, far from following these examples. Instead, he followed his "impulsive passion" (*thymos*), instead of conquering his enemy by magnanimity, generosity, and piety. The historian goes on to explain the necessity of war, but also the necessity of moderation:

> The customs and laws of war force us to do all this: to capture or to destroy the forts of the enemies, their harbors, their cities, their men, their ships, their crops, and other similar things, which will make the enemies weaker, but our interests stronger and our plans more forceful, if we deprive them of all this. But to destroy temples together with statues and all works of this kind without necessity, although this will neither result in any advantage in the present war to our own cause nor to any disadvantage to that of the enemy, who would not say that this is the work of a . . . spirit in rage?
>
> (Polyb. 5.11.3–4; trans. W. R. Paton)

Similar character studies against the background of wars are not uncommon in Polybios' work (e.g., 10.22–4).

The character of an entire community was also judged on the basis of its behavior during a war. Aigeira was taken by the Aitolians in 219 BC through the treason of a deserter. When the Aitolians started plundering the houses, their owners, surprised and terrified, fled out of the town and abandoned it. However, those Aigeiratans whose houses were still intact gathered in the citadel and started a counter-attack, putting the invaders to flight (Polyb. 4.57.5–58.11). Polybios' comment probably reflects common opinion on such events: "the Aigeiratans lost their city by their negligence, and recovered it again by their courage and valor, beyond expectation" (Polyb. 4.58.12).

The city of Aphrodisias owed its free status to its devotion to Octavian during the last civil wars of the Republic. The importance of this devotion is clearly expressed in a subscript sent by Octavian not to Aphrodisias, but to Samos, rejecting the Samian request to be awarded freedom:

> you yourselves can see that I have given the privilege of freedom to no people except the Aphrodisieis, who took my side in the war and were captured by storm because of their devotion to us. For it is not right to give the favor of the greatest privilege of all at random and without cause. I am well-disposed to you and should like to do a favor to my wife who is active in your behalf, but not to the point of breaking my custom. . . . I am not willing to give the most highly prized privileges to anyone without good cause.
>
> (trans. Reynolds 1982: no. 13; cf. *IG* XII 6.1, 160)

As in the case of decrees for individuals, here again we recognize a spirit of competition: Aphrodisias is compared to Samos, and if we possess this document it is not thanks to the Samians, who probably never inscribed this letter, but to the Aphrodisians, who included this text among the documents which were inscribed around 250 years later on the wall of the north parodos of their theater.

9.3. Naming Wars

The names given to wars is an indirect but valuable source for the way people thought about the wars they had experienced – though I am referring here only to contemporary reflections. Very often, a war which was still going on or had just ended was simply referred to as "the war" (*en toi polemoi, kata ton polemon*). Nevertheless, the frequency of wars, and their varying magnitude – such as the dimensions of the threat, the level of casualties, or the fame of the opponent – made distinctions necessary. For example, the "Lamian War" (*Lamiakos polemos*, 323–322 BC) owes its name to the decisive battles around Lamia; the "Social War" (*Symmachikos polemos*, i.e., the war of the allies, 220–217 BC) was started by the Hellenic Alliance under Philip V; the "(Second) Cretan War" (*Kretikos polemos*) was named after the aggressor, i.e., the Cretan League (*Koinon ton Kretaieon*).

One of the best examples is provided by the Galatian invasion, first in Greece (279/8 BC) and then in Asia Minor (278/7 BC), which contemporary Greeks saw as the greatest danger their nation had faced since the Persian Wars of the fifth century. Following the frequent practice of using ethnic names to name wars, this war was designated after the ethnic name of the barbarian aggressor as the "Galatian War" (*Galatikos polemos*). Other wars named after barbarian tribes are the "Olatian War" (*Olatikos polemos*), which refers to the war of Greek cities in the Black Sea region against the Thracian tribe of the Olatai (third century), and the "Pisidian War", which was fought between Attalos II and the Pisidians (ca. 143 BC). One has the impression that the very fact that a war was named gave it a particular celebrity, distinguishing it from the mass of anonymous conflicts which did not merit a name.

The names of wars fought against the non-Greeks expressed ethnic opposi-tions and ethnic solidarity. This is obvious in the Galatian wars, since the contemporary and later references to them never tire of stressing the god-less atrocities of the uncivilized enemy. In the case of the Pisidian War, things are more complex, since we find this name in a decree of Olbasa, which was herself a Pisidian town (*SEG* XLIV 1108; Savalli-Lestrade 2001: 86–9). But Olbasa was a strongly Hellenized city, which in this war had taken the side not of the Pisidians, but of the Pergamene King Attalos. One may conjecture that by adopting this name, the Olbaseis were underlining their solidarity with Attalos and their opposition to the rebellious Pisidians.

The name of a war could associate it with previous conflicts and evoke past glories. When Eumenes II named his war against the Galatians in 168–166 BC as the "Galatian War," he was most probably alluding to the great victories of his father Attalos I, which had legitimized monarchical rule in Pergamon (see chapter 4, section 1). It should be noted here that the Athenians called the "Lamian War" the "Hellenic War" (*Hellenikos polemos*) in order to stress the fact that it was fought for Greek freedom (*IG* II² 448, lines 43–5: "during the Hellenic War which the Athenian people started on behalf of the Hellenes").

In addition to solidarity and opposition, the names of wars also expressed superiority and pride. Many wars were named after the person, usually a monarch, who had started them. Frequently, the very name of the enemy (Mithridates VI of Pontos or Aristonikos) was so notorious and feared that the reference to the war recalled the dangers and the pain, but simultaneously gave the reassuring feeling of having overcome such a great danger.

9.4. Deciding and Justifying War

In cases of conflict, war is only one of the options. The public discussions on the Iraq War between September 2002 and March 2003 might offer future historians an excellent example of how the issue of war can be openly debated. Most probably, however, the relevant material will only be elec-tronically saved and at some point lost, so that future historians will be in the same position as a modern historian of the Hellenistic period, to whom more material about the justification of wars *after* they had been decided, or often after they had been fought, is left than about the reasoning for them being started in the first place.

For the major wars – those wars fought between and by kings – we have to rely on the reports of historians, who were of course not present at the debates prior to the conflict in question. Their reports – second-hand, filtered, and sometimes entirely fictitious – are not reliable, and even when such reports are found in the work of the best Hellenistic historian, Polybios, they can be taken as a plausible reconstruction of discussions at the most. This is certainly the case with his report on the considerations in the court of young Antiochos III in view of the revolt of Molon, satrap of Media (ca. 223 BC). The revolt itself is explained by Polybios as the result of a combination of motives: fear of the cruelty of Hermeias, Antiochos' chief minister ("in charge of affairs"), contempt towards the young and inexperienced king, and hope that the revolt would be successful, since Antiochos would face a second front in Asia Minor (Polyb. 5.41). These are psychological interpretations that seem plausible, but are not necessarily accurate. The hope concerning a front in Asia Minor may in fact be a *vaticinium ex eventu* (self-fulfilling prophecy). The report on a meeting between Antiochos and his advisers confronts us with similar questions. One of the king's "friends," Epigenes, advised him to immediately take control of the situation and to march to these provinces with an adequate army. Hermeias, who according to Polybios was Epigenes' enemy, was terrified at the prospect of a war in the upper satrapies, and hoped that the more fronts Antiochos had (Asia Minor, Media, and Koile Syria), the stronger his own position would be. He accused Epigenes of trying to expose the king's person to the rebels, and advised an attack on Koile Syria, a Ptolemaic possession, instead, "believing this would be a safe war because of Ptolemy's indolence" (Polyb. 5.41–2). Again, Polybios tries to read Hermeias' thoughts, probably based on a biased source (see Walbank 1957: 571). The historian himself had political experience and in his long life had attended similar councils, both in Achaia and in Rome; consequently, he knew well what types of argument were used on similar occasions and what kind of personal motives lay behind such arguments. But his personal experience makes his report plausible, not accurate; unfortunately, in history not only plausible things happen. Antiochos III ultimately fought all three wars (first in Koile Syria, then against Molon, in Koile Syria again, and finally against Achaios). What is interesting in Polybios' report is not his reconstruction of arguments and his psychological explanations, but the fact that no matter what decision Antiochos III took, there was an option which he did not have: to remain inactive. Even if he did not face the real threats to his kingdom, in Asia Minor and in the upper satrapies, because of the dangers involved, he had to fight another war somewhere. Decisions about war, at least in the context of monarchy, were not only based on pragmatism – response to threat, hope of gain – or on rational considerations – prospects of success – but also on general perceptions of monarchical power (see chapter 4), on the behavior expected from a king, and of course on notions of honor and shame.

The Hellenistic reports on how the wars of kings were decided are of a similar nature to the aforementioned example and confront us with similar problems of reliability. One of the very few exceptions is a documentary source – not the report of a historian, but a letter sent by King Attalos II to a priest of Kybele at Pessinous (Phrygia, ca. 156 BC), in which he summarizes the discussion in the Pergamene court as regards the Galatian danger in Asia Minor. The king and some of his advisers were in favor of a war, but Chloros, one of Attalos' friends, warned them against it:

> Chloros vehemently held forth the Roman factor and counseled us in no way to do anything without them. In this at first a few concurred, but afterwards, as day after day we kept considering, it appealed more and more, and to start something without them began to seem to hold great danger; if we were successful [there would be] envy and detraction and baneful suspicion – that which they felt also towards my brother – if we failed, certain destruction. As it is, however, [it seems that] if – may it not happen – we were worsted in any matters, having done everything with their approval, we would receive help and fight our way back, with the goodwill of the gods.
>
> (trans. Bagnall and Derow 2004: no. 50; cf. *RC* 61)

Attalos finally decided to continually consult the Romans and at the same time make preparations for defense. His situation was in some ways very particular, since he had to take into consideration the fact that the Romans limited the freedom of his actions. Nevertheless, and despite the fact that his report is filtered, since it is not a private memorandum but a letter to another person, we may still discern factors that were taken into consideration: an imminent danger, the chances of success, the general political situation, but also the behavior appropriate to the king – or any king. The unexpected, and probably unkingly, hesitation of Attalos explains why he decided to present his considerations at such length. All these are pragmatic considerations, but we may suspect that pragmatism was not the only factor at work. It cannot escape our attention that at the beginning, Chloros' warning was not taken seriously by most of the king's advisers; unfortunately, the letter does not reveal why they were in favor of immediate and vigorous action, but considerations of honor, shame, and revenge may have played some part in their attitude.

For the wars which were decided by citizen communities – cities and leagues – we hardly have any authentic reports of the discussions, but sometimes the relevant decrees reflect the arguments that may have been used in the assembly. The decree proposed by Chremonides (*IG* II² 687; Austin 1981: no. 49; Bagnall and Derow 2004: no. 19) gives us a vague impression of the discussions before the war against Antigonos Gonatas. Chremonides proposed to the popular assembly of the Athenians to ratify a treaty of alliance between Athens, Sparta, and many other Greek communities, which eventually led to the Chremonidean War (ca. 268 BC). The arguments presented are a combination of political pragmatism, historical analogies, and subtle propaganda:

The Athenians, the Lakedaimonians, and their respective allies had previously established a common friendship and alliance with each other and fought together many glorious battles against those who sought to enslave the cities; these battles won them fame and brought freedom to the other Greeks. Now that similar circumstances have afflicted the whole of Greece because of those who seek to subvert the laws and ancestral constitutions of each city, and King Ptolemy, following the policy of his ancestor and of his sister, conspiciously shows his zeal for the common freedom of the Greeks, the people of the Athenians have made an alliance with him and the other Greeks and have passed a decree to invite all to follow the same policy ... So that now a common concord has been established between the Greeks against those who are presently flouting justice and breaking the treaties with the cities, they may prove eager combatants with King Ptolemy and with each other and in future may preserve concord and save the cities.

The praise of Ptolemy is pure propaganda, whereas the subtle assimilation of the Persian invasion with the threat of the Macedonian king Antigonos (". . . now that similar circumstances have afflicted the whole of Greece") is a more intelligent strategy of persuasion, the application of a historical exemplum: united Athenians and Spartans defeated the Persians, winning fame and protecting freedom – united again we will prevail! Glory, justice, and fame appealed to the public morality of Greek citizens, and the reference to the danger to freedom and the constitution coming from Antigonos was an accurate representation of reality. What obviously worked was the combination of different strategies of persuasion.

Polybios, not unlike other (less reliable) Hellenistic historians, often summarizes discussions either among influential statesmen or in public assemblies, which were called to make decisions about war. His reports are not free of the problems of reliability mentioned above. We may observe, for example, that the manner in which he explains how the war of the Aitolians against the Messenians (221 BC) was decided by the Aitolians Dorimachos and Skopas, very much resembles his discussion of deliberations in Antiochos' court. According to Polybios (4.5; cf. Walbank 1957: 453), Dorimachos was motivated by his own lawlessness (*paranomia*) and arrogance (*skomma*). Having no valid pretext for the war (*axia logou prophasis*) and unable to exhort the Aitolians in their assembly (*kata koinon*) to make war against the Messenians, he approached Skopas, explaining to him that such a war would be a safe enterprise, since the Macedonian king was still young, the Spartans were hostile to the Messenians, and the Eleians were allies of the Aitolians. In addition to the perspective of success, Dorimachos also pointed to the potential gain: booty and popularity. Grievances could also be found, since the Messenians had wronged (*adikein*) the Aitolians by intending to ally themselves with the Macedonians. Grievances play a subordinate role in the context of this private deliberation, and pragmatism (the balance of power at that moment, the prospect of success) and psychological arguments (greed, love of power, lawlessness, and arrogance) are placed in the foreground. Polybios later describes (4.67.1–3) Dorimachos' attack against Dodona in Epeiros (219 BC) as the result of his impulsive nature (*thymikoteron*). This attack was extremely violent, and made not to secure booty for himself, but in order to inflict damage in a vindictive spirit.

Things were different when the option of war was a matter of public debate. This was the case shortly after the beginning of the Aitolian attack, when a meeting of the Hellenic League was held in Korinthos (221 BC) to discuss the attacks of the Aitolians against members of the League (Polyb. 4.25–6; see also Walbank 1957: 471–5). Grievances are here the most important issue. The representatives presented their grievances against the Aitolians: they had sacked cities, plundered sanctuaries, ravaged territories, and were planning more attacks. The delegates unanimously decided to make war against the Aitolians, who presented an imminent danger. The decree of the assembly reveals the pragmatism behind the decision and its concrete and plausible aims: territories occupied by the Aitolians from 229 BC onwards should be restored to their previous owners; cities which had been forced to join the Aitolian League against their will should regain their freedom and ancestral constitution; and the cities should be free of garrisons and tribute. The declaration of war was also linked to the sanctuary of Apollo in Delphi, which from 247 BC onwards was under Aitolian control: it should be restored to the Amphictyony, the league traditionally responsible for its administration. Polybios comments that the declaration of war in this case was a "justified" (*dikaia*) and "appropriate" (*prepousa*) response to the wrongs committed by the Aitolians.

In other public debates reported by Polybios, we find an analogous combination of pragmatism, historical exempla, moralizing arguments, and appeals to honor and revenge. The speeches of the representatives of Aitolia and Akarnania in Sparta (211 BC) belong to the most detailed presentations – or rather, reconstructions – of the type of argument in the popular assembly (9.28–39). The Aitolian representative Chlaineas, anxious to turn the Spartans against the Macedonian king, described at great length how Macedonian kings from the mid-fourth century onwards had enslaved Greek cities (9.28.1–29.6). After this historical example, he appealed to Spartan pride: the Spartans should not be grateful that Antigonos Doson had not destroyed their city when he could, but should hate the Macedonians for humiliating their prestige (*ten hymeteran hyperochen tapeinoson*) and for preventing them from attaining supremacy in Greece (9.29.7–12). Moralizing arguments follow: Philip's impiety in Thermon, his cruelty to men, his perfidy and his treachery (9.30.1–2). Then comes an appeal to gratitude: the Aitolians alone had saved Greece from the Galatian invasion (9.30.3–4). After Chlaineas had used all the necessary historical and moral arguments, he turned to practical considerations: the general strategic and military context and the balance of power which made success in war likely (9.30.5–9).

The representative of Akarnania, an ally of the Macedonians, responded to this speach with a similar combination of arguments, focusing on notions of safety (*asphaleia*; 9.32.4; 9.37.9–10), power (*hyperoche kai megethos tes dynameos*; 9.32.4), advantage (*sympheronta*; 9.32.4 and 10–11), freedom (9.37.7; 38.4), just cause (*dikaia*; 9.32.4 and 6; 9.36.9 and 11; 9.37.3; *hosion*: 9.36.12; *adikia*: 9.39.7), past benefactions of the Macedonians (9.33.2–34.3; 9.35.2–4; 9.36.1–6), past unjust and impious deeds of the Aitolians (9.34.4–11; 9.35.6–8), and the duty of solidarity with the Greeks rather than the barbarians – i.e., the Romans (9.37.6–39.6).

The emphasis on the justification, not simply the appropriateness, of violence is not a particular attitude of Polybios as a moralizing historian. In fact, it corresponds to the mentality of contemporary Greeks and Romans: those who fought wars had to be convinced – or had to convince others – that they were fighting for a just cause. This idea persisted until the late Hellenistic period. Even documents written after the end of a war frequently refer to the conditions under which the war had started, castigating the enemy's unjust or treacherous behaviour, and such phrases reflect the discussions during the war. A decree of Ilion in honor of Antiochos I (after 280 BC) reflects the way the king had justified his military actions in Asia Minor at the beginning of his reign:

> He has sought to bring back to peace and to their former prosperity the cities of the Seleukis which were suffering from difficult times because of the rebels from his rule, and after attacking those hostile to his affairs [*pragmata*, his kingdom], as was just, he sought to recover his ancestral rule; and therefore he has embarked upon an honorable and just enterprise, and with not only the zealous support of his friends and his military forces in his fight for his interests but also with the goodwill and collaboration of the deity, he has restored the cities to peace and the kingdom to its former state; and now he has come to the provinces this side of Mt. Tauros with all zeal and enthusiasm and has at once restored peace to the cities and has advanced his interests and the kingdom to a more powerful and more brilliant position.
>
> (Bagnall and Derow 2004: no. 16; cf. *OGIS* 219; *I.Ilion* 32; Austin 1981: no. 139)

Antiochos is portrayed as the victim of unjust hostility, which had caused him to lose part of what was lawfully his. His motivation was the recovery of his property, the restoration of peace, the defeat of rebels, and the strengthening of his kingdom. His just cause won him the favor of the gods. Similarly, one of the dedications made by Attalos II in the sanctuary of Athena Nikephoros in Pergamon (chapter 8, section 1) explains that the king had waged war against King Prousias of Bithynia, "after he had violated the treaties which were concluded with the mediation of the Romans" (ca. 154 BC; *OGIS* 327; Allen 1983: 82). Since the sanctuary of Athena Nikephoros had been plundered by Prousias in the first phase of this war (Polyb. 32.15; App. *Mithr.* 3), Prousias' defeat was presented as his just punishment.

Similar themes abound in Hellenistic sources (e.g., *I.Ephesos* 8; *Syll.*[3] 567; Migeotte 1992: no. 78). An Athenian decree of the time of the war against Kassandros (306/5 BC) refers to this war, pointing to the aggressor: "and now that Kassandros started a campaign against the Athenian people in order to [enslave] the city" (*IG* II[2] 469). A decree of Apollonia (*ISE* 129, ca. 200–150 BC) castigated the inhabitants of Mesembria for carrying out an undeclared war, occupying parts of the territory, and committing many and great acts of sacrilege against the sanctuary of Apollo. During the negotiations between Antiochos III, and Ptolemy IV (219 BC), the only subject discussed was the justification of their respective claims on Koile Syria, which went back to the rights of conquest established in 301 BC (Polyb. 5.67; see section 9.5). The honorary decree for Agathokles of Histria (*SEG* XXIV 1095; Austin 1981: no. 98) does not simply mention a danger- ous attack of Thracians, but also the fact that they "had broken their oath and the agreement." Similarly, in a victory monument dedicated in Pergamon after a war against King Prousias of Bithynia (ca. 154 BC), Attalos II of Pergamon justified his war – and at the same time explained the fortunate outcome of the war – by the fact that Prousias "had violated the treaties which were concluded with the mediation of the Romans" (*OGIS* 327; see chapter 8, section 1). To the envoys from Magnesia on the Maeander, who had come to Crete to arbitrate between Gortyn and Knossos (219 or 184 BC), the Knossians responded: "the Knossians fight a war against the Gortynians not of their free will (*hekontes*), but for their safety" (*I.Cret.* I,viii 9). Sim- ilarly, a Gortynian decree which approved a peace treaty between the two cities, which put an end to another of their frequent wars (ca. 168 BC), does not neglect to attribute the responsibility for the war to Knossian aggression (*I.Cret.* IV 181; Chaniotis 1996a: no. 43, pp. 292–3): "the Knossians should restore to the Gortynians the --- which they took, when they started an offen- sive war (*iontes epi polemoi*)." When envoys of Hierapytna, another Cretan city, appeared before the Roman senate to defend their claims over a disputed territory, they made sure to mention the fact that they had not attacked or wronged their adversary, Itanos (Ager 1996: no. 158 I, lines 6–8: *adikematon me ginomenon hyph' hemon*). Some vague references to the unjust or unlaw- ful occupation of a territory may in fact be connected with this line of argument (e.g., Polyb. 15.22.2 Ager 1996: no. 156, lines 23–4).

The best example of the eloquent and successful justification of a clearly unprovoked war is provided by the Third Macedonian War (171–167 BC). The last years of the third decade of the second century BC were full of hectic diplomatic activity. After the allies of Rome in the East, especially Eumenes II and Rhodes, had alarmed the Roman senate about the rising power of Perseus, the young king of Macedonia, Roman envoys toured Greece to ensure the support of the Greek cities and leagues in a war which had already been decided. The Roman envoys negotiated with almost everyone except the envoys of Perseus, whose efforts to meet with them and reach a peaceful arrangement were futile. Shortly before the beginning of the war, the Romans sent a letter either to the city of Delphi or to the Delphic Amphictyony, in which they summarize the grievances against Perseus (*Syll.*[3] 643; Austin 1981: no. 76; Bagnall and Derow 2004: no. 44, ca. 171 BC): Perseus had come with his army to Delphi during the sacred truce of the Pythian festival (174 BC); he had allied himself with the barbarians who lived across the Danube, the same barbarians who had once tried to enslave Greece and to sack the sanctuary of Apollo in Delphi; he had attacked friends and allies of the Romans; he had killed ambassadors who were sent to conclude treaties with Rome; he had attempted to poison the senate; and he had even tried to assassinate King Eumenes II, when he was visiting Delphi under the protection offered to sanctuaries and their visitors. In addition to all this, he had instigated confusion and strife in the Greek cities, corrupted the leading statesmen, tried to win the favor of the masses by promising cancellation of debts, and planned a war against Rome in order to deprive the Greeks of their protector and enslave them. The rest of the accusations (there were more) are not preserved, but were probably as false as those listed here.

Presenting grievances before an attack is a universally applied strategy of persuasion – the allegations against Saddam's secret weapons are only the most prominent among recent examples of this practice. Diodoros' narrative of how the famous siege of Rhodes by Demetrios the Besieger started in 305 BC (20.81.4–82.3) is very instructive with regard to the importance of grievances for the justification of war. The Rhodians avoided giving legitimate grievances (*dikaion enklema*) and, although they profited most from trade with Egypt, they retained good relations with all the kings. Antigonos the One-Eyed, wishing to separate the Rhodians from Ptolemy I, asked them to become his allies in his war against Ptolemy. When the Rhodians did not consent, he ordered one of his generals to seize the cargo of all the ships sailing from Rhodes to Egypt, and when the general was driven off by the Rhodians, Antigonos had his grievance, and accused them of starting an unjust war (*adikou katarchesthai polemou*). The Rhodians cautiously responded to this provocation by honoring the general and begging him not to force them to violate their treaties with Ptolemy and rush into war against him. Antigonos reacted by sending his son Demetrios with an army, and at that point the Rhodians agreed to fight against Ptolemy. However, when Demetrios demanded hostages and ordered the Rhodians to receive his fleet into their harbors, they realized that there was no way to avoid a war against Antigonos.

One of the fables of Babrius, which very much resembles this story, is an ironic commentary on the ritualized presentation of grievances (*enklemata*) before launching an attack which had long been decided:

Once a wolf saw a lamb that had gone astray from the flock, but instead of rushing upon him to seize him by force, he tried to find a plausible complaint [enklema euprosopon] by which to justify his hostility. "Last year, small though you were, you slandered me." "How could I last year? It's not yet a year since I was born." "Well, then, aren't you cropping this field, which is mine?" "No, for I've not yet eaten any grass nor have I begun to graze." "And haven't you drunk from the fountain which is mine to drink from?" "No, even yet my mother's breast provides my nourishment." Thereupon the wolf seized the lamb and while eating him remarked: "You're not going to rob the wolf of his dinner even though you do find it easy to refute all my charges" [pasan aitien].

(Babrius, *Fab.* 89; trans. B. E. Perry)

What this fable intends to show is that an attack has to be justified as reprisal for a previous act of injustice, even if the real cause is of a more material nature. This idea is deeply rooted in the Greek mentality. Thucydides begins his narration of the Peloponnesian War with a sharp distinction between the real cause of the war and the grievances (Thuc. 1.23.5–6) which were invoked in order to justify it. The Roman grievances against Perseus should be seen both in a profane and a religious setting. On the one hand, Perseus is presented as a real danger to the freedom of the Greeks and the security and concord of their cities; on the other hand, especially in a document which was inscribed in Delphi, the accusations of sacrilegious behaviour take a prominent position: "he came with his army to Delphi during the sacred truce"; he was an ally of the barbarians who earlier "had marched against the sanctuary of Pythian Apollo at Delphi, with the intention of sacking and destroying it, but they met a fitting punishment at the hands of the gods"; and he tried to assassinate Eumenes, "at the time when he went to Delphi to fulfill his vow, in complete disregard of the safety guaranteed by the god Apollo to all who come to visit him and attaching no importance to the sanctity and inviolability of the city of Delphi which has been recognized by all men, Greeks and barbarians, from the beginning of time." Perseus was worse than a barbarian – his behavior was beyond human custom, and those who fought against him fought not for Rome but for their own freedom and for the gods.

The justification of wars is connected with the idea that victory could not be achieved without the support of the gods, whose favor – no less than the favor of mortals – had to be won not only with the vow of a tithe from the booty, but also with moral arguments. The right of conquest is essentially based on this idea (see section 9.5). For this reason, before the beginning of hostilities, the enemy had to be portrayed as the aggressor and the wrongdoer, and after the end of the war had to be castigated for unprovoked hostilities, for violation of treaties and customs (e.g., *I.Ephesos* 8), and for sacrilegious deeds. An eloquent testimony is Demosthenes' oration *Against Ktesiphon*, where the orator denounces Philip's aggression. The Macedonian king had won by the spear some of the cities of the Athenians, "without having first suffered injustice [*ouden proadiketheis*] at the hands of the Athenian people" (Demosth. 18.181). The orator is not criticizing conquest in general, but unjustified, unprovoked conquest.

The importance of this distinction can be seen in a document of an entirely different nature – a curse tablet deposited in a grave in Oropos. An ordinary man, who cursed his opponents – probably in a conflict – made sure to inform the gods of the underworld that what he had written down and deposited with them should be acomplished, "having been wronged, and not having wronged first" (*SEG* XLVII 510, late third/early second century BC). Similar prayers for justice abound in the Greek and Roman world.

The significance attributed to the "just war" is clearly reflected in contemporary historiography – for example, in Polybios' moralizing views about wars which educated the unjust: "good men should not make war on those who do not care about right and wrong in order to destroy them, but in order to correct and reform their errors, nor should they destroy the things that do no wrong together with the wrong-doers, but rather save and deliver the guiltless together with those whom they regard as guilty" (5.11.5). The victorious party should practice moderation after the victory, for "to conquer the enemies by virtue [*kalokagathia*] and justice [*tois dikaiois*] is of no lesser, but of higher service than anything achieved by weapons. For the defeated yield to arms from necessity, but to virtue and justice from conviction" (5.12.2–3).

One can find examples of victorious generals whose treatment of the defeated seems consistent with Polybios' ideals – for example, the declaration of Greek freedom by Titus Flamininus after his victory over Philip V (197 BC). But the surprised reaction of the Greeks at this announcement during the Isthmian games (Polyb. 18.46) shows that moderation after a victory was beyond their normal expectations.

9.5. The Right of Conquest

The violent occupation of territory in war was under certain conditions regarded in ancient Greece as a legitimate source of property. The control of territories by Hellenistic kings was based on victorious wars, and it is precisely in this way that King Eumenes II justified his rights to territories in Asia Minor in letters sent to Tyriaion (cf. chapter 4, section 2; *SEG* XLVII 1745; Bagnall and Derow 2004: no. 43, ca. 187 BC). He had received the territory in question from the legitimate owners, the Romans, who in their turn had occupied it by defeating Antiochos III in war (*polemoi*) and on the basis of the treaty of Apameia (*kai synthekais*). War appears here as an equally legitimate means of appropriating territory as an interstate agreement.

Despite the lack of a written set of statutes of international law, the Hellenistic Greeks treated the violent occupation of territory in such a consistent way that we have to assume they had clearly defined concepts and principles. The right of conquest is unequivocally mentioned in the protocol of an arbitration of Magnesia on the Maeander between the Cretan cities of Hierapytna and Itanos in 112 BC (Ager 1996: no. 158 II). Before the judges gave their verdict, they provided a theoretical statement about the arguments that can be used to support a claim of ownership (*kyrieia*) over land: "Men have proprietary rights over land either because they have received the land themselves from their ancestors, or because they have bought it for money, or because they have won it by the spear, or because they have received it from someone of the mightier." There is much earlier evidence for this principle, of which Alexander the Great and the Successors made very liberal use. It is, however, necessary to make certain modifications, since the Hellenistic evidence shows that the right of conquest did not apply unconditionally.

Property is subject to changes by different means: purchase, conquest, donation, and inheritance. Although it is always evident who possesses a piece of property, it is far more difficult to determine who has a legitimate claim on it, precisely because of the many – and at least in theory mutually exclusive – means of acquisition of property. The question "who is the legitimate owner of a territory" very much depends on the *terminus a quo*, in other words on the historical moment which had been determined as the basis for the discussion (Marshall 1980: 648–9; Scuderi 1991; Chaniotis 2004d). Therefore, the question asked in the Hellenistic period in property conflicts was: "who was the lawful owner of a territory in a given historical moment and did the territory change hands in a lawful manner?" This is the legal background of the negotiations between Antiochos III and the Romans in 196 BC. The Romans asked Antiochos to retire from the cities previously subject to Philip V, who had been defeated by them in 197. According to Polybios (18.49–51), the Roman envoy argued: "It was a ridiculous thing that Antiochos should come in when all was over and take the prizes they had gained in their war with Philip." When the Romans raised a claim on these areas because of their victory over Philip, Antiochos did not question the principle itself, but moved the *terminus a quo* further into the past, saying that another, earlier, act of violence had established his claim – the victory of his ancestor, Seleukos I, in 281 BC. Again, Polybios summarizes his argument (18.51.3–6):

He said that he had crossed to Europe with his army in order to recover the area of Chersonesos and the cities of Thrace, for the sovereignty [*arche*] of these places belonged to him more than to anyone else. Originally, these areas were under the rule of Lysimachos, but when Seleukos went to war with him and defeated him, he won the entire kingdom of Lysimachos by spear [*doriktetos genesthai*]. But in the following years, when his ancestors had their attention deflected elsewhere, first Ptolemy captured and appropriated them [*paraspasamenon spheterisasthai*], and then Philip. As for himself, he was not by taking advantage of Philip's difficulties to take possession [*ktasthai*] of these areas, but he was *regaining* possession [*anaktasthai*], making also use of his right [*dikaia*].

In Antiochos' view, the victory at Kouropedion (281 BC) had established the righteous claim of his family on areas earlier occupied by the defeated party (Lysimachos). We may be certain that this was not only Antiochos' view. Part of the land acquired by Seleukos after this victory was sold by his son and successor Antiochos I to the city of Pitane. Later documents (Ager 1996: no. 146, lines 130–50) show that this transaction was regarded as lawful by Philetairos, Eumenes I, and the Pergamene arbitrators.

But if violence constitutes a legitimate form of acquisition of property, then why did Antiochos deny this right to the Romans? The explanation is that the exact circumstances of conquest affected the legitimacy of ownership through victory in war (see, e.g., Aeschines 2.33; *SEG* XXXIX 1426, lines 19–27). Whether the land was taken from its lawful owners in open war, or "robbed" in a moment in which they had their attention deflected elsewhere, and whether the war was just or unprovoked and unjust, affected the right of conquest. Violent occupation of land or property was regarded as a legitimate form of acquisition, no less legitimate than inheritence, purchase or donation. When the parties to a conflict based their claims on different arguments neither the arbitrators nor the adversaries gave priority to a certain type of argument over another (e.g., inheritance over conquest), but determined a *terminus a quo* for the possession. The exact conditions of the act of violence were important factors. Two questions played an important part: did the conquest take place in a direct confrontation between the owner and the aggressor (e.g., Dem. 18.181), and was the war justified? These distinctions in no way limited the validity of violence as a basis for property claims in international law. The right of conquest was not questioned or criticized. What was questioned were the circumstances, not the principle.

This idea that a victory in war establishes proprietary rights was connected with the belief that success – in violent activities such as war, piracy, or raids – could not be achieved without the support of the gods (cf. *I.Ilion* 32, lines 10–11: *kai to daimonion eunoun kai sunergon*; *Syll.*[3] 700: *enikesen ... meta tes ton theon pronoias*), who of course received their share of the booty (e.g., *SEG* L 936, lines 8–9). Victory was viewed as the punishment of the defeated party, as the expression "the verdict of victory" implies (Polyb. 13.3.4; Ager 1996: no. 74 I, lines 105–6).

In the Hellenistic period, the idea that victory in war establishes rights became one of the most important constituents of the ideology of Hellenistic monarchy. The representation of trophies on the coins of the Antigonids (Reinach 1913) or of military motifs (elephants, helmets) on those of the

Seleukids (Bikerman 1938: 217–19), the dedication of war booty in sanctuaries, and all the other forms of war memorial in the form of texts, images, monuments, and rituals (see chapter 11) focused on the image of the victorious warrior-king. Whether the war was justified or not could easily be forgotten under the much stronger impression of success. In the late second century, a prayer in Pergamon for the success of King Attalos III (*I.Pergamon* 246, line 31) expresses the wish that the gods give him victory and success not only in his defensive wars (*amynomenoi*), but also in his offensive campaigns (*archonti*).

9.6. Longing for Peace

Lists of annual civic magistrates survive from several Hellenistic cities. In Tenos, the civic officials used to have their names inscribed after their term of office, adding short notes at the end of each entry which commemorated important events – for example, "during their term of office there was health, good harvest, safe navigation" (*hygieia, eueteria, euploia; IG* XII.5 897), or "during their term of office there was health and peace" (*hygieia, eirene; IG* XII.5 902). Such "chronographical" notes show how relieved the officials of small communities were when they left their office without associating their names with any major disasters, but rather with the blessings of the gods: peace, health, and safety. To the best of our knowledge, only positive events are recorded, and there must have been magistrates who did not have their names so noted, not because of modesty, but because of the small or major calamities which had occurred during their time in office. A victorious war was no less a cause of pride and a blessing of the gods than a (rare) year of peace. Needless to say that when the magistrates of Tenos referred to peace, they only had in mind their one small island in the Kyklades.

The notion of peace in the Hellenistic world is a relative one. Peace does not appear as the ideal condition of mankind, but as the temporary relationship between two or more communities which had signed a peace treaty (or were not in a state of war), or as the geographically and chronologically limited interval between two wars. A standard formulation in decrees and treaties which asserts that the rights granted would be forever valid, under all circumstances, reads "both in war and in peace" (*kai en polemoi kai en eirenei*), and this expression implies that time is a succession of periods of war and periods of peace. Consequently, the appreciation of peace presupposes the reality of war. A speech of an anonymous envoy to Aitolia (207 BC) describes the feelings many Hellenistic Greeks must have had as regards the destructive power of war:

> As with fire, once one has set timber on fire the consequences are not at its discretion, but the fire spreads wherever chance directs it, conducted mainly by the winds and by the destruction of the timber with which it is fed, often

turning on the very persons who lit it, beyond reasonable expectation. So it is with war. Once it has been kindled by anyone, at times it destroys in the first place its authors and at times it advances destroying without any just cause everything it meets with, ever revived and ever blown anew into a blaze, as if by winds, by the folly of those who come near it.

(Polyb. 11.4.4–5; trans. W. R. Paton)

Consequently, references to peace are always understood in relation to a preceding war. When Hellenistic kings are praised for establishing peace, they are praised for defeating an enemy and thus putting end to a war. The same idea – that successful war against an enemy establishes peace – explains why the Rhodians named one of their warships *Eirene* ("Peace"; *IG* XII Suppl. 210 + *SEG* XXXIII 683). Peace treaties were concluded in order to end particular hostilities between two or more communities. Although the experience of war in the late fifth and early fourth century had led in the fourth century, before the campaigns of Alexander the Great, to the idea of a "common peace" (*koine eirene*) among the Greeks and to the cult of Eirene, the personification of peace (Jehne 1994; Perrin-Saminadayar 1999), this idea hardly played any part in the Hellenistic period. Hellenistic peace treaties were valid with regard to particular areas and were usually concluded "for all time" (e.g., *Staatsverträge* 428, 516), but this book would not have a subject if this clause had been taken literally. A general and unconditional renunciation of war and violence, like that pronounced by the Mauryan King Ashoka in the late third century (Thapar 2002), is unknown in Hellenistic public life.

This limited scope of the Hellenistic Greeks when referring to peace does not of course mean that peace was not regarded as a preferable condition – at least when the quick victory of one of the parties did not seem realistic. In such situations it was regarded as a great service if a friendly community (or a king; see chapter 4, section 4) intervened and attempted to arbitrate. This is what Magnesia on the Maeander in Asia Minor did on several occasions in the numerous Cretan wars. It successfully arbitrated in the Lyttian War (ca. 219 BC), the greatest war of Cretan history, possibly again in a war between Knossos and Gortyn (184 BC), and in wars between Itanos and Hierapytna (140 BC and 112 BC). The importance with which this service was regarded can be best seen in the fact that when Magnesia on the Maeander sent envoys to the Greek cities and leagues in order to promote the local festival of Artemis Leukophryene and to have the inviolability of the sanctuary recognized (208 BC), the successful appeasement in Crete was included among the great achievements of the Magnetes. It was mentioned in one breath with their contribution to the defense of Delphi during the Galatian attack of 278 BC (*I.Magnesia* 46; Bagnall and Derow 2004: no. 155).

Two fragmentary decrees of Gortyn and Knossos which refer either to the arbitration during the Lyttian War (Magnetto 1997: no. 43) or to the war of 184 BC (Chaniotis 1996a: no. 40) show that the reconciliation of neighboring communities was an honorable service. The Gortynian decree, which is better preserved but similar in content to the Knossian one, explains that the Magnetes had sent a decree and ambassadors asking the Gortynians to resolve their disputes with the Knossians, stop the war, and restore friendly relations. Magnesia is then praised:

> for it does what a friend and a kin of the Cretans should do; we also praise the ambassadors [--], son of Mikion, Charisios, son of Nikomachos son of Nika [--], because they explained well the good relations which exist between the Gortynians and the Magnetes from the beginning and because they did what was appropriate for the peace and did not fall short as regards love of honor; they did not hesitate to undertake a journey or another hardship in order to achieve what is advantageous for Crete and for Magnesia.
>
> (*I.Cret.* IV 176; Chaniotis 1996a: no. 40c)

Many years later, when in 112 BC Magnesian judges were again asked to arbitrate in a war between Itanos and Hierapytna, they narrated in a document their efforts to reconcile the two cities and the principles on which they based their decision (*I.Cret.* III. iv 9). This document opens with a condemnation of conflicts and a praise of peace and concord: as circumstances often bring even the closest relatives to a conflict, it is the duty of their friends to try their best to reconcile them (lines 14–17). It is for this reason that the Magnesians had willingly accepted the role of arbitrator (lines 26–31):

> When we were elected as judges, we immediately went up to the altar of Artemis Leukophryene and after the slaughter of a sacrificial animal we took an oath upon it, in the presence of the legal representatives of the two cities and the men who had come with them. And we took our seats in the sanctuary of Artemis Leukophryene and heard the conflicting parties to the end, allowing them [for their orations] not only the daytime, but also most part of the night, taking upon ourselves every laborious toil, so that neither of the adversaries might have any disadvantage in regard to justice.

After the representatives of Hierapytna and Itanos had presented their arguments, the judges made a last effort to reconcile them before taking a vote on the verdict.

The arbitration of the Knidians between Temnos and Klazomenai (*SEG* XXIX 1130 *bis*, ca. 200–150 BC) reveals the same spirit. The Knidians explain that their purpose was that "the friendship and the goodwill that had existed in the past may be maintained between the two cities, corresponding to the earlier friendly relationship, and that the conflict that came about concerning the disputed affairs will stop and there will be a secure re-establishment to friendship." The Knidians also observed that the accusations mutually made for the acts of violence which had occurred during the war would contribute to the enmity between the two sides, and for this reason they established an amnesty for everything which had occurred during the war, realizing that peace often requires a selective memory: remembering the sufferings, but forgetting who had caused them.

If peace does not appear as a general ideal for mankind, it nevertheless appears as an instrument of prosperity and safety. Peace and prosperity are mentioned in one breath in a letter of Eumenes II in response to honors awarded to him by the Ionian League (*RC* 52, 167/6 BC): "I had from the start chosen the finest actions and had shown myself a common benefactor of the Greeks; consequently I had undertaken many great struggles against the barbarians, exercising all zeal and forethought that the inhabitants of the Greek cities might always dwell in peace and the utmost prosperity." We find the same connection in the "hymn of the Kouretes" from Palaikastron in Crete (Furley and Bremer 2001: I 68–75, II 1–20). This hymn survives in a copy of the Imperial period, but was originally composed in the early Hellenistic period. It is generally agreed that it was sung by the ephebes of several Cretan cities, probably the cities which participated in the cult of Zeus Diktaios in eastern Crete, during the annual festival of Zeus. With this hymn the Cretans prayed to Zeus to appear, to protect their cities, their flocks, their ships, and their young men. The hymn also praises justice and "peace, which goes with prosperity" (*philolbos eirene*). At first sight, this seems a general praise of justice and peace, but considered in the context of the reality of Hellenistic Crete, the hymn more probably expressed the hope that peace might prevail only among the communities which participated in the cult.

The idea that peace among the Greeks was the best instrument for their protection from foreign enemies has its origins in the early fourth century. We find a distant reflection at the peace conference of Naupaktos (217 BC) which put an end to the "Social War." Here, Agelaos gave the Greeks the following advice: "Above all the Greeks should never go to war against each other, but give the gods hearty thanks if speaking all with one voice and joining hands together, as when crossing a river, they managed to repel the attacks of the barbarians and save themselves and their cities" (Polyb. 5.104.1; Austin 1981: no. 59).

For Agelaos, peace was not a desirable condition for all mankind, but an instrument which would guarantee the safety of the Greeks. The Greeks ignored this advice, and it took another two centuries of fighting before the Roman conquest established the *Pax Romana*.

Further Reading

9.1. War Reflections. *The report on the Third Syrian War: FgrHist* 160; cf. Austin 1981: no. 220.

9.2. War Reveals the Character of Men and Groups. e.g., Polyb. 10.22–4; 16.1; 16.21–2; 18.41; 21.9.

9.3. Naming Wars. *Anonymous wars*: SEG XXVI 1817: *ho polemos*; IG II^2 493: *epi tou polemou tou proterou*; *Syll.*^{3} 529: *sympolemesantes ton polemon*; see e.g., SEG XXXVI 777; XXIX 1130 bis; XXXIX 759; *Sardis* VII.1 2. *Named wars*: the Lamian War, 323–322 BC: *FgrHist* 239 B, section 9; Hellenic War: IG II^2 448, lines 43–5; 505, line 17; the Social War: e.g., Polyb. 4.26.1; the Cretan War: Polyb. 33.13; IG XII.3 103; the Galatian wars, 278–276 BC: *I.Laodikeia* 1 (*Galatikos polemos*); OGIS 748 (*ho polemos ho pros tous Galatas*); *I.Priene* 17 (*ho ton Galaton polemos*); the Galatian war of 168–166: RC 54 (*Galatikos polemos*); *Olatikos polemos*: *Syll.*^{3} 707 = Maier 1959: no. 86; Mithridates' War: OGIS 445 (*ho polemos ho Mithridatous*); OGIS 441 (*pros Mithridaten polemos*); cf. *I.Stratonikeia* 1333; SEG XLV 1825; Aristonikos' War: SEG XXXIV 1198 (*ho pros Aristonikon polemos*). Cf. *ho polemos ho pros tous klerouchous*: SEG XXVI 1022 (Samos); *ho poti Libyas kairos*: SEG XXVI 1817. Cf. Thompson 1999: 324–6, on the proverbial phrase "the audacity of Herchonesis", which was inspired by a native revolt in Ptolemaic Egypt.

9.4. Deciding and Justifying War. *Antiochos' wars*: Ma 2000a. *Bellum iustum*: Bickermann and Sykoutris 1928: 27–8; Mantovani 1990 (in the Roman Imperial period). *The Roman manifesto against Perseus*: *Syll.*^{3} 643 = Sherk 1969: no. 40 A = Austin 1981: no. 76 = Bagnall and Derow 2004: no. 44; cf. Livy 42.11–14; 42.40; see also Gruen 1984: 408–19; Jacquemin and Laroche 1995. *Discussions in the assembly described by Polybios*: e.g., 9.28–39; 11.4–6; 16.26; 20.3; 27.8; 29.23.8–26.2; 38.13.6; see also the descriptions of negotiations in 18.1–12; 18.50–1; 21.10 and 13–15. *Prayers for justice*: Versnel 1991; Chaniotis 2004e.

9.5. The Right of Conquest. *Selection of sources*: Thuc. 4.98.2–3; Xen., *Cyr. paed.* 7.5.73; Dem. 12.21; Polyb. 5.67.41–8; 28.20.6–22; Diod. 21.1.5; Livy 34.57.7; see also Bikerman 1938: 15; Müller 1972: 108–21; Mehl 1980/1; Boffo 2001; Chaniotis 2004c, 2004d. *The claims of Antiochos III*: Bickermann 1932; Boffo 2001: 239–40; Chaniotis 2004c; see also Ma 2000a: 82–102.

9.5. Longing for Peace. The notion of peace, in general: Lana 1989; Spiegel 1990. "*Chronographical notes of Tenos*": Wilhelm 1927: 342–5; Chaniotis 1988: 188–9; for similar texts from Delos see, e.g., IG XI.2 105, 108–11, 113–16, 120, 122, 124, 126, 128, 132–3; SEG L 724. *Common peace (koine eirene) in the fourth century*: Jehne 1994; Schmidt 1999. *Peace treaties*: in general: Keil 1916; Schaefer 1932: 58–63; in the Hellenistic period: Klose 1972: 160–1; Chaniotis 1996a: 61, 227–8 (on Crete). *International arbitration*: Ager 1996; Magnetto 1997; the arbitrations of Magnesia on the Maeander in Cretan wars: Chaniotis 1996a: 281–5, 307–10, 333–7; Ager 1996: nos. 58, 127, 158; Magnetto 1997: nos. 43, 53. Praise of kings, generals, and officers for preserving peace: IG II^2 672, line 9; 682, line 34; *F.Delphes* III.4 163, line 21; OGIS 6, lines 16–18; *I.Ilion* 32 (Bagnall and Derow 2004: no.16); *I.Iasos* 4; SEG XLVI 1565 (Pompey); see also the hymn for Demetrios (see chapter 4, section 5); prayers for peace: *I.Magnesia* 98; Furley and Bremer 2001: I 68–75, II 1–20.

10

AESTHETICS OF WAR

10.1. Images of Violence in Hellenistic Literature and Art

Theokritos is usually remembered as the poet of shepherds in love; he was also the poet of passionate women, of self-confident kings, but also of realistic descriptions of violence – for example, in his 22nd idyll, in which he describes the boxing match between Polydeukes and Amykos (lines 97–128):

> Drunk with the blows, he came to a standstill and spat crimson blood, while all the heroes shouted to see the grievous wounds about his mouth and jaws; and as his face swelled the eyes were narrowed to slits. Then did the prince confound him with feints on every hand, but when he marked him at a loss drove with the fist down on the brow above the center of the nose and skinned the whole forehead to the bone, and with the blow Amykos stretched on his back upon the flowery sward . . . Polydeukes slipped his head aside and with his stout fist struck below the left temple and put his shoulder into the punch; and from the gaping temple swift flowed the dark blood. Then with his left he landed on the mouth so that the close-set teeth rattled, and with an ever faster rain of blows savaged the face until the cheeks were crushed and Amykos, dizzy, stretched his length on the ground.
>
> (trans. A. S. F. Gow)

Such merciless representations of violence are not uncommon in Hellenistic art and literature (Fowler 1989: 33–5; see section 10.2). From the famous dying Gauls of Athens and Pergamon, to the irrational violence of the toddler who strangles a goose, from the long, detailed, and frequent representations of contemporary battles and the sacking and plundering of cities in Hellenistic historiography, to mythical narratives of violence in the epic poetry of Apollonios of Rhodes, from battle scenes in grave monuments or Homeric scenes on drinking bowls, to hunting scenes on mosaics, from fighting athletes and warriors, to the images of the mythical combat between the Olympians and Giants on the Great Altar of Pergamon, Hellenistic audiences were confronted with a variety of texts and images which represented violence.

Sometimes the representation was subtle – for example, in the image of two boys watching a cock fight; but more often violent scenes were described or shown in a highly realistic manner. Taken in isolation, such images may create the wrong impression that Hellenistic audiences found it entertaining to see others suffer – as audiences in the Roman arena did – or that they took the same pleasure in blood, wounds, and mutilated bodies as the audiences of modern movies. For most modern audiences, brutal violence is experienced on a screen; Hellenistic art and literature represented forms of violence which their audiences most likely had witnessed in real life. Hellenistic literature and art demonstrate an interest in realism, not in violence in itself, as this chapter will attempt to show.

Hellenistic realism and "Hellenistic baroque" (Pollitt 1986: 111–26, 141–7; Fowler 1989: 32–43) are only two of the predominant aesthetic tendencies of a long historical period which was anything but free of contradictions. These two trends, in addition to a sensibility towards passion, dramatic contrasts, and unexpected turns of fortune (Pollitt 1986: 1–4; Fowler 1989: 32), determine the way war was represented in contemporary art and literature. It is, of course, beyond the scope of this book to study Hellenistic aesthetics in general, but in this chapter, I will attempt to sketch how Hellenistic wars inspired art and literature and how the aforementioned general aesthetic tendencies of Hellenistic art and literature can be observed in the representation of war.

> Hellenistic poetry brought to Western literature many of the qualities which we think of as modern: an interest in animals (especially pets), babies, children, women, and grotesques; common or working people and the tools of their trades; landscapes; cities; the passions of romantic love and of sinning; pathos; burlesque. The literature parallels the subject matter of the visual arts, where we find fishermen, hunchbacks, dancing dwarfs, drunken old women, babies, dogs, women who have died in childbirth, kitchen utensils, and the expression of emotion in the faces of creatures as well as people.
>
> (Fowler 1989: 4)

If battle scenes and dying or triumphant warriors are absent from this excellent summary of the essential features of Hellenistic art and poetry, this is not the fault of the author of these lines. War is indeed not very well represented in Hellenistic poetry, the more so if we take into consideration the quantity of warfare in this period, as it has been surveyed in the preceding chapters. War was primarily a subject for historians, not for poets, a subject for public recitation, not for private reading. A similar observation can be made in the case of visual art: representations related to war primarily (and quite naturally) invaded public space: sanctuaries and market-places are the areas in which we find war monuments, and only a single private space invited images of war: the grave (e.g., Smith 1991: figs. 217–18). War may have been ubiquitous in the "real world" of the Hellenistic Greeks, but it did not dominate their entire culture.

Of course, subjects related to warfare are to be found in many areas of Hellenistic art, at least in an indirect way. Some of the best known and admired works of Hellenistic art owe their existence to wars. Good examples are the Nike of Samothrake (Pollitt 1986: 114–16, fig. 117; Smith 1991: 77–9, fig. 97) and the Colossus of Rhodes, now lost, which was a war memorial of the Rhodians (see chapter 11, section 6). The representations of the dying Gauls on the altar of Zeus in Pergamon commemorated the triumph of the Pergamene kings over the barbarian invaders. Hellenistic warfare bequeathed to world literature the *miles gloriosus*, the boastful professional soldier who is represented in contemporary comedy, but also on terracotta statuettes (Ducrey 1986: 138–9, fig. 98). We have already seen that the wars that followed the death of Alexander the Great are the background of many of Theophrastos' *Characters* (see chapter 9, section 2). The great interest in technical virtuosity, which has been recognized as an important feature of the Hellenistic aesthetic (Fowler 1989: 5–22), is closely connected with the detailed descriptions of ships and war machines (e.g., Athen. 209 c). Among Kallimachos' epigrams one finds some written for soldiers (e.g., epigr. 24, 37, and 62), and many other epigrams of anonymous poets were written on the graves of war dead. The encomiastic poem for King Ptolemy II, composed by another great Hellenistic poet, Theokritos (*Idyll* 17), does not lack references to military success. Two historical epics, by Leschides ("The deeds of Eumenes," *FgrHist* 172) and Simonides of Magnesia ("The deeds of Antiochos and the battle against the Gauls," *FgrHist* 163) were dedicated to victories over the Gauls. Of course, only a vague impression of the encomiastic elegies inspired by the Galatian wars can be given by two small poetic fragments (*Supplementum Hellenisticum* 958, 969; Barbantani 2001; cf. Barigazzi 1974). Similarly, the genre of poetic laments for the destruction of cities is almost entirely lost, with the exception of a epigram of Antipatros of Sidon about the sack of Korinth (*Anth. Gr.* 9.151; see section 10.2).

For no other literary genre was war so important as for historiography, and no other genre is so well preserved as historiography (see chapter 11, section 2). For this reason, the following pages primarily explore the way historians presented war to their audiences, but they also draw attention to the convergence between this literary genre and contemporary aesthetic trends.

10.2. Blood is Beautiful: Realism and Subtlety in the Representation of Violence

The Hellenistic historian Phylarchos (*apud* Plut., *Pyrrhos* 28.4–5; cf. Beston 2000: 316–17) gives a very dramatic description of a critical moment in

Sparta, when the troops of Pyrrhos attacked and almost seized the city (cf. chapter 6, section 3):

> The young Akrotatos saw the danger, and running through the city with three hundred men got round behind Ptolemy without being seen . . . The elderly men and the host of women watched his deeds of bravery . . . And when he went back again through the city to his allotted post, covered with blood and triumphant, elated with his victory, the Spartan women thought that he had become taller and more beautiful than ever and envied Chilonis her lover.

Akrotatos does not appear beautiful *although* he is covered with blood, but *because* he is covered with blood. We are not told whether the blood which covered his body was his own or that of the enemies he had killed; the Spartan context, where part of the training of youths consisted in their being flogged near the altar of Artemis Orthia, renders the former assumption plausible, without of course excluding the latter. The beauty of Akrotatos is the beauty acquired by a man through heroism; no wounds or scars can diminish it. Hellenistic historians and honorary decrees often mention in contexts of admiration and praise the fact that a king or a benefactor had been severely wounded.

In a world in which the ideal of *kalokagathia* – the combination of visible beauty (*kalos*) and virtue (*agathos*) – remained valid until the coming of Christianity (e.g., *SEG* XXXI 903, third century AD), it would be a discrepancy if the visible proof of virtue – i.e., the wounds which a man received while fulfilling the ideal of bravery – was regarded as ugly. And yet – with the exception of Alexander's father, Philip II – neither the royal portraits nor the images of warriors let the spectator imagine that the idealistic heads and bodies had received scars in wars; and this despite the fact that realism is one of the central tendencies of Hellenistic art and poetry (Pollitt 1986: 141–7). The exaggerated realism which can be observed, for example, in the famous statue of a seated boxer in the Museo Nazionale delle Terme in Rome, with damaged ears, broken nose, overdeveloped back, scarred cheek and forehead, and broken teeth, is not allowed in the case of kings and men who died heroic deaths. The contradiction between the idealization, evident in royal portraits, funerary monuments, honorary statues, or dedicatory reliefs, and the merciless naturalism which one observes in "genre scenes," with old fishermen or drunk old women, or the burlesque representations of crippled persons, is only one of the many contradictions one observes in the Hellenistic aesthetic – and in the Hellenistic world in general. The representations of battles or of the consequences of war, whether in historiographical narratives, in poetry, or in art, also cover the entire range, from brutal realism to subtlety.

Battle scenes occupy a central position in historiographical narratives, and this is not surprising, since Hellenistic historiography is primarily the historiography of war (see chapter 11, section 2). The historians who were inspired by the conquests of Alexander the Great naturally described battles in great detail. The never-ending wars that followed Alexander's death offered the next generations of historians plenty of opportunities to show their talents in the narratives of campaigns and battles. A *locus classicus* for the representation of war in Hellenistic historiography is Polybios' description of the defeat and death of Machanidas, Sparta's king (or regent), in 207 BC (Polyb. 11.11–18), and for this reason that narrative will be discussed here in some detail.

At the beginning of the narrative, Polybios prepares the reader for the apocalyptic dimensions of this war: the general of the Achaians, Philopoimen, gathers his troops to Mantineia "to start the struggle against the tyrant for the liberty of all the inhabitants of the Peloponnese" (11.10.9). Polybios leaves no doubt for whom his heart beats. The tyrant is represented at the beginning at the hight of his power; so much farther his fall will therefore be. Already we recognize the interest of contemporary audiences in dramatic changes of fortune, an interest which is of course prominent also in the New Comedy (the comedy of the Hellenistic period).

Filled with confidence, Machanidas regards the Achaian attack as a fulfillment of his prayers to the gods (11.11.1). In the next paragraphs Polybios, the conscientious preacher of pragmatic historiography and an experienced military commander himself, describes in detail how and where Philopoimen and Machanidas put up their troops and of which units these troops consisted (11.11.2–7). Such detailed descriptions in historical narratives correspond exactly to the contemporary interest in technical details and virtuosity (see Fowler 1989: 5–22).

The next scene – often repeated in epic films (e.g., in *Braveheart* and *Lord of the Rings: The Return of the King*), alas (as far as we know) without knowledge of Polybios' narrative – is the classical exhortation of the troops by the good commander. Philopoimen rides along the divisions addressing the soldiers in a few brief words: in the present battle the enemy were fighting for shameful and ignominious slavery, while they were fighting for imperishable and noble liberty. His words are hardly heard, for the soldiers' affection for their general, their ardour, zeal, and enthusiasm were so great that they exhorted him to lead them on, being of good heart (11.12.1–3). From the first movement of Machanidas, Philopoimen recognizes the enemy's plan and opens the attack, obliging the enemy to do likewise. At first the battle of a confused crowd seems equally balanced, but after some time the tyrant's mercenaries prevail, due to their superior numbers and better professional training, as Polybios finds it necessary to explain (11.13.3). The Achaian troops flee in disorder towards the city of Mantineia, and everything seems lost. The historian intervenes again, indirectly pointing to three essential elements of such narratives, which one finds also in contemporary decrees: the role of central figures (here, the two commanders), the dramatic situation caused by the imminent danger, and the unexpected success (*to paradoxon*): "Most accomplishments in war are due to the experience or again the lack of experience *of the commanders*... Indeed we often see that those who already *seem to have gained the day*, totally fail shortly afterwards, whereas those who at first seemed to have failed turn the tables and *unexpectedly* succeed in everything by their intelligence" (11.14.2–4; trans. W. R. Paton).

In his moment of triumph, Machanidas makes a fatal mistake: instead of remaining on the field in order to strike the decisive blow, he follows his mercenaries and runs after the fugitive enemies, behaving like an undisciplined boy. The commander moves from leader to follower. The true character of a person is revealed in war (see chapter 9, section 2), and the behavior of Philopoimen is directly opposed to that of Machanidas. The lucid description of the calm, self-controlled, and ingenious commander is now a striking contrast to the confusing and chaotic scenes of the battle (11.13.1–2: "they were mixed up; they were fighting all over the field in a confused crowd and man to man"; 11.14.1: "they left in disorder"). First Philpoimen calls the leaders of his own mercenaries by name; when he realizes that the pressure is too strong, he posts himself on the wing, lets the pursuers pass by and then occupies the field they have left, thus cutting off the pursuers from the rest of their army. At the right moment he gives the order for a general attack.

The contrasts between the confusion inherent in a mass slaughter and the clarity in the description of Philopoimen skillfully makes the reader concentrate on the protagonist and underlines the role of the great personality. We may observe the same technique not only in other texts, but also in contemporary images of battle scenes. In the famous "Alexander mosaic" in the Museum of Naples (Pollitt 1986: 3–4, fig. 2), confusing scenes of mass slaughter coexist with and form the background for the depiction of the protagonists, Alexander and Dareios. This applies to some extent to the so-called "Alexander sarcophagus" in Istanbul (Winter 1912), and can be observed in a different way in the monument of Aemilius Paullus in Delphi (Pollitt 1986: 155, fig. 162; Smith 1991: 185, fig. 209). Here the bronze equestrian statue of Paullus placed on the pillar's top separates and elevates the general from the confusing battle, thus stressing the role of the great individual.

In the description of the final combat, Polybios contrasts the two armies: the Achaians with one heart (*homothymadon*) and with a loud, terrifying cheer (*meta krauges kataplektikes*) rush on their foes, who descend into a ditch around the walls of Mantineia, where they perish, killed either by the Achaians or by each other (11.16.2–3). And then, once again, he changes the perspective, leaving the confusing slaughter in the ditch and focusing on the two protagonists. Such close-ups are frequent in representations of battle scenes, whether in Homer, Thucydides, the "Alexander mosaic" or

Akira Kurosawa. Polybios first describes the desperate attempts of Machanidas to escape. He initially tries to force his way through the pursuers with the remainder of his mercenaries; they, however, lose heart and abandon him, attempting to save themselves as best as they can.

> Meanwhile the tyrant, losing hope of making his way across the bridge, rode along the ditch vigorously trying to find a crossing. Philopoimen, recognizing Machanidas by his purple cloak and the ornaments of his horse, left Alexidamos and his men, ordering them to guard the passage carefully and spare none of the mercenaries, for they had always increased the power of the Spartan tyrannies. Taking with him Polyainos of Kyparissia and Simias, who were at that time his aides-de-camp, he followed the tyrant and those with him – two men had joined him, Arexidamos and one of the mercenaries – along the opposite side of the ditch. When Machanidas, on reaching a place where the ditch was easily passable, set spurs to his horse and forced it across, Philopoimen turned to meet him. He first wounded him seriously with his spear and added another wound with the lower end of it, thus killing the tyrant hand to hand. Arexidamos suffered the same fate at the hands of those who were riding with Philopoimen, but the third man, despairing of crossing, escaped the danger while the other two men were being slain. When both had fallen, Simias' companions stripped the bodies of the dead, taking together with the armor also the head of the tyrant and rushing back to the pursuers, eager to show to the troops those proofs of the death of the enemies' commander . . .
>
> (11.17.7–18.7; trans. W. R. Paton, modified)

The tragic ironies in this report would not have escaped the notice of the ancient reader: the purple garment and the luxurious horse trappings, arrogant symbols of superiority, betray Machanidas, and the pursuer becomes, because of his own insolence, the pursued. If this description of the showdown resembles a hunting scene, it is not only because hunting was the favorite occupation of the nobleman Polybios and his readers, but possibly an intentional humiliation of the hated enemy. He is killed like a wild boar with Philopoimen's spear; the tyrant's head is triumphantly shown (*epideixai*) like the head of a hunted animal. There is yet another tragic irony: the death of Machanidas and Arexidamos saved the third man's life.

The war which started as a struggle between tyranny and liberty (11.10.9) ends in a close-up, where Hellenistic historiography meets the epic war films of Hollywood. The battle culminates in a face-to-face combat between the two protagonists: the tyrant and the champion of liberty. The modern reader is left to decide whose actor's face he chooses to give Philopoimen – Mel Gibson being my personal preference.

Polybios must have heard of this combat between Philopoimen and Machanidas from eye-witnesses, possibly from Philopoimen himself. Hellenistic men enjoyed narrating their exploits in war, and references to warriors killing their opponents hand to hand (*en cheiron nomais, kata cheiras*) in

195

Figure 10.1 Battle scene between a Macedonian horseman and a Persian infantry-man in the painted "Kinch tomb" (Naousa, third century BC; courtesy of the Department of Antiquities of Pella).

honorary decrees certainly originate in the stories told by the soldiers when they returned home after a battle. A prominent citizen of Aphrodisias was praised in the first century precisely for killing 60 enemies (Reynolds 1982: no. 28; see also Robert 1937: 313–14).

There can be little doubt that these stories were elaborated with all the brutal details; the wounds of the enemy somehow healed the trauma of the danger which had just been overcome. An impression of such personal narratives is given by the grave epigram of Apollonios of Tymnos (ca. 250 BC; *SGO* I 01/02/01; see chapter 2, section 2). The epigram mentions the great number of enemies Apollonios had killed in person and the innumerable spears which he "firmly stuck into the flesh of the enemies." This text brings to mind a typical representation of battle scenes in contemporary art, inspired by the iconography of Alexander the Great: the mounted warrior with raised spear strikes the enemy who falls on the ground (**see** figure 10.1; see also e.g., Pollitt 1986: 43–4, figs. 36–8; Smith 1991: fig. 204.2). In this case, we can be certain: blood is beautiful when it is the blood of others.

Blood is visible in colorful works of Hellenistsic art. The statues of the dead Gauls – and also of dead mythical figures – do not only show the open wounds, with drops of blood in low relief (e.g., Flower 1989: 38–9, figs. 23–6), they were also painted. These bodies, who are familiar to us as white marble figures, were shown to contemporary audiences covered with blood (see e.g., the reconstructions of "Alexander's sarcophagus" in Brinkmann 2003).

The elements which we have seen in Polybios' narrative reappear, sometimes in the same density, in other battle descriptions. Dramatic suspense and unexpected changes are one of the most prominent features of contemporary historiography (see section 10.3). The description of the enemy's death is pitiless in the miracle of Panamara (see chapter 8, section 4). Brutal descriptions of violence are also not unknown to Hellenistic poetry (Fowler 1989: 35, 39–40 and section 10.1). The contrast between confusion in the mass slaughter of enemies and the clarity of single combat between two protagonists already had a long tradition before it was adopted by Hellenistic authors. And, despite the fact that historians' sympathies can easily be recognized – even the sympathies of such a preacher of objectivity as Polybios – they did not hesitate to underline the bravery, good training, and of course greater numbers of defeated opponents when this could render the victory of their troops all the more glorious.

We may recognize some of these elements in a documentary description of military action during the Sixth Syrian War between Ptolemy VIII Euergetes II and Ptolemy VI Philometor, who allied himself with Antiochos IV (170–168 BC). The following narrative was not written by a historian, but by a general – though of course the two disciplines were closely interrelated in the Hellenistic period (see chapter 11, section 2). An anonymous officer of Euergetes describes how the troops of Philometor attempted to capture a fort, but got trapped in ditches and were defeated (ca. 169 BC). The similarity to the Spartan defeat near Mantineia is striking:

> They [the enemy] mounted a vigorous spear attack, as a result of which it turned out that [some of them] rather overpowered our men, prevailing with their bravery, and being [brave men] and worthy of their native lands they got control of the palisade and [entered; but] they were thrown into confusion by their own ranks because inside they were cut off and [had] no means of escape, and falling into ditches and canals, they perished by suffocation and . . . so that if anyone attempted to hide . . . by our cavalry because it was easy to overpower them thanks to the spaciousness . . . [They were so many] of the distinguished among them, it would be too long to enumerate them.
>
> (trans. Bagnall and Derow 2004: no. 46)

If reading or listening to narratives of how aggressors were destroyed gave their enemies a sense of relief, the descriptions of scenes of horror, especially during the destruction of cities, when the victims were not just warriors, but also women and children, fulfilled a different function: cathartic and didactic, very similar to the function of tragedy. With a long chain of rhythmically arrayed questions, Antipatros of Sidon laments the sack of Korinth (146 BC), bitterly stressing the ephemeral nature of power and the destructive power of war:

Dorian Korinth, where is your admired beauty, where are the crowns of your towers, where is your old wealth? Where are the temples of the Blessed? Where are the palaces? Where are the wives, and the myriads of men, the descendants of Sisyphos? Not a single trace has been left of you, most miserable. For war has seized and devoured everything.

(*Anth. gr.* 9.151)

Polybios' description of the siege and ultimate sack of Abydos (16.30–4, 201 BC) stands out due to its detailed description of fearlessness, hope, and despair. In this case the baddie, from Polybios' point of view – Philip V of Macedon – prevailed: another form of unexpected fortune. As the historian himself comments (16.30.3), it was not the nature of the siege that made this event "worthy of being remembered and described to posterity," but the exceptional bravery of the besieged. The tragic dimensions of these events are, again, underlined in a subtle way by the historian, who starts his narrative by commenting on the self-confidence (*pisteuontes hautois . . . erromenos*) of the Abydenoi and their initial success. When, however, their fortune turned and Philip demanded their surrender, they decided to die fighting, together with their women and children:

> They decided first to free the slaves, in order to have men who would unhesitantly fight with them, then to assemble all the women in the temple of Artemis and the children together with the nurses in the gymnasium, and finally to collect all the silver and the gold in the market-place and to place all valuable garments in the quadrireme of the Rhodians and the trireme of the Kyzikenoi.
>
> (16.31.2–3; trans. W. R. Paton)

Fifty of the older and most trusted citizens were asked to swear to kill all the women and children and to destroy all the property as soon as they saw the inner wall in the possession of the enemy. After the cross wall had fallen, the defenders continued the fight, almost bringing Philip to despair:

> For the foremost of the Abydenes mounted the bodies of their dying enemies and fought with the utmost courage; not only did they fight desperately with sword and spear alone, but whenever any of these weapons was damaged and became useless or when they were forced to drop it, they took hold of the Macedonians with their hands and threw them down in their armor, broke their pikes and stabbed them repeatedly with the fragments . . . or struck them on the face or the exposed parts of the body with the points and threw them into total confusion.
>
> (16.33.2–3; trans. W. R. Paton)

Most of the defenders were dead or exhausted from wounds and toil when night came, and together with darkness also treason. A few of the elderly citizens broke their oath and surrendered the city to Philip. But the majority of the Abydenes fulfilled their oath, killing the women, children, and themselves:

> When he [Philip] saw the number and the fury of those who were killing themselves and the children and the women, by cutting throats, burning, hanging, throwing into wells and off the roofs, he was amazed and sad at what was happening; he announced that he granted a respite of three days to those who wished to hang themselves and cut their throats. The Abydenes, remaining faithful to their original decision and regarding themselves as almost traitors to those who had fought and died for their country, by no means accepted to live, except those whose hands had been stayed by fetters or similar forcible means; all the rest of them rushed without hesitation in whole families to their death.
>
> (16.34.9–12; trans. W. R. Paton)

Polybios adds that this incident of desperate heroism was not unique: on earlier occasions (early fifth century) the Phokians and the Akarnanians had resolved to take similar measures, which they, however, had not been forced to carry out, since they had defended themselves successfully. The historian does not fail to observe the tragic quality of the daring courage shown by the Abydenes – as a matter of fact he uses in this context the word *peripeteia*, which describes sudden changes of fortune in ancient drama:

> In the case of the sudden change of fortune [*peripeteia*] of the Abydenes one feels inclined to blame Fortune [*Tyche*] at the most, who, as if in pity, set right at one the misfortunes of the aforementioned peoples [i.e., the Phokians and Akarnanians], by granting both victory and safety to those who had lost hope; in the case of the Abydenes, however, she chose to do the opposite. For the men were killed, the city was taken, and the children together with their mothers fell into the enemy's hands.
>
> (16.32.5–6; trans. W. R. Paton)

The description of the siege of Abydos and the tragic fate of its population finds close parallels in the description of the sack of Xanthos in 42 BC (App. *b. civ.* 4.76–82; Plut., *Brutus* 30–1; Cassius Dio 47.34; Schaps 1982: 200–2).

The visual qualities in battle scenes narrated in Hellenistic historiography are quite evident in the few texts quoted here. We find references to dust and fire, to sudden movements, to the color of clothes. We have also seen that the scene in which Philipoimen kills Machanidas with his spear corresponds to contemporary representations of single combat. The mention of blood in Theokritos' poetry is matched by the images of fallen warriors with bleeding wounds, painted red, in sculpture. In this respect, textual and visual narratives are close to each other. We observe an analogous convergence in the representation of cruel scenes of violence. Of course, direct scenes of war brutality are not frequent (Pfuhl and Mobius 1977/9: 306–9). A clay statuette in the Louvre (Ducrey 1986: 104, fig. 75, third century) which represents a war elephant as it crushes under its feet a Galatian warrior, or the statue of a Galatian warrior – a nobleman, possibly a king – in Pergamon ("the Ludovisi Gaul"; Smith 1991: 101 with fig. 118), who kills himself by piercing his throat with his sword, with thick blood flowing out of the wound, or the Capitoline Dying Gaul, who sits on his fallen shield and turns his eyes to a large mortal wound (Mattei 1987; Smith 1991: 101 fig. 19), are all exceptions. One of the funerary reliefs from Bithynia with battle scenes inspired from the campaign of King Prousias I against the Galatians (216 BC) distinguishes itself from the frequent representations of combat (see figure 10.2). The Galatian is represented still on the back of his wounded horse; a spear is stuck under the horse's neck, and a second spear is stuck in the Galatian warrior's neck. A dead horse between the Galatian and the Bithynian warrior completes the scene of merciless violence (Peschlow et al. 2002: 434, fig. 2d).

That in these cases we are dealing with barbarians is not a coincidence. Greek and barbarian opponents were not treated in the same manner (see chapter 11, section 3). Representations of battles among Greeks were rather rare, whereas representations of battles against the Persians and the Gauls, or battles between Macedonians and Romans (from the perspective of the victorious Romans) are far more common.

Of all the wars fought in the Hellenistic period, the wars against the Galatians undoubtedly present the most traumatic experience, and the battles with the invading barbarians were often narrated by historians and sung by epic poets. Hellenistic artists did portray battles between Greeks and Galatians – for example, in Ephesos (Smith 1991: fig. 208) – although they more frequently chose a more subtle way to commemorate a victory over such an awesome enemy. Among the monuments which were dedicated to commemorate the defeat of the foreign tribe, those dedicated by the Attalid kings in Pergamon and in Athens (ca. 230–220 BC) are best known, primarily through later copies (Smith 1991: 99–104, figs. 118–32). Sculptors preferred to focus not on the turning point of battles, but on the moment thereafter: on the desperate reactions following the realization of defeat or on the dead bodies of the barbarians. The famous statues of the dying Galatians ("the Large Gallic Group") dedicated by Attalos I probably in the temple of Athena in Pergamon do not depict direct confrontation with the enemy; the central image, instead, is a Galatian warrior who has just killed his wife and is now killing himself (see figure 10.3). He is still standing, the sword opening a deep wound in his throat, from which thick strains of blood are emerging. Such images would have inspired feelings of joy in the populations of Asia Minor and northern Greece, coming from the pleasure of survival, but they also evoked a certain respect for heroic death. The extraordinary dimensions of this war were, again, underlined in a subtle way in the "Small

Figure 10.2 Funerary relief from Bithynia with a battle scene between a Bithynian horseman and a Galatian warrior (Peschlow et al. 2002: 434, fig. 2d).

Gallic Group," an Attalid dedication in Athens (perhaps under Attalos I), through the inclusion of representations of Giants and Persians (Smith 1991: 102–3, figs. 123–32). Attalid victories were associated with the victories of the Olympians over the Giants and of the Greeks over the Persians (see chapter 11, section 3), and the Pergamene kings appeared as the new defenders of Hellenism (Smith 1991: 103).

Figure 10.3 Reconstruction of "the Large Gallic Group" dedicated by Attalos I in the temple of Athena in Pergamon (Schober 1938).

The representation of Herakles clubbing a Gaul in a votive relief in Kyzikos (Smith 1991: fig. 211) similarly alludes to the more than human dimension of the struggle against the Galatians.

Subtlety in the representation of victory is more evident in the earliest works of art inspired by the victory near Delphi. The statue which was dedicated there does not survive, but it is known from a copy found in Delos. It is a statue of Apollo, triumphantly stepping on the symbol of the Galatians: a small shield (*thyreos*). The god is represented naked, with his right arm raised above his head, in a gesture of relaxation; his left arm rests on a tree, and his gaze is turned away from the symbol of the most hated enemy (see figure 10.4). The image, with this relaxed attitude, gives the impression almost of a lack of interest in a negligible opponent. The statue dedicated by the Aitolians in Delphi is similar: a seated woman, representing Aitolia, with a spear in one hand and a winged Victory in the other, steps

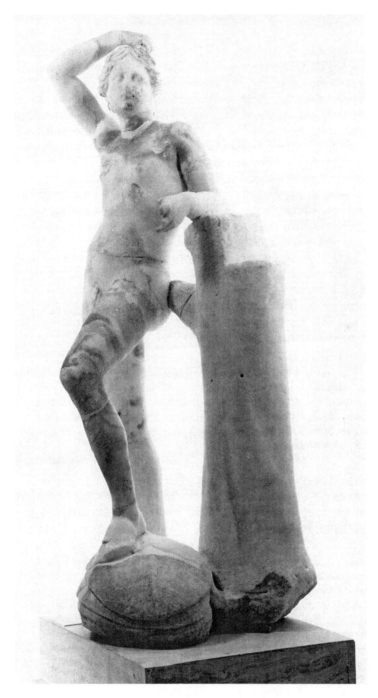

Figure 10.4 Statue of Apollo dedicated in Delphi after the victory over the
Galatians (278/7 BC). The god steps on a small Galatian shield (*thyreos*).
Marble copy found in Delos. Delos Archaeological Museum (courtesy of the
Ecole Française d'Athènes).

on Galatian shields (see figure 2.1). Unlike the Pergamene dedications, these images show contempt, not fear; they do not depict the toils of direct combat, but feeling of superiority after victory.

If we leave the area of public representation of war and warriors, which is dominated by the works of the historians, the honorary decrees, and the public war monuments, and come to the private area of funerary references to war, we may observe a clearer preference for subtle allusions rather than direct images. Many funerary epigrams, especially for children, for women who died in childbirth, or for other people who died a premature death, appeal to the compassion of the passer-by, focusing on the painful moment and the tragic circumstances of death. In the case of warriors, the relatives of the departed frequently did not wish to provoke compassion, but rather the admiration of the spectator. They therefore requested epigrams or images which kept in memory the exploits of the deceased warrior during his lifetime. The funerary epigram for Thrasymachos ("the bold one in battle"), the son of Leontios ("the lion") of Knossos, a citizen warrior killed in one of the wars of the late second century, focuses on the moment of his heroic death, but only in order to overcome the sorrow of the loss with the expectation of eternal glory:

> You have not lost the glory of your valor, not even after your death, but the fame which honors you brings you up from Hades' chambers, Thrasymachos. Someone of the later generations will sing about you, recalling that impetuous chivalry, when near windy Elaion you, alone among the Cretans, broke a squadron during the battle of the cavalry, in your effort to accomplish deeds worthy of your father Leontios.
>
> (*I.Cret.* I.viii 33; cf. *I.Cret.* I.xvi 48 = *SEG* XXVIII 749)

The same idea is even more directly expressed in the two funerary epigrams written for the Bithynian officer Menas, who was killed in a battle at Kouropedion (Nikaia, 281 or rather 190 BC):

> Although a long tomb contains my bones, stranger, I did not shrink back in view of the heavy weight of the enemies. Although I fought on foot I stood my ground in front of riders among those who fought in the first line, when we battled in the plain of Kouros. After I had hit a Thracian in his armor and a Mysian, I died because of my great bravery. For this, may someone praise the swift Menas, the son of Bioeris, the Bithynian, an excellent officer.
>
> One may come and pour tears on the tombs of cowards, who have died an inglorious death through illness. But earth has received me, who fought near the flow of the Phrygian river for my fatherland and for my parents, as a man who died while fighting with others in the first line, having first slain many enemies. For this, may someone praise the Bithynian Menas, the son of Bioeris, who exchanged light [life] with bravery.
>
> (*SGO* I 09/05/16; Pfuhl and Möbius 1977/9: no. 1269)

Figure 10.5 The grave relief and epigram of the Bithynian officer Menas, who was killed in a battle at Kouropedion (Nikaia, 281 or rather 190 BC) (Mendel 1914).

Above the two epigrams a sculptor represented the exploits of Menas (**see** figure 10.5). Although only the lower part of the relief is preserved, one may still recognize him standing on the right side, with his right leg stepping on a fallen shield. The left side of the relief is occupied by the two enemies he has killed, who lie on the ground covered with their weapons. Both the epigram and the relief transform the moment of death

Figure 10.6 Representations of the weapons of the Macedonian soldiers Lyson and Kallikles decorate their tomb in Lefkadia (ancient Mieza, ca. 200 BC). (Courtesy of the Department of Antiquities of Pella.)

into a moment of eternal glory, for which one should not pity Menas or the relatives bereft of him.

In the case of many warriors' tombs we cannot tell whether they died in action, because the monuments are not accompanied by an explanatory inscription. Sometimes, military activity is alluded to through the representation of weapons, as in the case of the painted Macedonian tomb of Lyson and Kallikles at Lefkadia (ancient Mieza, ca. 200 BC; Miller 1993; see figure 10.6). The deceased is sometimes represented in scenes of successful military action – for example, in the metopes with a battle scene in Taras (Pollitt 1986: 112, figs. 114–15; Smith 1991: fig. 204.2, early third century) and in the painted Macedonian tombs at Lefkadia and Naousa (ca. 300 BC; Pollitt 1986: 189–90, fig. 201; Miller 1993: pl. 8a, fig. 13) – but it is striking that warriors are more frequently represented in isolation. This may be connected with the general trend towards individualism in the Hellenistic period (see Zanker 1993: 228). Aristonautes ("the excellent sailor") appears in his monument in Athens in full armor and in motion without, however, an opponent (late fourth century); the occupant of a tomb in Taras is represented seated, inactive, surrounded by his weapons (Smith 1991: fig. 204.1); the grave relief of a young soldier in Rhodes shows him standing, but in a relaxed position, supported by a column, watching the helmet he holds in his hands

(Smith 1991: fig. 218, early third century; see figure 11.2). All these images isolate – and according to Zanker they *elevate* – the warrior. At any rate they make the spectator concentrate on a single figure, on the protagonist who stands on the stage the funerary monument forms.

10.3. The Beauty of the Unexpected: Peripeteia and the Paradoxon in Narratives of War

It has long been observed, as a matter of fact during the Hellenistic period, that one of the central characteristics of Hellenistic historiography is the great influence excercised by rhetoric and drama. Rhetorical elements (orations in the assembly or exhortations before a battle) are, of course, not a new element in Hellenistic historiographical works; similarly, a convergence between drama and historical narrative can be observed as early as Herodotos. The strong impressions left by the campaigns of Alexander the Great only strengthened such tendencies towards theatricality, and Hellenistic historiography is often called "tragic history." Life was conceived as a spectacle by contemporary thought, and a similar attitude also characterizes Hellenistic literature, which often adopted a theatrical vocabulary to describe the many different situations of life. A sense of dramatic change is predominant in historiography, and not only in Douris or Phylarchos – even the greatest critic of "tragic history," Polybios, did not remain indifferent to the peripeteias in the life of individuals and in the life of states, attributing to the sudden changes of fortune that others experienced (*hai ton allon peripeteiai*) a great instructive value (e.g., 1.1.2; 1.35.7; 5.75.5; cf. Walbank 1938: 64; Sacks 1981: 132–44). In a speech, which he put into the mouth of Philip V, he even mentions drama along with mythology and history as a source of moral instruction (23.11.1: "you should not only read tragedies, myths, and historical narratives, but know well and ponder over such things"; cf. Walbank 1979: 234).

Similar trends have also been recognized in Hellenistic art, with the architect's "fondness for dramatic settings and for surprising mysterious inner spaces" and the "exaggeratedly massive, tension-filled bodily forms and pathetic facial expressions that seem to echo the masks of tragic drama" (Pollitt 1986: 7).

Not only Hellenistic thinkers and artists were interested in the unexpected sufferings and joys of humans, delivered to the invisible powers of Fortune. Everything that occurred beyond expecation (*paradoxon*) attracted the attention of the Hellenistic spectators of life. A double victory in an athletic competition gave an athlete the attribute *paradoxos* (victor beyond reasonable expectations); the unexpected cures accomplished by physicians were stressed in honorary decrees (e.g., *I.Perge* 12, lines 32–3: *polla kai paradoxa therapeumata*) as no less than miraculous rescues due to divine intervention (see chapter 8, section 4). Similarly, Hellenistic historians tried to detect (or invent) the incredible, admirable, and unexpected in the deeds of the protagonists of their works. What makes the First Punic War so interesting for Polybios is the fact that there was hardly any other war which demonstrated such great changes of fortune (3.97.8). When the same historian explained how the pro-Macedonian group under Askondas and Neon prevailed in Boiotia in the late third century, during the reign of Antigonos Doson, he repeatedly pointed to unexpected elements (20.5.6–11): Askondas and Neon got the upper hand owing to a sudden change of fortune (*genomenes tinos peripeteias*); an unexpectedly low tide kept the Macedonian ships on the land at Larymna; the Boiotian troops under Neon did not attack them "contrary to what they expected" (*para ten prosdokian*), thus winning Antigonos' favor for not attacking him "during his change of fortune" (*kata ten peripeteian*).

An episode of Hellenistic history – the sack of Pellene in the Peloponnese (ca. 241 BC) – narrated by Plutarch (*Aratos* 31–2), but based on a Hellenistic historian's account (possibly Phylarchos), illustrates the pleasure contemporary narrators took in the portrayal of the unexpected. The Aitolians suddenly (*exaiphnes*) attacked and seized the small Achaian town, immediately beginning to plunder it. While the soldiers were fighting with one another over the booty, the officers seized the women, putting on their heads their own helmets, thus showing to whom each woman belonged. Aratos, the Achaian general, exploited precisely this moment of the enemy's victory. Taking advantage of the disorder and of the insolence (*hybris*) – a central theme of tragedy – he attacked the town:

> In the midst of this confusion [*tarachos*] . . . it occurred by chance [*etyche*] that the daughter of Epigethes, a distinguished man, and herself conspicuous for her beauty and the stateliness of her body, was sitting in Artemis' sanctuary, where she had been placed by the officer who had seized her for himself and had placed his three-crested helmet upon her head. But suddenly [*aphno*] she ran forth towards the tumult, and as she stood in front of the gate of the sanctuary and looked down upon the combatants from on high [*anothen*], with the three-crested helmet on her head, she appeared to the citizens themselves as a vision of more than human majesty, while the enemy thought they saw an apparition from heaven and were struck with amazement and terror, so that no one among them thought of defending himself.
>
> (*Aratos* 32.1–2; trans. B. Perrin, modified)

This is a small drama staged by Fortune (*etyche*) in which the insolence (*hybris*) of the victorious enemies prepares their destruction. The arrogant and wanton officer makes the defenseless woman into his own ruin by placing his helmet on her head and by bringing her to the sanctuary. Plutarch (or his source) dramatically contrasts the confusion of the battle (*tarachos*) and the individual figure of Epigethes' daughter, who stands out as she, almost like an actress, appears in a costume (the soldier's helmet), which changes her identity and makes her resemble Artemis. And as she comes into sight on the high stage (*anothen*) formed by the gate of the sanctuary, she becomes a *dea ex machina*. Plutarch adds another version of the story, according to which it was the goddess' statue, carried away by the priestess, which terrified the enemy. These dramatic descriptions show not only the interests of Hellenistic historians, but also their inventiveness. For, as Plutarch explains, Aratos, the general involved in this battle, "makes no mention of such a thing" in his memoirs (*Aratos* 32.5). A lost painting of Timanthes portrayed the battle in a vivid manner (*emphantikos*), again with no reference to Epigethes' daughter.

The interest in dramatic descriptions of attacks and battles can be seen in honorary decrees of this period as well. We may discern the attraction of the unexpected even in the laconic phrase of a decree of an Athenian *deme* in honor of elite soldiers (ca. 319 BC): "when during the night the enemies came close even to the city walls, they defeated them in a battle and threw them out, killing or capturing many of them; they stripped them of their weapons, which they dedicated on the acropolis" (*IG* II^2 1209, ca. 319 BC).

A list of magistrates in Tenos (*IG* XII Suppl. 315), which mentions the most important event during their term in office, is almost identical in content: "when some men noticed those who had sailed against [the city] and had climbed up the walls and had occupied the lower parts of the town, Onesas and the guards formed themselves in battle-order within the city and threw the enemies out by storm."

An honorary decree from Aigiale describes a similar attack, with a happy end of a different kind (Bielman 1994: no. 38, late third century BC):

> During the night, pirates landed in our territory and virgins and [married] women and other persons, both free and slaves, were captured – a total of more than thirty persons; and (the pirates) destroyed the ships in the harbor and captured the ship of Dorieus, with which they departed carrying away both the persons and the rest of the booty; when this occurred, Hegesippos and Antipappos, the sons of Hegesistratos, who were among the captives, jointly persuaded the leader of the pirates, Sokleidas, who was sailing along with them, to release the free persons, also some of the freedmen and the slaves, while they offered themselves as hostages.

When the necessary ransom was paid, the local heroes were freed.

All these texts, and this is but a small selection, convey the same message: when everything seems lost, the courage of "a few good men" can save the day. The dramatic descriptions in these honorary decrees is a means by which both the contribution of the "heroes" and the relief of the people are maximized. If we take into consideration the fact that in similar narratives related to a miraculous rescue (see chapter 8, section 4) the savior is a god, we understand why the achievements of some of these men assimilated them with superhuman beings.

Philopoimen, for example, was posthumously the recipient of divine honors (see chapter 2, section 5); for the inhabitants of the villages Neon Teichos and Kiddiou Kome near Laodikeia of Lykos, the services of Banabelos and Lachares, two officials in the service of Achaios during the Galatian wars (267 BC), were so important that they honored them with the establishment of a cult (*I.Laodikeia* 1).

Occasionally, such dramatic narratives in honorary decrees are lengthier and resemble small biographies. We have already seen how the decree for Kallias of Sphettos (see chapter 2, sectoin 5) describes in detail his contributions, which saved Athens from a desperate situation. The decree of Chersonesos (Black Sea) for Diophantos of Sinope, a general of King Mithridates Eupator (late second century) is one of the best examples of how honorary decrees approach in style and content contemporary historiography. A passage of this decree best exemplifies this trend (*IOSPE* I² 352; trans. Bagnall and Derow 2004: no. 56, modified):

> Upon his [the king's] request he took upon him the war against the Skythians; after arriving at our city, he crossed over with manly spirit together with all the troops to the opposite coast. When Palakos, the king of the Skythians, suddenly [*aiphnidios*] launched an attack, he drew up his men in battle order in stress [*en chreiai*] and after putting the Skythians, who were believed to be unbeatable [*tous anypostatous dokountas eimen*], to flight, he let king Mithridates Eupator set up a first trophy from their defeat. After he had subdued the neighboring Taurians and united the population in a city which he founded at that site, he proceeded to the areas of Bosporos and, after accomplishing many and great deeds in a short time, he returned to our area, took with him the adult citizens and marched into the interior of Skythia. When the Skythians handed over to him the royal dwellings Chabaioi and Nea Polis, it occurred that almost all [of them] subdued themselves to King Mithridates Eupator. In gratitude for these deeds the people honored him with the appropriate honors, as if already relieved from the dominance of the barbarians.
>
> (lines 5–15)

After stressing the extraordinary nature of Diophantos' achievements, the authors of the decree create the impression that the war is over, only to underline the sudden change of fortune to which they then turn:

> The Skythians demonstrated the faithlessness which is inherent in their nature, revolting from the king and bringing the affairs to a change [*eis metabolan agagonton*]. For these reasons King Mithridates Eupator again sent Diophantos with troops, and although the season was closing in and winter was approaching, Diophantos took his own men and the most able among the citizens and marched against the very capitals of the Skythians. As he was hindered because of stormy weather, he returned to the coastal areas, seizing Kerkinitis and the "Walls" and starting to besiege those who inhabit Kalos Limen. When Palakos thought that the weather was giving him an advantage and gathered all his

troops, inviting in addition to them also the tribe of the Rheuxinaloi, the Virgin, patron of the Chersonesians on all occasions, who then was present next to Diophantos, foretold the deed which was about to be accomplished through the signs which occurred in her sanctuary, filling the entire troops with bravery and daring courage. Diophantos prudently drew up his troops in battle order and so it ocurred that a fair victory, worthy of memory for all time, was won for King Mithridates Eupator. For hardly any of the infantry [of the enemy] was saved, and of the riders only a few escaped.

(lines 15–28)

The narration continues in this way, with more toils, unexpected perils, rescues, and glorious victories. We observe in this decree the same interest in dramatic contrasts as in literature and art: the contrast between the sudden attack of the enemy and the hasty but successful marshalling of Diophantos; between the expectation of peace and the renewed danger; between the confidence of Palakos and his disastrous defeat. Diophantos appears with the traits of a hero: he not only fights against treacherous and uncivilized barbarians, but defies the powers of nature; he not only exterminates his opponents, but also introduces urban life, a main feature of Greek civilization, as a city-founder in Tauris. This brings to mind the mythical heros, as the protection he offers in a subtle way is assimilated into the patronage of the Virgin, who was "present together with Diophantos" (line 24: *symparousa Diophantoi*). If the goddess' contribution consisted of the courage she gave to the warriors, it was his prudent marshalling (*diataxamenou sophronos*) that brought the victory.

Long narratives, which stress sudden changes and the tragic contrast between expectation and outcome, are possible in historiography and in such honorary decrees. This can also be achieved, at least to a limited extent, in visual arts as well – for example, in friezes or in large paintings. A famous example is the "Alexander Mosaic" in Pompeii, based on a Hellenistic painting. As has been observed (Pollitt 1986: 3–4, fig. 2):

> its dominant figure, both from the standpoint of composition and dramatic interest, is not Alexander but rather the Persian ruler Darius. It is the harried figure of the Great King, torn between the need to save himself on the one hand and compassion for his fallen comrades on the other, which most stirred the imagination of the artist who created the picture. Perhaps this was because it was Darius whose fortune had reached a crisis and a point of incipient collapse, while Alexander's irresistible *daimon* pressed steadily onward.

The Alexander Mosaic painting portrays precisely an imminent change of fortune. In the case of the statues of the Galatians, the change of fortune had already taken place. The artists chose to represent them after the realization of defeat: committing suicide or already dead. The muscular body of the dead barbarian in Venice, part of the "Small Gallic Group" (Fowler 1989: 38, fig. 23; Smith 1991: fig. 132) still reveals after death the might

211

and the greatness of the danger: the Gaul lies on the ground, with arms and legs outstretched, as if in a last posthumous effort to occupy space, the space he violently, but unsuccessfully, had invaded. His fallen body evokes awe, to some perhaps also compassion, because with its mighty limbs and the mortal wound near the heart it reveals the height from which it had been overthrown – and the toilsome struggle which had been necessary.

In a period in which spectacles were all the rage, and in a culture which can be characterized as "a culture of onlookers" (Chaniotis 1997: 248–54), both historical narratives and pictorial representations of war created a stage on which dramatic contrasts and unexpected changes of fortune could be presented. This theatricality in the representation of war was so intensively felt that the honorary decree of Araxa (Lykia) for the "local hero" Orthagoras uses three times the verb *protagonistein* ("play the first part in a play") to describe his achievements in wars (*SEG* XVIII 570, lines 10, 30–1, 49, ca. 180 BC; cf. *SEG* XXXIV 1198). Unlike the audiences of drama, who saw on stage the sufferings of heroes in mythological times, most of the audiences of Hellenistic literary and pictorial narratives had experienced the same or similar scenes in real life. The feelings which the representations of suffering (*pathos*) and unexpected changes (*to paradoxon*) provoked were at least in part the same feelings to which Aristotle's *Poetics* attributes the cathartic effect of tragedy: *eleos* (compassion) and *phobos* (fear). But in many cases another feeling was brought into play as well: the affirmative feeling of superiority after the deliverance from peril.

Hellenistic audiences may have wished to be simply audiences of war; more often they were on the stage themselves. A phrase in Diodoros (20.83.2) expresses this ambivalence, as the historian describes how Demetrios' fleet approached the city of Rhodes at the beginning of the famous siege (305 BC):

> The soldiers of the Rhodians occupied the walls awaiting the approach of the enemy fleet, while the old men and the women watched from their houses, as the city is built like a theater [*theatroeidous*]; and all of them terrified at the size of the fleet and at the bright light reflected by the shining weapons were in great agony.

In this passage, the besieged Rhodians are at the same time the spectators of their own war and the spectacle for the historian's readers.

Further Reading

10.1. Images of Violence in Hellenistic Literature and Art. *Hellenistic aesthetic, in general*: Pollitt 1986; Fowler 1989. *Scenes of violence in Hellenistic art*: Toddler strangles a goose: Pollitt 1986: 128, fig. 132; Fowler 1989: 14, fig. 10. Hunting scenes: Pollitt 1986: 41–2, figs. 34–5, 130, fig. 136, 201, fig. 214. Fighting athletes and warriors: Smith 1991: 53, 183–4, figs. 52–4, 204. Cock fight: Fowler 1989:

14, fig. 9. *Battle scenes in art*: Alexander mosaic: Andreae 1977; Cohen 1997. Alexander sarcophagus: Winter 1912; von Graeve 1970; Pollitt 1986: 38–45; Smith 1991: 190–2; Brinkmann 2003. The monument of Aemilius Paullus (Delphi): Kähler 1965; Pollitt 1986: 155, fig. 162; Smith 1991: 185, fig. 209; Boschung 2001. The Large Gallic Group (Pergamon): Schober 1938: 126–49; Bieber 1961: 73–82; Künzl 1971; Robertson 1975: 527–46; Wenning 1978; Pollitt 1986: 83–90. The Small Gallic Group (Athens): Stewart 1979: 19–23; Palma 1981: 45–84; Pollitt 1986: 90–3. Combat between Olympians and Giants on the Great Altar of Pergamon: Pollitt 1986: 97–107; Smith 1991: 158–64.

10.2. Blood is Beautiful: Realism and Subtlety in the Representation of Violence. *Wounded kings and benefactors*: SEG XXVIII 60 = Austin 1981: no. 44; *OGIS* 220 = Bagnall and Derow 2004: no. 79; Polyb. 10.49; Plut., *Cato major* 14. *The wounds of the boxer of Terme*: Pollitt 1986: 146, fig. 157; Fowler 1989: 34–5, fig. 21; Smith 1991: 54–5, fig. 62. *Battle descriptions in Hellenistic historiography*: Phylarchos *FgrHist* 81 F 59; Polyb. 5.82.5–5.86.6; 11.11.1–18.10; 16.2–9; 18.18–33; 29.14–19; Diod. 19.83–4; 20.22–3, 20.48–52; see also Sage 1996: 213–20; Beston 2000: 325–8. *The battle of Mantineia and the death of Machanidas*: Walbank 1967: 282–94. *The siege of Abydos*: Walbank 1967: 538–44; Pritchett 1991: 222. *Funerary inscriptions for fallen warriors*: Stecher 1981: 39–47; Themelis 2001; e.g., IG IX 1.4², 929 (Korkyra); *I.Cret.* I.viii 33; I.xvi 48 (*SEG* XXVIII 749); *Syll.*³ 1225 (Rhodes); *SGO* I 01/01/96 (Knidos); 01/06/01 (Smyrna); 03/01/05 (a Messenian mercenary in Priene); 04/19/01 (Iaza); 06/01/01 (Elaia); 06/02/30 (Pergamon); *SGO* II 08/01/40 (Kyzikos); 09/05/16 (Nikaia); *SEG* XXXVIII 1101 (Stratonikeia); *Greek Anthology* 6.132; 7.208, 232, 724. *Images of warriors, military themes, and battle scenes in funerary monuments*: Bean and Harrison 1967: 42, no. 8; Carter 1970 (Taras); Fraser 1977: 34, 39, 127, 133; Pfuhl and Möbius 1977/9: e.g., nos. 1269–78, 1430, 1432, 1439–40; Pollitt 1986: 112; Rumscheid and Held 1994 (see also *SGO* II 09/06/18); Ma 2004; Zanker 1993: 228; Peschlow et al. 2002: 433–36 nos. 103–5 (scenes of battle between Galatians and the Bithynian troops of Prousias I, 216 BC). *Individualism*: Pollitt 1986: 7–10.

10.3. The Beauty of the Unexpected: Peripeteia and the Paradoxon in Narratives of War. *Theatricality in Hellenistic thought*: Pollitt 1986: 4–7, 230–42; Chaniotis 1997 (with further bibliography). *Tragic history*: Walbank 1955, 1960; Meister 1975: 94–126; Sacks 1981: 144–70. *Tragic elements in Hellenistic historiography*: Words related to the theater in Polybios: *ektheatrizo* (3.91.10; 5.15.2; 11.8.7), *ektragodeo* (6.15.7; 6.56.8), *hypokrisis* (35.2.13), *peripeteia* (1.13.11; 3.85.9; 3.97.8; 5.75.5; 6.2.5; 9.12.6; 16.6.9; 20.5.6; 32.8.4; 38.9.2); see also Wunderer 1909: 52–5; Foucault 1972: 31, 231, 233. *The sack of Pellene*: *FgrHist* 231 F 2 (with the commentary of F. Jacoby). *Dramatic descriptions in honorary decrees*: e.g., IG II² 1209; IG XII Suppl. 315; IGR III 34; IG V.2 16.

11

THE MEMORY OF WAR

11.1. The Memory of War: Individual, Collective, Cultural

Bouchetion is a small town near the city of Kassope in Epeiros. Some 40 years after the Roman conquest of this region (167 BC), the news arrived at Kassope and Bouchetion that Marcus Perpena, the Roman consul of the year 130, was campaigning against Aristonikos in order to subdue his revolt in Asia Minor. Three wealthy men of noble birth, Philotas, Hipparchos, and Kylisos, joined the Roman troops, probably when they were crossing the Adria, *en route* to Asia. After Aristonikos' defeat, one year later, they returned to their native city and thanked Herakles, their savior in battle, by dedicating a statue to him in Kassope. Their dedicatory epigram survives in an inscription (*SEG* XXXVI 555):

> Herakles, the son whom Zeus brought forth, they publicly proclaimed as their Savior, those men from Kassope who went to Asia with chariots, when Markos, the general, led an army against Aristonikos; having defeated him in battle these men of Bouchetion bring back home strength. The descendants of Oxylos, the old inhabitant of this land, offered a sacrifice upon their safe return to their fatherland and erected this statue of Herakles, who stood beside them in all battles.

We can imagine how their countrymen, who had never seen Asia, eagerly asked Philotas, Hipparchos, and Kylisos to tell them about the war, about the battles, and about the god's miraculous assistance on the battlefield. We can also imagine how, many years after these events, the three men narrated their youthful adventures at drinking parties.

In the Hellenistic Age the commemoration of wars was to a great extent an individual affair: the storytelling of old men in the symposium (see Dosiadas *FgrHist* 458 F 2) and the work of historians, who practiced historiography not as a "profession," but either at their leisure or as part of their engagement in public life. We can never tell whether ordinary people knew more about wars, recent and old, from the narratives of individuals than from attending the public lectures of historians, but we shall be on the safe side if we do not place a lot of emphasis on the contribution of the

214

reading of historiographical works to the historical knowledge of Hellenistic Greeks. The significance of indirect means through which historical
information was transmitted should not be underestimated. The visitors to
a sanctuary would not only admire a dedication, they would also read the
dedicatory inscription – or they would have someone explain to them the
dedication's background. Other indirect means of transmitting historical
knowledge are closely connected with public life: the erection or restoration
of a monument, the honoring of a historian or the invitation to a historian
to give a public lecture; the celebration of a commemorative anniversary;
the orations on the occasion of festivals or the annual honors paid to the
war dead (e.g., in the Athenian festival *Epitaphia*); the annually repeated
announcement of honors bestowed upon a benefactor. All these public, oral
performances provided civic audiences with historical information, admittedly vague, often inaccurate, and always filtered. The institutionalized forms
of communal commemoration, especially the commemorative anniversaries,
are extremely important for our understanding of how the memory of past
wars became part of the collective and cultural memory of urban populations,
and contributed to the construction of identities.

In the following discussion a distinction should be made between *collective*
and *cultural memory*, following Jan Assmann's (1992) theoretical definitions. The *collective memory* of war refers to the wars that a community has
jointly experienced – i.e., wars of the recent past. By contrast, the *cultural
memory* of a community consists of events of the mythical or the remote
past, the knowledge of which is obscured by time. Cultural memory is
abstract, reduced to a few key words, but it is, nevertheless, very effective as
a means of communication. An anecdote narrated by Plutarch (*Sulla* 13)
presents a perceptible example of the mechanisms of cultural memory in a
Hellenistic context.

In 87 BC, during the war against Mithridates VI, Sulla was besieging
Athens, then governed by the tyrant Aristion. After a year of siege, Aristion
sent envoys to Sulla: "But after a long time, at last, he sent out two or three
of his fellow-revellers to negotiate for peace; when they made no demands
which could save the city, but proudly talked about Theseus and Eumolpos
and the Persian Wars, Sulla said to them: 'Go away, blessed men, and take
these speeches with you; for I was not sent to Athens by the Romans to
fulfill love of knowledge, but to subdue rebels.'"

Anecdotes are exaggerated reflections of reality. These few lines encapsu-
late not only the confrontation of two cultures, but also of two cultural
memories. On one level, Plutarch presents us with the confrontation between
the ritualized use of history as an argument in Greek diplomacy on the one
hand, and the pragmatism of a Roman general, who is not interested in a
historical lecture, on the other. But on another level this anecdote of a *ritus
interruptus* demonstrates the failure of communication, based on the cultural
memory of one party that the other party could not possibly understand.

The oration of the Athenian envoys consisted of the most glorious chapters of Attic history, the best known components of their self-representation.

In our context, it is important to examine what constituted the cultural memory of the Hellenistic Athenians. We immediately observe that Plutarch simply mentions the names of two heroes (Theseus and Eumolpos) and the Persian Wars, with no further details. He obviously presupposed that his reader (or the reader of his source) would understand the significance of these names without any explanation. He was certainly right in his assumption. Perhaps not every Athenian would have been in a position to list all of Theseus' adventures, not every Athenian would have known the name of the mythical king who had defended Athens against the Thracian invasion under Eumolpos, and it is doubtful whether many Athenians would have been in a position to place the Persian Wars in an accurate historical context. Nevertheless, Theseus, Eumolpos, and the Persian Wars, in this particular constellation (three victorious wars), and in this particular context (the siege of Athens by a foreign army), conveyed to every Athenian a message that could easily be understood: Athens had often been attacked by foreign armies (the Amazons, the Thracians, the Persians), but it had always prevailed. From Plato's *Menexenos* (fourth century BC) to Aelius Aristides' *Panathenaic Oration* (second century AD), these three victories, of Theseus over the Amazons, of King Erechtheus over the Thracians of Eumolpos, and of the Athenians over the Persians, were stereotypically alluded to as the pillars of Athenian self-representation.

Cultural memory is abstract and vague with regard to historical events, but unequivocal as a means of communication. An event is reduced to a few essential points and becomes a sign that can be activated through the mention of a word or a name. Naturally, cultural memory can serve as communication only to those who share it. For the Athenians, the mention of Theseus, Eumolpos, and the Persian Wars was unequivocal, because these three events were always mentioned in the particular context of the glorification of Athens, as the most important Athenian victories that had saved Greece from invading barbarians. What the Athenians did not take into consideration was the fact that Sulla was not an ordinary recipient of this type of argument: he was just another of the non-Hellenic aggressors; and he was not part of the circle that shared the same cultural memory. Nothing could interest him less than the Athenian contributions to the defense of Greece. More than two centuries earlier, Alexander the Great had not destroyed Athens, thus paying his respect precisely to these achievements. Alexander knew and understood the Athenian traditions; Sulla did not.

It is important to note that this very selective cultural memory of the Athenians was the memory of wars, which created a clear distinction between the Athenians (or the Greeks) and the "others"; it constructed identities.

We will explore these aspects by studying, in the sections that follow, the means by which the memory of war was preserved.

216

11.2. War in Hellenistic Historiography

Writing history in ancient Greece to a great extent means writing about wars, especially about wars that the historian himself had experienced (Momigliano 1972; Fornara 1983, 62–3, 99–100, 175). Only one treatise about "How one should write history" survives – a work by Lucian. Although this work was composed in the late second century AD, it draws heavily upon the ideals of Classical historiography (Zecchini 1985). With the Parthian Wars of his time as a starting point, Lucian exclusively discusses the historiography of war, using as an example the history of the Peloponnesian War by Thucydides. His ideal historian should deal with a war he had himself experienced; he should be a military expert himself, and he is expected to narrate the events either on the basis of autopsy or after the questioning of eye-witnesses. These ideals can be followed back to the Hellenistic period, especially to the historiographical theory of the only Hellenistic historian whose work survives to such an extent as to allow a better understanding of method, philosophy of history, and subject matter: Polybios.

Polybios personifies in many respects Lucian's ideal historian. Before he started writing history, he had served as a cavalry commander in the Achaian League. He not only lived history, he was one of its protagonists. After the end of the Third Macedonian War, he lived as a hostage in Rome, where he had the opportunity to carry out an extensive survey of the oral and written sources and to become acquainted with leading Roman statesmen. In 151 BC, he accompanied Scipio Aemilianus to Spain and Africa, and of course the subject of his historiographical work is the history of wars – the wars that made Rome the ruler of the known world. It was Polybios' conviction that war reveals the advantages and disadvantages of a constitution, the strengths and weaknesses of a community or a nation; it demonstrates the unexpected element in history, the impact of secret forces that lie completely outside human control and cannot be rationally comprehended (*tyche*); the historiography of war educates the future statesman (e.g., 2.35.5–9, 3.7.5, 3.31). For this reason, Polybios' *pragmatike historia*, "serious" history with an educational purpose, is military and political history (Walbank 1957: 8).

If we leave aside Diodoros, who wrote his work in the late first century, and Memnon of Herakleia (*FgrHist* 434), who may have been a contemporary of Diodoros (or a historian of the early Imperial period), Polybios is the only Hellenistic historian with substantial parts of his work surviving to the present day, and he was probably the best, but he was not the only author of historical narratives. We know the names, sometimes also the titles of the works of more than 200 Hellenistic historians, and the date of several hundred others cannot be determined with certainty. Most of them directly or indirectly wrote about wars, either dealing with contemporary political history or reconstructing local history. The campaigns of Alexander the

Great alone inspired more than 30 historians of his lifetime or of the Hellenistic period (cf. *FgrHist* 117–45), and the Wars of the Sucessors were an equally great source of inspiration for contemporary historians – for example, Hieronymos of Kardia and Nymphis of Herakleia (*FgrHist* 154 and 432).

In addition to "universal" Greek histories (*Historiai*, *Hellenika*), the Hellenistic historians also wrote about particular wars or the wars ("deeds," *praxeis*) of individual kings – for example, the wars of Pyrrhos, Antiochos I, Eumenes I, Philip V, and Perseus, or the wars against the Galatians in Asia Minor. Unfortunately, of these works we know little more than the title. This is a shame, as we know that some of them were of a substantial length. Demetrios of Byzantion, for example, narrated "The crossing over of the Galatians from Europe to Asia" (i.e., the wars of 280–277 BC) in 13 "books" (chapters).

Many of these historians would have easily fulfilled Lucian's demands, at least to the extent that they were people who had held military office, had military experience, and often wrote about the wars they had actively fought in (Meißner 1992: 316–61). The Athenian Demochares (*FgrHist* 75, late third/early second century), author of a contemporary history, served as a general (*strategos*) and organized the defense of Athens during the war against Kassandros. Hieronymos of Kardia (*FgrHist* 154), the most important historian of the Wars of the Successors, participated actively in the wars of Antigonos the One-Eyed. The Thessalian philosopher and rhetorician, Kineas (*FgrHist* 603), epitomized the military writings of Aineias the Tactician and possibly composed a local history of Thessaly. The account of the campaigns of Pyrrhos (*Hypomemata*) may have been composed by the king himself with Kineas' assistance (Meißner 1992: 355–6, 476). To the historians who wrote about the wars of their times, in which they themselves held military positions, we may also add Antandros of Syracuse (late third/early second century, *FgrHist* 565), Patrokles, and Demodamas, generals in the service of Seleukos I (*FgrHist* 712, 428).

In addition to Ptolemy I's history of Alexander the Great and the accounts of Pyrrhos' wars which the king himself is said to have written, it is very probable that an account describing events of the Laodikean War (Third Syrian War) was written by King Ptolemy III (see chapter 9, section 1). Aratos, general and political leader of the Achaian League in the second half of the third century BC, also wrote his memoirs (*FgrHist* 231).

If an understanding of military matters and personal experience are two of Lucian's requirements which many Hellenistic historians fulfilled, the postulate of objectivity hardly inspired any of them. Because of the ideological implications of military victories, valor and leadership in war, in particular for the legitimacy of royal power and for the privileged position of elites (see chapter 2, sections 6–7), the positive representation of military achievements (and, when necessary, the concealment of the failure and weakness of kings, but also of cities and their statesmen), were features highly appreciated by those who profited from such filtered representations. An honorary decree for the local historian of the Tauric Chersonesos, Syriskos (third century), proposed by the historian's father, explains why he should be honored with a golden crown (*FgrHist* 807 T 1; Chaniotis 1988: 300–1): "because Syriskos, son of Herakleidas, laboriously wrote the miracles of the Virgin and read them aloud [in lectures] and also narrated the events concerning the kings of Bosporos and narrated the acts of kindness towards the cities in a kind [or suitable] manner for the people." The qualities praised are diligence and a favorable disposition towards the people. That Syriskos' narrative corresponded to the truth was mentioned in the text read during the crowning: "he wrote down the miracles of the Virgin and narrated in a truthful and kind manner towards the city the past acts of kindness towards the other cities and the kings." Here again, not truth alone is praised, but also a kind attitude towards the homeland. Similarly, Leon, son of Ariston of Samos (second century), was honored in Samos for glorifying his native city in his local history. As the honorary epigram states, Leon praised Hera and narrated how the Samians had decorated her sanctuary with booty won in maritime expeditions (*IG* XII.6 285; *FgrHist* 540 T 1; Chaniotis 1988: 308–9).

As already mentioned, the works of Hellenistic historians are primarily known from fragments. The lengthier among them reveal the propagandist, at times polemical, at times apologetic, character of the historiography of war. A characteristic example is provided in the way the beginning of the battle at Pydna (167 BC) is described by an opponent of the Macedonian king (Polyb. 29.18) and by an opponent of the Romans (Poseidonios, *FgrHist* 169), both of them quoted by Plutarch:

> The king of the Macedonians, as Polybios states, as soon as the battle began showed cowardice and rode back to the city, pretending that he wanted to offer a sacrifice to Herakles, although this god neither accepts cowardly sacrifices from cowards nor accomplishes improper prayers . . . A certain Poseidonios, however, who says that he lived in those times and was present in these events, and who has written a history of Perseus in many books, says that it was not out of cowardice nor using the sacrifice as an excuse that he went away, but because a horse had kicked him on the leg on the day before the battle. In the battle, he says, although he was in a bad condition and his friends were deterring him, he ordered a pack-horse to be brought to him, mounted it and joined the soldiers in the phalanx without a breastplate; and while missiles of every kind were flying on all sides, a javelin made entirely of iron smote him, not touching him with its point, but coursing along his left side with a oblique stroke, passing with such a force, that it tore his tunic leaving a red bruise upon his flesh, the mark of which remained for a long time. This is what Poseidonios writes in defence of Perseus.
>
> (Plut., *Aemilius* 19.3–10; trans. B. Perrin, modified)

It has long been observed that the story of Perseus' early withdrawal "is to be treated with suspicion" (Walbank 1979: 390), and there is obviously no way we can find out whether Perseus withdrew in order to sacrifice or because of cowardice, or whether Polybios placed an incident at the beginning of the battle which in fact occured later, in order to underline the contrast with the Roman commander. Despite the obscurity of this story, its exploitation for reasons of propaganda remains evident. The anti-Perseus version was adopted by Roman historians in such an exaggerated form that by the time of Florus (1.28.8) in the early second century AD it is simply the arrival of Aemilius Paullus that terrifies Perseus and makes him take flight. The exaggerations of anti-Macedonian historiography explain the apologetic nature of Poseidonios' work, although this does not justify his own possible distortions.

From the beginning of historiography, numbers of troops and casualties have always been manipulated for the purposes of propaganda. Another of the few surviving fragments of Poseidonios (*FgrHist* 169 F 3) exemplifies this practice: according to him, 100 Romans fell in the battle at Pydna (Plut., *Aemilius* 21.3), whereas according to Cornelius Nasica, who fought in this battle, the Roman casualties were only 80.

These few examples indicate both the central position held by narratives of war in Hellenistic historiography and their importance as a means of propaganda. Similar "convenient distortions" are also evident in the monumental historiography of war – i.e., in historiographical works that were written on stone. It is to this that we now turn.

11.3. The Monumental Historiography of War

Around 250 BC, Herakleitos, an Athenian citizen in the service of King Antigonos Gonatas as general of the Macedonian garrison in Piraeus, dedicated to Athena Nike, the patron of victory, a monument of an unknown nature ([*graph*]as or [*stel*]as) that "contained memorials [*hypomnemata*] of the king's deeds against the barbarians for the salvation of the Greeks" (*IG* II² 677; Chaniotis 1988: 301). Although the fragmentary preservation of the inscription does not allow us to determine with certainty the nature of the dedication – a written historical narrative (stelai) or paintings (*graphai*) representing the battles of Antigonos Gonatas against the Gauls (278/7 BC) – the significance of the monument becomes evident when we take a closer look at its background. The victories of Antigonos over the Gauls helped him to establish his rule in Macedonia and at the same time these victories contributed to the rescue of the Greeks from the barbarian invasion. For the Macedonian king, this victory was in a double sense a constitutive element of his rule: it established his kingship and at the same time provided him with the ideological basis for his position in Greece (see chapter 4, section 1).

He was not alone in the exploitation of this victory for the purposes of propaganda. The Delphic Amphictyony (after 278 BC) and the Aitolians (ca. 245 BC) organized festivals to celebrate their contribution to the defense of Greece (see section 11.5), and later Magnesia on the Maeander recalled to memory "the military assistance given by their ancestors to the sanctuary in Delphi, when they defeated in battle the barbarians who had campaigned against the sanctuary in order to loot the god's property" (*I.Magnesia* 46; Bagnall and Derow 2004: no. 155) in her effort to acquire privileges. Two historical epics, by Leschides ("The deeds of Eumenes," *FgrHist* 172) and Simonides of Magnesia ("The deeds of Antiochos and the battle against the Galatians," *FgrHist* 163) were also dedicated to victories over the Galatians. The initiative of Herakleitos should be seen within the context of the competition of kings, cities, and federal states for the military glory that legitimizes leadership and privileges.

There is more to be observed in the written or painted representations of Antigonos' deeds. The location of the dedication was the ideal setting for a monument that aimed at conveying an important message: Antigonos was the savior of the Greeks from the barbarians. The dedication was made to the goddess who was at the same time the patron of Athens (Athena) and the patron of victory (Athena Nike). Her sanctuary was on the acropolis of Athens, where buildings and sculptures commemorated the victories of the Greeks (and the Athenians) over the barbarians. In this setting, Herakleitos' monument subtly incorporated the victory of the Macedonian king into the Greek tradition of military victories. Here, the collective memory of the war against the Galatians met the cultural memory of the Greeks.

If in the case of Herakleitos we are not certain whether he dedicated inscriptions with historical narratives, there is enough evidence for this practice elsewhere. The historical narratives written on stone, for which I use here the term "monumental historiography," were set up in public places and were funded both by the community and by individual citizens. Thanks to their monumental form they addressed a larger audience than literary works. The representation of wars, especially of wars of the past, was one of the most common subjects. A biography of the famous Parian poet Archilochos (seventh century BC) inscribed on a monument in his native city (*SEG* XV 517; ca. 250 BC) treated not only his life as a poet, but also his participation in the wars of his island, and this holds true for another biography of the same poet inscribed on the same monument. The biography by Sosthenes (*FgrHist* 502; *IG* XII.5 454) consists in fact of quotations from Archilochos' poems as sources for the wars of Paros against the Thracians.

Around 203 BC, the authorities of Magnesia on the Maeander published a local history on the walls of a gate in the market of their city (*I.Magnesia* 17; Chaniotis 1988: 34–40). One of the major subjects it treated was the war against the Galatians. Wars are also the background of the majority of the dedications listed in the "Lindian Chronicle" as well as of the miracles of Athena Lindia narrated in the same inscription (*I.Lindos* 2; Higgbie 2003). This stele was set up in the sanctuary of Athena Lindia in 99 BC in order to re-establish the memory of various personalities who had adorned the sanctuary with dedications that no longer existed. This is hardly surprising, since most of them had allegedly been made by protagonists of ancient myths (including Kadmos, Minos, Herakles, Menelaos, and Helena). The dedications listed in this text were primarily dedications of war booty. The following entries give an impression of the content of this text: "those who participated in a campaign in Lykia together with Kleoboulos dedicated eight shields and a gold crown for the statue, as narrated by Timotheos in the first book of his *Chronicle* and by Polyzalos in the fourth book of his *Histories*" (XXIII); "the Lindians made the golden crown and the necklaces and the largest part of the decoration, which the [cult] statue used to have, from the war booty from Crete, as a tithe, as Xenagoras states in the thirtieth book of his *Chronicle*" (XXXIV); and "the people dedicated a shield in accordance with an oracle that predicted that the war, which had broken out at that time against Ptolemy Philadelphos, would come to an end when the dedication is made to Athena; and it was fulfilled, as stated by Timokritos in the fourth book of his *Chronicle*." "The following text was inscribed on the shield: 'The Rhodian people to Athena Lindia in accordance to an oracle'" (XXXVII).

Two of the three miracles that are preserved in this inscription are connected with important wars: the siege of Rhodes by the Persian Datis (494 or 490 BC) and the siege by Demetrios Poliorketes (305–304 BC). The aim of the inscription was to increase the sanctuary's fame, and consequently local glory (lines 2–4: "the sanctuary of Athena Lindia is extremely old and revered, and it has been adorned with many and beautiful dedications from the oldest times because of the manifestation of the goddess' power; it has, however, occured, that the oldest of the dedications have been destroyed, together with their inscriptions, due to time").

The best known specimen of monumental historiography is the "Parian Chronicle," a list of important events in Greek myth and history from Kekrops, running to ca. 264 BC (*IG* XII.5 444; *FgrHist* 239). The anonymous author of this text, which was probably set up in a gymnasium, was primarily interested in wars (Chaniotis 1988: 165). Here are some of the entries for 322–318 BC:

> [9] From the Lamian War fought by the Athenians against Antipater, and from the sea battle fought and won by the Macedonians against the Athenians at Amorgos, 59 years; and Kephisodotos was archon in Athens. [10] From the time when Antipatros captured Athens, and Ophellas was sent by Ptolemy to take over Kyrene, 58 years; and Philotas was archon in Athens. [11] From the time when Antigonos crossed to Asia, and Alexander was laid to rest in Memphis, and Perdikkas invaded Egypt and was killed, and Krateros and

Aristotle the philosopher died at the age of 50, 57 years; and Archippos was archon at Athens; and Ptolemy made an expedition to Kyrene. [12] From the death of Antipatros, and the withrawal of Kassandros from Macedon, and from the siege of Kyzikos by Arrhidaios, and from the time when Ptolemy took over Syria and Phoinikia, 55 years; and Apollodoros was archon at Athens. And in the same year the Syracusans chose Agathokles to be general with full powers over the strongholds in Sicily.

(transl. Austin 1981: no. 21, modified)

Wars, battles, sieges, and the fall of cities are not only memorable events, they are points of reference in the collective memory and are often chosen as the beginning of a new era (see Leschhorn 1993). The capture of Babylon by Seleukos I in 312 BC (App., *Syr.* 54) was the point of reference for chronology in the East until the Roman period, competing only with the Actian era, which took the sea battle at Actium as its point of reference. In Tenos, inscriptions commemorated every year the names of the chief magistrates, stereotypically mentioning that under their magistracy health and fortune was given by the gods (see chapter 9, section 6). One of these texts is, however, supplemented with the narrative of an attack, probably by pirates (first century): "During their term of office there was [health? And they also retained] the existing concord. When some men noticed those who had sailed against us and had climbed on the walls and had occupied the lower part of the city, Onesas and the guards arranged themselves in order of battle within the city and with all their might they threw out the enemies" (*IG* XII Suppl. 315).

These narratives share some common features. The monumental historiography of the Hellenistic period, not unlike other contemporary forms of transmission of historical knowledge, shows a strong interest in wars, especially wars in which Greek cities (or the Greeks) fought against representatives of a different culture (Trojans, Persians, Thracians, Galatians). Consequently, their victories not only mean rescue from danger, but also underline the cultural identity of the victorious party, and sometimes herald the beginning of a new era. For Antigonos Gonatas the victory over the Galatians meant the beginning of his rule, but also the introduction of the Macedonian king to the circle of the legendary or historical figures that had rescued the Greeks from the barbarians. The poems of Archilochos, which were extensively quoted in his biographical inscriptions, reminded the Parians of their wars against the Thracians during the colonization of Thasos; they kept the memory of a heroic "founders' age" alive. The wars alluded to in the "Lindian Chronicle" are, again, the wars that shaped Greek identity: the Trojan War, the wars of the time of colonization, and the Persian Wars.

As we have already seen (see section 11.1), the cultural memory of a community has to be selective in order to be effective as a means of identity. The subjects treated by the monumental historiography of war express this selectivity.

11.4. Oral Commemoration of War

In the late second century BC, Bombos of Alexandreia Troas visited the city of Larisa in Thessaly. His activity is described in a decree issued to honor him (Chaniotis 1988: 310): "Bombos, son of Alpheios, an Aiolian from Alexandreia, spent several days in our city and organized many performances/lectures in the gymnasium, having great success with his treatises; he recalled the glorious events that have occured with regard to the Lariseans, increasing the goodwill and the friendship between both cities, as he reminded of the beneficient things that exist between the Aiolians and the Lariseans." The "glorious events" were probably, but not necessarily, wars. Two points are interesting in this decree: the oral form of the presentation – the lecture – and the place of the performance – the gymnasium, the place where youth exercised and learned.

Historical lectures (*akroaseis*) became very popular in the Hellenistic period, which can be seen as the golden age of Greek historiography in terms of quantity – though certainly not in terms of quality. Polybios' criticism of the historians of his time is to a great extent the result of the character inherent in a historiography which was to be orally performed in civic public spaces by historians eager to receive praise, honors, and material gain. In the mid-second century BC the Delphians honored the historian Aristotheos of Troizen (*F.Delphes* III.3 124; *FgrHist* 835 T 1; Chaniotis 1988: 309–10), and there can be no misunderstanding about the reasons: "Aristotheos, son of Nikotheos, an author of histories [*historiographos*], came to our city and conducted his stay in a manner worthy of [our] sanctuary and his own city; he presented his treatises in lectures for many days, and in addition to this he read out encomiastic orations for the Romans, the common benefactors of the Greeks." Aristotheos' subject was probably recent history (the Third Macedonian War) – hence, the writing of history and the encomiastic presentation of recent events were in the hands of the same author.

Although there are numerous references to historical lectures in the Hellenistic inscriptions, no text is preserved. From references in honorary decrees we may assume that the subjects treated in these lectures were "deeds of glory" (*endoxa*: Chaniotis 1988: 310, no. E18; 312, no. E20) – i.e., wars, foundation myths, and the miracles of local gods – again, often during wars (see chapter 8, section 4). It is only by coincidence that a small fragment of an *enkomion* for Athens survives – a fragment of an oration delivered by Hegesias, a local historian of Rhodes and an orator (Strabo 9.1.16, C 396): "I see the acropolis and, there, the sign of the miraculous trident; I see Eleusis, and I have been initiated in the sacred rites; the Leokorion is there, here Theseus' sanctuary. I cannot describe everything in detail, for Attika belongs to the gods, who laid claim on the land, and to the ancestors, who are honored as heroes." The orator alludes with a few words to standard elements of Athenian self-glorification: foundation myths (the contest between Athena and Poseidon, and Theseus), the Eleusinian mysteries, deeds of self-sacrifice (the Leokorion was the monument for the daughters of a king who sacrificed themselves to save Athens from hunger), and the heroic deeds of ancestors. His references can be short and allusive, since the sites, people, and events to which he refers were integral parts of the Athenian cultural memory.

Besides the public lectures of historians, the orations held during commemorative anniversaries of wars (see section 11.5), the hymns sung at festivals, and the explanations given in sanctuaries by local guides about the historical background of dedications and monuments, we may observe another, rather unexpected, form of oral transmission of the memory of wars: the discussions in the assembly (see chapter 9, section 4). In no other period of Greek history was the assembly summoned so often, and in so many cities. The decrees, which are often preserved in inscriptions, give us an impression of the discussions, the proposals, the arguments used, and the part played by oral historical narratives in the debates. Historical examples and historical arguments were an effective means of persuasion, used by local statesmen and foreign envoys alike. Chremonides of Athens convinced his countrymen to ally themselves with the Spartans against King Antigonos Gonatas in 268 BC (see chapter 9, section 4; see also section 11.5) not only with pragmatic arguments, but also by reminding them that in the past (i.e., during the Persian Wars), under similar conditions, Spartans and Athenians had fought glorious battles against those who wished to enslave their cities.

A historical narrative of a war was the central argument of the Kytenian envoys to Xanthos, where they were seeking financial assistance to rebuild their city wall (*SEG* XXXVIII 1476). In 206 BC, envoys of the small city of Kytenion in Doris (central Greece) arrived in Xanthos in Lykia (Asia Minor) and, probably very much to the surprise of the assembled Xanthians, explained that they were relatives, since Apollo was born in Xanthos and his son Asklepios in Doris. In order to document the good relations between the cities, the envoys also explained how Xanthian colonists had been assisted by Aletes, an ancestor of the Kytenians, in a war (lines 24–30): "they also demonstrated that Aletes, one of the Heraclids, took care of the colonists who were sent out from our land by Chrysaor, the son of Glaukos, the son of Hippolochos; for Aletes, starting from Doris, helped the colonists when they were being warred upon and, putting an end to the danger that had surrounded them, he married the daughter of Aor, the son of Chrysaor." It was now the Xanthians' turn to assist the Kytenians financially, and despite the terrible financial situation in Xanthos, the assembly approved (a very modest) aid of 500 drachma (see chapter 7, section 1). We cannot tell with certainty whether the legend of Aletes was invented for the purpose of this embassy or corresponded to an already existing myth. What is certain is that the oral narrative in the assembly of Xanthos and, later, the engraving of this document on stone, made the mythological war part of the common cultural memory of the Xanthians and Kytenians.

This is not an isolated case. In the second century BC envoys of Apollonia on the Rhyndakos (south coast of the Black Sea) came to Miletos in order to establish relations based on ancestry. The relevant document explains (Curty 1995: 143–5 no. 58):

> The Milesians listened to the envoys favorably and, after examining the historical narratives about this issue as well as the other documents, they responded that our city [Apollonia] has truly been a colony of their city. Their ancestors did this, when they sent an army to Hellespontos and to Propontis, defeated in war the barbarians that inhabit these places and founded the other Greek cities and our own; Apollo of Didyma was their leader in this campaign.

It is, again, an oral presentation and discussion in the assembly, accompanied by a study of written documents, that brings an old war back to memory. The event concerns, as in many other cases (see section 11.5), a war against barbarians in the times of the founders.

The aforementioned examples of oral narratives concern wars of the remote past, but oral accounts of recent wars were no less common and played a prominent part in honorary decrees. The proposals, orally presented in the assembly, included a justification (*narratio*) which is often a narrative of heroic deeds in battles. If these oral reports have survived, it is because many decrees were inscribed on stone upon approval. In many cases the honors were periodically announced in the theater or in athletic competitions, thus perpetuating the memory of military achievements. A decree of Apollonia in honor of Histria (ca. 200–150 BC) is an instructive example of this practice (*ISE* 129; Curty 1995: 39–41, no. 21):

> It occured that the inhabitants of Mesembria carried out an undeclared war against us, occupied our territory beyond the sea, committed many and great acts of sacrilege against the sanctuary of Apollo, and brought our city to the greatest dangers. But the Histrians, who are our relatives and friends and have a favorable disposition towards our people, sent ships and soldiers to help us.

The decree – including this narrative that presented the enemy in the darkest colors as a cowardly, unjust, and impious aggressor – was not only to be inscribed on the base of the statue of the victorious general but also read aloud during the contests that took place in Histria "forever" (*aei*). Such decrees sometimes contain detailed narratives and dramatic descriptions of battles – usually with a reassuring happy end (see chapter 10, section 3). Their authors were very conscious of the effect these announcements had, as two documents from Entella in Sicily show. Entella had suffered greatly during a war against Carthage; its population even had to abandon the city temporarily. A series of honorary decrees was issued after the population had returned to Entella to honor the cities which had helped in a time of need – among them Herbita and Gela (*SEG* XXX 1117–1118). Their citizens were invited to the contests and sacrifices in Entella, in order to keep the memory of these events alive ("so that we demonstrate to future generations that we remember those who helped our city"). As we know from similar documents, the guests of honor were invited by the herald to take their seats, and this invitation in front of the assembled population included a reference to the event for which the honor had been awarded. The memory of wars – often abstract, distorted, and idealized – was transmitted to future generations of citizens by means of these annual announcements no less than through the work of local historians.

11.5. Commemorative Anniversaries

Festivals interrupt the normal course of things and the routine of everyday life. In the Hellenistic period, festivals seem at first sight to *be* everyday life. This impression is to a great extent misleading, and it is created by the large number of existing documents that concern themselves with the establishment of new celebrations – documents that were published on stone and have, therefore, survived. There can be no doubt that hundreds of new festivals were established in the Hellenistic cities (Chaniotis 1995), but sometimes only to replace existing ones.

However, it is true that Hellenistic civic culture was one of celebration. Festivals attracted the interest of officials, citizens, and kings, they were a subject of discussion in the popular assembly, they competed with other festivals in glamor and innovative devices. Celebrations not only structured the course of the year, but provided an opportunity for a community to celebrate its gods, its kings, and above all the community itself. Festivals also gave foreigners – traders, artists, shoppers, and thieves – a good reason to visit a major civic center.

Among the new festivals established in the Hellenistic period, commemorative anniversaries take a prominent position. In a sense, every Greek festival was a commemorative anniversary, since it was supposed to commemorate an event of the mythical past, a deed of a god or a hero. Commemorative anniversaries, in a narrower sense of the term, are celebrations that commemorate historical events. Such celebrations are known already from the Classical period (Chaniotis 1991a). Most of them were anniversaries of war victories – for example, the battles of Marathon, Thermopylai, Salamis, and Plataia. Some of these anniversaries, especially those connected with the Persian Wars, continued to be celebrated for centuries, being part of the festive culture of commemoration of the Hellenistic Greeks.

The many wars of the Hellenistic period naturally added new anniversaries to existing ones. One of them continues to be celebrated today: the Jewish Hanukkah festival commemorates a victory over the Seleukid king, Demetrios.

Commemorative anniversaries shared some common features:

- they commemorated victories;
- the opponents were usually not ordinary enemies, but representatives of a different culture – i.e., barbarians or enemies that threatened the freedom or very existence of a community; and
- the victory marked salvation from great danger and/or the beginning of a new era.

Consequently, anniversaries of battles became an important element of cultural identity and gave rise to competition among communities. We may observe these features in the small selection of commemorative anniversaries presented below.

The Delphic festival of the *Soteria* ("the festival of the Salvation") presents an instructive case study. This festival commemorated the defeat of the invading Galatians in 279 BC. It was established for the first time by the Delphic Amphictyony – i.e., by the commonwealth of tribal communities and cities that administered the cult of Demeter at Thermopylai and that of Apollo at Delphi – some time after the defeat of the Galatians. A contemporary Koan decree, which establishes a thanksgiving sacrifice to Apollo in Kos (*Syll.*[3] 398; Austin 1981: no. 48; Bagnall and Derow 2004: no. 17, 278 BC), attributes the defeat of the Galatians to Apollo's miracle, precisely as later literary sources do (Paus. 10.23.1–9; Just., *epit.* 24.7.6 and 8.3–7). Immediately after the defeat of the Galatians, the religious dimension prevailed, and this is also expressed in the name of the Delphic festival, which derives from the epithet of Apollo Soter ("the Savior"), the god whose miraculous intervention was the focal point of the celebration. However, when in the mid-third century BC the Aitolian League took over control of the Delphic sanctuary, the festival was not only reorganized as a pentaeteric contest (i.e., a contest that took place every four years), this time under the auspices of the Aitolians, but the historical tradition was also reshaped (Champion 1995). The divine elements are conspicuously absent in the decrees issued by Greek communities to declare their acceptance of the pentaeteric contest in 246/45 (*IG* II[2] 680; *F.Delphes* III.1 481–3; III.3 215). These decrees emphasize instead the piety of the Aitolians. The historical event is represented as a massive invasion repulsed by the Aitolians before Delphi, and interestingly, in these decrees Zeus Soter (not Apollo Pythios) occupies the most prominent position.

The commemorative anniversary of the battle at Plataia (478 BC), which continued to be celebrated until Plutarch's day, 600 years after the event, is another good example of the way in which festivals became grounds for competition between communities and formed a vital part of cultural life. The festival's name, *Eleutheria*, derives from Zeus Eleutherios, the patron god of freedom. But the focal point of attention was not the god, but the war heroes buried at Plataia and the idea of freedom, which explains why the service of slaves was not allowed on this occasion. A detailed description survives in Plutarch's life of Aristeides:

> On the sixteenth of the month Maimakterion, which corresponds to the Boiotian month Alalkomenios, they held a procession, which is led forth, at break of day, by a trumpeter who sounds the signal for battle; wagons filled with myrtle and wreaths follow, then a black bull, then free-born youths who carry libations of wine and milk in jars and pitchers of oil and myrrh; for no slave is permitted to assist in this service, since the men had died for freedom; and at the end comes the chief magistrate of the Plataians, who may not at other times touch iron or dress himself with any other garment than white, but on this occasion wears a purple tunic, carries a water-jar from the city's archive, and marches, sword in hand, through the city to the graves. Then he takes water from the spring, washes with his own hands the stelae and anoints them with myrrh; then he slaughters the bull at the pyre and praying to Zeus and Hermes Chthonios he invites the brave men who died for Greece to come to the banquet and the offerings of blood. Then he mixes a mixer of wine and makes a libation saying: "I drink to the men who died for the freedom of the Greeks." The Plataians observe these rites down to this very day.
>
> (Plut., *Aristeides* 21.3–6; trans. B. Perrin, modified)

An interesting detail of this festival was a rhetorical competition (*dialogos*, "debate") between the two leading powers of the Greeks during the Persian Wars, Athens and Sparta. The representative of Athens tried to prove that the contribution of his native city to the victory was more significant than that of Sparta, and the representative of Sparta tried to prove the opposite. A pan-Hellenic jury decided who had made the most convincing argument, and the winner was honored by his countrymen; his city had the privilege of leading the procession (*propompeia*; Robertson 1986). This rhetorical contest was introduced in the second century BC, and continued to take place even in the Roman period. An inscription found in Athens preserves a fragment of a speach delivered on this occasion (*IG* II^2 277; Chaniotis 1988: 42–8, late second century).

This was not the only competition during this festival. Races took place as well, but on the battlefield, not in an ordinary stadium. The starting point was the trophy of victory, and the races ended at the altar of Zeus Eleutherios.

The subtext of this festival – a common culture and a common ideal of freedom – did not remain entirely unchanged in the course of the centuries, and it is particularly interesting to observe that during a Hellenistic war a new element was emphasized in the anniversary: the concord of the Greeks. The Chremonidean War (268–261 BC) united Ptolemy II and several Greek states, including Athens and Sparta, against the enemy of Greek freedom, King Antigonos Gonatas of Macedon. The decree proposed by Chremonides (Austin 1981: no. 49; Bagnall and Derow 2004: no. 19) reminded the

Greeks that together "they had fought many glorious battles against those who wished to enslave the cities" (i.e., against the Persians), thus winning fame and assuring freedom. Now that similar circumstances prevailed, as King Antigonos threatened the freedom and the ancestral constitutions, the Greeks were urged to ally themselves with Ptolemy, the defender of "the common freedom of the Greeks," and to preserve concord (*homonoia*). This was the lesson taught by the Persian Wars. The interdependence of freedom and concord in connection with the Persian Wars and with the war against Antigonos is expressed directly in a decree which was moved by the league of the Greeks that participated in the festival of the *Eleutheria* during the celebration itself (Étienne and Piérart 1975; Austin 1981: no. 51, ca. 261–246 BC). On the very battlefield where the concord of the Greeks prevailed over the enemies of freedom, the decree praises Glaukon, an Athenian in the service of Ptolemy II, who "had contributed to making more lavish the sacrifice to Zeus Eleutherios and Concord and the contest which the Greeks celebrate on the tomb of the heroes who fought against the barbarians for the freedom of the Greeks." This is the earliest reference to an altar of *Homonoia* (Concord) that stood next to that of Zeus Eleutherios (Thériault 1996: 102–22), serving as a reminder that freedom can be best defended through concord. We do not know if the cult of *Homonoia* was introduced in Plataia during the Chremonidean War or earlier, but we can be certain that during and after this war the emphasis of the *Eleutheria* was shifted from the notion of freedom to the combination of concord and freedom. It is interesting to observe that the surviving fragment of a speach delivered by an Athenian representative on the occasion of this festival in the late second century (*IG* II² 2778; Chaniotis 1988: 42–8), castigates the Spartans for abandoning this concord immediately after the battle and not participating in the subsequent wars against the Persians. The result was that Greek cities fell under the rule (*despoteia*) of the Persians.

Commemorative anniversaries of wars could be continually adapted to new circumstances and were one of the occasions on which the Hellenistic statesmen urged their countrymen to learn from history. In Pergamon, the festival of the Nikephoria (the festival of Athena Nikephoros, "the goddess who brings victory") was founded by Attalos I around 220 BC to commemorate the victory of the Pergamene rulers over the Galatians in Asia Minor (Jones 1974). Just like the festival at Plataia, it stressed the opposition between Greeks and barbarians, but unlike the *Eleutheria* it did not propagate the idea of freedom, but the ideology of the victorious king (see chapter 4). It was enlarged as a pentaeteric contest in 182/1 BC, but was eclipsed after the end of the Attalid dynasty by the wars that followed. It was re-established after the Mithridatic Wars (69 BC) by the local statesman and benefactor Diodoros Pasparos. The name remained unchanged, but, even if some Pergamenes did not forget the festival's origins, the function of the festival in its last phase was not to legitimize monarchical rule, but to praise victory in a more general sense, and thus to contribute to the identity and self-confidence of the Pergamenes. A decree of Pergamon (*I.Pergamon* 246; *SEG* XXXIV 1251) concerns the festivities of a commemorative anniversary for a victory of Attalos III, but the opponent is, unfortunately, not known.

While at Plataia the Greeks could jointly celebrate their pan-Hellenic identity, they did not lack opportunities to separately celebrate the memory of their conflicts as well. Interestingly, the commemorative anniversaries of Greek wars in the Hellenistic period do not concern the wars between Greek cities, but the wars against or between kings. There are a few exceptions – for example, the commemorative anniversaries celebrated in the Cretan city of Lyttos, known from a (still unpublished) inscription of the late second century. One of them commemorated the re-foundation of the city after its destruction during the Lyttian War (ca. 220 BC), the other commemorated the destruction of the neighboring city of Dreros (late third/early second century). A neighbor is often the worst enemy, and not only in Hellenistic Greece, but this particular anniversary meant more to the Lyttians than just a victory over a traditional enemy. During the Lyttian War the Drerians had sworn never to stop fighting against the Lyttians (see chapter 3, section 1); the destruction of the enemy was in Lyttian collective memory intrinsically connected with survival, revenge, and the beginning of a new era.

But apart from this festival, the Hellenistic commemorative anniversaries of wars and battles are connected with the wars of kings – and were usually short-lived. The Samians introduced the festival Antigoneia and Demetria in 306 BC upon the announcement of the victory of Demetrios at the sea-battle of Salamis in Cyprus (*IG* XII.6 56; *epi tois euangeliois*). The Athenians introduced in 304 BC a sacrifice to Agathe Tyche ("Good Fortune") and to kings Antigonos the One-Eyed and Demetrios the Besieger after the latter's victory in the Peloponnese during one of the Wars of the Successors (*SEG* XXX 69). The campaigns of Philip V of Macedon in Asia Minor (ca. 204–200 BC), the dangers for the Karian cities, and their rescue from this danger are the most probable background of festivals in Knidos (*SEG* XXXVIII 812) and Bargylia (*I.Iasos* 613; cf. *SEG* XLV 1508 A/B) that commemorated the miracles of Artemis. The festival of Artemis Kindyas at Bargylia was continually enlarged until the late second century, commemorating not only this particular war, but also other miracles (*epiphaneiai*) of Artemis during later wars. Two other contemporary festivals, this time in Thessaly, also focused on defeats of Philip V. The *Eleutheria* of Larisa, dedicated to Zeus Eleutherios, was a contest of the Thessalian League established when it acquired its autonomy after the Roman victory at Kynos Kephalai (ca. 197 BC; *IG* IX.2 525–6, 528–30, 534; *Syll.*³ 613). After the battle at Pydna, which heralded the end of the Macedonian kingdom, the city of Larisa established another competition to honor its cavalrymen who had risked their lives fighting (*tois prokindyneusasin*) with the Romans against King Perseus at the Tempe in 171 BC (*IG* IX.2 527, 531–3; Robert and Robert 1964: 176–82). The program of this latter contest is primarily military in nature. The disciplines in which the Lariseans competed included races of men and children, horse races, a competition of trumpeters and heralds, bull hunting, torch races on horses, and competitions between infantry and cavalry. Both commemorative festivals were still celebrated in the Roman Imperial period, but possibly with interruptions (see *IG* IX.2 531–2). A commemorative festival of a similar nature was celebrated in Kyzikos in the late first century (*IGR* IV 159; Robert and Robert 1964: 180). This was a thanksgiving contest (*eucharisterioi agones*) which honored Asklepiades and the other citizens of Kyzikos who had fought with Caesar against Ptolemy XIII in Alexandria in 47/46 BC. The contest included a competition in incursion (*katadrome*). When the festival Amphiaraia in honor of Amphiaraos in Oropos was refounded around 85 BC after Sulla's victory over Mithridates VI, it was not only given a second name (*Amphiaraia* and *Rhomaia*), but was also enlarged with a competition in honor of the "good tidings of the victory of the Romans" (*euangelia Rhomaion nikes*; *I.Oropos* 521, 525, 529).

The evident preference for anniversaries of victories over kings (Philip V, Perseus, Ptolemy XIII) certainly reflects the dedication of citizen communities to the ideal (and the illusion) of freedom and autonomy until the end of the Hellenistic Age. It should be remarked in this context that military victories in civil wars were also celebrated when they were connected with the abolition of repressive regimes (tyrannies, oligarchies), the introduction of democracy, or the establishment of freedom. We know of such festivals, for example, in Priene, after the violent expulsion of a tyrant (*I.Priene* 11; 297 BC), and in Sikyon after the liberation of the city by Aratos in 251 BC (Plut., *Aratos* 53.4).

Almost all Greek commemorative anniversaries had an aggressive character (Chaniotis 1991a: 140–1), and naturally this aggressive element is particularly clear in war anniversaries. The aggressive celebration of superiority and success, often with military overtones (e.g., in the contests), is intrinsically connected with the function of these celebrations: they were one of the most effective means by which identity was constructed and transmitted to later generations. A common identity can be based on common suffering, but it is more effective when it is based on the memory of success. When the Athenians wanted to show Sulla who they were, they narrated the history of their great victories which rescued Greece and Greek culture; when Athenians and Spartans stressed their common Greek identity, an identity based on freedom no less than on common culture, they looked back to the victories of the Persian Wars; and when the Lyttians wished to strengthen their friendship with the Oluntians, they invited them to their most important festivals, to the memorials of their success:

the anniversary of the victory over Dreros and the anniversary of the refoundation of their city. The feeling of togetherness arose in the Hellenistic cities and leagues, no less than in other communities, from shared toil, shared suffering, and shared victories. The Hellenistic historical anniversaries strengthened identities, and by so doing they also constructed otherness: they underlined the barriers that separated the Greeks from the barbarians (Amazons, Thracians, Persians, Galatians) and the free cities from the repressive kings.

Finally, there is a clear preference for events that in some sense mark the beginning of a new era: the Persian Wars, the wars that established the rule of kings (Antigonos Gonatas, Attalos I), the refoundation of Lyttos, and the re-establishment of freedom (e.g., the *Eleutheria* of the Thessalian League).

Among the many anniversaries of Hellenistic wars, only those that could be understood as marking the beginning of a new era survived the end of the Hellenistic period: the Thessalian *Eleutheria*, the Pergamene *Nikephoria* (of Diodoros Pasparos), and the anniversary of the battle that marks the end of the Hellenistic Age itself: the sea battle of Actium. Among the many anniversaries of earlier battles (of the fifth and fourth centuries) only those connected with the Persian Wars did not fall into oblivion: the battles at Marathon, Plataia, Salamis, and Thermopylai. The Persian Wars remained until the Imperial period a constituent of Greekness, a central element of self-representation not only of individual communities, but of the Hellenes as a whole. As late as the fifth century AD, long after the victory of Christianity, a pagan priest with the characteristic name Helladios had an inscription written on the cenotaph of the dead of the Persian Wars in Megara that records that his city still offered (or offered again) a sacrifice to these heroes. Helladios demonstrated Greekness by defying the Christian prohibitions (*IG* VII 53).

11.6. War Monuments

According to ancient custom the victorious army erectred a trophy at the turning point of a battle, the *trope*. At least in early times this consisted of the trunk of an oak tree on which the arms of the defeated enemy were hung (see figure 11.1). Zeus Tropaios was recipient of the dedication, as the patron of victory. The religious nature of the dedication forbade the destruction of trophies (see Cassius Dio 42.48.2), which consequently sometimes survived for centuries. Given the number of battles from the Archaic period onwards and the fact that this practice continued in the Hellenistic period, trophies cannot have been a very unusual sight for a traveler in Hellenistic Greece. A trophy at Las that commemorated a victory of Spartans over a Macedonian detachment in 218 BC could still be seen there 400 years later (Paus. 3.24.6). This battle is otherwise unknown (see Polyb. 5.19.4), and it is reasonable to assume that if its memory survived in Lakonia (and

Figure 11.1 Tetradrachm of Agathokles. Nike, the goddess of victory, sets up a trophy (© British Museum).

in local historiography), it was primarily because of the existence of the trophy. Similarly, Sulla's trophy at Chaironeia (86 BC) still stood in Plutarch's day, two centuries later (Plut., *Sulla* 19.10).

But in addition to the trophies spontaneously erected immediately or soon after a battle, there were also permanent, monumental trophies erected years later, often not in the exact location of the battle. Their monumental form enabled them to survive for centuries, and the trophy at Las may have been just such a monument. Trophies were part of the cultural memory of the Hellenistic Greeks, providing a reminder of great battles, especially battles of the Persian Wars or local conflicts. The trophy at Plataia still existed in the late second century AD, probably also later, and it was incorporated into the rituals of the commemorative anniversary for this battle.

Forgetting about a war was sometimes as important as remembering it. An amnesty clause was not unusual in agreements concluded after civil strife or a war (e.g., Quillin 2002; Wolpert 2002). The Knidians who arbitrated between Temnos and Klazomenai after a war forbade, for example, the two parties to raise accusations about things that had ocured during their war and guaranteed amnesty (Herrmann 1979: 259–60; *SEG* XXIX 1130 *bis*, ca. 200–150 BC), and a similar clause is found in the peace treaty between Magnesia and Miletos (*Syll.*[3] 588; Ager 1996: no. 109; ca. 183 BC).

If trophies celebrated the victory of a city, at the same time they served as a reminder of the defeat of another, thus contributing to enmity. For the imaginative Greeks, the religious prohibition against the destruction of a trophy could be overcome by sophistical arguments or by cunning. As a trophy erected by an enemy could not be destroyed, the Rhodians just built a building around it that prevented it beeing seen (Vitruvius 2.8.15). This attitude shows that trophies were taken very seriously.

The dedication of war booty and the erection of memorials of victories in sanctuaries is another practice of early origin, which has a religious background and helped to keep the memory of wars alive. As we have already seen, the dedications listed in the "Lindian Chronicle" are primarily connected with wars. New dedications, especially commemorating naval victories, continued to be made in the sanctuary of Athena Lindia in the Hellenistic period (e.g., *I.Lindos* 88). Visitors to civic or pan-Hellenic sanctuaries were continually confronted with such memorials. Inscriptions explained the historical background, as in the dedication made by Achaian soldiers in Aigion in 209 BC (*SEG XXXVI* 397): "The Achaians and general Kyliadas, son of Damaretos from Pharai, to the gods after he won a victory together with the Macedonians." We may discern in this dedication a tension between collective and individual achievement ("the Achaians and general," "he won a victory"; see section 11.7). It should also be stressed that only defeated barbarians are explicitly named (see e.g., Ameling et al. 1995, no. 105: Galatians; no. 107: Romans; no. 110: Thracians; no. 201: Dardanians), with Greek opponents frequently remaining anonymous.

To the dedications of cities, leagues, and generals in sanctuaries, the Hellenistic Greeks added two new categories: dedications in pan-Hellenic sanctuaries (Olympia, Delos, Delphi) made by kings as a medium of their imperial propaganda (Bringmann 2000: 64–78) and, later, dedications by victorious Roman generals (e.g., Pollitt 1986: 155–8). A dedication of a Pergamene king in Athens demonstrates the competitive nature and aims of such dedications. Attalos I or II dedicated on the Athenian acropolis representations of mythical battles (the Gods fighting against the Giants, the Athenians fighting against the Amazons), but also of the battle of Marathon, and of the Pergamene victory over the Galatians (Paus. 1.25.2; Ameling et al. 1995: 66–8). In this way the victory of the Attalids was on the one hand subtly associated with the Gigantomachy and the Amazonomachy and on the other was given the status of a pan-Hellenic victory, similar to that against the Persians.

Did the monument commemorating the victory of Antigonos Gonatas against the Galatians still stand on the Athenian acropolis when the monument of the rival dynasty of the Attalids was erected at the same site? We do not know, but the similarity of the two dedications is striking. Both of them concern a victory over barbarians (the same barbarians); both of them mark the beginning of a royal dynasty; and both of them are aimed at presenting kings as saviors of the Greeks.

Not many users of the word "colossal" or its variants in other modern languages realize that they are using a word that goes back to a victory monument of the Hellenistic period. When Demetrios ended the siege of Rhodes which gave him his name "Besieger" (305/4 BC), the Rhodians sold the siege equipment and with the proceeds funded the construction of a 33-meter high bronze statue of Helios, the patron of Rhodes, as "a memorial of his power and their own bravery" (Plut., *Demetr.* 20.9; see also Plut., *mor.* 183 b). The statue was probably erected on their acropolis – and not, as widely believed, in one of the harbors (Rice 1993: 235–9; Hoepfner 2003). The Colossus was destroyed by the great earthquake of 238 BC and never re-erected, in accordance with an oracle. Although short-lived, it became one of the Seven Wonders of the world, and this fame overshadowed the historical event that it was intented to commemorate. If the occasion of this dedication was forgotten, this may be due to the fact that the monument itself did not allude in any way to the historical event.

This also holds true in the case of another victory monument, the famous Nike of Samothrake, the statue of Victory standing on the prow of a ship. The monument probably commemorated a naval victory of the Rhodians (Rice 1991; Mark 1998: 190). And yet, other victory monuments were far more explicit in the messages they conveyed, for example, ships dedicated in sanctuaries to commemorate sea battles (Rice 1991). Antigonos Gonatas dedicated a trireme in Delos after his victory in the sea battle at Kos (Athen. 5.209 e; Ameling et al. 1995: nos. 133, 432). Usually an inscription provided viewers with the necessary information.

Monuments were often erected in the capitals of kingdoms in order to celebrate victories in wars and at the same time to legitimize monarchical rule. The victory monument of the Attalids of Pergamon that commemorated their victory over the Galatians consisted of bronze statuary groups on the acropolis of Pergamon. They no longer survive, but they are known from copies (Pollittt 1986: 79–110). The numerous dedications of the Attalids in the sanctuary of Athena Nikephoros ("the one who brings victory") made specific reference to the military events (e.g., *OGIS* 281: "a first-fruit offering from the spoils from Aigina"; 283: "from the sea-battle near Chios against Philip and the Macedonians"; 284: "from the occupation of Oreos"; 285: "from the captured weapons"; 298: "from the battle at Lypedron against the Bithynians and the Galatians"; cf. *OGIS* 273–9 = Austin 1981: no. 197), thus contributing to the glorification of the Attalid dynasty and the commemoration of its success.

The practice of honoring the dead with war memorials has a long tradition in Greek history. The *demosion sema* (public grave monument) in Athens and the Funeral Oration of Perikles are archaeological and literary testimonies to this practice, but this evidence is not limited to Athens.

Philon of Byzantion (A 86, ed. Garlan 1974: 300) recommends the construction of grave monuments and cenotaphs for war dead in the form of towers "so that both the city will be more safe and those who distinguished themselves for their valor and those who died for the fatherland will be well buried in their very fatherland."

One should distinguish between the representations of warriors, sailors, and riders on private epitaphs and the public or communal erection of war memorials for the dead. The latter practice is attested by the Hellenistic memorial for the Milesian warriors who lost their lives in a war against Megara in the Archaic period (Herrmann 1997: 732; *SGO* I 01/20/08), and the grave monument erected by the Rhodian district of the Kasareis for three men who lost their lives fighting against Tyrrhenian pirates (*Syll.*[3] 1225; cf. *I.Stratonikeia* 1333).

Individuals were also honored with memorials – for example, the Macedonian officer Alketas, a brother of Perdikkas, one of the Successors. Alketas killed himself in order to avoid capture in 319 in Termessos in Pisidia, and although his death did not occur in combat, it was heroic and impressed the young Termessians. They recovered his body and provided for a memorable burial, which perhaps can be identified with a grave found in Termessos (Fedak 1990: 94–6; Rice 1993: 234–5). Apollonios, the commander of the troops of Metropolis during the Aristonikos War (133 BC), was honored with a statue in the market-place after his heroic death in battle, and the names of 13 young men who fell in the same battle were inscribed on the base of his statue (Dreyer and Engelmann 2003: 41). In Sparta, the old tradition of setting up inscribed gravestones only for those who had died in war (*en polemoi*) continued into the Hellenistic period (e.g., *SEG* XXXII 397).

War memorials, whether a dedication in a sanctuary, a trophy on the battlefield, or a monumental tomb, were often accompanied by inscriptions that explained to passers-by the historical background of the monument. As "places of memory" (*lieux de mémoire*) they attracted visitors and were used as the location for rituals, especially on commemorative anniversaries or other celebrations.

The ephebic inscriptions of Athens (see chapter 3, section 1) demonstrate the importance of war monuments for the transmission of cultural memory and identity to youth. One of these texts honors the ephebes of the year 123 BC and describes their various activities (*IG* II[2] 1006). The nucleus of ephebic training was instruction in fighting, but it also included a historical component – i.e., instruction in the use of old weapons which in a sense were "historical monuments" themselves. More interesting in our context is the list of festivals in which the ephebes participated. They attended the procession for Artemis Agrotera on the 6th of Boedromion, which was at the same time the anniversary of the battle at Marathon (Plut., *mor.* 349 e); and they also sacrificed to Athena Nike, the patron of military victory. "On the *Epitaphia* [the funeral contest in honor of the war dead] they held a

Figure 11.2 Grave relief of a young soldier in Rhodes. Archaeological Museum of Rhodes (courtesy of the Museum).

race in armor, both the race that starts at the *polyandreion* and the other obligatory races." The *polyandreion*, the common burial place of the Athenians who had died in the sea battle of Salamis, was one of the most important historical monuments in Athens.

On the festival of the Theseia, which honored Theseus as the legendary founder of the Athenian state and as an archetypical ephebe, and on the

Epitaphia, the ephebes performed excersises with weapons; the armed ephebes toured the frontier of the Athenian territory, which they had to defend, and visited the extra-urban sanctuaries. One of these excursions brought them to another *lieu de mémoire* connected with the Persian Wars: the tomb at Marathon. "When they reached the tomb in Marathon, they crowned it and sacrificed to those who were killed in the war for the liberty of the Greeks." Since prayers and hymns were parts of sacrifices, it is not unreasonable to assume that on this occasion there was some oral reference to the historical events, probably even an oration, as in their next visit, to the sanctuary of Amphiaraos, where the ephebes testified to (*historesan*) the ancestral claim of their city on the sanctuary. The ephebes also sailed to the trophy erected by the Athenians after the sea battle at Salamis, and sacrificed there to Zeus Tropaios. On the occasion of the Aianteia, which honored Aiax, the hero of Salamis, the ephebes organized a regatta, a procession, and a sacrifice. This ephebic inscription resembles an itinerary that brings the young Athenians to the sacred and historical sites of their city. The sites that are related to battles – trophies and graves of the war dead – occupy a prominent position, showing how historical monuments were integrated into rituals of memory.

We should remark here the correspondence of the elements of cultural memory in this inscription (Theseus, Persian Wars) with those in the anecdote of Plutarch (see section 11.1). They also correspond to the elements of cultural memory that we find in another inscription which concerns the restoration of sanctuaries in Attica (*IG* II² 1035; *SEG* XXVI 121). According to this decree, the sanctuaries and precincts should be restored to the gods and heroes to whom they originally had been dedicated; this should happen "for the everlasting glory of the people" (line 26). The list of these sacred places, compiled by the hoplite general Metrodoros, also contains references to historical monuments and events. Although the date of this decree is not known – the dates suggested range from the time immediately after Sulla's destruction of Athens to the mid-first century AD – this does not diminish its value as evidence for the cultural memory of the Athenians. The historical references in connection with these places of memory concern the mythical period and the founders' times (Ajax, Theseus, and Solon), the Persian Wars, the Peloponnesian War, and the war against the Galatians (Attalos I); there is also a reference to a "Magnus" (line 47; perhaps meaning Pompey the Great):

- Ajax and the foundation of Salamis (lines 31–2);
- Theseus, founder of the Athenian state (line 48);
- Solon, founder of the ancestral constitution (lines 31, 35);
- the victorious war of the Athenians against Megara for the occupation of Salamis (line 34: "where they sacrificed during the war against the Megarians for the island");

- the Persian Wars (line 33: "where the trophy of Themistokles against the Persians is as well as the common tomb of those who were killed in the battle"; line 45: "the sanctuary of Athena Herkane, founded by Themistokles before the sea battle at Salamis");
- the Peloponnesian War (line 41: ". . . during the Peloponnesian War . . .");
- dedications of king Attalos I (line 25: "dedications and statues dedicated by king Attalos for the safety of [---]"; possibly a dedication commemorating the victory over the Galatians; see Ameling 1995: no. 26a).

With the exception of the Peloponnesian War, the events alluded to in this inscription share the same features that we have observed in our study of other expressions of war memory. One notes a preference for events that mark the beginning of new eras (Theseus, Solon, the Persian Wars), for wars against barbarians (Persians, Galatians), and for victories that legitimize claims (the occupation of Salamis).

The ephebic decree and the decree concerning the restoration of sanctuaries clearly show that monuments, trophies, and tombs are places where memory rests, a memory that could be reactivated by means of visits, pilgrimages, contests, inscriptions, and orations. Let us examine again in this context Hegesias' Athenian oration (see section 11.4): "I see the acropolis and, there, the sign of the miraculous trident; I see Eleusis, and I have been initiated in the sacred rites; the Leokorion is there, here Theseus' sanctuary. I cannot describe everything in detail, for Attika belongs to the gods, who laid claim on the land, and to the ancestors, who are honored as heroes." The starting point of each of Hegesias' allusions to a mythical or historical event is a place or a monument: the acropolis alludes to the contest between Athena and Poseidon, Eleusis to the invention of agriculture in Attika, the Leokorion to the sacrifice of a king's daughters, the Theseion to the founder of Athens. No further explanation was necessary for his audience. Short allusions to *lieux de mémoire* suffice to bring to mind the origins and the achievements of the Athenians.

It is because such places of remembrance functioned as agents of cultural and collective memory that Hellenistic communities were concerned with their maintenance – or their destruction. The "Lindian anagraphe", which renewed the memory of old dedications, the veil thrown by the Rhodians over the trophy of their enemy, the ephebic excursions of the Athenians – all these measures reveal how intensely Hellenistic communities felt the need to keep the memory of war alive as an important component of their collective identity.

11.7. Collective Identity and the Glorification of the Individual

At the very end of the Hellenistic period, a statue of Philippos of Pergamon, a historian of the contemporary wars of the Late Republic, was erected in

Epidauros (see chapter 1, section 3). The beginning of his historical work is quoted on the statue's base:

> With my pious hand I delivered to the Greeks the historical narrative of the most recent deeds – all sorts of sufferings and a continual mutual slaughter having taken place in our days in Asia and Europe, in the tribes of Libya and in the cities of the islanders; I did this, so that they may learn also through us, how many evils are brought forth by courting the mob and by love of profit, by civil strifes and by the breaking of faith, and thus, by observing the sufferings of others, they may live their lives in the right way.

Not unlike Polybios or Chremonides, Philippos was convinced that the Greeks could learn from history. His narrative of the recent wars followed Thucydides' ideal of historiography as *magistra vitae*. Altough this was undoubtedly one of the primary motivations of Hellenistic historians, it seems that the greatest gain civic communities had from the memory of war was not education, but togetherness. The principal function of the commemoration of military conflicts, both those of the remote past and those of more recent times, was the construction of identity.

This survey has hopefully made clear that war is a central theme of the Hellenistic culture of commemoration. It is by far the most important – often the only – subject of contemporary historiography. Military conflicts, together with stories about the foundation of cities (*ktiseis*), the miracles of gods (*epiphaneiai*), and new inventions (*heuremata*), are also the most popular subjects in local historiography and in chronicles (Chaniotis 1988: 162–73). Wars attracted the interest of audiences in historical lectures and monopolized the subject of commemorative anniversaries. A substantial amount of Hellenistic monumental art is directly or indirectly related to military events: kings, leagues, and cities gave thanksgiving dedications in sanctuaries after victorious wars, donated to the gods their share of booty, and erected monuments, trophies, and warriors' tombs. Honorary decrees inscribed on stone and read aloud in festive gatherings aimed at keeping the memory of war alive, and with this memory also the glory of brave soldiers, prudent leaders, trustworthy friends, beneficent kings, and savior gods.

This chapter has, however, also suggested that the memory of war is selective. Among the wars of the mythical past, the conflicts of the heroic "founders' days," the countless hostilities among the Greek communities or between Greeks and barbarians in the Archaic and Classical periods, and the never-ending Hellenistic military conflicts, only a few wars seem to have been remembered for generations, becoming part of the cultural memory of Hellenistic communities. The surviving evidence suggests that those wars that denoted the beginning of a new era or expressed cultural differences were effective agents of identity, and as such were transmitted to the coming generations. It is only natural therefore that a large part of the evidence for the conveyance of war memories concerns the ephebes.

How important the experience of war, danger, and salvation could be for a community can be seen in the events that were selected by the Lyttians as their most important comemmorative anniversaries, also as the festivals to which the allies of Lyttos were invited in the late second century: the destruction of the nearest enemy (Dreros) and the refoundation of Lyttos after the Lyttian War (ca. 220 BC). Although Lyttos claimed to be one of the oldest Cretan cities – a colony of Sparta – in the late Hellenistic period, its citizens founded their identity primarily on the collective memory of recent wars and on the triumph over a crisis that had threatened their very existence.

We may observe a similar phenomenon in another Hellenistic city, Aphrodisias in Karia (Chaniotis 2004b). Aphrodisias acquired the status of a city probably in the early second century and joined the neighboring city of Plarasa in a sympolity, forming one community with one citizenship (*ho demos ho Plaraseon kai Aphrodisieon*), but with two urban centers. This community faced a great crisis during the wars of the Late Republic, when the "Plaraseis and Aphrodisieis" decided to take the side of Rome in the Mithridatic War in 88 BC and when, one generation later, they supported Octavian (Reynolds 1982: 3–20, 48–54, 96–113). In the long term, they proved to have made the right choices, but around 40 BC Aphrodisias was attacked, captured, and looted by the troops of the renegade Roman general Labienus. The public documents of the Late Republican and early Imperial periods continually stress exposure to danger, military achievements, and self-sacrifice (Reynolds 1982: nos. 2–3, 10–13, 28, 30); the members of the local elite were praised both for heroism in these wars (Reynolds 1982: nos. 28 and 30) and as the descendants of those "who had jointly founded the city" (Reynolds 1982: 164–5). As in Lyttos, the remembrance of a new beginning and the experience of war constituted the identity of the Aphrodisians both in their foreign contacts and in their public conduct in their own city.

The memory of war is, however, not only a matter of collective identity. The Hellenistic Age was the golden age of protagonists, and this is also reflected in the emphasis given to great individuals in the commemoration of war: kings, generals, and leaders. The media used for the glorification of communities were often different to those used for the praise of individuals. The achievements of a collective were primarily the subject of local historiography, of historical anniversaries, trophies, collective tombs for dead warriors, dedications of booty. On the other hand, honorary decrees, statues, and private dedications in sanctuaries emphasized the contributions of individuals. Heroic or even divine honors could be established for some exceptional military commanders, and the victorious king was the focal point in works of contemporary historiography, in war monuments in capitals, in the civic ruler cult, in dedications in pan-Hellenic sanctuaries, and in coinage.

This shift from communal achievements to individual contributions has been observed in war memorials as well. While war memorials of the Classical period emphasized civic communities, those of the Hellenistic period increasingly focused on the contribution of protagonists: the charismatic ruler or the great military commander (Pollitt 1986: 19; see also Rice 1993: 225–7).

The conspicuous part played by war in historical texts and monuments is intrinsically connected with its glorification. It is not death, destruction, and loss that are in the foreground of commemorations, but superiority, salvation, success, and divine protection. The cult of Concord in Plataia did not aim at establishing peace, but at the more effective conduct of war against an enemy of the Greeks. As battles and wars were associated with abstract ideas – victory, salvation, freedom, heroism – they were isolated from their specific historical contexts. We can best observe this in the case of commemorative anniversaries. In the framework of a staged festival, there was no place for historical details – the periodicity of celebration transformed the unique event into a diachronic ideal, with which a community could identify itself, generation after generation. Freed from their ephemeral contexts, wars were also deprived of their historical dimensions.

Of course, any keen-sighted observer could recognize behind this façade of self-glorification the contradiction between past achievements and the present state of Greek cities. Already at the begining of the Hellenistic Age an anonymous geographer ("Herakleides of Crete") noticed that the Plataeans had nothing else to say than that they were Athenians and that the last decisive battle of the Persian Wars was fought near their city (Herakleides fr. 11 ed. Pfister); and his contemporary, the comic poet Poseidippos (fr. 29 ed. Edmonds) described Plataia with the following verses:

> It has two temples, a stoa, and its name,
> a bath and the fame of Serambos.
> Most of the time it is a desert,
> and only at the festival of the Eleutheria
> does it become a city.

Further Reading

11.2. War in Hellenistic Historiography: *Polybios*: Meister 1975; Sacks 1981; Derow 1994. A selection of Hellenistic historians who wrote about Hellenistic wars: Timaios of Tauromenion, "The events concerning Pyrrhos" (*FgrHist* 566); Proxenos, "Concerning Pyrrhos" (*FgrHist* 703); Zenon, "Concerning the campaign of Pyrrhos in Italy" (*FgrHist* 158); Demetrios of Byzantion, "The crossing over of the Galatians," "The events concerning Antiochos" (*FgrHist* 162); Eratosthenes of Kyrene, "The Galatian Wars" (*FgrHist* 745); Phylarchos of Athens, "The events concerning Antiochos and Eumenes of Pergamon" (*FgrHist* 81); Straton, "The deeds of Philip and Perseus" (*FgrHist* 168); Poseidonios, "Concerning Perseus" (*FgrHist* 169).

11.3. The Monumental Historiography of War: Chaniotis 1988: 14–182 (collection and discussion of historiographical texts written on stone). *Wars in the vitae of*

Archilochos: Chaniotis 1988: 23–34, 57–68; Berranger 1992; Costa 1997: 108–15. *The "Lindian Anagraphe":* Blinkenberg 1915 [1980]; Chaniotis 1988: 52–7 (with bibliography); Ameling et al. 1995: nos. 194, 197, 201, 204, 214; Scheer 1996; Bresson 1999: 100–2; Higbie 2003.

11.4. Oral Commemoration of War: *Public lectures of historians:* Chaniotis 1988: 365–82. *Wars of the past used as historical arguments:* Curty 1995; Jones 1999.

11.5. Commemorative Anniversaries: Robert and Robert 1964: 176–82; Chaniotis 1991a. *The Delphic Soteria:* Nachtergael 1977; Champion 1995. *The Eleutheria of Plataia:* Étienne and Piérart 1975; Robertson 1986; Thériault 1996: 102–22; see also Burkert 1983: 56–8. *The Nikephoria of Pergamon:* Jones 1974; see also Ohlemutz 1940: 33–5. *The festival of Artemis Kindyas in Bargylia:* Robert 1937: 459–67; Pugliese Carratelli 1987: 122; Zimmermann 2000.

11.6. War Monuments: Trophies, Memorials, Dedications, Warriors' Tombs: *Trophies in the Hellenistic period:* e.g., *IOSPE* I² 352; Polyb. 4.8.6; Diod. 18.15.4; 18.32.2; 20.39.4; 21.2.3; Plut., *Sulla* 19.10. Representations of trophies: Soteriadis 1906: 75–6; Pantos 1985: 124–5, no. 100, fig. 18. *Dedication of war booty in sanctuaries:* Jacquemin 1999b; e.g., *SEG* XXXIV 878; *SGO* I 01/01/13 (Knidos); *by kings:* Launey 1987: 901–1000; Ameling et al. 1995: nos. 11, 105, 107–10, 135, 137–8, 201, 204, 261; Bringmann 2000: 64–78; Schmidt-Dounias 2000: 85–90, 98–102; Bagnall and Derow 2004: no. 38. *Royal war monuments in pan-Hellenic sanctuaries:* Ameling et al. 1995: nos. 133, 432 (Antigonos Gonatas in Delos), no. 174 (Attalos I in Delos). *War monuments in Delphi:* Jacquemin 1999a. *Epitaphia (festival of the war dead) in Athens:* Pélékidis 1962: 235–6; see also *SEG* XXXVIII 107 lines 14–15 (Rhamnous, ca. 229 BC; "the customary rites for those who died for the fatherland"). *Battle scenes and military themes in private grave monuments:* see chapter 10, section 2 (further reading). *Inscriptions for warrior dead:* see chapter 10, section 2 (further reading); cf. *SGO* II 08/01/40 (the statue of a young warrior, who was killed in action, dedicated by his father to Sarapis and Isis in Kyzikos, 2nd/1st century). *War Memorials:* e.g., *I.Slide* 227 (for the dead of a war between Side and Aspendos, late fourth century); Themelis 2001 (memorial for the dead of a battle at Makistos, erected in the gymnasium of Messene, late third century); Chaniotis 2005. *Victory monuments of kings:* Rice 1993: 231–3. *Victory monuments of the Rhodians:* Rice 1993: 235–42, with the suggestion that a chariot of Helios dedicated in Delphi was also a dedication after the siege of Demetrios the Besieger. *War monuments in royal capitals:* Pollitt 1986: 79–110. *Restoration of Attic sanctuaries:* Culley 1975; Pritchett 1985: 129–31; Baldassarri 1998: 242–6 (*SEG* XXVI 121; XXXI 107; XXXIII 136; XXXIV 99; XXXVII 96; XLIV 55; XLVIII 116).

12

BREAKING BOUNDARIES: HOW WAR SHAPED THE HELLENISTIC WORLD

The invasion of foreign territory is one of the most frequent forms of Hellenistic warfare. Precisely this aspect, the crossing of a (natural) boundary, is underlined in the *res gestae* of Ptolemy III (see chapter 4, section 1; *OGIS* 54; Bagnall and Derow 2004: no. 26, ca. 241 BC): "he crossed the River Euphrates and subdued Mesopotamia, Babylonia, Sousiane, Persis, Media and the rest of the land as far as Baktria . . ." Naturally, one of the consequences of this practice was the continual change of frontiers among states, which is often mentioned by historians and equally often recorded in delimitations.

War broke boundaries in a very physical sense: through invasion, through the destruction of fortification walls, and through the occupation of forts which made the boundary between a community and the next neighbor visible. Invisible boundaries – legal, social, cultural – are more difficult to break, but once broken the results are both more fundamental and more lasting than those of territorial expansion or external rule. This final chapter summarizes precisely these indirect, slow, but lasting effects of war on social and cultural mobility.

In times of crisis, hierarchies and social positions tend to be confirmed and strengthtened, as both groups and individuals are asked to fulfill different duties assigned to them by law or custom. In war, the young and the old, the officers and the ordinary soldiers, men and women, foreigners and citizens, free men and slaves not only play different parts, but their lives can also be affected in different ways. If defeat means for men the loss of life – and if they are fortunate, the loss of freedom and property – for women it means captivity, and for slaves either a change of master or a chance to run away. A victory may be welcome to all, but the symbolic and material gain it will bring to a victorious general will be substantially higher than that of an ordinary soldier.

The way in which wars confirmed social roles can be best seen in the case of women, whose powerlessness becomes even more evident when they are regarded as part of the "baggage" of mercenaries, when they are led to captivity by victorious armies, or when they are killed by their own fathers and husbands during the sack of a city, along with the destruction of the rest of their property (see chapter 6, section 3). The expression "women, children, and property" comprises what citizens value, but also what is entirely subject to their decisions and actions. Even Hellenistic prayers, which wish to place the entire population of a territory under the protection of the gods, underline the existence of social and legal boundaries by listing different level of status. A prayer in Magnesia on the Maeander, for example, was made "for the rescue of the city and the territory and the citizens and their wives and children and the others who inhabit the city and the territory" (*I.Magnesia* 98, early second century BC). Similarly, a Koan decree concerning a subscription for the defense of the city (*PH* 10; Migeotte 1992: no. 50) appeals to the contribution of all, explicitly stating at the same time the legal differences: "male and female citizens, illegitimate children, foreign residents and foreigners."

Wars affected the wealthy and the poor differently, but they also confronted them with different demands. Because of wars, tensions among groups separated by existing boundaries could increase and provoke civil strife (see chapter 1, section 3). Bearing in mind that, in this sense, wars confirmed and sometimes even strengthened boundaries, we can still observe that under certain conditions the Hellenistic wars also broke boundaries, even though they hardly ever subverted the existing order in a radical and fundamental manner.

No matter whether a war confronted a monarch, a league, or a citizen community, victory or defeat did not only determine the gain or loss of territory or other material gains; many wars decided the very existence of a community. For a king, defeat could mean the loss of prestige, the throne, or life itself – in that order (e.g., Demetrios the Besieger) or simultaneously (e.g., Prousias of Bithynia). The defeat of a league weakened internal coherence and encouraged cesessions. The impact on the life of a polis was more substantial, ranging from the loss of human resources, territory, or autonomy to total extinction.

In these crucial moments, when everything is at stake, and the sack of a city means death for all free males and slavery for the rest of the population, when every other concern is overshadowed by the elementary issue of survival, the traditional boundaries between legal statuses, social classes, and genders can be reconsidered, and new priorities prevail. Time and again it occurred that in these desperate situations debts were cancelled, land was redistributed, foreigners were enfranchised, slaves were freed, and women fought and died like men. Or the traditional "constitutional" barriers were forgotten, and an individual rose to a position above the rest of the citizen body, as Apollodoros of Berenike did, to whom his city entrusted full authority over it and the countryside (see chapter 2, section 5).

Finally, even the fundamental boundary between mortals and immortals could be broken. For example, a heroic death or an achievement which surpassed human standards, could raise a man's status to that of the gods.

War naturally appears as an external force which divides and destroys. This destructive force is clearly expressed in the Drerian oath, which obliged young men to fight against an enemy until its final destruction (see chapter 3, section 2). The Drerians were not the only Hellenistic youths who were raised with a belief in a never-ending hatred against an ancestral foe and who died with and for this belief, but Hellenistic history would be much easier to study and to teach if there had been more such cases of traditional enmity. The only invariable, however, in Hellenistic history is the *renversement des alliances* which transformed a former enemy into an attractive ally for a new enterprise, and the ally in a successful war into the next potential opponent. We may observe such developments in relations among the Successors, between Aitolians and Antigonids, Antigonids and Achaians, Gortynians and Knossians, and Romans and Aitolians. In a paradoxical sense, the Hellenistic wars made alliances and diplomatic enterprises necessary to a greater extent than in any preceding historical period, thus substantially contributing to the creation of an extensive network of political relations which brought distant communities into close interaction. The "interweaving" (*symploke*) of historical processes from Spain to the Euphrates was the result of warfare.

The ultimate result of the *symploke* was Roman expansion in the East. The plundering of Greek sanctuaries and cities by the victorious Roman troops, particularly during the Third Macedonian War (167 BC) and during the sack of Korinth (146 BC) and Athens (88 BC) brought hundreds of works of art – sculptures and paintings – to Rome, thus revolutionizing Roman art (Pollitt 1986: 150–63; Pritchett 1991: 166). Similar effects can be observed in the area of technology. The inventiveness of humans in finding new and more effective ways to harm each other is unlimited, as are the applications of devices invented for warfare. Our electronic mail goes back to military communications, and similarly Hellenistic kings promoted "applied science" for the sake of warfare. Ship building and the construction of ports, architecture and medicine, but above all mechanics, advanced at least in part thanks to the military applications of new inventions (Green 1990: 467–79).

Another important effect of Hellenistic wars was the redistribution of wealth, which took many forms (see chapter 7, section 4): territories changed owners; war booty enriched royal treasuries, paid mercenaries, rewarded royal friends, and increased the greed of Roman generals (see chapter 7, section 3); the enslavement or ransoming of captives generated sunstantial profit for populations which lived on raids; the expenses for the defense of cities had a detrimental effect on their finances and increased their dependence on local and foreign lenders and donors (see chapter 7, section 1), but also their dependence on kings (see chapter 4, section 4).

The rescuing measures of benefactors and kings presuppose the dangers of war. Kings owed their authority, within and without their realm, to the fact that they appeared as saviors (*Soteres*) in times of war and no other factor contributed as substantially to the establishment of the rulers' cult than warfare (csee chapter 4, section 5).

Leaving the domains of politics and economics, where the changes caused by war can easily be observed, and coming to the area of legal and social change, the case of women presents an interesting example. We have already seen that in desperate situations, when even the slaves were mobilized, women broke the boundaries of their traditional roles and actively contributed to the defense of their city, encouraging the warriors, sacrificing themselves, or making financial contributions to the defense of the city (see chapter 6, section 3). By fulfilling the obligations reserved for men – financial obligations in particular – some women (usually wealthy women belonging to the leading families, such as Kourasio of Aspendos, Timessa of Amorgos, and Archippe of Ilion) rose above the customary position of their gender and at least in part contributed to the more active, albeit still limited, participation of women in public life (see van Bremen 1996).

Foreign inhabitants of cities faced a similar situation. During one of the most troubled periods of Athenian history, in 302/1 BC, the Athenian assembly voted a decree in honor of two foreigners:

> Nikandros, son of Antiphanes, from Ilion, and Polyzelos, son of Apollophanes, from Ephesos, have always remained well disposed towards the people of the Athenians and those who inhabit Athens and have shown themselves useful in many of the affairs which are advantageous for the people; year after year, from the archonship of Themistokles to the archonship of Kephisodoros [347/6–323/2], they had contributed to the collection of ten talents for the building of the docks and of the arsenal in a fair and zealous manner; when voluntary contributions were imposed [?] for the preparation of the war and the rescue of the city [ca. 322 BC], both of them gave 1,000 drachmas; and during the archonship of Koroibos [305 BC], when the general Hegesias asked them and requested that they take upon themselves together with others the dangers and participate in the construction of the towers of the south wall, which had been assigned to them, they constructed in a fair and generous manner their section; and they participated in all campaigns on sea and on land, fighting together with the people in a fine and zealous manner at their own expense . . .
>
> (*IG* II² 505 lines 7–39; cf. Adak 2001: 81–4, 195–6)

For almost half a century (347–302 BC), these two foreigners had continually shown their solidarity with the citizen community, which hosted them without, however, accepting them as equals. For their services during the Lamian War (323–322 BC) they had already received crowns of honor (lines 23–7), but it took another 20 years and more wars for them to be promoted to a more privileged group of foreigmers as *isoteleis* ("bearing equal burdens" as the citizens) and to be given the right to own a house and land and to participate in campaigns and military contributions on the same terms as the citizens. Even then, they never actually attained citizen status.

The request for financial contributions often gave foreigners an opportunity to be part of the joint defense efforts (see chapter 7, section 1; Migeotte 1992: 358–63; e.g., *IG* VII 4263 = Maier 1959: no. 26). The aforementioned example concerns two individuals; a massive and far more radical breaking of legal boundaries was effected by the liberation, occasionally even the enfranchisement, of slaves as the ultimate effort to prevent a defeat (see chapter 2, section 2).

In the realm of monarchies, such measures were unlikely to occur at a comparable scale, but even here a great crisis could trigger measures which had lasting effects. The outstanding services of professional soldiers in a crisis promoted their careers and the position of their families (see chapter 4, section 2). This form of social mobility was natural, frequent, but not massive, unlike the measures taken by Ptolemy IV, when he recruited native Egyptians – the so-called *machimoi* – into his army for the first time, during the Fourth Syrian War (219 BC). These measures had a lasting impact on the lives of thousands, and the self-confidence won by the Egyptian *machimoi* because of their contribution to victory at the Battle of Rhaphia ultimately led to the native revolts of the second century (Thompson 2003: 115).

In a much more material sense, mobility in the Hellenistic age meant the massive movement of populations: the carrying away of prisoners of war (women and children in particular), the migration of populations of destroyed cities, the relocation of captives or hostages (Amit 1970), deserters, and runaway slaves, the expulsion of unpleasant intellectuals (Fraser 1972: 86–8; Austin 2001: 90), and the service of mercenaries. With the notable exceptions of mercenary service and the settlement of populations in military colonies, the mobility of people caused by Hellenistic wars was involuntary and frequently huge. Mobility caused by war had significant social implications, since its specific form depended on gender (e.g., fugitive men, captured women), age (children versus adults), and status (citizen versus non-citizen, free versus enslaved, wealthy versus poor).

Sometimes the relocation of individuals or larger groups was only temporary, but more frequently it was lasting. Examples of mass relocations should not make us forget about the fate of individuals – for example, the story of Epikles of Axos. His tale is narrated in a letter sent by the Cretan city of Axos to the Aitolians (early second century BC; *Syll.*³ 622 B = *I.Cret.* II.v 19; see chapter 6, section 4). In this letter the magistrates of Axos claimed on behalf of their citizen Epikles citizen rights in Aitolia on the basis of a treaty. To justify this claim, they tell of the adventures of Epikles' family. Eraton, a citizen of Axos, had come as a mercenary to Cyprus, where he married a woman of unknown name and origin. This woman gave birth to two sons,

Epikles and Euagoras. After Eraton's death in Cyprus, his widow and his older son, Epikles, were captured (by pirates or enemies). Epikles was sold as a slave in the Aitolian city of Amphissa – his mother's fate is not mentioned. In Amphissa he was somehow able to pay the necessary ransom and settled there, taking a wife (again of unknown name and origin), who gave birth to two sons (Erasiphon and Timonax) and one daughter (Melita). The letter of the Axians, obviously written more than 30 years after Eraton's departure for Cyprus, shows how strong the legal ties of Epikles were to his father's city, which he himself had probably never visited. This text also attests to the impact war had on migration in the life of two generations of the same family: first the voluntary migration of Eraton, as a mercenary, to Cyprus; then the involuntary transfer of his son Epikles, as a slave, to Amphissa.

The impact of this mass relocation of populations on Hellenistic culture is more complex than the terms *Hellenistic koine* (common culture) and *syncretism* (religious interpenetration) allow us to recognize (cf. Green 1990: 312–35). Both terms express the positive impact of the conquests of Alexander the Great and the subsequent creation of extensive networks of political, economic, and cultural interaction; the emergence of a new culture, the roots of which can be found both in Hellenic civilization and in the cultures of the indigenous populations. This undoubtedly is one of the most important phenomena of Hellenistic history, but not only *koine* and *syncretism* characterize the Hellenistic Age, but also local particularities – for example, the persistence of local dialects (Bubenik 1989), and ethnic and cultural confrontations.

In the Hellenistic garrisons, men from very different areas served together, lived together, drank together, and sometimes died together. A list of mercenaries serving in the Ptolemaic army in Laodikeia in Syria (*SEG* XXVII 973 *bis* + XXIX 1596, ca. 250–200 BC) includes men from central Greece (Athens, Boiotia, Phokis, and Thessaly), Macedonia, Thrace, and Ionia (Miletos), Pamphylia (Aspendos), Pisidia, and Cyprus (Salamis), Libya (Kyrene), and Palestine (Philoteria). A similar list from Samos (*IG* XII.6.1 217, shortly after 280 BC) shows a comparable diversity, with men from Achaia, Boiotia, Malis, Akarnania, Aitolia, Phokis, Euboia, Crete, Kolophon, and Egypt (cf. *IG* II² 1956: *I.Tralleis* 33). The Ptolemaic garrison at Paphos on Cyprus in 224/223 BC included men from Mytilene, Kadyanda, Limyra, Myra, Patara, Xanthos, and Tlos. In roughly the same period we encounter men from Pamphylia, Thessaly, Euboia, and Thrace in the garrison at Kition, and the Attalid garrison at Lillaia (208 BC) brought together soldiers from the Peloponnese (Sikyon, Sparta, Arkadia, Achaia), Eretria, Lokris, Phokis, Aitolia, Thessaly, Kalymnos, Crete, Macedonia, Thrace, various regions of Asia Minor (especially Mysia), Sicily, and Massalia (Chaniotis 2002: 100). These few examples remind us that Hellenistic armies were an important conduit for the exchange of ideas and the widening of Greek geographical and cultural horizons.

The forms and content of cultural interaction ranged from setting up an inscription with the names of the months of the Egyptian calendar in Samos, probably to serve the needs of the members of the Ptolemaic garrison (*IG* XII.6.1 218), to mixed marriages among the family members of soldiers of different origins (see chapter 6, section 2), to the introduction of new cults. The dedication to a Pisidian god with a Greek name (Ares Nikephoros Euagros) somewhere in the Egyptian desert, the worship of the gods of Samothrake in Koptos in Egypt and of Egyptian gods in Crete by Therean and Roman officers of the Ptolemies respectively, or the cult of Artemis in the Arabian Gulf, are only a few examples of the religious complexities to which Hellenistic armies contributed (see chapter 8, section 2).

The impact was, naturally, stronger and more lasting in military settlements. The new settlers from Macedonia and the Greek city states brought new institutions (e.g., the gymnasium, athletic and musical competitions) and cults (see chapter 8, section 2). They became accustomed to local practices, as evidence from Ptolemaic Egypt suggests, thanks to the numerous papyri. After a few generations, the settlers interacted with the native population, adopted Egyptian names, and even learned the native language. Mixed marriages became more common, and the amalgamation of Greek and Egyptian cultural elements gradually intensified. We have already observed this development in the family of Dryton of Crete (see chapter 6, section 2), and another example is provided by the four daughters of Ptolemaios of Kyrene, who lived in Pathyris (ca. 147–127 BC) and adopted Egyptian names next to their Greek one: Apollonia-Semmonthis, Ammonia-Semminis, Herakleia-Senapathis, and Herais-Tasris (*SB* 4638; Launey 1987: 676; Pomeroy 1984: 103–24).

But no matter how abundant the evidence for a multifaceted interaction between the natives and foreign mercenaries, garrison troops or settlers (see chapter 5, section 4), or between soldiers of different origins may be, it cannot entirely overshadow the evidence for ethnic and cultural confrontation triggered by war and military mobility. The assimilation of the Macedonian King Antigonos Gonatas with the Persians by his enemies on the eve of the Chremonidean War, his stigmatization as an enemy of Greek freedom, and his implicit exclusion from the Hellenic world is a rather harmless case of ethnic discrimination.

Many other cases of "ethnic stereotyping" are directly related to warfare: the Cretans were characterized with the cliché of being "ever brigands and pirates, not righteous" because of their raids (*Anth.Gr.* 7.654; see Perlman 1999), and the same activity made the Aitolians famous for their "inherent greed, enslaved by which they always lead a life of greed resembling wild beasts, regarding no one as a friend and everyone as their enemy" (Polyb. 4.3.1, see chapter 7, section 3), while a decree of Chersonesos refers to the faithlessness of the Skythians which is inherent in their nature (*IOSPE* I^2 352). The revolt of the Maccabees in the Seleukid kingdom may not have had its origins primarily in the opposition of conservative Jews to the process of Hellenization, but it was already in Antiquity perceived as such, and the Egyptian revolts of the second century BC were a clear case of ethnic confrontation (see chapter 1, section 3).

Ethnic confrontation is more evident in the case of the Galatians, who are presented in our sources as a rabble of bloodthirsty, godless, and uncivilized barbarians. The Galatian invasion, the greatest external threat Greece and Asia Minor had faced since the Persian Wars, triggered off a new sentiment of "Greekness" and revived the opposition between Greeks and barbarians (Mitchell 2003: 284–7). Looking at things from the perspective of our Greek sources (both literary and documentary) we are, naturally, accustomed to view the settlement of innumerable soldiers in territories conquered by Alexander the Great and defended by his successors as a process of civilization, and the attempts of non-Greeks to occupy territories as the destructive invasions of barbarian tribes. It is only in recent years that archaeological and epigraphic research in Galatia, the area which the Celts occupied, has increased our awareness of their accomplishment: the formation of a new state and the preservation of their distinct culture for centuries (Mitchell 2003).

Perhaps the most fundamental boundary broken by Hellenistic wars is that separating mortals from the gods. Wars did not only make mortals into gods, they also brought gods to earth. Around 291 BC, the desperation of the Athenians after a long period of wars and their frustration at the fact that the Amphictyonic sanctuary of Delphi was controlled by the impious Aitolians made them willingly sing a hymn for Demetrios the Besieger, in which the very existence of gods was doubted: "The other gods are either far away, or they do not have ears, or they do not exist, or do not take any notice of us" (see chapter 4, section 5). Terrified by the Galatian attack against the same sanctuary of Delphi 12 years later, the Greeks were convinced that their gods had at last taken notice of their earthly sufferings: the defeat of the Galatians was regarded the result of divine intervention, and mythical heroes were seen fighting next to the Greeks. Almost two centuries later (129 BC), two men from Epeiros dedicated a statue of Herakles "who had stood beside them in all battles" (*SEG* XXXVI 555; see chapter 8, section 1, chapter 11, section 1). If power, victory, and protection gave a monarch divine properties, unexpected rescues were interpreted as miracles (*epihaneiai*), thus restoring belief in the gods in a period in which the plundering of sanctuaries – not to mention other catastrophes – could easily justify any doubts as to their existence (see chapter 8, section 4).

A goddess who seems to have preferred to stay away was Eirene (Peace), a personified idea worshipped as a god long before the Hellenistic period. Her altar was erected in Athens in 374 BC at the latest (Isocrates 15.109–10). We do not know of any altars or temples of Eirene erected in the Hellenistic period – on the contrary, the Aitolian pirate Dikaiarchos is known

252

to have set up altars for sacrifices to Impiety (Asebeia) and Lawlessness (Paranomia; Polyb. 18.54.10; Walbank 1967: 626). The Hellenistic populations never stopped praying for peace, but they also never stopped fighting. A sacrifice offered to Zeus in Magnesia on the Maeander in the early second century had a clear aim: "for the rescue of the city and the territory and the citizens and their wives and children and the others who inhabit the city and the territory, for peace and wealth and the productiveness of grain and all the other crops and the animals" (*I.Magnesia* 98). Even the "hymn of the Curetes" from Crete, which was sung by ephebes, praises "peace, which goes with prosperity" (Furley and Bremer 2001: I 68–75, II 1–20).

Despite the explicit longing for peace, all the wars of the Hellenistic period failed to create among the Hellenistic Greeks either an ideology of peace or the mechanisms which could effectively establish it. In this respect they appear as incapable as we are to "live our lives in the right way... by observing the sufferings of others," to put it in the words of one of the last Hellenistic historians, Philippos of Pergamon (*IG* IV 1² 687; *FgrHist* 95 T 1; Goukowski 1995). But this has never convinced any historian that the hope that people may learn from history is entirely unjustified.

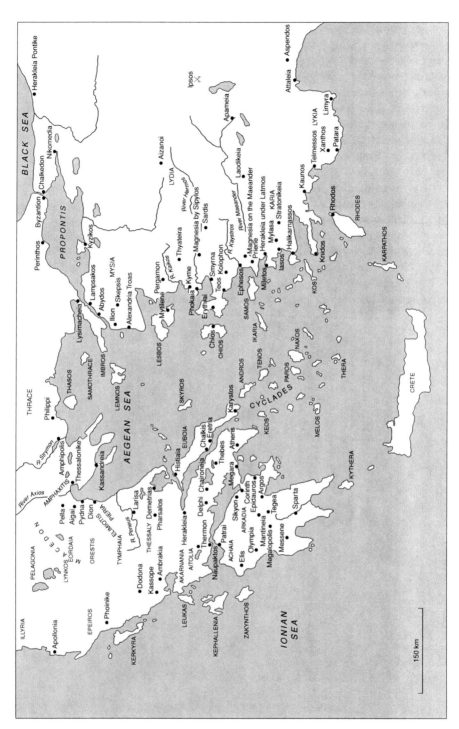

Map 4 Mainland Greece, the Aegean, and Asia Minor

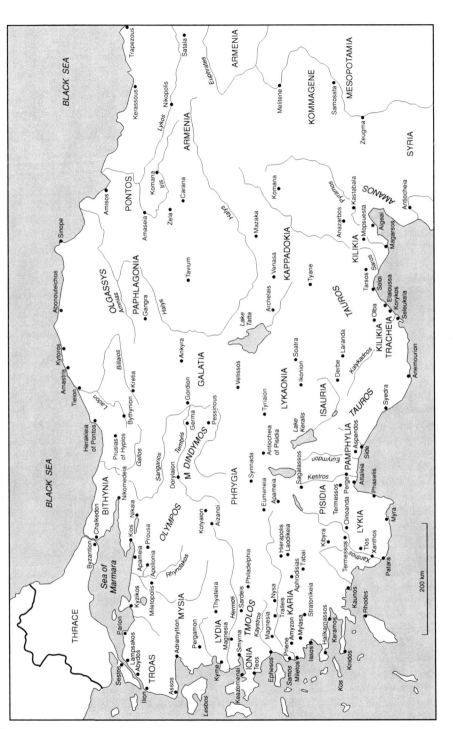

Map 5 Asia Minor

BIBLIOGRAPHY

Adak, M. (2003) *Metöken als Wohltätet Athens. Untersuchungen zum sozialen Austausch zwischen ortsansässigen Fremden und der Bürgergemeinde in klassischer und hellenistischer Zeit (ca. 500–150 v. Chr.)*, Munich.

Ager, S. L. (1996) *Interstate Arbitration in the Greek World, 337–90 B.C.*, Berkeley, Los Angeles, London.

Alcock, S. E. (1993) *Graecia capta: The Landscapes of Roman Greece*, Cambridge.

Allegro, N. and Ricciardi, M. (1999) *Gortina IV. Le fortificazioni di eta ellenistica*, Padova.

Allen, R. A. (1983) *The Attalid Kingdom, a Constitutional History*, Oxford.

Ameling, W., Bringmann, K. and Schmidt-Dounas, B. (1995) *Schenkungen hellenistischer Herrscher an griechische Städte und Heiligtümer, Teil 1, Zeugnisse und Kommentare*, Berlin.

Amit, M. (1970) Hostages in ancient Greece, *Rivista di Filologia e di Istruzione Classica*, 98: 129–47.

Amouretti, M.-C. (1986) *Le pain et l'huile dans la Grèce antique*, Paris.

Andreae, B. (1977) *Das Alexandermosaik aus Pompeji*, Recklinghausen.

Andreau, J., Briant, P. and Descat, R. (eds) (2000) *Économie antique 5. La guerre dans les économies antiques*, Saint-Bertrand-de-Comminges.

Aneziri, S. (2003) *Die Vereine der dionysischen Techniten im Kontext der hellenistischen Gesellschaft*, Stuttgart.

Anochin, V. A. and Rolle, R. (1998) Griechische Schleuderbleie bei den Mauern von Olbia, in R. Rolle and K. Schmidt (eds), *Archäologische Studien in Kontaktzonen der antiken Welt*, Göttingen: 837–49.

Antonetti, C. (1990) *Les Étoliens. Image et religion*, Besançon, Paris.

Ashton, S. A. (2001) *Ptolemaic Royal Sculpture from Egypt: The Interaction Between Greek and Egyptian Traditions*, Oxford.

Assmann, J. (1992) *Das kulturelle Gedächtnis. Schrift, Erinnerung und politische Identität in frühen Hochkulturen*, Munich.

Austin, M. M. (1981) *The Hellenistic World from Alexander to the Roman Conquest: A Selection of Ancient Sources in Translation*, Cambridge.

Austin, M. (1986) Hellenistic kings, war and the economy, *Classical Quarterly*, 80: 450–66.

Austin, M. (2001) War and culture in the Seleucid Empire, in Bekker-Nielsen and Hannestad (eds): 90–109.

Aymard, A. (1957) Le partage des profits de la guerre dans les traités d'alliance antiques, *Revue Historique*, 217: 233–40.

Badian, E. (1972) *Publicans and Sinners*, Baltimore.

Bagnall, R. S. (1976) *The Administration of the Ptolemaic Possessions outside Egypt*, Leiden.

Bagnall, R. S. and Derow, P. (2004) *Historical Sources in Translation: The Hellenistic Period*, Oxford (second edition).

Baker, P. (1991) *Cos et Calymna 205–200 a.C. Esprit civique et défence nationale*, Québec.

Baker, P. (1999) Les mercenaires, in Prost (ed.): 240–55.

Baker, P. (2000a) Coûts des garnisons et fortifications dans les cités à l'époque hellénistique, in Andreau et al. (eds): 177–96.

Baker, P. (2000b) La cause du conflit entre Mélitéa et Narthakion: Une note à propos de IG IX 2, 89, in L. Dubois and E. Masson (eds) *Philokypros. Mélanges de philologie et d'antiquités grecques et proches-orientales dédiés à la mémoire d'Olivier Masson*, Salamanca: 33–47.

Baker, P. (2001) La vallée du Méandre au IIe siècle: relations entre les cités et institutions militaires, in Bresson and Descat (eds): 61–75.

Baker, P. (2003) Warfare, in Erskine (ed.): 373–88.

Baldassarri, P. (1998) Σεβαστῶι Σωτῆρι. *Edilizia monumentale ad Atene durante il Seaculum Augustum*, Rome.

Baldwin Bowsky, M. W. (1989) Portait of a Polis: Lato pros Kamara (Crete) in the Late Second Century B.C., *Hesperia*, 58: 331–47.

Baldwin Bowsky, M. W. (1994) Cretan connections: the transformation of Hierapytna, *Cretan Studies*, 4: 1–44.

Baltrusch, E. (1994) *Symmachie und Spondai. Untersuchungen zum griechischen Völkerrecht der archaischen und klassischen Zeit (8.–5. Jh. v. Chr.)*, Berlin, New York.

Bar-Kochva, B. (1976) *The Seleucid Army*, Cambridge.

Bar-Kochva, B. (1989) *Judas Maccabaeus*, Cambridge.

Barbantani, S. (2001) *Phatis nikephoros. Frammenti di elegia encomiastica nell'età delle Guerre Galatiche: Supplementum Hellenisticum 958 e 969*, Milano.

Barigazzi, A. (1974) Un frammento dell'inno a Pan di Arato, *Rheinisches Museum*, 117: 221–46.

Barry, W. D. (1996) Roof tiles and urban violence in the Ancient World, *Greek, Roman, and Byzantine Studies*, 37: 55–74.

Baslez, M.-F. (1996) Le premier presence romaine à Delos (vers 250–149), in A.D. Rizakis (ed.) *Roman Onomastics in the Greek East: Social and Political Aspects*, Athens: 215–24.

Baslez, M.-F. (1997) Le sanctuaire de Délos dans le dernier tiers du IVe siècle. Étude historique des premiers inventaires de l'indépendance, *Revue des Études Anciennes*, 99: 345–56.

Bean, G. E. (1955) The defences of Hellenistic Smyrna, *Anadolu Arastirmalari*, 1: 43–55.

Bean, G. E. (1966) *Aegean Turkey: An Archaeological Guide*, London.

Bean, G. E. and Fraser, P. M. (1954) *The Rhodian Peraea and Islands*, London.

Bean, G. E. and Harrison, R. M. (1967) Choma in Lycia, *Journal of Roman Studies*, 57: 40–4.

Bekker-Nielsen, T. and Hannestad, L. (eds) (2001) *War as a Cultural and Social Force: Essays on Warfare in Antiquity*, Copenhagen.

Bengtson, H. (1937–52) *Die Strategie in der hellenistischen Zeit*, Munich.

Bernand, A. (1972) *El Paneion d'El-Kanais. Les inscriptions grecques*, Leiden.

Bernand, A. (1984) *Les portes du désert*, Paris.

Bernand, A. (1987) *Pan du désert*, Leiden.

Bernand, E. (1994) Réflexions sur les proscynèmes, in D. Conso, N. Fick and B. Poulle (eds) *Mélanges François Kerlouégan*, Paris: 43–60.

Berranger, D. (1992) *Recherches sur l'histoire et la prosopographie de Paros à l'époque archaïque*, Clermont-Ferrand.

Berthold, R. M. (1984) *Rhodes in the Hellenistic Age*, Ithaca, London.

Bertman, S. (ed.) (1976) *The Conflict of Generations in Ancient Greece and Rome*, Amsterdam.

Bertrand, J.-M. (1990) Formes de discourse politiques: décrets des cités grecques et correspondence des rois hellénistiques, in C. Nicolet (ed.) *Du pouvoir dans l'antiquité: mots et réalités*, Paris: 101–15.

Beston, P. (2000) Hellenistic military leadership, in van Wees (ed.): 315–35.

Bickermann, E. (1927) Der Heimatsvermerk und die staatsrechtliche Stellung der Hellenen im ptolemäischen Ägypten, *Archiv für Papyrusforschung*, 8: 216–39.

Bickermann, E. (1932) Bellum Antiochicum, *Hermes*, 67: 46–76.

Bickermann, E. (1950) Remarques sur le droit des gens dans la Grèce classique, *Revue Internationale des Droits de l'Antiquité*, 4: 99–127 (reprinted as: Bemerkungen über das Völkerrecht im klassischen Griechenland, in F. Gschnitzer, ed., *Zur griechischen Staatskunde*, Darmstadt 1969: 474–502).

Bickermann, E. and Sykoutris, J. (1928) *Speusipps Brief an König Philipp*, Leipzig.

Bieber, M. (1961) *The Sculpture of the Hellenistic Age*, New York (second edition).

Bielman, A. (1994) *Retour à la liberté. Libération et sauvetage des prisonniers en Grèce ancienne*, Paris.

Bielman, A. (2002) *Femmes en public dans le monde hellénistique, IVe-Ier s. av. J.-C.*, Paris.

Bikerman, E. (1938) *Institutions des Séleucides*, Paris.

Bilde, P., Engberg-Pedersen, T., Hannestadt, L. and Zahle, J. (eds) (1996) *Aspects of Hellenistic Kingship*, Aarhus.

Bile, M. (1992) Les termes relatifs à l'initiation dans les inscriptions crétoises (VIIe-Ier siècles av. J.-C.), in A. Moreau (ed.) *L'initiation. Actes du colloque international de Montpellier, 11–14 Avril 1991*, Montpellier: 11–18.

Billows, R. A. (1995) *Kings and Colonists: Aspects of Macedonian Imperialism*, Leiden.

Blinkenberg, C. (1915) *Die lindische Tempelchronik*, Bonn (reprinted as: *Timachidas of Lindus, The Chronicle of the Temple of Athena at Lindus*, prefatory note by R. Clairmont, introduction by G.C. Richards, Chicago 1980).

Blümel, W. (2000) Ein dritter Teil des Kultgesetzes aus Bargylia, *Epigraphica Anatolica*, 32: 89–94.

Boardman, J. (1995) *Greek Sculpture: The Late Classical Period*, London.

Boffo, L. (2001) Lo statuto di terre, insediamenti e persone nell'Anatolia ellenistica. Documenti recenti e problemi antichi, *Dike*, 4: 233–55.

Bonfante, L. (1989) Nudity as a Costume in Classical Art, *American Journal of Archaeology*, 93: 543–70.

Bonfante, L. (2000) Classical nudity in Italy and Greece, in D. Ridgway et al. (eds) *Ancient Italy in its Mediterranean Setting: Studies in Honour of Ellen Macnamara*, London: 271–93.

Borchardt, J. and Stanzl, G. (1990) Ein hellenistischer Bau des Herrscherkultes: Das Ptolemaion in Limyra, in *Götter, Heroen, Herrscher in Lykien*, Vienna: 79–84.

Boschung, D. (2001) Überlegungen zum Denkmal des L. Aemilius Paullus in Delphi, in C. Evers and A. Tsingarida (eds) *Rome et ses provinces. Genèse e diffusion d'une image du pouvoir*, Brussels: 59–72.

Bosworth, A. B. (2002) *The Legacy of Alexander: Politics, Warfare and Propaganda under the Successors*, Oxford.

Braund, D. (2003) After Alexander: the emergence of the Hellenistic World, 323–281, in Erskine (ed.): 19–34.

Bravo, B. (1980) Sulân. Représailles et justice privée contre des étrangers dans les cités grecques, *Annuario della Scuola Normale Superiore di Pisa*, 10: 675–987.

Brelich, A. (1961) *Guerre, agoni e culti nella Grecia arcaica*, Bonn.

Brelich, A. (1969) *Paides e parthenoi*, Rome.

Bresson, A. (1999) Rhodes and Lycia in Hellenistic Times, in Gabrielsen et al. (eds): 98–131.

Bresson, A. and Descat, R. (eds) (2001) *Les cités d'Asie Mineure occidentale au IIe siècle a.C.*, Paris.

Briant, P. (1973) *Antigone le Borgne. Les débuts de sa carrière et les problèmes de l'assemblée Macédonienne*, Paris.

Briant, P., Brun, P. and Varinlioglu, E. (2001) Une inscription inédite de Carie et la guerre d'Aristonicos, in Bresson and Descat (eds): 241–59.

Bricault, L. (1999) Sarapis et Isis, sauveurs de Ptolémée IV à Raphia, *Chronique d'Égypte*, 74: 334–43.

Bringmann, K. (1983) *Hellenistische Reform und Religionsverfolgung in Judäa. Eine Untersuchung zur jüdisch-hellenistischen Geschichte (175–163 v.Chr.)* (Abhandlungen der Akademie der Wissenschaften in Göttingen, Phil.-hist. Klasse, 3. Folge, Nr. 132), Göttingen.

Bringmann, K. (1993) The king as benefactor: some remarks on ideal kingship in the Age of Hellenism, in Bulloch et al. (eds): 7–24.

Bringmann, K. (2000) *Geben und nehmen. Monarchische Wohltätigkeit und Selbstdarstellung im Zeitalter des Hellenismus*, Berlin.

Brinkmann, V. (2003) Die blauen Augen der Perser. Die farbige Skulptur der Alexanderzeit und des Hellenismus, in V. Brinkmann and R. Wünsche (eds) *Bunte Götter. Die Farbigkeit antiker Skulptur. Eine Ausstellung der Staatlichen Antikensammlungen und Glyptothek München in Zusammenarbeit mit der Ny Carlsberg Glyptothek Kopenhagen und den Vatikanischen Museen, Rom*, Munich: 166–79.

Brulé, P. (1978) *La piraterie crétoise hellénistique*, Paris.

Brulé, P. (1990) Enquête démographique sur la famille grecque antique. Étude de listes de politographie d'Asie mineure d'époque hellénistique (Milet et Ilion), *Revue des Études Anciennes*, 92: 238–42.

Brulé, P. (1999) La mortalité de guerre en Grèce classique. L'exemple d'Athènes de 490 à 322, in Prost (ed.): 51–68.

Brun, P. (2004) Les cités grecques et la guerre: l'exemple de la guerre d'Aristonikos, in Couvenhes and Fernoux (eds): 21–54.

Bubenik, V. (1989) *Hellenistic and Roman Greece as a Sociolinguistic Area*, Amsterdam.

Bugh, G. R. (1988) *The Horsemen of Athens*, Princeton.

Bulloch, A., Gruen, E. S., Long, A. A. and Stewart, A. (eds) (1993), *Images and Ideologies: Self-Definition in the Hellenistic World*, Berkeley.

Bunge, J. G. (1976) Die Feiern Antiochos' IV. Epiphanes in Daphne im Herbst 166 v.Chr., *Chiron*, 6: 53–71.

Buraselis, K. (1982) *Das hellenistische Makedonien und die Ägäis. Forschungen zur Politik des Kassandros und der drei ersten Antigoniden im Ägäischen Meer und in Westkleinasien*, Munich.

Buraselis, K. (2000) *Kos between Hellenism and Rome. Studies on the Political, Institutional and Social History of Kos from ca. the Middle Second Century B.C. until Late Antiquity*, Philadelphia.

Burkert, W. (1983) *Homo Necans: The Anthropology of Ancient Greek Sacrificial Ritual and Myth*, Berkeley, Los Angeles, London.

Burkert, W. (1985) *Greek Religion*, Cambridge, Mass.

Burzacchini, G. (1999) L'epigraphie de Passaron (SEG XXXVII, 1987, 170 n. 529), in P. Cabanes (ed.), *L'Illyrie méridionale et l'Épire dans l'Antiquité. III. Actes du IIIe colloque international de Chantilly (16–19 Octobre 1996)*, Paris: 127–34.

Cabanes, P. (1991) Recherches épigraphiques en Albanie: péripolarques et peripoloi en Grèce du Nord-Ouest et en Illyrie à la période hellénistique, *Comptes Rendues de l'Academie des Inscriptions et Belles Lettres*: 197–221.

Cabanes, P. and Drini, F. (1995) *Corpus des inscriptions grecques d'Illyrie méridonale et d'Épire. I. Inscriptions d'Épidamne-Dyrrhachion et d'Apollonia. 1. Inscriptions d'Épidamne-Dyrrhachion*, Athens.

Calame, C. (1982/3) Morfologia e funzione della festa nell'antichità, *Annali dell'Istituto universitario orientale di Napoli. Sezione Filologico-letteraria*, 4–5: 3–23.

Calame, C. (1990) *Thésée et l'imaginaire athénien*, Lausanne.

Callot, O. (1989) *Failaka à l'époque hellénistique*, in T. Fahd (ed.) *L'Arabie préislamique et son environment historique et culturel. Actes du Colloque du Strasbourg*, Strasbourg: 127–44.

Carney, E. D. (1987) Olympias, *Ancient Society*, 18: 35–62.

Carney, E. (2000) *Women and Monarchy in Macedonia*, Norman, Va

Carter, J. C. (1970) Relief sculptures from the necropolis of Taranto, *American Journal of Archaeology*, 74: 125–37.

Carter, J. C. (1975) *The Sculpture of Taras (Transactions of the American Philosophical Society, 65.7)*, Philadelphia.

Cartledge, P. and Spawforth, A. (1989) *Hellenistic and Roman Sparta: A Tale of Two Cities*, London, New York.

Champion, C. (1995) The Soteria at Delphi: Aetolian propaganda in the epigraphical record, *American Journal of Philology*, 116: 213–20.

Chandezon, Chr. (1999) L'économie rurale et la guerre, in Prost (ed.): 195–208.

Chandezon, Chr. (2000) Guerre, agriculture et crises d'après les inscriptions hellénistiques, in Andreau et al. (eds): 231–52.

Chandezon, Chr. (2003) *L'élevage en Grèce (fin V^e-fin Ier s. a.C.). L'apport des sources épigraphiques*, Bordeaux.

Chaniotis, A. (1988) *Historie und Historiker in den griechischen Inschriften: Epigraphische Beiträge zur griechischen Historiographie*, Stuttgart.

Chaniotis, A. (1990) Zur Frage der Spezialisierung im griechischen Theater des Hellenismus und der Kaiserzeit, *Ktema*, 15: 89–108.

Chaniotis, A. (1991a) Gedenktage der Griechen: Ihre Bedeutung für das Geschichtsbewußtsein griechischer Poleis, in J. Assmann (ed.) *Das Fest und das Heilige: Religiöse Kontrapunkte zur Alltagswelt*, Gütersloh: 123–45.

Chaniotis, A. (1991b) Von Hirten, Kräutersammlern, Epheben und Pilgern: Leben auf den Bergen im antiken Kreta, *Ktema*, 16: 93–109 (reprinted in G. Siebert (ed.) *Nature et paysage dans la pensée et l'environnement des civilisations antiques: Actes du Colloque de Strasbourg, 1992*, Paris 1996: 91–107).

Chaniotis, A. (1995) Sich selbst feiern? Die städtischen Feste des Hellenismus im Spannungsfeld zwischen Religion und Politik, in Wörrle and Zanker (eds): 147–72.

Chaniotis, A. (1996a) *Die Verträge zwischen kretischen Städten in der hellenistischen Zeit*, Stuttgart.

Chaniotis, A. (1996b) Conflicting authorities: Greek asylia between secular and divine law in the Classical and Hellenistic poleis, *Kernos*, 9: 65–86.

Chaniotis, A. (1997) Theatricality beyond the theater: staging public life in the Hellenistic World, in B. Le Guen (ed.) *De la scène aux gradins. Théâtre et représentations dramatiques après Alexandre le Grand dans les cités hellénstiques. Actes du Colloque, Toulouse 1997 (Pallas, 41)*, Toulouse: 219–59.

Chaniotis, A. (1998a) Inscriptions from Bucak Köyü, *American Journal of Archaeology*, 102: 248–50.

Chaniotis, A. (1998b) Willkomene Erdbeben, in E. Olshausen and H. Sonnabend (eds) *Stuttgarter Kolloquium zur historischen Geographie des Altertums 6, 1996. Naturkatastrophen in der antiken Welt*, Stuttgart: 404–16.

Chaniotis, A. (ed.) (1999a) *From Minoan Farmers to Roman Traders: Sidelights on the Economy of Ancient Crete*, Stuttgart.

Chaniotis, A. (1999b) Milking the mountains: economic activities on the Cretan uplands in the Classical and Hellenistic period, in Chaniotis (ed.): 181–220.

Chaniotis, A. (1999c) The epigraphy of Hellenistic Crete. The Cretan Koinon: new and old evidence, in *Atti del XI Congresso Internazionale di Epigrafia Greca e Latina*, Rome I: 287–300.

Chaniotis, A. (2002) Foreign soldiers – native girls? Constructing and crossing boundaries in Hellenistic cities with foreign garrisons, in Chaniotis and Ducrey (eds): 99–113.

Chaniotis, A. (2003a) Vom Erlebnis zum Mythos: Identitätskonstruktionen im kaiserzeitlichen Aphrodisias, in E. Schwertheim and E. Winter (eds) *Stadt und Stadtentwicklung in Kleinasien*, Bonn: 69–84.

Chaniotis, A. (2003b) The divinity of Hellenistic rulers, in Erskine (ed.): 433–45.

Chaniotis, A. (2004a) Mobility of persons during the Hellenistic wars: state control and personal relations, in C. Moatti (ed.) *La mobilité des personnes en Méditerranée, de l'antiquité à l'époque moderne. II. La mobilité négociée. Procédures de contrôle et documents d'identification*, Rome (forthcoming).

Chaniotis, A. (2004b) Inscriptions of Aphrodisias, *American Journal of Archaeology*, 108 (forthcoming).

Chaniotis, A. (2004c) Victory' verdict: the violent occupation of territory in Hellenistic interstate relations, in J.-M. Bertrand and P. Schmitt-Pantel (eds) *La Violence dans les mondes grec et romain* (forthcoming).

Chaniotis, A. (2004d) Justifying territorial claims in Classical and Hellenistic Greece: the beginnings of international law, in E. Harris and L. Rubenstein (eds) *The Law and the Courts in Ancient Greece*, London: 185–213.

Chaniotis, A. (2004e) Under the watchful eyes of the gods: aspects of divine justice in Hellenistic and Roman Asia Minor, in S. Colvin (ed.) *The Greco–Roman East*, Cambridge: 1–43.

Chaniotis, A. (2005) The ritualised commemoration of war in the Hellenistic city, in P. Low and G. Oliver (eds) *Cultures of Commemoration: War Memorials, Ancient and Modern*, Oxford (forthcoming).

Chaniotis, A. and Ducrey, P. (eds) (2002) *Army and Power in the Ancient World*, Stuttgart.

Chankowski, A. S. (1993) Date et circonstances de l'institution de l'éphébie à Érétrie, *Dialogues d'Histoire Ancienne*, 19.2: 17–44.

Chankowski, A. S. (2004a) L'entraînement militaire des éphébes dans les cités grecques d'Asie Mineure à l'époque hellénistique: nécessité pratique ou tradition atrophée? in Couvenhes and Fernoux (eds): 55–76.

Chankowski, A. S. (2004b) *L'éphébie hellénistique: étude d'une institution civique dans les cités grecques des îles de la Mer Égée et de l'Asie Mineure (IVᵉ-Iᵉʳ siècles avant J.-C.)*, Paris.

Charneux, P. (1991) En relisant les décrets argiens II, *Bulletin de Correspondance Hellénique*, 115: 297–323.

Coarelli, F. (1990) La pompè di Tolemeo Filadelfo e il mosaico nilotico di Palestrina, *Ktema*, 15: 225–51.

Cohen, A. (1997) *The Alexander Mosaic: Stories of Victory and Defeat*, Cambridge.

Cohen, G. M. (1978) *The Seleucid Colonies: Studies in Founding, Administration, and Organization*, Wiesbaden.

Cohen, G. M. (1995) *Hellenistic Settlements in Europe, the Islands, and Asia Minor*, Berkeley, Los Angeles, Oxford.

Cohn-Haft, L. (1956) *The Public Physicians of Ancient Greece*, Northampton, Mass.

Cole, S. G. (1984) *Theoi Megaloi: The Cult of the Great Gods at Samothrace*, Leiden.

Cordiano, G. (2001) La ginnasiarchia a Cirene. I. Dall'eta tolemaica fino all'epoca augustea, *Minima Epigraphica et Papyrologica* 6: 255–296.

Costa, V. (1997) *Nasso dalle origini al V sec. a.C.*, Rome.

Couvenhes, J.-C. (1999) La réponse hénienne à la violence territoriale aux IVe et IIIe siècles av. J.-C., *Cahiers du Centre Gustave-Glotz* 10: 189–207.

Couvenhes, J.-C. (2004) Les cités grecques d'Asie Mineure et le mercenariat à l'époque hellénistique, in Couvenhes and Fernoux (eds): 77–113.

Couvenhes, J.-C. and Fernoux, H.-L. (eds) (2004) *Les cités grecques et la guerre en Asie Mineure à l'époque hellénistique*, Tours.

Criscuolo, L. (1998) Il dieceta Apollonios e Arsinoe, in H. Melaerts (ed.) *Le culte du souverain dans l'Égypte ptolémaïque au IIIᵉ siècle avant notre ère*, Leuven: 61–72.

Culley, G. R. (1975) The restoration of sanctuaries in Attica: I.G., II, 1035, *Hesperia*, 44: 207–23.

Curty, O. (1995) *Les parentés légendaires entre cités grecques*, Geneva.

Daubner, F. (2003) *Bellum Asiaticum: Der Krieg der Römer gegen Aristonikos von Pergamon und die Einrichtung der Provinz Asia*, Munich.

Daverio Rocchi, G. (1988) *Frontiera e confini nella Grecia antica*, Rome.

Davies, J. K. (1984) Cultural, social, and economic features of the Hellenistic World, *CAH*, VII.1²: 257–320.

de Callataÿ, F. (1989) Des trésor royaux achéménides aux monnayages d'Alexandre: espèces immobilisées et espèces circulantes, *Revue des Études Ancienne*, 91: 25–74.

de Callataÿ, F. (2000) Guerres et monnayages à l'époque hellénistique. Essai de mise en perspective suivi d'une annexe sur le monnayage de Mithridate VI Eupator, in Andreau et al. (eds): 337–64.

de Foucault, J.-A. (1972) *Recherches sur la langue et le style de Polybe*, Paris.

de Souza, P. (1999) *Piracy in the Graeco-Roman World*, Cambridge.

Debord, P. and Descat, R. (eds) (1994) *Fortifications et défense du territoire en Asie Mineure occidentale et méridionale. Table ronde CNRS, Istanbul, 20–27 Mai 1993 (Revue des Études Anciennes*, 96), Bordeaux.

Delemen, I. (1999) *Anatolian Rider-Gods: A Study on Stone Finds from the Regions of Lycia, Pisidia, Isauria, Lycaonia, Phrygia, Lydia and Caria in the Late Roman Period*, Bonn.

Dell, H. J. (1967) The origin and nature of Illyrian piracy, *Historia*, 16: 344–58.

Derow, P. (1994) Historical explanation: Polybius and his predecessors, in S. Hornblower (ed.) *Greek Historiography*, Oxford: 73–90.

Derow, P. (2003) The arrival of Rome: from the Illyrian Wars to the fall of Macedon, in Erskine (ed.): 51–70.

Detienne, M. (1973) L'olivier: Un myth politico-religieux, in M. I. Finley (ed.) *Problèmes de la terre en Grèce ancienne*, Paris-La Haye: 293–306.

Dietze, G. (2000) Temples and soldiers in southern Ptolemaic Egypt, in L. Mooren (ed.) *Politics, Administration and Society in the Hellenistic and Roman World. Proceedings of the International Colloquium, Bertinoro 19–24 July 1997*, Leuven: 77–89.

Dirscherl, H.-C. (2000) Die Verteilung von kostenlosem Getreide in der Antike vom 5. Jh. v. Chr. bis zum Ende des 3. Jhs. n. Chr., *Münstersche Beiträge zur antiken Handelsgeschichte*, 19.1: 1–33.

Dreyer, B. (1999) *Untersuchungen zur Geschichte des spätklassischen Athen (322–ca. 230 v. Chr.)*, Stuttgart.

Dreyer, B. and Engelmann, H. (2003) *Die Inschriften von Metropolis. Teil I. Die Dekrete für Apollonios. Städtische Politik unter den Attaliden und im Konflikt zwischen Aristonikos und Rom*, Bonn.

Ducrey, P. (1970) Nouvelles remarques sur deux traités attalides avec des cités crétoises, *Bulletin de Correspondence Hellénique*, 94: 637–59.

Ducrey, P. (1977) L'armée, facteur de profits, in *Armées et fiscalité dans le monde antique, Paris, 14–16 Octobre 1976*, Paris: 421–32.

Ducrey, P. (1985) *Warfare in Ancient Greece* (trans. by Janet Lloyd), New York.

Ducrey, P. (1999) *Le traitement des prisonniers de guerre dans la Grèce antique des origines à la conquête romaine*, Paris (second edition).

Dunand, F. (1978) Sens et fonction de la fête dans la Grèce hellénistique. Les cérémonies en l'honneur d'Artémis Leucophryéné, *Dialogues d'Histoire Ancienne*, 4: 201–15.

Eckstein, A. (1995) *Moral Vision in the Histories of Polybius*, Berkeley.

Engelmann, H. (1993) Der Kult des Ares im ionischen Metropolis, in G. Dobesch and G. Rehrenböck (eds) *Die epigraphische und altertumskundliche Erforschung Kleinasiens: Hundert Jahre Kleinasiatische Kommission der Österreichischen Akademie der Wissenschaften. Akten des Symposiums vom 23. bis 25 Oktober 1990*, Vienna: 171–6.

Errington, R. M. (1969) *Philopoemen*, Oxford.

Errington, R. M. (1978) The nature of the Macedonian state under the monarchy, *Chiron*, 8: 77–133.

Errington, R. M. (1986) *Geschichte Makedoniens*, Munich.

Erskine, A. (ed.) (2003) *A Companion to the Hellenistic World*, Oxford.

Esser, A. A. M. (1942) Invaliden – und Hinterblibenenfürsorge in der Antike, *Gymnasium*, 52: 25–9.

Étienne, R. and Knoepfler, D. (1976) *Hyettos de Béotie et la chronologie des archontes fédéraux entre 250 et 171 av. J.-C.*, Paris.

Étienne, R. and Piérart, M. (1975) Un décret du Koinon des Hellènes à Platées en l'honneur de Glaukon, fils d'Éteoclès, d'Athènes, *Bulletin de Correspondance Hellénique*, 99, 51–75.

Étienne, R. and Roesch, P. (1978) Convention militaire entre les cavaliers d'Orchomène et ceux de Chéronée, *Bulletin de Correspondance Hellénique*, 102: 359–74.

Evans, J. A. S. (1991) *Herodotus, Explorer of the Past*, Princeton.

Fantasia, U. (1989) Finanze cittadine, liberalità privata e sitos demosios: considerazioni su alcuni documenti epigrafici, *Serta Historica Antiqua*, 2, 47–84.

Faraone, Chr. A. (1991) Binding and burying the forces of evil: the defensive use of "voodoo dolls" in Ancient Greece, *Classical Aniquity*, 10: 165–205.

Faraone, Chr.A. (1992) *Talismans and Trojan Horses: Guardian Statues in Ancient Greek Myth and Ritual*, New York, Oxford.

Fedak, J. (1990) *Monumental Tombs of the Hellenistic Age*, Toronto.

Fernández Nieto, F. J. (1997) Los reglamentos militares griegos y la justicia castrense en época helenística, in G. Thür and J. Vélissaropoulos-Karakostas (eds) *Symposion 1995. Vorträge zur griechischen und hellenistischen Rechtsgeschichte (Korfu, 1.–5. September 1995)*, Cologne, Weimar, Vienna: 213–44.

Fernoux, H.-L. (2004) Les cités s'entraident dans la guerre: historique, cadres institutionnels et modalités pratiques des conventions d'assistance dans l'Asie Mineure hellénistique, in Couvenhes and Fernoux (eds): 115–76.

Ferrary, J.-L. (2001) Rome et les cités grecques d'Asie Mineure au IIe siècle, in Bresson and Descat (eds): 93–106.

Feyel, M. (1942a) *Contribution à l'épigraphie béotienne*, Paris.

Feyel, M. (1942b) *Polybe et l'histoire de Béotie au IIIe siècle avant notre ère*, Paris.

Fleischer, R. (1991) *Studien zur seleukidischen Kunst. I. Herrscherbildnisse*, Mannheim.

Forbes, C. A. (1933) *Neoi: A Contribution to the Study of Greek Associations*, Middletown, Conn.

Fornara, C. W. (1983) *The Nature of History in Ancient Greece and Rome*, Berkeley, Los Angeles, London.

Forrest, W. G. (1975) An Athenian generation gap, *Yale Classical Studies*, 24: 36–52.

Foulon, E. (1996) Contribution à une taxinomie des corps d'infanterie dans les armées hellénistiques, *Les Études Classiques*, 64: 227–44, 317–38.

Fowler, B. H. (1989) *The Hellenistic Aesthetic*, Madison.

Foxhall, L. (1993) Farming and fighting in ancient Greece, in Rich and Shipley (eds.) 1993: 134–45.

Fraser, P. M. (1972) *Ptolemaic Alexandria*, Oxford.

Fraser, P. M. (1977) *Rhodian Funerary Monuments*, Oxford.

Fuks, A. (1972) Isokrates and the social-economic situation in Greece, *Ancient Society*, 3: 17–44.

Furley, W. D. and J. M. Bremer (2001) *Greek Hymns*, Volume I: *The Texts in Translation*; Volume II: *Greek Texts and Commentaries*, Tübingen.

Gabrielsen, V. (1997) *The Naval Aristocracy of Hellenistic Rhodes*, Aarhus.

Gabrielsen, V. (2001a) Naval warfare: its economic and social impact on Greek cities, in Bekker-Nielsen and Hannestad (eds): 72–89.

Gabrielsen, V. (2001b) Economic activity, maritime trade, and piracy in the Hellenistic Aegean, *Revue des Études Anciennes*, 103: 219–40.

Gabrielsen, V. (2003) Piracy and the slave-trade, in Erskine (ed.): 389–404.

Gabrielsen, V. et al. (eds) (1999) *Hellenistic Rhodes: Politics, Culture, and Society*, Aarhus.

Gaebel, R. E. (2002) *Cavalry Operations in the Ancient Greek World*, Norman.

Garlan, Y. (1972) Les esclaves grecs en temps de guerre, in *Actes du colloque d'histoire sociale de Besançon, 1970*, Besançon: 29–62.

Garlan, Y. (1973) Cités, armées et stratégie à l'époque hellénistique d'après l'ouevre de Philon de Byzance, *Historia*, 22: 16–33.

Garlan, Y. (1974) *Recherches de poliorcétique grecque*, Paris.

Garlan, Y. (1977) Le partage entre alliés des dépenses et des profits de guerre, in *Armées et fiscalité dans le monde antique. Paris, 14–16 Octobre 1976*, Paris: 149–164.

Garlan, Y. (1978) Signification historique de la piraterie grecque, *Dialogues d'Histoire Ancienne*, 4: 1–31.

Garlan, Y. (1984) Hellenistic science: its application in peace and war, in *CAH* VII.1²: 353–62.

Gauthier, Ph. (1982) Notes sur trois décrets honorant des citoyens bienfaiteurs, *Revue de Philologie*, 56: 215–31.

Gauthier, Ph. (1985) *Les cités grecques et leurs bienfaiteurs (IVe-Ier siècle avant J.-C.). Contribution à l'histoire des institutions*, Paris.

Gauthier, Ph. (1989) *Nouvelles inscriptions de Sardes II*, Geneva.

Gauthier, Ph. (1991) Ateleia tou somatos, *Chiron*, 21, 49–68.

Gauthier, Ph. (1995a) Notes sur le rôle du gymnase dans les cités hellénistiques, in Wörrle and Zanker (eds): 1–11.

Gauthier, Ph. (1995b) Du nouveau sur les courses aux flambeaux d'après deux inscriptions de Kos, *Revue des Études Grecques*, 108: 576–85.

Gauthier, Ph. (1996) Bienfaiteurs du gymnase au Létôon de Xanthos, *Revue des Études Grecques*, 109: 1–34.

Gauthier, Ph. (2000a) Le décret de Thessalonique pour Parnassos. L'evergète et la dépense pour sa statue à la basse époque hellénistique, *Tekmeria*, 5: 39–61.

Gauthier, Ph. (2000b) Les institutions politiques de Delphes au IIe siècle a.C., in A. Jacquemin (ed.) *Delphes cent ans après la Grande Fouille. Essai de bilan. Actes du Colloque International organisé par l'École Française d'Athènes, Athènes-Delphes, 17–20 septembre 1992*, Paris.

Gauthier, Ph. (2003) De nouveaux honneurs cultuels pour Philétairos de Pergame: à propos de deux inscriptions récemment publiées, in B. Virgilio (ed.) *Studi ellenistici*, XV, Pisa: 9–24.

Gauthier, Ph. and M. B. Hatzopoulos (1993) *La loi gymnasiarchique de Beroia*, Athens.

Gawantka, W. (1975) *Isopolitie. Ein Beitrag zur Geschichte der zwischenstaatlichen Beziehungen in der griechischen Antike*, Munich.

Gehrke, H.-J. (1982) Der siegreiche König. Überlegungen zur hellenistischen Monarchie, *Archiv für Kulturgeschichte*, 64: 247–77.

Gehrke, H.-J. (1997) Gewalt und Gesetz. Die soziale und politische Ordnung Kretas in der Archaischen und Klassischen Zeit, *Klio*, 79: 23–68.

Gehrke, H.-J. (2003) *Geschichte des Hellenismus*, Munich (third edition).

Girone, M. (2003) Una particolare offerta di chiome, *Epigraphica Anatolica*, 35: 21–42.

Golden, M. (1998) *Sport and Society in Ancient Greece*, Cambridge.

Goukowski, P. (1995) Philippe de Pergame et l'histoire des guerres civiles, in C. Brixhe (ed.) *Hellenika Symmeikta II* (*Études d'archéologie classique* 8), Paris: 39–53.

Grac, N. (1987) Ein neu entdecktes Fresko aus hellenistischer Zeit in Nymphaion bei Kertsch, in H. Franke (ed.) *Skythika. Vorträge zur Entstehung des skytho-iranischen Tierstils und zur Denkmälern des Bosporanischen Reichs anläßlich einer Ausstellung der Leningrader Ermitage in München 1984*, Munich: 87–95.

Graeve, V. von (1970) *Der Alexandersarkophag und seine Werkstatt*, Berlin.

Graf, F. (1984) Women, war, and warlike divinities, *Zeitschrift für Papyrologie und Epigraphik*, 55: 245–54.

Graf, F. (1995) Bemerkungen zur bürgerlichen Religiosität im Zeitalter des Hellenismus, in Wörrle and Zanker (eds): 103–14.

Granier, F (1931) *Die makedonische Heeresversammlung*, Munich.

Grassl, H. (1986): Behinderte in der Antike. Bemerkungen zur sozialen Stellung und Integration, *Tyche*, 1: 118–26.

Green, P. (1990) *Alexander to Actium: The Historical Evolution of the Hellenistic Age*, Berkeley, Los Angeles.

Grottanelli, C. (1991) Do ut des?, in G. Bartoloni, G. Colonna and C. Grotanelli (eds), *Atti del convegno internazionale Anathema. Regime delle offerte e vita dei santuari nel mediterraneo antico, Roma 15–18 Giugno 1989* (*Scienze dell'antichità* 3–4, 1989/90), Rome: 45–55.

Gruen, E. S. (1984) *The Hellenistic World and the Coming of Rome*, Berkeley, Los Angeles.

Gruen, E. (1985) The coronation of the Diadochoi, in J. W. Eadie and J. Ober (eds) *Essays Ch. G. Starr*, Lanham, New York, London: 253–71.

Gruen, E. S. (2003) Jews and Greeks, in Erskine (ed.): 264–79.

Gschnitzer, F. (1981a) *Griechische Sozialgeschichte von der mykenischen bis zum Ausgang der klassischen Zeit*, Wiesbaden.

Gschnitzer, F. (1981b) *Zur Normenhierarchie im öffentlichen Recht der Griechen*, in P. Dimakis (ed.) *Symposion 1979. Actes du IVe colloque international de droit grec et hellénistique, Égine 3–7 Septembre 1979*, Athens, 143–64. (Reprinted (2003) in F. Gschnitzer, *Uleine Schriften zum griechischen und römischen Aetertum*, Stuttgart, 153–74.)

Günther, W. (1971) *Das Orakel von Didyma in hellenistischer Zeit. Eine Interpretation von Stein-Urkunden*, Tübingen.

Guizzi, F. (1997), Conquista, occupazione del suolo e titoli che danno diritto alla proprietà: L'esempio di una controversia interstatale cretese, *Athenaeum*, 85: 35–52.

Guizzi, F. (2001) Hierapytna. Storia di una polis cretese dalla fondazione alla conquista romana, *Memorie dell'Accademia Nazionale dei Lincei*, Serie IX 13.3: 277–444.

Habicht, Chr. (1970) *Gottmenschentum und griechische Städte*, Munich (second edition).

Habicht, Chr. (1982) *Studien zur Geschichte Athens in hellenistischer Zeit*, Göttingen.

Habicht, Chr. (1984) Zur Vita des Epikureers Philonides (P Herc 1044), *Zeitschrift für Papyrologie und Epigraphik*, 74: 211–4.

Habicht, Chr. (1995) Ist ein "Honoratiorenregime" das Kennzeichen der Stadt im späteren Hellenismus? in Wörrle and Zanker (eds): 87–92.

Habicht, Chr. (1997) *Athens from Alexander to Antony*, Cambridge, Mass.

Hamilton, C. D. (1999) The Hellenistic world, in K. Raaflaub and N. Rosenstein (eds) *War and Society in the Ancient and Medieval Worlds: Asia, The Mediterranean, Europe and Mesoamerica*, Cambridge, Mass, London: 163–91.

Hammond, N. G. L., Griffith, G. T. and Walbank, F. W. (1972) *A History of Macedonia*, Vol. I, Oxford.

Hammond, N. G. L., Griffith, G. T. and Walbank, F. W. (1979) *A History of Macedonia*, Vol. II, Oxford.

Hammond, N. G. L., Griffith, G. T. and Walbank, F. W. (1989) *A History of Macedonia*, Vol. III, Oxford.

Hanson, V. D. (1983) *Warfare and Agriculture in Classical Greece*, Pisa.

Harvey, P. (1986) New harvests reappear: the impact of war on agriculture, *Athenaeum*, 64: 205–18.

Hatzfeld, J. (1919) *Les trafiquants italiens dans l'Orient hellénique*, Paris.

Hatzopoulos, M. B. (1994) *Cultes et rites de passage en Macédoine*, Athens.

Hatzopoulos, M. B. (1996) *Macedonian Institutions under the Kings. A Historical and Epigraphic Study*, Athens.

Hatzopoulos, M. B. (2001) *L'organisation de l'armée macédonienne sous les Antigonides. Problèmes anciens et documents nouveaux*, Athens.

Hauben, H. (1983) Arsinoe II et la politique extérieure de l'Égypte, in *Egypt and the Hellenistic World. Proceedings of the International Colloquium Leuven, 24–26 May 1982*, Louvain: 99–127.

Hazzard, R. A. (2000) *Imagination of a Monarchy: Studies in Ptolemaic Propaganda*, Toronto, Buffalo, London.

Heinen, H. (1976) Zur Sklaverei in der hellenistischen Welt I, *Ancient Society*, 7: 127–49.

Helly, B. (1999) Modèle, de l'archéologie des cités à l'archéologie du paysage, in M. Brunet (ed.) *Territoires des cités grecques. Actes de la table ronde internationale organisée par l'École française d'Athenes, 31 Octobre–3 Novembre 1991*, Paris: 99–124.

Hennig, D. (1985) Die Militärkataloge als Quelle zur Entwicklung der Einwohnerzahlen der boiotischen Städte im 3. und 2. Jh. v. Chr., *La Béotie antique*, Paris, 333–42.

Hennig, D. (1995) Staatliche Ansprüche an privaten Immobilienbesitz in der klassischen und hellenistischen Polis, *Chiron*, 25: 235–82.

Hennig, D. (2003) Sicherheitskräfte zur Überwachung der Wüstengrenzen und Karawanenwege im ptolemäischen Ägypten, *Chiron*, 33: 145–74.

Herrmann, P. (1965) Antiochos der Große und Teos, *Anadolu*, 9: 29–159.

Herrmann, P. (1979) Die Stadt Temnos und ihre auswärtigen Beziehungen in hellenistischer Zeit, *Mitteilungen des Deutschen Archäologischen Instituts (Abteilung Istanbul)*, 29: 249–71.

Herrmann, P. (1987) Milesier im Seleukidenhof. Prosopographische Beiträge zur Geschichte Milets im 2. Jhdt. V. Chr., *Chiron* 17: 171–192.

Herrmann, P. (1997) *Inschriften von Milet. Teil 1*, Berlin.

Herrmann, P. (2001) Milet au IIe siècle a.c., in Bresson and Descat (eds): 109–118.

Higbie, C. (2003) *The Lindian Chronicle and the Greek Understanding of their Past*, Oxford.

Höckmann, O. (1999) Naval and other graffiti from Nymphaion, *Ancient Civilisations from Scythia to Siberia*, 5: 303–56.

Hoepfner, W. (2003) *Der Koloss von Rhodos und die Bauten des Helios. Neue Forschungen zu einem der Sieben Weltwunder*, Mainz.

Holleaux, M. (1938a) *Études d'épigraphie et d'histoire grecques*, I, Paris.

Holleaux, M. (1938b) *Études d'épigraphie et d'histoire grecques*, II, Paris.

Holleaux, M. (1942) *Études d'épigraphie et d'histoire grecques*, III, Paris.

Honigman, S. (2003) Politeumata and ethnicity in Ptolemaic and Roman Egypt, *Ancient Society*, 33: 61–102.

Hülden, O. (2000) Pleistarchos und die Befestigungsanlagen von Herakleia am Latmos, *Klio*, 82: 382–408.

Huttner, U. (1997) *Die politische Rolle der Heraklesgestalt im griechischen Herrschertum*, Stuttgart.

Hyldahl, N. (1991) The Maccabean Rebellion and the Question of "Hellenization" in P. Bilde, T. Engberg-Pedersen, L. Hannestad and J. Zahle (eds) *Religion and Religious Practice in the Seleucid Kingdom*, Aarhus: 188–203.

Irby-Massie, G. L. and Keyser, P. T. (2002) *Greek Science of the Hellenistic Era*, London, New York.

Isager, S. and Skydsgaard, J. E. (1992) *Ancient Greek Agriculture: An Introduction*, London, New York.

Jacquemin, A. (1999a) *Offrandes monumentales à Delphes*, Paris.

Jacquemin, A. (1999b) Guerres et offrandes dans les sanctuaires, in *Guerres et sociétés dans les mondes grecs à l'époque classique. Colloque de la Sophau, Dijon, 26, 27, et 28 Mars 1999 (Pallas* 51), Toulouse: 141–57.

Jacquemin, A. (2000) *Guerre et religion dans le monde grec (490–322 av. J.-C.)*, Liège.

Jacquemin, A. and Laroche, D. (1995) Delphes, le roi Persée et les Romains, *Bulletin de Correspondance Hellénique*, 119: 125–36.

Jameson, M. H., Runnels, C. N. and van Andel, T. H. (1994) *A Greek Countryside: The Southern Argolid from Prehistory to the Present Day*, Stanford.

Jeffery, L. H. (1966) Two inscriptions from Iria, *Archaiologikon Deltion, Meletai* 21: 18–25.

Jehne, M. (1994) *Koine Eirene. Untersuchungen zu den Befriedungs- und Stabilisierungsbemühungen in der griechischen Poliswelt des 4. Jh. v. Chr.*, Stuttgart.

Jeppesen, K. (1989) *Ikaros. The Hellenistic Settlements. Vol. 3: The Sacred Enclosure in the Early Hellenistic Period. With an Appendix on Epigraphical Finds*, Aarhus.

Jobst, W. (1978) Hellenistische Aussenfortifikationen um Ephesos, in S. Sahin, E. Schwertheim and J. Wagner (eds) *Studien zur Religion und Kultur Kleinasiens. Festschrift für F.K. Dörner zum 65. Geburtstag, I*, Leiden: 447–56.

Jones, C. P. (1974) Diodoros Pasparos and the Nicephoria of Pergamon, *Chiron*, 4: 183–205.

Jones, C. P. (1999) *Kinship Diplomacy in the Ancient World*, Cambridge, Mass., London.

Jones, C. P. and Habicht, C. (1989) A Hellenistic inscription from Arsinoe, *Phoenix*, 43: 317–46.

Jonnes, L. and Ricl, M. (1997) A new royal inscription from Phrygian Paroreios: Eumenes II grants Tyriaion the status of a polis, *Epigraphica Anatolica*, 29: 1–29.

Jost, M. (1999) Les divinités de la guerre, in Prost (ed.): 163–78.

Jung, F. (2001) *Soter: Studien zur Rezeption eines hellenistischen Ehrentitels im Neuen Testament*, Munich.

Kähler, H. (1965) *Der Fries vom Reiterdenkmal des Aemilius Paullus in Delphi*, Berlin.

Kantzia, C. (1999) Ἔνα ἀσυνήθιστο πολεμικὸ ἀνάθημα στὸ ἱερό τῆς ὁδοῦ Διαγοριδῶν στὴ Ῥόδο, in Ῥόδος 2.4000 χρόνια. Ἡ πόλη τῆς Ῥόδου ἀπὸ τὴν ἴδρυσή της μέχρι τὴν κατάληψη ἀπὸ τοὺς Τούρκους (1523). Διεθνὲς ἐπιστημονικὸ συνέδριο, Ῥόδος, 24–29 Ὀκτωβρίου 1993. Πρακτικά I, Athens: 75–82.

Keil, B. (1916) *Eirene. Eine philologisch-antiquarische Untersuchung*, Leipzig.

Kennell, N. M. (1995) *The Gymnasium of Virtue. Education and Culture in Ancient Sparta*, London.

Kirsten, E. (1942) *Das dorische Kreta. I. Die Insel Kreta im fünften und vierten Jahrhundert*, Würzburg.

Kleijwegt, M. (1991) *Ancient Youth. The Ambiguity of Youth and the Absence of Adolescence in Greco-Roman Society*, Amesterdam.

Klose, P. (1972) *Die völkerrechtliche Ordnung der hellenistischen Staatenwelt in der Zeit von 280–168 v. Chr. Ein Beitrag zur Geschichte des Völkerrechts*, Munich.

Knoepfler, D. (1991) L. Mummius Achaicus et les cités du golfe euboïque. À propos d'une nouvelle inscription d'Érétrie, *Museum Helveticum*, 48: 252–80.

Knoepfler, D. (1993) Les kryptoi du stratège Epicharès à Rhamnonte et le debut de la guerre de Chrémonidès, *Bulletin de Correspondance Hellénique*, 118: 327–41.

Kohl, M. (2004) Sèges et défense de Pergame. Nouvelles réflexions sur sa topographie et son architecture militaires, in Couvenhes and Fernoux (eds): 177–98.

Kosmetatou, E. and Waelkens, M. (1997) The "Macedonian" Shields of Sagalassos, in M. Waelkens and J. Poblome (eds) *Sagalassos IV: Report on the Survey and Excavation Campaigns of 1994 and 1995*, Leuven: 277–91.

Kotsidu, H. (2000) *Time kai doxa. Ehrungen für hellenistische Herrscher im griechischen Mutterland und in Kleinasien unter besonderer Berücksichtigung der archäologischen Denkmäler*, Berlin.

Kralli, I. (2000) Athens and the Hellenistic kings (338–261 BC): the language of the decrees, *Classical Quarterly*, 50(1): 113–32.

Kreuter, S. (1992) *Außenbeziehungen kretischer Gemeinden zu den hellenistischen Staaten im 3. und 2. Jh. v. Chr.*, Munich, 18–34.

Krischen, F. (1922) *Die Befestigungen von Herakleia am Latmos* (*Milet* III.2), Berlin, Leipzig.

Künzl, E. (1971) *Die Kelten des Epigonos*, Würzburg.

Labarre, G. (2004) *Phrourarques et phrouroi des cités grecques d'Asie Mineure à l'époque hellénistique*, in Couvenhes and Fernoux (eds): 221–48.

Lana, I. (1989) *Studi sull'idea della pace nel mondo antico* (*Memorie dell'Accademia delle scienze di Torino. Classe di scienze morali, storiche e filologiche*, Serie 5,13, 1–2), Torino.

Landucci Gattinoni, F. (1990) La morte di Antigono e di Lisimaco, in M. Sordi (ed.) *"Dulce et decorum est pro patria mori", La morte in combattimento nell'antichità*, Milano: 111–26.

Laronde, A. (1987) *Cyrène et la Libye hellénistique. Libykai Historiai de l'époque républicaine au principat d'Augustus*, Paris.

Laubscher, H. P. (1985) Hellenistische Herrscher und Pan, *Mitteilungen des Deutschen Archäologischen Instituts (Abteilung Athen)* 100: 333–53.

Launey, M. (1987) *Recherches sur les armées hellénistiques*. Reimpression avec addenda et mise à joure en postface par Y. Garlan, P. Gauthier and C. Orrieux, Paris.

Le Bohec, S. (1985) Les philoi des rois Antigonides, *Revue des Études Grecques*, 98: 93–124.

Lebessi, A. (1985) Τὸ ἱερὸ τοῦ Ἑρμῆ καὶ τῆς Ἀφροδίτης στὴ Σύμη Βιάννου. *I.1. Χάλκινα κρητικὰ τορεύματα*, Athens.

Lebessi, A. (1991) Flagellation ou autoflagellation. Données iconographiques pour une tentative d'interpretation, *Bulletin de Correspondance Hellénique*, 115: 99–123.

Lebessi, A. (2002) Τὸ ἱερὸ τοῦ Ἑρμῆ καὶ τῆς Ἀφροδίτης στὴ Σύμη Βιάννου. *III. Τὰ Χάλκινα ἀνϑρωπόμορφκ εἰδώλια*, Athens.

Lebrun, R. (1994) Syncrétismes et cultes indigènes en Asie Mineure Méridionale, *Kernos*, 7: 145–57.

Lefèvre, F. (1998) Traité de paix entre Démetrios Poliorcète et la confédération étolienne, *Bulletin de Correspondance Hellénique*, 122: 109–41.

Lefèvre, F. (2002) *Corpus des inscriptions de Delphes. IV. Documents amphictioniques*, Paris.

Legras, B. (1999) *Néotês. Recherches sur les jeunes grecs dans l'Égypte ptolémaique et romaine*, Geneva.

Lehmann, G. A. (2000) Polis-Autonomie und römische Herrschaft an der West-küste Kleinasiens: Kolophon/Klaros nach der Aufrichtung der Provincia Asia, in L. Mooren (ed.) *Politics, Administration, and Society in the Hellenistic and Roman World*, Leuven: 215–38.

Lehmann, G. A. (2003) Ἀνδρολήψιον. Rom und der Menschenfang –Streit zwischen Kolophon und Metropolis, *Zeitschrift für Papyrologie und Epigraphik* 114: 79–86.

Leitao, D. D. (1995) The perils of Leukippos: initiatory transvestism and male gender ideology in the Ekdusia of Phaistos, *Classical Antiquity*, 14: 130–63.

Lendon, J. E. (2004) War and society in the Hellenistic World and the Roman Republic, in H. van Wees, P. Sabin, and M. Whitby (eds) *Cambridge History of Greek and Roman Warfare*, Cambridge (forthcoming).

Leschhorn, W. (1984) *"Gründer der Stadt." Studien zu einem politisch-religiösen Phänomen der griechischen Geschichte*, Stuttgart.

Leschhorn, W. (1993) *Antike Ären. Zeitrechnung, Politik und Geschichte im Schwarzmeerraum und in Kleinasien nördlich des Tauros*, Stuttgart.

Lévêque, P. (1968) La guerre à l'époque hellénistique, in J.-P. Vernant (ed.) *Problèmes de la guerre en Grèce ancienne*, Paris: 261–87.

Lévêque, P. (1991) Monarchie et idéologies. Le cas des gréco-bactriens et des gréco-indiens, in *L'idéologie du pouvoir monarchique dans l'antiquité. Actes du colloque (Lyon et Vienne 26–28 juin 1989)*, Paris: 39–51.

Lévy, E. (1978) La monarchie macédonienne et le mythe d'une royauté démocratique, *Ktema*, 3, 201–25.

LiDonnici, L. R. (1995) *The Epidaurian Miracle Inscriptions. Text, Translation, and Commentary*, Atlanta.

Loman, P. (2004) No woman, no war: women's participation in ancient Greek warfare, *Greece & Rome*, 51(1): 34–54.

Loots, L., Waelkens, M. and Depuydt, F. (2000) The city fortifications of Sagalassos from the Hellenistic to the Late Roman period, in M. Waelkens and L. Loots (eds) *Sagalassos V. Report on the Survey and Excavation Campaigns of 1996 and 1997*, Louvain: 595–634.

Ma, J. (1994) Black hunter variations, *Proceedings of the Cambridge Philological Society*, 40: 49–80.

Ma, J. (2000a) *Antiochos III and the Cities of Western Asia Minor*, Oxford (cf. the enlarged paperback edition in 2002).

Ma, J. (2000b) Seleukids and speech-acts: performative utterances, legitimacy and negotiation in the world of the Maccabees, *Scripta Classica Israelica*, 19, 71–112.

Ma, J. (2000c) Fighting poleis of the Hellenistic World, in van Wees (ed.): 337–76.

Ma, J. (2002) "Oversexed, overpaid and over here": a response to Angelos Chaniotis, in Chaniotis and Ducrey (eds): 115–22.

Ma, J. (2003) Kings, in Erskine (ed.): 177–95.

Ma, J. (2004) Une culture militaire en Asie Mineure hellénistique?, in Couvenhes and Fernoux (eds): 199–220.

Magnelli, A. (1992/3) Una nuova iscrizione da Gortyna (Creta). Qualche considerazione sulla neotas, *Annuario della Scuola Italiana di Archeologia d'Atene*, 70/71: 291–305.

Magnelli, A. (1994/5) Il santuario delle divinità egizie a Gortyna: L'evidenza epigrafica, *Annuario della Scuola Italiana di Archeologia d'Atene*, 72/73: 33–52.

Magnetto, A. (1997) *Gli arbitrati interstatali greci. Introduzione, testo critico, traduzione, commento e indici, Volume II. Dal 337 al 196 a.C.*, Pisa.

Maier, F. G. (1959) *Griechische Mauerbauinschriften. Erster Teil. Texte und Kommentare*, Heidelberg.

Maier, F. G. (1961) *Griechische Mauerbauinschriften. Zweiter Teil. Untersuchungen*, Heidelberg.

Manakidou, E. (1996) Heroic overtones in two inscriptions from ancient Lete, in E. Voutiras (ed.) Ἐπιγραφὲς τῆς Μακεδονίας. Γ΄ Διεθνὲς Συμπόσιο γιὰ τὴ Μακεδονία. 8–12 Δεκεμβρίου 1993, Thessalonike: 85–98.

Manganaro, G. (2000) Kyme e il dinasta Philetairos, *Chiron*, 30, 403–14.

Manning, J. G. (2003) *Land and Power in Ptolemaic Egypt. The Structure of Land Tenure*, Cambridge.

Mantovani, M. (1990) *Bellum Iustum. Die Idee des gerechten Krieges in der römischen Kaiserzeit*, Bern, Frankfurt.

Marasco, G. (1996) Les médecins de cour à l'époque hellénistique, *Revue des Études Grecques*, 109: 435–66.

Mark, I. S. (1998) The Victory of Samothrace, in O. Palagia and W. Coulson (eds) *Regional Schools in Hellenistic Sculpture. Proceedings of a Conference held at the American School of Classical Studies at Athens, March 15–17, 1996*, Oxford: 157–65.

Marsden, E. W. (1969) *Greek and Roman Artillery: Historical Development*, London.

Marsden, E. W. (1971) *Greek and Roman Artillery: Technical Treatises*, Oxford.

Marshall, A. J. (1980) The survival and development of international jurisdiction in the Greek World under Roman rule, *Aufstieg und Niedergang der römischen Welt*, II.13, Berlin, 626–61.

Masson, O. (1965) Notes d'anthroponymie grecque et asianique, *Beiträge zur Namenforschung* 16: 166–79 (= *Onomastica Graeca Selecta*), Paris, I: 69–73.

Massar, N. (2001) Un savoir-faire à l'honneur. "Médecins" et "discours civique" en Grèce hellénistique, *Revue belge de philologie et d'histoire*, 79: 175–201.

Mattei, M. (1987) *Il Galata Capitolino*, Rome.

Mauritsch, P. (2002) Das Frauenbild als Teil der Geschlechterrollen-Konzeption bei Polybios, in Chr. Ulf and R. Rollinger (eds) *Geschlechter – Frauen – Fremde Ethnien in antiker Ethnographie, Theorie und Realität*, Innsbruck: 315–30.

McGing, B. C. (1997) Revolt Egyptian style: internal opposition to Ptolemaic rule, *Archiv für Papyrusforschung*, 43: 273–314.

McNicoll, A. W. (1997) *Hellenistic Fortifications from the Aegean to the Euphrates*, Oxford.

Mehl, A. (1980/1) Doriktetos Chora. Kritische Bemerkungen zum "Speererwerb" in Politik und Völkerrecht der hellenistischen Epoche, *Ancient Society*, 11/12: 173–212.

Meißner, B. (1992) *Historiker zwischen Polis und Königshof. Studien zur Stellung der Geschichsschreiber in der griechischen Gesellschaft in spätklassischer und frühhellenistischer Zeit*, Göttingen.

Meister, K. (1975) *Historische Kritik bei Polybios*, Wiesbaden.

Mélèze-Modrzejewski, J. (1984) Dryton le crétois et sa famille, ou Les marriages mixtes dans l'Égypte hellénistique, in *Aux origines de l'Hellénisme. La Crète et la Grèce. Hommage à Henri van Effenterre*, Paris, 353–76.

Mendel, G. (1914) *Catalogue des sculptures grecques, romaines et byzantines III*, Istanbul, no. 1072.

Menu, M. (2000) *Jeunes et vieux chez Lysias. L'akolasia de la jeunesse au IVe siècle av. J.-C.*, Rennes.

Merkelbach, R. (2000) Der Überfall der Piraten auf Teos, *Epigraphica Anatolica*, 32: 101–14.

Migeotte, L. (1984) *L'emprunt public dans les cités grecques. Recueil des documents et analyse critique*, Québec.

Migeotte, L. (1991) Le pain quotidien dans les cités hellénistiques: A propos des fonds permanents pour l'approvisionnement en grain, *Cahiers du Centre G. Glotz*, 2: 19–41.

Migeotte, L. (1992) *Les souscriptions publiques dans les cités grecques*, Quebec, Geneva.

Migeotte, L. (1994) Ressources financières des cités béotiennes, in J.M. Fossey (ed.) *Boeotia Antiqua* IV, Amsterdam: 3–15.

Migeotte, L. (1995) Les finances publiques des cités grecques: bilan et perspectives de recherche, *Topoi*, 5: 7–32.

Migeotte L. (2000a) Retour à la grande souscription publique de Cos des années 205–201 avant J.-C., in Τιμαὶ Τριανταφυλλοπούλου, Athens: 159–72.

Migeotte, L. (2000b) Les dépenses militaires des cités grecques: essai de typologie, in Andreau et al. (eds): 145–76.

Mileta, C. (1998) Eumenes III. und die Sklaven. Neue Überlegungen zum Charakter des Aristonikosaufstandes, *Klio*, 80: 47–65.

Miller, S. G. (1993) *The Tomb of Lyson and Kallikles: A Painted Macedonian Tomb*, Mainz.

Mitchell, S. (1993) *Anatolia: Land, Men, and Gods in Asia Minor*, Oxford.

Mitchell, S. (2003) The Galatians: representation and reality, in Erskine (ed.): 280–93.

Mittag, P. F. (2000) Die Rolle der hauptstädtischen Bevölkerung bei den Ptolemäern und Seleukiden im 3. Jh., *Klio*, 82: 409–25.

Momigliano, A. (1972) Tradition and the classical historian, *History and Theory*, 11: 279–93 (reprinted in *Quinto contributo alla storia degli studi classici e del mondo antico*, Rome 1975, I: 13–31).

Mooren, L. (1975) *The Aulic Titulature in Ptolemaic Egypt. Introduction and Prosopography*, Brussels.

Mooren, L. (1977) *La hiérarchie de cour Ptolémaique. Contribution à l'étude des institutions et des classes dirigeantes à l'époque hellénistique*, Louvain.

Morrison, J. S. and Coates, J. F. (1994) *Greek and Roman Oared Warships, 399–31 BC*, Oxford.

Mossé, C. (1991) Women in the Spartan revolutions of the third century BC, in S.B. Pomeroy (ed.) *Women's History and Ancient History*, London: 138–53.

Müller, C. (1999) La défense du territoire civique: stratégies et organisation spatiale, in Prost (ed.): 16–33.

Müller, H. (1975) Φυγῆς ἕνεκεν, *Chiron*, 5: 129–56.

Müller, H. (1989) Ein neues hellenistisches Weihepigramm aus Pergamon, *Chiron*, 19: 499–553.

Müller, O. (1972) *Antigonos Monophthalmos und "Das Jahr der Könige". Untersuchungen zur Begründung der hellenistischen Monarchien 306–4 v. Chr.*, Saarbrücken.

Musti, D. (1984) Syria and the East, in *CAH* VII.1^2: 175–220.

Nachtergael, G. (1977) *Les Galates en Grèce et les Sotéria de Delphes. Recherches d'histoire et d'épigraphie hellénistique*, Brussels.

Narain, A. K. (1989) The Greeks of Bactria and India, in *CAH* VII.3^2: 388–421.

Nilsson, M. P. (1906) *Griechische Feste von religiöser Bedeutung mit Ausschluß der attischen*, Lund.

Oakley, J. H. and Sinos, R. H. (1993) *The Wedding in Ancient Athens*, Madison.

Ober, J. (1985) *Fortress Attica. Defence of the Athenian Land Frontier, 404–322 BC*, Leiden.

Ober, J. (1989) *Mass and Elite in Democratic Athens. Rhetoric, Ideology and the Power of the People*, Princeton.

Oetjen, R. (2004) *Die Garnisonsinschriften als Quelle für die Geschichte Athens im dritten Jahrhundert v. Chr.* (PhD dissertation), Heidelberg.

Ogden, D. (1996) *Greek Bastardy in the Classical and Hellenistic Periods*, Oxford.

Ohlemutz, E. (1940) *Die Kulte und Heiligtümer der Götter in Pergamon*, Würzburg.

Palagia, O. (1992) Cult and allegory: the life story of Artemidoros of Perge, in J. M. Sanders (ed.) *Philolakon: Lakonian Studies in Honour of Hector Catling*, London: 171–7.

Palma, B. (1981) Il picolo donario pergameno, *Xenia*, 1/2: 45–84.

Pantos, P. (1985) Τὰ σφραγίσματα τῆς Αἰτωλικῆς Καλλιπόλεως, Athens.

Parker, R. (2000) Sacrifice and battle, in van Wees (ed.): 299–314.

Parker, R. and Obbink, D. (2000) Aus der Arbeit der "Inscriptiones Graecae" VI. Sales of priesthoods on Cos I, *Chiron*, 30: 415–49.

Paton, W. R. (1900) Sites in E. Karia and S. Lydia, *Journal of Hellenic Studies*, 20, 57–80.

Pélékidis, Chr. (1962) *Histoire de l'éphébie attique des origines à 31 avant Jésus-Christ*, Paris.

Perlman, P. (1996) Πόλις ὑπήκοος. The dependent polis and Crete, in M. H. Hansen (ed.), *Introduction to an Inventory of Poleis*. Symposium, 23–26 August 1995, Copenhagen: 233–87.

Perlman, P. (1999) Κρῆιες ἀεὶ ληιβιαί? The marginalization of Crete in Greek thought and the role of piracy in the outbreak of the First Cretan War, in Gabrielsen et al. (eds): 132–61.

Perrin-Saminadayar, E. (1999) Si vis pacem, gere bellum. L'aspiration à la paix dans la société athénienne, de la guerre du Péloponnèse à la guerre lamiaque, in Prost (ed.): 147–62.

Peschlow, U., Peschlow-Bindokat, A. and Wörrle, M. (2002) Die Sammlung Turan Beler in Kumbaba bei Sile (II). Antike und byzantinische Denkmäler von der bithynischen Schwarzmeerküste, *Mitteilungen des Deutschen Archäologischen Instituts (Abteilung Istanbul)*, 52: 429–522.

Petrakos, V. C. (1997) La forteresse de Rhamnonte, *Comptes Rendus de l'Academie des Inscriptions et Belles Lettres.* 605–30.

Petrakos, V. C. (1999) Ὁ δῆμος τοῦ Ραμνοῦντος. Σύνοψη τῶν ἀναβκαφῶν Καὶτῶν ἐρευνῶν (1813–1998). I. Ἡ τοπογραφία. II. Οἱ ἐπιγραφές. Athens.

Petropoulou, A. (1985) *Beiträge zur Wirtschafts- und Gesellschaftsgeschichte Kretas in hellenistischer Zeit*, Frankfurt.

Pfister, F. (1951) *Die Reisebilder des Herakleides*, Vienna.

Pfuhl, E. and Möbius, H. (1977/9) *Die ostgriechischen Grabreliefs*, Mainz.

Piejko, F. (1988) The Inscriptions of Icarus-Failaka, *Classica & Mediaevalia*, 39: 89–116.

Pimouguet, I. (1995) Défense et territoire: L'exemple Milésien, *Dialogues d'Histoire Ancienne*, 21(1): 89–109.

Pimouguet-Pédarros, I. (2000) *Architecture de la défense. Histoire des fortifications antiques de Carie. Époques classique et hellénistique*, Besançon.

Pimouguet-Pédarros, I. (2003) Le siège de Rhodes par Démétrios et "l'apogée" de la poliercétique grecque, *Revue des Études Anciennes*, 105: 371–92.

Pohl, H. (1993) *Die römische Politik und die Piraterie im östlichen Mittelmeer vom 3. Jahrhundert bis zum 1. Jahrhundert v. Chr.*, Berlin, New York.

Poliakoff, M. B. (1987) *Combat Sports in the Ancient World*, New Haven.

Pollitt, J. J. (1986) *Art in the Hellenistic Age*, Cambridge.

Pomeroy, S. B. (1984) *Women in Hellenistic Egypt from Alexander to Cleopatra*, New York.

Potts, D. T. (1990) *The Arabian Gulf in Antiquity*, Oxford.

Préaux, C. (1939) *L'économie royale des Lagides*, Brussels.

Price, S. R. F. (1984) *Rituals and Power: The Roman Imperial Cult in Asia Minor*, Cambridge.

Pritchett, W. K. (1974) *The Greek State at War: Part II*, Berkeley, Los Angeles, Oxford.

Pritchett, W. K. (1979) *The Greek State at War: Part III*, Berkeley, Los Angeles, Oxford.

Pritchett, W. K. (1985) *The Greek State at War: Part IV*, Berkeley, Los Angeles, Oxford.

Pritchett, W. K. (1991) *The Greek State at War: Part V*, Berkeley, Los Angeles, Oxford.

Pritchett, W. K. (1996) *Greek Archives, Cults, and Topography*, Amsterdam.

Prost, F. (1999) *Armées et sociétés de la Grèce classique. Aspects sociaux et politiques de la guerre aux Ve et IVe s. av. J.-C.*, Paris.

Pugliese Carratelli, G. (1987) Epigrafi di Cos relative al culto di Artemis in Cnido e in Bargylia, *La Parola del Passato*, 42, 110–23.

Quass, F. (1993) *Die Honoratiorenschicht in den Städten des griechischen Ostens. Untersuchungen zur politischen und sozialen Entwicklung in hellenistischer und römischer Zeit*, Stuttgart.

Queyrel, F. (2003) *Les portraits des Attalides. Fonction et représentation*, Paris.

Quillin, J. M. (2002) Achieving amnesty: the role of events, institutions, and ideas, *Transactions of the American Philological Association*, 132, 71–107.

Rackham, O. and Moody, J. (1996) *The Making of the Cretan Landscape*, Manchester.

Raeck, W. (1995) Der mehrfache Apollodoros. Zur Präsenz des Bürgers im hellenistischen Stadtbild am Beispiel von Priene, in Wörrle and Zanker (eds): 231–40.

Ramelli, I. (2001) La dialettica tra guerra esterna e guerra civile da Siracusa a Roma, in M. Sordi (ed.) *Il pensiero sulla guerra nel mondo antico*, Milano: 45–63.

Rauh, N. K. (1993) *The Sacred Bonds of Commerce: Religion, Economy, and Trade Society at Hellenistic Roman Delos*, Amsterdam.

Reed, N. (1998) *More than a Game: The Military Nature of Greek Athletic Contests*, Chicago.

Reger, G. (1993) The public purchase of grain on independent Delos, *Classical Antiquity*, 12: 300–34.

Reger, G. (1999) The relations between Rhodes and Caria from 246 to 167 BC, in Gabrielsen et al. (eds): 76–97.

Reger, G. (2003) The economy, in Erskine (ed.): 331–53.

Reinach, A. J. (1913) Trophées macédoniens, *Revue des Études Grecques*, 26: 347–98.

Reinmuth, O. W. (1971) *The Ephebic Inscriptions of the Fourth Century B.C.*, Leiden.

Reinmuth, O. W. (1974) A New Ephebic Inscription from the Athenian Agora, *Hesperia* 43: 246–59.

Reynolds, J. (1982) *Aphrodisias and Rome*, London.

Rice, E. (1983) *The Grand Procession of Ptolemy Philadelphus*, Oxford.

Rice, E. (1991) The Rhodian navy in the Hellenistic Age, in W.R. Roberts and J. Sweetman (eds) *New Interpretations in Naval History*, Annapolis: 29–50.

Rice, E. (1993) The glorious dead: commemoration of the fallen and portrayal of victory in the Late Classical and Hellenistic World, in Rich and Shipley (eds) *War and Society in the Greek World*, London, New York: 224–57.

Rich, J. and G. Shipley (eds.) (1993) *War and Society in the Greek World*, London, New York.

Ricl, M. (1997) *The Inscriptions of Alexandreia Troas*, Bonn.

Rigsby, K. J. (1996) *Asylia. Territorial Inviolability in the Hellenistic World*, Berkley, Los Angeles, London.

Ritter, H.-W. (1965) *Diadem und Königsherrschaft. Untersuchungen zu Zeremonien und Rechtsgrundlagen des Herrschaftsantritts bei den Persern, bei Alexander dem Großen und im Hellenismus*, Munich, Berlin.

Robert, J. and Robert, L. (1954) *La Carie. Tome II. Le plateau de Tabai et ses environs*, Paris.

Robert, J. and Robert, L. (1964) *Bulletin épigraphique, Revue des Études Grecques*, 77, 127–259.

Robert, J. and Robert, L. (1976) Une inscription grecque de Téos en Ionie. L'union de Téos et de Kyrbissos, *Journal des Savants*, 153–235.

Robert, J. and Robert, L. (1983) *Fouilles d'Amyzon en Carie. Tome I. Exploration, histoire, monnaies et inscriptions*, Paris.

Robert, L. (1926) Notes d'épigraphie hellénistique, *Bulletin de Correspondance Hellénique* 50: 469–522 (reprinted in L. Robert, *Opera Minora Selecta* I, Amsterdam 1969: 33–86).

Robert, L. (1927) Études d'épigraphie gecque, *Revue de Philologie* 1: 97–132 (reprinted in L. Robert, *Opera Minora Selecta* II, Amsterdam 1969: 1052–87).

Robert, L. (1928) Notes d'épigraphie hellénistique, *Bulletin de Correspondance Hellénique* 52: 426–43 (reprinted in L. Robert, *Opera Minora Selecta* I, Amsterdam 1969: 108–125).

Robert, L. (1937) *Études anatoliennes. Recherches sur les inscriptions grecques de l'Asie Mineure*, Paris.

Robert, L. (1944) Hellenica, *Revue de Philologie* 18, 5–56 (reprinted in L. Robert, *Opera Minora Selecta* III, Amsterdam 1969: 1371–1422).

Robert, L. (1945) *Le sanctuaire de Sinuri près de Mylasa*, Paris.

Robert, L. (1949) Les chèvres d'Héracleia, *Hellenica*, 7: 161–70.

Robert, L. (1955) Péripolarques, *Hellénica X*, Paris: 283–92.

Robert, L. (1967) Sur des inscriptions d'Ephése, *Revue de Philologie* 41: 7–84 (reprinted in L. Robert, *Opera Minora Selecta* V, Amsterdam 1989: 347–424).

Robert, L. (1970) Review of Meier 1959, *Gnomon* 42: 580–603 (reprinted in L. Robert, *Opera Minora Selecta* VI, Amsterdam 1989: 629–53).

Robertson, M. (1975) *A History of Greek Art*, Cambridge.

Robertson, N. (1986) A point of precedence at Plataia. The dispute between Athens and Sparta over leading the procession, *Hesperia*, 55, 88–102.

Roesch, P. (1982) *Études béotiennes*, Paris.

Rosivach, V. J. (1987) The cult of Zeus Eleutherios in Athens, *Parola del Passato*, 42: 262–87.

Rostovtzeff, M. (1941) *The Social and Economical History of the Hellenistic World*, Oxford.

Roueché, Ch. and Sherwin-White, M. (1985) Some aspects of the Seleucid Empire: The Greek inscriptions from Failaka in the Persian Gulf, *Chiron*, 15: 1–39.

Roussel, P. (1930) Un nouveau document relatif à la guerre Démétriaque, *Bulletin de Correspondance Hellénique*, 54: 268–82.

Roussel, P. (1939) La pérée samothracienne au IIIe siècle avant J.-C., *Bulletin de Correspondance Hellénique*, 63: 133–41.

Rousset, D. (1999) Centre urbain, frontière et espace rural dans les cités de Grèce centrale, in M. Brunet (ed.) *Territoires des cités grecques. Actes de la table ronde internationale organisée par l'École française d'Athenes, 31 Octobre–3 Novembre 1991*, Paris: 35–77.

Roy, J. (1998) The masculinity of the Hellenistic king, in L. Foxhall and J. Salmon (eds), *When Men were Men: Masculinity, Power and Identity in Classical Antiquity*, London, 111–35.

Rudhardt, J. (1958) *Notions fondamentales de la pensée religieuse et actes constitutifs du culte dans la Grèce classique*, Geneva.

Rumscheid, F. and Held, W. (1994) Erinnerungen an Mokazis, *Mitteilungen des Deutschen Archäologischen Instituts (Abteilung Istanbul)* 44: 89–106.

Rumscheid, F. (1999) Mylasas Verteidigung: Burgen statt Stadtmauer? in E.-L. Schwandner and K. Rheidt (eds) *Stadt un Umland. Neue Ergebnisse der archäologischen Bau- und Siedlungsforschung*, Mainz: 206–22.

Sacco, G. (1979) Sui neaniskoi dell'età ellenistica, *Rivista di Filologia e di Istruzione Classica*, 107: 39–49.

Sacks, K. (1981) *Polybius on the Writing of History*, Berkeley.

Sage, M. M. (1996) *Warfare in Ancient Greece: A Sourcebook*, London, New York.

Sahin, S. (1994) Piratenüberfall auf Teos. Volksbeschluß über die Finanzierung der Erpressungsgelder, *Epigraphica Anatolica*, 23: 1–36.

Salazar, Chr. (2000) *The Treatment of War Wounds in Graeco-Roman Antiquity*, Leiden.

Samama, E. (2003) *Les médecins dans le monde grec. Sources épigraphiques sur la naissance d'un corps médical*, Genève.

Savalli-Lestrade, I. (1996) Courtisans et citoyens: le cas des philoi attalides, *Chiron*, 26, 149–81.

Savalli–Lestrade, I. (1998) *Les philoi royaux dans l'Asie hellénistique*, Geneva.

Savalli–Lestrade, I. (2001) Les Attalides et les cités grecques d'Asie Mineure au IIe siècle a.C., in Bresson and Descat (eds): 77–91.

Savalli-Lestrade, I. (2003) Remarques sur les élites dans les poleis hellénistiques, in M. Cébeillac-Gervasoni and L. Lamoine (eds) *Les élites et leurs facettes. Les élites locales dans le monde hellénistique et romain*, Rome-Clermont-Ferrand: 51–64.

Schaefer, H. (1932) *Staatsform und Politik. Untersuchungen zur griechischen Geschichte des 6. und 5. Jh.*, Leipzig.

Schalles, H.-J. (1985) *Untersuchungen zur Kulturpolitik der pergamenischen Herrscher im dritten Jahrhundert v. Chr.*, Tübingen.

Schaps, D. (1982) The women of Greece in wartime, *Classical Philology*, 77, 193–213.

Schas, G. P. and Spencer, N. (1994) Notes on the topography of Eresos, *American Journal of Archaeology*, 98: 411–30.

Scheer, T. S. (1996) Ein Museum griechischer "Frühgeschichte" im Apollontempel von Sikyon, *Klio*, 78, 353–73.

Schmidt, K. (1999) The peace of Antalcidas and the idea of the *Koine Eirene*. A panhellenic peace movement, *Revue Internationale de droits de l'antiquité*, 46: 81–96.

Schmidt-Dounias, B. (2000) *Geschenke erhalten die Freundschaft. Politik und Selbstdarstellung im Spiegel der Monumente*, Berlin.

Schmitt, H. H. (1964) *Untersuchungen zur Geschichte Antiochos' des Großen und seiner Zeit*, Wiesbaden.

Schnapp, A. (1997a) *Le chasseur et la cité. Chasse et érotique dans la Grèce ancienne*, Paris.

Schnapp, A. (1997b) Images of young people in the Greek city state, in G. Levi and J.-C. Schmitt (eds) *A History of Young People in the West. Ancient and Medieval Rites of Passage, Vol. I*, Cambridge: 12–50.

Schober, A. (1938) Epigonos von Pergamon und die pergamenische Kunst, *Jahrbuch des Deutschen Archäologischen Instituts*, 53: 126–49.

Scholl, R. (1988) Drytons Tod, *Chronique d'Égypte*, 63: 141–4.

Scholten, J. B. (2000) *The Politics of Plunder: Aitolians and Their Koinon in the Early Hellenistic Era, 279–217 B.C.*, Berkeley.

Scholten, J. B. (2003) Macedon and the mainland, 280–221, in Erskine (ed.): 134–58.

Schuler, C. (1999) Kolonisten und Einheimische in einer attalidischen Polisgründung, *Zeitschrift für Papyrologie und Epigraphik*, 128: 124–32.

Scuderi, R. (1991) Decreti del senato per controversie di confine in età repubblicana, *Athenaeum*, 69, 371–415.

Sekunda, N. (1997) Nearchus the Cretan and the foundation of Cretopolis, *Anatolian Studies*, 47, 217–23.

Shear, T. L. Jr. (1978) *Kallias of Sphettos and the Revolt of Athens in 287 B.C.*, Princeton.

Sherk, R. K. (1969) *Roman Documents from the Greek East*, Baltimore.

Sherwin-White, S. and Kuhrt, A. (1993) *From Samarkhand to Sardis. A New Approach to the Seleucid Empire*, London.

Shipley, G. (2000) *The Greek World after Alexander, 323–30 BC*, London.

Sion–Jenkis, K. (2001) La disparition du mercenariat en Asie Mineure occidentale au IIe siècle a.c.: éléments de réflexion, in Bresson and Descat (eds): 19–35.

Smith, R. R. R. (1988) *Hellenistic Royal Portraits*, Oxford.

Smith, R. R. R. (1991) *Hellenistic Sculpture: A Handbook*, New York.

Sokolowski, F. (1955) *Lois sacrées de l'Asie Mineure*, Paris.

Sokolowski, F. (1962) *Lois sacrées des cités grecques. Supplément*, Paris.

Sokolowski, F. (1969) *Lois sacrées des cités grecques*, Paris.

Soteriadis, G. (1906) Ἐκ τάφων τῆς Αἰτωλίας, *Archaiologike Ephemeris*, 45: 67–88.

Spiegel, N. (1990) *War and Peace in Classical Greek Literature*, Jerusalem.

Spyridakis, S. (1969) The Itanian cult of Tyche Protogeneia, *Historia*, 18: 42–8.

Stecher, A. (1981) *Inschriftliche Grabgedichte auf Krieger und Athleten. Eine Studie zu griechischen Wertprädikationen*, Innsbruck.

Sternberg, R. H. (1999) The transport of sick and wounded soldiers in Classical Greece, *Phoenix*, 53: 191–205.

Stewart, A. (1979) *Attika: Studies in Athenian Sculpture of the Hellenistic Age*, London.

Stewart, A. (1993) *Faces of Power. Alexander's Image and Hellenistic Politics*, Berkeley.

Strauss, B. S. (1993) *Fathers and Sons in Athens. Ideology and Society in the Era of the Peloponnesian War*, London.

Strobel, K. (1991) Die Galater im hellenistischen Kleinasien, in J. Seibert (ed.), *Hellenistische Studien. Gedenkschrift für Hermann Bengtson*, Munich: 101–34.

Stroud, R. S. (1971) Greek inscriptions: Theozotides and the Athenian orphans, *Hesperia*, 40: 280–301.

Stroud, R. S. (1998) *The Athenian Grain-Tax Law of 374/3 BC*, Princeton.

Tarn, W. W. (1951) *The Greeks in Bactria and India*, Cambridge (second edition).

Taylor, M. V. (1997) *Salamis and the Salaminioi. The History of an Unofficial Athenian Demos*, Amsterdam.

Taylor, M. C. (1998) When the Peiraieus and the city are reunited, *Zeitschrift für Papyrologie und Epigraphik*, 123: 207–22.

Thapar, R. (2002) The role of the army in the exercise of power in early India, in Chaniotis and Ducrey (eds): 25–37.

Themelis, P. (2001) Monuments guerriers de Messène, in R. Frei-Stolba and Gex, K. (eds) *Recherches récentes sur le monde hellénistique. Actes du colloque international organisé à l'occasion du 60ᵉ anniversaire de Pierre Ducrey (Lausanne, 20–21 novembre 1998)*, Bern: 199–215.

Thériault, G. (1996) *Le culte d'Homonoia dans les cités grecques*, Lyon-Québec.

Thompson Crawford, D. J. (1984) The Idumeans of Memphis and the Ptolemaic Politeumata, in *Atti del XVII Congresso Internazionale di Papirologia*, Naples: 1069–75.

Thompson, D. J. (1999) "When Egypt divorced itself": Ptolemaic *tarache* and the *elpis* of Harchonesis, in A. Leahy and J. Taits (eds) *Studies on Ancient Egypt in Honour of H. S. Smith*, London: 321–6.

Thompson D. J. (2000) Philadelphus' procession: dynastic power in a Mediterranean context, in L. Mooren (ed.) *Politics, Administration and Society in the Hellenistic and Roman World. Proceedings of the International Colloquium, Bertinoro 19–24 July, 1997*, Louvain, 365–88.

Thompson, D. J. (2003) The Ptolemies and Egypt, in Erskine (ed.): 105–20.

Thorne, J. A. (2001) Warfare and agriculture: the economic impact of devastation in Classical Greece, *Greek, Roman, and Byzantine Studies*, 42: 225–53.

Trebilco, P. R. (1991) *Jewish Communities in Asia Minor*, Cambridge.

Turner, V. (1967) *The Forrest of Symbols*, Ithaca, London.

Turner, V. (1974) *The Ritual Process*, Harmodnsworth (second edition).

Tzifopoulos, I. Z. (1998) "Hemerodromoi" and Cretan "Dromeis": athletes or military personnel? The case of the Cretan Philonides, *Nikephoros*, 11: 137–70.

Uebel, F. (1968) *Die Kleruchen Ägyptens unter den ersten sechs Prolemäern*, Berlin.

van Bremen, R. (1996) *The Limits of Participation. Women and Civic Life in the Greek East in the Hellenistic and Roman Periods*, Amsterdam.

van der Spek, R. J. (2000) The effect of war on the prices of barley and agricultural land in Hellenistic Babylonia, in Andreau et al. (eds): 293–13.

van Effenterre, H. (1942) Querelles crétoises, *Revue des Études Anciennes*, 44: 31–51.

van Effenterre, H. (1948) *La Crète et le monde grec de Platon à Polybe*, Paris.

van Effenterre, H. (1949) *Fortins crétois, in Mélanges d'archéologie et d'histoire offerts à Charles Picard à l'occasion de son 65ᵉ anniversaire*, Paris: 1033–46.

van Effenterre, H. and Ruzé, F. (1994) *Nomima. Recueil d'inscriptions politiques et juridiques de l'archaïsme grec.* I, Rome.

van Gennep, A. (1960) *The Rites of Passage*, London.

van t' Dack, E. (1977) *Sur l'evolution des institutions militaires lagides, in Armées et fiscalité dans le monde antique. Paris, 14–16 octobre 1976*, Paris: 77–105.

van Wees, P. (1996) Heroes, knights and nutters: warrior mentality in Homer, in A. B. Lloyd (ed.) *Battle in Antiquity*, London: 1–86.

van Wees, P. (ed.) (2000) *War and Violence in Ancient Greece*, London.

Vandorpe, K. (2000) Negotiators' laws from rebellious Sagalassos in an early Hellenistic inscription, in M. Waelkens and L. Loots (eds) *Sagalassos V. Report on the Survey and Excavation Campaigns of 1996 and 1997*, Leuven: 489–508.

Vatin, C. (1970) *Recherches sur le mariage et la condition de la femme mariée à l'époque hellénistique*, Paris.

Vérilhac A.-M. and Vial, C. (1998) *Le mariage grec du VIe siècle av. J.-C. à l'époque d'Auguste*, Paris.

Versnel, H. S. (1991) Beyond cursing: the appeal to justice in judicial prayers, in Chr. A. Faraone and D. Obbink (eds) *Magika Hiera: Ancient Greek Magic and Religion*, New York, Oxford: 60–106.

Versnel, H. S. (1994) *Inconsistencies in Greek and Roman Religion. 2. Transition and Reversal in Myth and Ritual*, Leiden.

Vidal-Naquet, P. (1981) *Le chasseur noir. Formes de pensée et formes de societé dans le monde grec*, Paris.

Vidman, L. (1969) *Sylloge Inscriptionum Religionis Isiacae et Sarapiacae*, Berlin.

Vinogradov, J. G. (1999) Der Staatsbesuch der "Isis" im Bosporos, *Ancient Civilisations from Scythia to Siberia*, 5: 271–302.

Virgilio, B. (1983) Eumene I° e i mercenari di Feletereia e di Attaleia, *Studi Classici e Orientali* 32: 97–140.

Virgilio, B. (1988) *Epigrafia e storiografia. Studi di storia antica*, Pisa.

Virgilio, B. (1993) *Gli Attalidi di Pergamo. Fama, eredità, memoria* (*Studi Ellenistici*, 5), Pisa.

Virgilio, B. (2003) *Lancia, diadema e porpora. Il re e la regalità ellenistica*, Pisa (second edition).

Viviers, D. (1999) Economy and territorial dynamics in Crete from the Archaic to the Hellenistic period, in Chaniotis (ed.): 221–34.

Volkmann, G. (1990) *Die Massenversklavung der Einwohner eroberter Städte in der hellenistisch-römischen Zeit*, Stuttgart (second edition by G. Horsmann).

Vollgraff, W. (1908), Praxitèle le jeune, *Bulletin de Correspondance Hellénique*, 32: 236–58.

Vollmer, D. (1990) *Symploke. Das Übergreifen der römischen Expansion auf den griechischen Osten*, Stuttgart.

Walbank, F. W. (1938) Philippos tragoidoumenos. A Polybian experiment, *Journal of Hellenic Studies*, 58: 55–68.

Walbank, F. W. (1955) Tragic history: a reconsideration, *Bulletin of the Institute of Classical Studies*, 2: 4–14.

Walbank, F. W. (1957) *A Historical Commentary on Polybius. Volume I. Commentary on Books I–VI*, Oxford.

Walbank, F. W. (1960) History and tragedy, *Historia*, 9: 216–34.

Walbank, F. W. (1967) *A Historical Commentary on Polybius. Volume II. Commentary on Books VII–XVIII*, Oxford.

Walbank, F. E. (1975) *Symploke*: its role in Polybius, in D. Kagan (ed.) *Studies in the Greek Historians in Memory of Adam Parry*, Cambridge: 197–212.

Walbank, F. W. (1979) *A Historical Commentary on Polybius. Volume III. Commentary on Books XIX–XL*, Oxford.

Walbank, F. W. (1984) Monarchies and monarchical ideas. Macedonia and Greece. Macedonia and the Greek Leagues, *CAH*, VII.1², 62–100, 221–56, 446–481.

Walbank, F. W. (1987) Könige als Götter. Überlegungen zum Herrscherkult von Alexander bis Augustus, *Chiron*, 17, 365–82.

Walbank, F. W. (1996) Two Hellenistic processions: a matter of self-definition, *Scripta Classica Israelica*, 15, 119–30.

Waldner, K. (2000) *Geburt und Hochzeit des Kriegers. Geschlechterdifferenz und Initiation in Mythos und Ritual der griechischen Polis*, Berlin, New York.

Walsh, J. J. (2000) The disorders of the 170s BC and Roman intervention in the class struggle in Greece, *Classical Quarterly*, 50: 300–3.

Wenning, R. (1978) *Die Galateranatheme Attalos I.*, Berlin.

Wheatley, P. (2001) The Antigonid campaign in Cyprus, 306 BC, *Ancient Society*, 31: 133–56.

Wheeler, E. L. (1984) Sophistic interpretations and Greek treaties, *Greek, Roman, and Byzantine Studies*, 25: 253–74.

Whitehead, D. (1990) *Aineias the Tactician. How to Survive under Siege*, Oxford.

Wiemer, H.-U. (2002) *Krieg, Handel und Piraterie. Untersuchungen zur Geschichte des hellenistischen Rhodos*, Berlin.

Wilhelm, A. (1927) Inschrift aus Tenos, in *Epitymbion H. Swoboda dargebracht, Reichenberg*: 336–45.

Will, E. (1962) Les premières anées du règne d'Antiochos III, *Revue des Études Grecques*, 75: 72–129.

Will, E. (1975) Le territoire, la ville et la poliorcétique grecque, *Revue historique*, 253: 297–318.

Will, E. (1979) *Histoire politique du monde hellénistique*. Tome 1, Nancy.

Will, E. (1982) *Histoire politique du monde hellénistique*. Tome 2, Nancy.

Will, E. (1984) The succession of Alexander: the formation of the Hellenistic kingdoms, CAH VII.1: 23–61, 101–17.

Willetts, R. F. (1962) *Cretan Cults and Festivals*, London.

Willetts, R. F. (1977) The Cretan system of maintaining armed forces, in *Armées et fiscalité dans le monde antique*, Paris, 14–16 Octobre 1976, Paris: 65–75.

Winnicki, J. K. (1972) Ein ptolemäischer Offizier in Thebais, *Eos*, 60: 343–53.

Winter, F. (1912) *Der Alexandersarkophag aus Sidon*, Strasbourg.

Winter, F. E. (1994) Problems on tradition and innovation in Greek fortifications in Asia Minor, late fifth to third century BC, *Revue des Études Anciennes*, 96: 29–52.

Wörrle, M. (2000a) Eine hellenistische Inschrift aus Gadara, *Archäologischer Anzeiger*: 267–71.

Wörrle, M. (2000b) Pergamon um 133 v. Chr., *Chiron*, 30: 543–76.

Wörrle, M. and P. Zanker (eds.) (1995) *Stadtbild und Bürgerbild im Hellenismus*, Munich.

Wolpert, A. ((2002) *Remembering Defeat. Civil War and Civil Memory in Ancient Athens*, Baltimore, London.

Wunderer, C. (1909) *Polybios-Forschungen. III. Teil. Gleichnisse und Metaphern bei Polybios nach ihrer sprachlichen, sachlichen und kulturhistorischen Bedeutung bearbeitet*, Leipzig.

Zanker, P. (1993) The Hellenistic grave stelai from Smyrna: identity and self-image in the polis, in Bulloch et al. (eds): 212–30.

Zecchini, G. (1985) Osservazioni sul presunto modello del "come si deve scrivere la storia" di Luciano, in *Xenia. Scritti in onore di P. Treves*, Rome, 247–52.

Ziebarth, E. (1914) *Aus dem griechischen Schulwesen*, Leipzig, Berlin (second edition).

Zimmermann, K. (2000) Späthellenistische Kultpraxis in einer karischen Kleinstadt. Eine lex sacra aus Bargylia, *Chiron*, 30, 451–85.

NAME INDEX

SUBJECT INDEX

acclamation, 62–3, 75
admiral, 65
aesthetic of war, 189–213
age, age-class, 47–8, 50; age
  qualification, 93
agon, *see* competition
agriculture, 14, 116, 121–9, 140–1;
  burning of fields, 123; damage on,
  92, 122–5, 128; destruction of
  agricultural products, 122–3, 127–8;
  interruption of cultivation, 29, 123,
  125; protection of, 33, 120–2,
  141; transportation of agricultural
  products, 39, 90, 116, 121–2;
  agricultural terracing, 127, 141
alliance, 20, 28–9, 41, 133–4, 175, 247
amnesty, 84, 92, 126, 187, 234
amphictyony, 147, 176, 179, 221, 228
anniversary, commemorative, 49, 52–3,
  215, 225, 227–33, 237, 242–4
arbitration, 12, 15, 19, 71, 76, 130,
  178, 182–3, 185, 188
archery, archers, 21–3, 50–1, 78–9,
  97–8
aristocracy, 41
army, assembly, 62–3, 66, 75–6;
  citizen army, 21, 23, 38, 42, 78–9,
  116; relation to king, 62–8, 75–6;
  royal a., 79; *see also* archer, artillery,
  barrack, billeting, bodyguard,
  camp, campaign, catalog, cavalry,
  commander, condottieri, discharge,
  discipline, elephants, elite troop,
  garrison, guard, light-armed,
  mercenaries, military service,
  mutiny, officer, patrol, regulation

art, 189, 196, 199–200, 206–7, 211;
  painting, 209; royal portraits, 75,
  192; sculpture, 189, 196–7, 200,
  202, 205–6, 211–12, 236; works of
  art brought to Rome, 247
artillery, artillerists, 21, 28, 34, 50, 61,
  68, 79, 84, 98–9
assembly, popular, and discussion about
  war, 174–7, 188, 226
association, cult, 162; private, 23;
  of soldiers, 64, 94–5, 144, 152–3;
  see also club
athletic training, 48–50; athletic
  competition, *see* competition
autonomy, 13, 16, 18–20, 23, 41, 71,
  232
award, for bravery, 43; *see also* crown,
  decoration, reward

bandits, 34, 46
barbarians, 6–7, 13–14, 69–70, 90,
  160, 169, 177, 179, 200, 210–11,
  216, 220–1, 223, 226, 228, 230,
  233, 235, 240, 252
barrack, 85, 89; *see also* billeting, camp
battle, description of, 192–3, 197,
  219; humor in, 95; representation in
  art, 196, 206; *see also* death, killing,
  street fight, surprise attack
belt, 46, 48, 54; *see also* clothes
benefactor, 30, 36–9, 41, 43, 51, 69,
  119, 121, 154, 170, 248
billeting, 70, 92, 124–5, 137, 141
blood, 192, 196–7, 199–200
boasting, 95–6, 144
bodyguard, 64, 66

293

3 Greek terms

SOURCE INDEX